Life *of* Bryant

by

Chris Bryant

Grosvenor House
Publishing Limited

This book is published by
Grosvenor House Publishing Ltd
Link House
140 The Broadway, Tolworth, Surrey, KT6 7HT.
www.grosvenorhousepublishing.co.uk

A CIP record for this book
is available from the British Library

ISBN 978-1-83975-404-3

LIFE OF BRYANT

This book is dedicated to my wonderful
wife Debs & my beautiful daughter Amber.

A special thanks to all those who made this book
possible including Kyra Nicholson, (Graphic Designer)
Josh Redman, (Photographer) and fellow climbing enthusiast
Rhys Williams, who came up with this
books' pun-tastic title. I salute you all.

Prologue

'The only thing constant is change,' so said the Greek philosopher Heraclitus. He lived his life in the city of Ephesus, an ancient settlement that once sat off the coast of Ionia. Appropriately enough, this city first fell to the Persian empire, then the Roman Empire and finally the Ottoman Empire, before being abandoned at the end of the fifteenth century. During its life, it was beset by famine, earthquakes and the silting-up of its harbour from the Küçük Menderes River. And yet, this was no inconsequential settlement: this city was built for the temple of Artemis, one of the seven wonders of the ancient world. It went on to become one of the largest cities in the Roman empire, referenced in the Book of Revelation, and was the setting for various Christian councils that went on to form the basis of much of Western World religion. The ruins of the city are now a tourist attraction in present-day Turkey. If Heraclitus were around to see it today, he no doubt would have mused upon the fate that was bestowed upon his beloved city in the same way that he mused upon everything else in his life, with a thoughtful melancholy, and appropriate metaphor close at hand. 'Everything changes and nothing remains still, you cannot step twice into the same stream.'

Ephesus is not unique in this regard. Babylon was once the centre of Mesopotamian civilization for thousands of years, and yet today 99% of people couldn't place it on a map. It is, in fact, a crumbling ruin of mud brick buildings and debris, fifty miles south of Baghdad. It was so unknown that in 2003

US troops levelled part of the site for a helipad and car park, in preparation for the Iraq invasion, destroying artefacts over 2000 years old. Other ancient settlements like Corinth, Athens, and Pylos survive as thriving cities and towns, suggesting that it's not the age of these settlements that contributed to their demise, it is something else. Without effort and care, everything crumbles to dust – the streets, the buildings, and sometimes even the memories.

The idea that our lives as human beings are inconsequential is, in equal parts, terrifying and enchanting. What will be my legacy when I leave this earth? How long until I am forgotten? What will be beneath my feet in 50, 500, 5000 years' time? During the long process of writing this book, these thoughts kept returning to me. I always felt that my life was pretty ordinary and that the things that have interested me during this time would unlikely be of interest to others. I have lost count of the number of autobiographies I have read where the writer insists on recounting tales of 'the good old days' and all the various hijinks and merriment that accompanied them. That was something I have endeavoured to avoid. I wanted to write something that, yes, was from the heart, but also more than that. I wanted to create something that could sit as a tiny time capsule for my insignificant life. Something that would give the reader a sense of what life was like at the end of the 20th century and first part of the 21st.

The impetus for writing this book was a dawning realisation of this process of change. As I have grown older (35, at the time of writing this chapter), I have noted with increasing regularity that people don't recognise or, worse, have a growing ambivalence to things that I grew up with and once took for granted. Whether or not these next few words mean anything to a future reader, I cannot say, but my eureka moment happened whilst I was sitting at a family friend's house. We were indulging in a few drinks and chatting aimlessly when her two-year-old daughter came into the room.

She waddled straight up to the TV, put her finger on the screen, and tried to move the picture in a confident swiping motion. At first, I wasn't sure what she was doing, but then she tried again and again. Her mum laughed and turned round to me. 'She still hasn't figured out how the TV works.' This was a child who could barely speak, but already had such exposure to technology that she thought the TV was touch-sensitive (in 2018). This is something that I never envisaged could happen. This was a television, a staple of households for 60 years, and this child had a completely different relationship to it. This child, I realised, would grow up in an era so removed from my own, where drones, AI, and technologies not even yet dreamt of, might be commonplace. When I bought my first iPhone at the age of 32, I couldn't swipe; it was an action that didn't come naturally. It took me days to perfect a technique that a two-year-old was now doing in front of me. I don't even recall seeing a computer until I was 12. No doubt every generation says the same thing, but the pace of this change is something that profoundly shocked me. And for possibly the first time in my life, I no longer felt young. I felt out of place, slightly out of time, as though the world was continuing to turn without me. It was such a small thing, but as an American politician once remarked, 'While it may seem small, the ripple effect of small things is extraordinary.'

I mused on my mortality and wondered what kind of world my children and grandchildren would grow up in. And so, my 'time capsule story' was born. I wanted to record some of these things before they were forgotten, so this isn't so much a trip down memory lane, more an insurance policy for travelling down Alzheimer's avenue. It's not a rollercoaster ride by any means, but hopefully an accurate, enlightening, and amusing representation of my life (so far). I hope you will find it intriguing and have as much fun reading it as I most assuredly have had writing it.

CHAPTER 1

Born in the Eighties

I was born on 20th March, 1984, at the Queen Elizabeth Hospital in Margate. I weighed a very respectable eight pounds and four ounces – roughly the weight of an average adult head. Or alternatively, four-fifths of the average domestic cat. The only famous person of note that I can ascertain was born on the same day as me is the Spanish football player, Fernando Torres. Depending on how you calculate the UK charts (the date itself being a Tuesday), the no.1 single on that day was either the brilliant *99 Red Balloons* by Nena, or the cringeworthy *Hello* by Lionel Ritchie. It would be some strange Kafkaesque nightmare if I were to have come out singing, 'Hello, is it me you're looking for?'

My parents were Trevor James Bryant and Maureen Reardon. (My mum was never given a middle name for some reason.) They met in Nottingham where my mum was studying

Modern European History, before moving down south. I was born out of wedlock, which was pretty unusual at the time. They got married two-and-a-bit years later, on 15th July, 1986, at Ramsgate Registry Office, followed by the birth of my brother, Matthew Charles Bryant, in November. My dad worked as a record and music merchandise seller, whilst my mum had a revolving door of jobs as we grew up.

We lived above my dad's record shop, number 1 Turner Street, which stood just off Ramsgate High Street. It was a traditional early 1900s-style building, typical of the Edwardian housing stock along the Kent coastline. My parents rented both the shop and the flat for two years before buying it; astonishingly, the rent was £140 per month for the shop and £140 per month for the flat. My earliest memories are of that flat in Turner Street. It was a pretty cramped dwelling with only three rooms of note: a tiny bedroom that I shared with my younger brother; my parents' slightly larger bedroom; and a central area connecting the two, that served as a living/dining space and occasional playroom. The kitchen (if you could call it that) was no more than five feet wide, with a single toilet behind a paper-thin wall. There was no real bathroom. Essentially, the flat was an upstairs storage space for the shop below; not really adequate for a family of four, plus a rather large dog (more on that later). Connecting the two was this beautifully ornate Victorian-style cast iron spiral staircase, which still exists to this day. The staircase was a death trap for two young kids – not that I thought about it at the time. I have memories of me and my brother having sword fights with rolled-up posters, tearing up and down it like we were storming a castle. To call it a health and safety nightmare would be an understatement.

My recollections of that time are, perhaps not surprisingly, pretty hazy. I remember the toys that I used to play with, particularly a garage set and a penguin slide toy. I remember waking up early on Christmas Day to unwrap a toy police car, which was incredibly exciting. It had this loud siren noise, so I couldn't resist bursting into my parents' bedroom at 5am with this deafening siren blaring. Safe to say, they were not that impressed. Apparently, I was obsessed with The Smiths' song *Panic* when I was two. This was released as a standalone single in 1986, and I would jump around the flat singing the refrain 'hang the DJ' incessantly. My mum said words to the effect of 'Hang that bloody DJ and be done with it.'

Another event that I don't recall, but which has since gone down in Bryant family legend, was a situation involving me releasing some birds. For some unfathomable reason, my mum decided to buy two budgies which lived in a cage in our living room, making one hell of a racket. Whenever I've looked back at the old family videos, they are always squawking away and drowning out all the other noise. One day, I somehow managed to climb up onto the top of the sofa and open the cage, whereupon they proceeded to fly out into the living room and then straight out of the open window. As my mum tried in vain to catch them before they flew out into the big wide world, I uttered the immortal words, 'Never mind, plenty more birdies.' Which in a strange kind of way was quite profound; my version of 'there's plenty more fish in the sea'. It's become something of a motto throughout my life.

When I was about two years old, just after my brother was born, my parents decided to get a guard dog for the shop. Maybe it was the shock of losing the budgies and needing a swift animal replacement. Just behind the shop was a small yard, and my parents thought having a dog stationed there would be a great deterrent for would-be burglars. At that time, Ramsgate wasn't the thriving creative seaside town that it is today. It was a poverty-stricken, gloomy place, shivering on the east Kent coast. It was part of the Isle of Thanet – an area of land that used to be separated from the mainland by a 600-metre channel. This had silted up long ago, with the last ship sailing through in 1672. But it still retained that sense of being adrift from the rest of Kent, with a melange of characters who certainly looked like they'd never left the isle; 'Thanet of the Apes' my dad would ruefully refer to it as. Unemployment was high, and there were a number of unsavoury characters who you wouldn't want to meet down a dark alley. It was a ringing endorsement for Thatcher's Britain. In this climate, getting a fierce guard dog as a deterrent made sense. My parents found an Alsatian at the local pet store and proudly brought her home as our fearsome protector. Unfortunately, she was anything but. She was a quivering wreck, scared of being left alone, and probably no braver than our dearly departed budgies. I think she managed two nights in the kennel outside before her howling brought down the wrath of the neighbours upon us. She had manifestly failed in her role, and from that day onwards she lived inside with us.

On 15th October, 1987, the south coast of England was hit by a violent extra-tropical cyclone, better known as a hurricane to most, but generally referred to by the press as 'The Great Storm'. Winds of up to 122mph battered the Home Counties and caused huge amounts of damage, resulting in excess of £2billion in insurance claims. Around 15million trees across the country were damaged, including a variety of rare specimens in places like Kew Gardens and Wakehurst Place. Whilst researching this book, I learned that the Kent town of Sevenoaks was named after seven ancient oak trees dating back to 800AD, six of which were destroyed by the storm. Ramsgate did not escape unscathed either. I was three years and seven months old when the storm struck, and I can remember the power flickering on and off. The National Grid was badly damaged, resulting in power outages across the country. Apparently, my parents woke up to find me screaming 'too many dark' at the top of my voice. By the morning, the storm had died down and we ventured out to investigate. I do recall, as a toddler, it feeling like the end of the world. The sign which had hung above the record shop had been torn away by the strong winds, as if it were nothing more than a piece of cloth. The streets were deserted, with tree branches, rubble and all manner of detritus strewn everywhere with people pottering around not quite sure what to do with themselves. I guess as a nation we are so unprepared for extreme weather events that when they actually happen people are unsure how to respond. It's funny how the expression 'the calm before the storm' came about, as the calm after an actual storm is so much spookier and more evocative. To my young mind, it was rather like the scene early on in Danny Boyle's film *28 Days Later*, in which a coma victim walks through a London that's been abandoned due to zombies. As luck would have it, we later found the bruised and battered sign for my dad's record shop. It had been blown about a mile away, and we stumbled across it whilst taking the dog for a walk along the beach a couple of days later.

Another of my earliest memories is eating fish and chips along the seafront, though minus the fish. (I was a fussy eater as a child.) I used to think that every morning the staff behind the counter would amble down to the shoreline and collect the salt from the seawater. Back then, with food safety standards laws relatively lax, it was still common practice to wrap fish and chips up in newspapers. This obviously saved the fish and chip shops money and could be considered an early form of recycling. I distinctly remember this, and the occasional random words where the ink would seep into the chips, imprinting them with the day's news. This practice was phased out during the 1980s and became illegal in 1990 with the Food Safety Act. I found out recently that there is a company that produces fake newspaper wrappings to satisfy those who still want to eat their fish and chips from a newspaper.

The record shop itself held no interest for me – it wouldn't for any young child – but I do remember being slightly scared by the black & white Siouxsie Sioux (from Siouxsie and The Banshees) posters that dotted the walls. The street outside was a relatively safe space for us to play as kids; it was just off the pedestrianised high street, so there weren't many cars around. There was a Woolworths about 50 metres from the shop which felt like heaven whenever my mum took me and my brother in there. I remember the Pick'n'Mix section and the excitement of all those different coloured sweets. It was an Aladdin's cave of enamel-erasing ebullience. Woolworths was such an important high street staple when I was growing up, but it wasn't just sweets. You went there for absolutely everything; Clothing, electronics, books, home furnishings, garden paraphernalia. It really was the Westfield's of its day. It was a deeply sombre occasion when it went into liquidation in November 2008. I visited the store with my parents on the final day before it ceased trading, to buy a couple of bits. I also came away with a branded Woolworths' basket which the cashier had no idea whether or not to charge me for. I think, after some debate, I paid 50p for it. I still have it to this day.

From a young age, I loved drinking tea. I can't remember what age exactly but it was something of a family ritual, mainly after dinner when you would allow your food to digest. Tea was the answer to everything: if you wanted to wake up, relax, plan something, get warm – it was always the prudent thing to do. 'Everything stops for tea,' my mum still says. I think it's probably the only thing that I'm addicted to. I still associate it with being a child, wrapped up in a blanket and watching *The Krypton Factor*. Not that much has changed really, though now it's more likely to be *Newsnight* that I'm engrossed in. I remember the first cup of tea that I made for myself. Either I couldn't reach the kettle, or I was nervous about turning it on. Either way, I substituted the kettle for the hot water tap, so the fruits of my labour was a disgusting cup of excessively milky warm water with probably five tablespoons of sugar thrown in for good measure.

The first major news I remember was the fall of the Berlin Wall in 1989. Obviously, I was far too young to understand what was going on, but it was quite a powerful image watching all these men with sledgehammers tear through this imposing concrete structure. Being an island nation, Britain doesn't really have a visible border, so I assumed that any country that wasn't an island had these gigantic walls circling them. I guess it's pretty logical for a five-year-old to come to that conclusion. I have always been fascinated by the sea. Perhaps it's the fact that I'm not a strong swimmer or that I get easily seasick. Whatever the rationale, I always feel humble standing beside the waves, looking out at an endless expanse of undrinkable water that is calm and tranquil but equally vicious and untameable. Living just a stone's throw from the coastline, you were always aware of its presence; this colossal infinity pool being held back by the concrete structures of Ramsgate harbour. As young children, we would toddle along the western arm of the marina and my dad would dangle us over the edge of the raised wall. Beneath my flailing legs I would see the crashing waves below me, whilst feeling the salty spray upon my face. The foam produced by the swell of the sea always used to remind me of a Mr Whippy ice cream. It was exciting and scary in equal measure.

My memories are of the sea in Ramsgate always being grey. Any body of water reflects the colour of the sky, so a dreary autumnal day becomes that much drearier when living by the coast. Ramsgate, in general, seemed to be shrouded in perpetual greyness. I don't really know why. Maybe that's purely retrospective, or maybe we had a non-existent summer one year. Whatever the reason, the world seemed to become so much brighter once we left, like we were moving from black and white to technicolour.

It had become apparent that the flat was far too cramped for a growing family. I would be starting school soon and the education in Ramsgate wasn't exactly first rate, plus neither my mum nor dad were particularly enamoured with the area. They had actually bought both the flat and the shop for the princely sum of £30,000 in 1987. A year later, they sold it to a gentleman called Martin Ellis for £67,000 – essentially doubling their money within a year. He turned it into a shoe repair and key-cutting shop, which (as of 2021) is still there. With the finance in place, they then began the search for somewhere to move to.

Upstreet, a small village about five miles away, was briefly considered before they settled on Canterbury. They knew the city fairly well. Six years earlier, they had both worked at the Cathedral Gate Hotel, a small establishment which simultaneously backed onto the expansive cathedral grounds and overlooked the Buttermarket. It's one of those places that our transatlantic cousins would refer to as 'quaint', being as it is kitted out with beamed ceilings, sloping floors, and crooked doors. At that time, my dad worked in the kitchen and my mum toiled as a waitress, whilst living in the guest rooms above. Clearly, living in the hustle and bustle of tourist town hadn't put them off.

I've spent so much of my life in and around Canterbury that I'm pretty much immune to its charms. I was pretty indifferent to it when I was growing up, and as a teenager it was as dull as dishwater. In reality it's a charming city, full of character and a history that stretches back over a thousand years. It was originally known as Durovernum Cantiacorum. The first part comes from the Romano-British word 'duro', which means walled town. The 'cantii' were an Iron Age Celtic people, living in Britain before the Romans invaded, so part of the name derives from a pre-Roman era. The name then went through several iterations over the centuries, being referred to as Cant-wara byrg, Cantuaria, and finally Canterbury, which was established around the time of the Norman Conquest. Most people wrongly assume that the name is derived from the word 'canter', when in actual fact the reverse is true – the word was named after the city. The word comes from the phrase 'Canterbury gallop', because in the Middle Ages pilgrims used to ride by horse to visit the cathedral at the pace of a canter, i.e. an easy rate of speed.

Canterbury is world-famous for its cathedral, but there are a plethora of other historical structures, including the city walls and St Augustine's Abbey, that attract thousands of visitors each year. It is also home to various buildings which are famous for being 'the oldest'. For instance, St Martin's Church is the first church founded in England, making it the oldest church in the English-speaking world, dating back to 601. There is also the oldest extant school in the world, The King's School, which was established in 597AD.

I remember as a child being terrified by an ancient-looking tree that sat in the Westgate Gardens. It's called an Oriental Plane tree, in excess of 200 years old and, you guessed it, the oldest specimen in the country. The branches were spindly and misshapen, stretching out above you like the tentacles of a kraken. The trunk itself was bulbous and knobbly, with swollen bark that made it look as if it were covered in boils ready to burst. There was a rumour that the tree had completely engulfed a metal seat that once surrounded it. I can't remember who told me this, but I heard it mentioned on more than one occasion. I don't think I realised that if this were true, it would have happened gradually over many decades. I had visions of this tree coming to life in the dead of night (*à la Lord of The Rings*) and devouring this bench. I had freaky nightmares about being swallowed up by this sprawling tree for weeks afterwards.

My parents purchased their new home for £56,000 in June 1989. It was an old Edwardian terrace which was in dire need of repair: no hot water, no electricity, but space-wise it was a massive step-up from the old flat. A separate living room and dining room; a front and back garden; a functioning bathroom! I still shared a bedroom with my brother (which I would do until I was 18), but it was much larger, with actual beds as opposed to bunk beds. It was in a lovely dead-end street called Lansdown Road, a 15-minute stroll from the centre of Canterbury. I remember bits of the move – the journey down on the train with our dog, and seeing all our possessions piled up in the middle of the dining room floor, like some gigantic jumble sale. It all felt like one big adventure.

CHAPTER 2

Primary School

Due to the recent upheaval, I had missed the start of the school year. My mum, however, was never one to blindly follow the rules. Usually, you would look within your catchment area for a suitable school. Instead, my mum chose the best primary school in Canterbury, strode right in and demanded to speak with the Headmaster, somehow convincing him that our background was Protestant Christianity (it was a Methodist primary school), and I was in.

I didn't realise at the time quite how well renowned a school it was, but during the 1990s it was frequently nominated as one of the best in the South East. Its small size helped – there was only one class per year, maximum of thirty, so there were less than two hundred children in the entire school. It was relatively spacious, with a tarmacked playground, a small sports field and a well-maintained orchard area. It had originally been built as a Sunday School in 1871, with a narrow passageway connecting the church to the main brick building. When the school expanded in the 1970s, these horrendous grey mobile classrooms were constructed to house the excess pupils. The outer walls of them were coated in an Artex-like substance, with a texture that resembled sharp sandpaper. I was continually scraping my hands on them when charging around during the lunch break. I think these types of mobile classrooms were later banned when it was discovered that they contained asbestos. Questionable aesthetic choices aside, it was a beautifully cared-for little school.

By this point, my dad had abandoned the idea of owning a record shop. Although the footfall in Canterbury was much greater, so too were the ground rents. The Cathedral owned a huge amount of land in the city centre and the rents reflected that. Instead, my dad hired space inside a series of indoor markets. First, at a place called the Harvey Centre, which was based in Love Lane and then Stour Street, followed by a market just off the main high street, called Rastro's. These three places were basically all the same – a series of makeshift stalls selling everything and anything. Most of them were focused on antiques, but there were also stalls that sold vintage clothing, books, collectables, and jewellery. There were many days during the school holidays when Matt and I would spend time there. Mostly, it was pretty dull, though occasionally we would find things to keep us entertained. Using the scaffolding that encased the building as a makeshift climbing frame was a frequent time-draining pastime. There was also a stall that had old vintage comic books that I would spend hours reading. I loved the old *Beano* comics; even though they were 20-30 years old, somehow I found them much more interesting than the modern incarnations. I loved Dennis the Menace, Roger the Dodger, and especially the Bash Street Kids.I pretty much ignored the Superhero comics. I never really understood the superhero craze, and to this day I find Superhero films (X-Men/ Batman, etc.) incredibly dull. I think I found the old *Beano* and *Dandy* comics more exciting because you could relate a lot more to the characters. I always found Dennis the Menace's latest scheme to steal an apple pie much more engrossing than Superman saving the world from crazed dictators.

When I was young, I assumed that almost every adult worked in high street shops. In much the same way that some children think their teachers live in schools, I thought that when people grew up, everyone worked in a WH Smith or a Marks & Spencers. I knew from cartoons that there were other jobs, i.e. Postmen (Postman Pat) and Firefighters (Fireman Sam), but by and large I thought that the majority of people ended up working in a high street shop. I guess that was quite a logical thing to think in pre-internet days. I think my dream was to work at the Pick'n'Mix counter at Woolworths.

I was a pretty quiet child at primary school. I didn't like being the centre of attention, preferring to blend into the background. I never played football, for instance, although I was quite energetic and enjoyed running around. British Bulldog was a game I loved playing, until all the schools in England decided to ban it after a few injuries caused a moral panic in the press. The rules were pretty simple:

'1 player is selected to be the bulldog who stands in the middle of the play area. All remaining players stand at one end of the area (the home). The aim of the game is to run from one end of the field of play to the other, without being caught by the bulldog. When a player is caught via physical contact, they become a bulldog themselves, so the number of bulldogs exponentially increases. The winner is the last player left.'

In fairness, trying to rugby tackle other children on a tarmacked playground is fraught with danger, and I do remember seeing a few bruised knees (as well as bruised egos).

My best friend at primary school was a guy called Richard Bore. We didn't have much in common other than our dislike of football and a shared love of dinosaurs. We would have in-depth conversations about the most nuanced dinosaur facts: which breed was larger; how fast they could run; and what the correct palaeontological name was for a Brontosaurus. (It's Brachiosaurus.) We also used to collect these dinosaur magazines which were a slightly bizarre pre-Jurassic Park cocktail of cartoon imagery, hard science, and surprisingly graphic comic strips. With each issue you would get a piece of plastic bone that you could eventually build into a model dinosaur. I remember the sense of achievement in finally building it after two years of my mum buying the magazines for me at a (relatively speaking) exorbitant cost. I haven't heard from Richard in over twenty years, but I know he's now a high-flying city lawyer, most famous for selling off the previously British brand Weetabix to a company based in the US.

My other close friend was a boy from Nigeria called Chioma Rouse Armadi. He was also a very bright and precocious boy, though his mother had a very controlling personality. She pushed him incredibly hard from a very young age. He was always near the top of the class but that was never enough for his mum. She actually broke into the school during lunchtime and went through his exercise books to check that he wasn't lying and that he actually was the top of the class. Once, when he was maybe fifteen or so he wrote her a birthday card but accidentally spelt 'birthday' wrong. She was livid and locked him in the house for a couple of days after that, telling my mum that he was a terrible son and would never amount to anything. It was quite sad as he had such a lovely temperament and I remember thinking how lucky I was to have parents that weren't that overbearing. We are still in contact, although he now lives in New Zealand as a Buddhist monk.

Academically, I did pretty well at primary school. I really enjoyed English and the Humanities subjects (Geography/

History). I was also pretty good at spelling. I remember being inconsolable when I couldn't spell the word 'elephant' correctly. I think I assumed that all my classmates had got it right in a spelling test, so my mum's efforts at consoling me were in vain. From then onwards, I became pretty good at spelling, and by the time I finished at St Peter's the teachers were sometimes asking me how to spell. I remember telling our Year 5 tutor how to spell 'discombobulated'. There was no spell check in those days, so being able to spell difficult words quickly was a real skill; it was too time-consuming to continually refer to a dictionary. This is definitely something that has been lost over the years with spell check and predictive text on phones rendering spelling prowess largely irrelevant. Consequently, my spelling has now regressed again, probably to the time when I was around 13/14. Still, I will always have that happy memory of telling my teacher how to spell discombobulated.

From what I recall, the teachers at St Peter's were excellent. I remember the first time that we were left alone by a teacher at around nine years of age. Even then, you weren't allowed to leave children that young unsupervised, but our teacher said she needed to make an urgent phone call. This was in the days before mobiles, so making important calls was always a thorny issue. The nearest phone was located on the other side of the school, so she made us promise that we would behave ourselves, carry on with our work, and not get up to any mischief. Of course, as soon as she left, people started chatting, jumping up on tables, and running riot around the room. One of the kids went into the teachers' stationary cupboard and pulled out a staple gun, before turning around to another pupil, 'I dare you to let me staple your hand to the wall.'

'Okay,' he responded, in that naively innocent voice that all prepubescent children have. He then proceeded to let the boy attach his finger to the wall. That was swiftly followed by the most piercingly high-pitched scream one could imagine. The teacher came running back into the room to see a child stapled to the wall, screaming in pain, as blood was oozing out from his index finger. All these globules, the colour of tomato ketchup, were dripping down the Year 4 Roman history display. She never left us alone after that.

At primary school, there were two major toy crazes I remember – Pogs and Boglins. Pogs were an updated version of milk caps, a game that originated in Hawaii in the 1920s. As the name would suggest, it was originally played using the caps of milk bottles, and later, fruit drinks. In fact, the initials of POG stood for passion fruit, orange, and guava – a brand of juice drink that was marketed as being great for playing milk caps. When the craze was revived in the 1990s, it was a massive success. We collected them like other kids collected football stickers. You had two types of POG – the traditional cardboard discs with a variety of ornate artworks, and slammers (marketed as Kinis), which were thicker discs made of plastic. I was obsessed with collecting them. These were pre-internet days, so no-one had any idea how many variations/designs there were. We kept on spending our pocket money trying to find that elusive design that no-one else had. I remember once getting a gold coloured pen and tracing round the outline of a design to create this unique hybrid which I then swapped for ten others. The object of the game was to steal as many of your opponent's caps as possible by slamming the Kini into the cardboard discs and attempting to turn them over.

Gameplay:

Each player has his/her own collection of milk caps and one or more slammers. Before the game, players decide whether or not to play 'for keeps', i.e. players get to keep the milk caps that they win during the game, and must forfeit those that have been won by other players. The game can then begin as follows:

- The players each contribute an equal number of milk caps to build a stack, with the pieces face down, which will be used during the game.
- The players take turns throwing their slammer down onto the top of the stack, causing it to spring up and the milk caps to scatter. Each player keeps any milk caps that land face-up after they have thrown.
- After each throw, the milk caps which have landed face down are then re-stacked for the next player.
- When no milk caps remain in the stack, the player with the most pogs is the winner.

As you can imagine, any game that potentially involved losing what you had spent months of precious pocket money on caused endless arguments. There was even a piece on the BBC News about incensed parents who accused other children of stealing their toys. I remember watching it and being more interested in the designs that briefly flashed up on screen. In the end, they were a victim of their own success. Schools ended up banning them, and eventually we all moved on to other things.

Boglins were the other craze I remember. These were a series of toy puppets made out of flexible rubber that were designed to look like little monsters, similar to the Gremlins craze a few years earlier. I only owned a handful but James, the kid across the street, had loads. We had great fun destroying them, particularly melting them onto bonfires, where they would twist and turn into even more grotesque shapes. Because they were designed to be stretched and used as hand-puppets, they easily got damaged. That, coupled with the fact they weren't tied into any TV show or comic book, and as such no individual design was manufactured in any great quantity, meant they are now incredibly rare. If you look on eBay, you'll find Boglins worth hundreds if not thousands of pounds, and to think we spent most of our time blithely disfiguring and destroying them.

From an early age, I suffered from travel sickness. Neither of my parents drove, so I never rode in a car until I was maybe eight or so. The occasional coach trips we took when I was at primary school felt like hell to me. I'm sure I was sick every time, much to the girls' horror and the boys' amusement. Travel sickness tablets were always ineffectual, the only remedy seemed to be eating and drinking as little as possible on the day. That wasn't always possible when my mum insisted on force-feeding me mushrooms on toast for breakfast. Years later, I discovered that my sickness was due to an ear imbalance, when I went to the doctor's after suffering a perforated eardrum. I recall one instance when we took a coach trip to the Natural History Museum in London. Some of the kids were taking bets at which point of the journey I would throw up. We pulled into Victoria Coach Station and came to a standstill. One of the other kids shouted, 'He's made it!' and patted me on the back, at which point I threw up all down the aisle. As you can imagine, I usually sat alone on these trips.

Travel sickness aside, I really enjoyed primary school. In all honesty, I didn't work that hard, but I could get away with it because I absorbed information really easily. My very first school report (written on a typewriter) states that 'Chris tends to rush his work in order to be allowed to play with the Lego'. That was basically the case for the first five years of primary school, although when it came to homework. I would substitute Lego with TV.

Television was a big part of my life as a child. I watched Kids TV, of course (*ChuckleVision*, *Teenage Mutant Hero Turtles,* and *Live & Kicking* were all big favourites), but I loved game shows most of all, especially *The Crystal Maze* and *Gladiators*. Many years later, I would get to live my dream and do the Crystal Maze for real in 2016. I became obsessed with *Doctor Who* a bit later on, and would spend hours reading all the books and writing out comics in between those magical birthdays and Christmases when my parents would buy me the videos. I also loved the family shows that I would watch with my parents, things like *Only Fools & Horses*. These were the days when you would gather around TVs to watch shows together, and plan your day accordingly. For instance, we would have dinner at a predetermined time, leave twenty minutes to clear up, unplug the phone, and draw the curtains so as not to be disturbed. It sounds so antiquated now, but there were only four channels in our house (BBC1, BBC2, ITV, & Channel 4) and no such thing as streaming or on demand catch-ups. You either had to watch a show live or set up the video recorder.

Setting up a video recorder was a surprisingly complex operation. I became a bit of an expert at it, but even then, things could go wrong. For starters, blank videotape wasn't cheap, so you only had a certain amount of space. You had to try and squeeze as many shows as possible onto one tape, which required precision timing. You had to pause and then remember to un-pause during the advert breaks, cut out the recaps (if there were any), and sometimes excise the ending credits, depending on the duration. You then had to write on the tape the length of the recording, so that you knew exactly how much longer you had left. If you wanted to go out you had to set the timer, which didn't always work. If, for instance, a football match went into extra time, it was hit and miss whether or not the VCR would be smart enough to realise.

This could also prove to be a problem if you then wanted to record over the next hour of excess programming, as the quality would begin to degrade after two or three shows had been re-recorded over. To make matters even more complex we didn't have a standard electricity supply. We had a metered key, which meant my parents needed to remember to go and buy 'top up electricity' every few days. There were many occasions when they would forget, and the electricity supply would literally turn itself off as if there were a power failure. To remedy this, you needed to reset the electric box in the hallway, which would then take you into the reserve power. This was sufficient for a few hours until you went to the shop to 'top up'. I recall one occasion when my dad was recording an episode of Jools Holland and the power went off. Suddenly, it was a mad scramble to get to the box, get back, and reset the VCR. So many of our videos had bizarre 'snowstorm' gaps that lasted a minute or so as a result of this.

The feeling of gathering around a television to watch a programme is now something that is lost to time. It was probably the scarcity of content that made it such an important bonding experience. I guess the only parallel left is live sport when, for instance, you go and watch a World Cup or Wimbledon match. You wouldn't get quite the same sensation if you watched it a few days later, already knowing what the score was. That's the equivalent of how all TV was back then. There were no digital channels, no catch-up services, no YouTube, no internet at all in family homes. You didn't want to be the only kid in school who couldn't join in because you'd missed a certain show and it was probably the same for adults with their work colleagues. I remember one time when half of my class (not the half I was in) brought in cakes to raise money for Children In Need. We were told that all the names of the kids were going to be mentioned by Terry Wogan live on air. For whatever reason, one of my classmates forgot about it and was absolutely distraught the following day when everyone else was discussing it. He was sobbing his eyes out because he'd missed his big TV debut. The teacher made a point of asking the class if any of our parents had recorded it, and so began a frantic search to find a version of it. It took days. I think another teacher eventually found a copy, and he finally got to see his blink-and-you'll-miss-it moment.

Canterbury wasn't a particularly exciting town, although occasionally celebrities would drop by. The first celebrity I ever saw was Tony Robinson. Not exactly 'big league', but I recognised him off the TV. They were filming an episode of *Time Team* in Stour Street just outside my dad's market. They were excavating in preparation for a new housing development, so I got taken along to go and watch them dig up the site. In truth, there wasn't much to see – a few exposed foundations and middle-aged men dusting bricks with brushes. The best bit was on the local news that evening when they ran a small piece on the dig and I saw myself in the crowd. To a young child being on TV, even just in the background for a split second, was very exciting.

In my childhood, there was never a school fête or weekend outing that passed without me consuming a significant percentage of my own body weight in Panda Pops. These were small bottles of fizzy drink that were the poor man's Coke or Tango. Brightly coloured liquid that was stuffed with E numbers and more chemical stimulants than Ozzy Osbourne's bathroom cabinet. Panda Pops never tasted quite the same as the real stuff; in fact, I don't think I ever even had a chilled one. They were as sweet and sticky as it was possible for a drink to be. They came in a variety of flavours, none of which bore any resemblance to the natural product they were trying to emulate. I think the cherry flavour was my favourite. At five pence a bottle, they were always the cheap bulk buy item, so were frequently the worst available tombola prize. I remember at the St Peter's summer fair one year when they hosted a fancy hat competition, my mum had made me this yellow stove pipe-type hat out of paper and card, which I proudly wore throughout the day. It was almost as tall as I was. I won some kind of prize token for it which I could exchange for various food and drink items. I opted for quantity over quality – it was Panda Pops all round. Me and my friends then spent the next sugar-crazed hour chasing each other around like over-excited Tasmanian Devils. As a bonus, you could then refill the bottles with tap water and create makeshift water pistols, an imminently more sensible purchase than a couple of fairy cakes. It seemed to be much more socially acceptable to give kids junk food in those days. I don't think it was even a class thing; everyone loved a McDonald's birthday party, for instance. I think people knew that these processed items were bad for children but parents were just more relaxed about it. This was many years before all the moral panics around obesity and Jamie's Oliver's quest to improve the nutritional content of school dinners. Years later, Panda Pops became one of the many casualties of a new health conscious public and were banned in the UK.

Later that same summer, my brother had a nasty accident involving a pan of boiling water. It's strange that certain events you can recall in intimate detail, whilst other memories melt away like a snowman on a mild winter's morning. I recall what I was wearing (blue shorts), what I was eating (a mandarin), and exactly where I was sitting (on the concrete step in the back garden). Mum and I heard this ear-piercing scream, and she darted inside to see what had happened. Matt, who was around seven or eight at the time, had reached up onto the stove and grabbed the handle of a saucepan that was on the boil, tipping the liquid contents over himself. Every parent's worst nightmare, I imagine. He was incredibly lucky in that he missed his face, with the water splashing down onto his arms and upper torso. The scarring is still there, but in the grand scheme of things he was pretty fortunate.

When I was ten years old, I came third in a regional poetry competition for children. I remember it feeling like a meritorious achievement having some creative writing recognised outside of St Peter's. My Mum and I were invited to a special award ceremony at one of Canterbury's top secondary schools – Simon Langton. I recall walking in and it feeling really imposing. We got lost trying to fathom out where we were supposed to be going, as we walked down seemingly endless rows of corridors with these towering banks of lockers. It reminded me of *Grange Hill* (a kids' TV programme from the early 90s, set in a London school), so I associated it with bullying and scary older kids. I think it was then that I decided that I never wanted to attend this terrifying school. We eventually found the room where they had laid on this buffet spread for all the guests. According to my mum, I didn't stop gobbling up the food for the next hour. There was one official photo taken of me on stage when I collected my certificate, but all the other photos my mum took were of me gorging at the buffet stand. It was incredible. Things I'd never eaten before like buffalo wings, vol-au-vents, and all these delicious types of pastries. I think it was supposed to be a networking event where kids and their parents talked about their aspirations and routes into Oxbridge – and I came in, devouring the catering like some half-starved orphan from Dickens.

We would go and visit my grandparents fairly regularly when I was younger. I remember the shock of arriving in London for the first time and witnessing how different it was from quaint, conservative Canterbury. Victoria train station was almost like a grotty Cathedral with its towering pillars and frosted glass roof. I had never seen a train station with more than four platforms, never mind 24. Victoria Bus station, just outside, was a maze of choking traffic fumes and unintelligible noise. I was profoundly shocked by all the dazzling diversity. At St Peter's, almost everyone in the entire school was white. Apart from Chioma, I think there were only two other kids that came from non-white backgrounds. Here, it seemed like there were people from every corner of the globe. The bus route we took was the number 16, which my mum used to call the banana bus because they always came in bunches of three. Because of my travel sickness I would always sit on the top deck and try and aim (like all kids do) for the front seat. Almost as soon as we got out of the bus station, London suddenly became a lot smarter, as we drove round Buckingham Palace, past the Wellington Arch, down Park Lane, and around Marble Arch. I loved looking at all the statues – it all seemed so regal, dead faces from a bygone imperial era. My imperial illusions were then shattered as we drove down Edgeware Road. Nowadays, I think this part of London is referred to as shabby chic, but it certainly wasn't chic then, just shabby. Full of overflowing bins, homeless people, strange market stalls, and call girl stickers plastered everywhere.

Edgeware Road once formed part of an ancient trackway that stretched all the way from the River Severn in the West Midlands down to the port of Dover in Kent. The Romans later incorporated part of this track into Watling Street, stretching all the way to Canterbury and past my dad's shop – that used to blow my mind! The section in London is an almost perfectly straight ten-mile road which goes all the way out to the M25. Sitting on that bus, it certainly felt like it went on forever, probably a combination of the terrible traffic and my nervous nausea. I vividly recall my brother and I fidgeting as we sat under Hammersmith flyover waiting for the lights to change. Once we reached Maida Vale, the traffic died down a little and the area became a bit more pleasant again.

My mum's parents lived in a ground floor council flat set back from the road by a narrow green strip of land. As it had a staircase and a back garden, it didn't really feel like a flat. Nowadays, it would be marketed as a maisonette. It was fairly modest, though it did have two bedrooms and two toilets – so a generous size for two elderly people. As well as the small garden area, it backed onto a shared green space full of apple trees. Me and my brother used to have great fun scrambling up and down them whenever our cousins, Sarah and Kylie, came to visit. My grandparents, Charlie and Eileen, had lived there pretty much their whole lives and rather infuriatingly had refused to buy the flat even when the council offered it to them. I imagine that a ground floor maisonette with two bedrooms, a garden, and a shared orchard that's a thirty-minute stroll from Hyde Park, must now be worth something with six zeros in it.

I don't have many recollections of my Grandmother Eileen, as she died when I was only ten years old. My Grandad Charlie lived for another fifteen years after that. I remember her being very kind and gentle – the complete opposite of my grandad, who my mum would affectionately term 'the old git'. He had been an alcoholic most of his life and behaved quite aggressively to his family. He was perfectly fine with me and my brother, though I suspect it was probably age that had mellowed him slightly. The only occasion I remember him being slightly off with me was a few years later, when he was shocked that I didn't have a job (I was still at school at the time), and he started having a go at my mum saying I was a layabout and she hadn't brought me up properly. I can't have been any older than 14 or 15. That was probably a generational thing, where if you hadn't started work by the time you were 13, you would have starved in 1930s London. On a more positive note, he did his best to look after us whenever we stayed, though breakfast was exclusively beans on toast.

The worst thing about staying over was the tobacco smoke. He smoked like an absolute chimney. I remember always walking into that flat and struggling to breathe. You'd open the door and the smoke fumes would disperse in front of you, like the parting of the Red Sea. It would cling to every item of furniture in a permanent state of noxious embrace. It was also one of the more toxic brands of tobacco with no filters and never an open window, not even on the hottest summer's day. Any excuse to go outside, whether to go and climb on the apple trees or take a trip to the local garage, we would grasp with both hands just so we could get a literal breather. The other thing I recall about the house were the pillows that me and my brother referred to as 'sandbag pillows'. He was such a make-do-and-mend hoarder that it wouldn't have surprised me if they were literal sandbags leftover from the war. I remember trying to sleep on those bloody things, giving up and throwing one to the floor, whereupon it made this massive thud sound. Pillows should never go thud.

Every trip to my grandad's resulted in my mum receiving a goody-bag. Somehow my grandfather would always receive the same items straight off the back of a lorry. It was always John West tuna, Pantene Shampoo, these tinned mints called Altoids, and Werther's Originals. Never one for diplomacy, he would also inevitably give my mum some skin cream and say, 'There you go, girl, that's for your wrinkles.' If my parents' house was stuck in a 1970s' time warp, my grandparents' abode was perpetually trapped in the 1940s. Everything was as basic as could be – no luxuries like toasters or washing machines. There was a wireless that only had three or four stations and a television that had to be seen to be believed. Not only was it not colour (he would never pay the extra for a colour TV licence), it wasn't even black & white! Some strange distortion had turned it black and a hideous shade of Frankenstein green. Watching snooker was certainly out of the question. He had worked most of his life as a newspaper vendor, but had various little businesses on the sidelines. I remember him telling my mum about the Coronation of Elizabeth II in 1953. Because the crowds were so vast, he made a fortune by going round the streets and selling people empty boxes, so that they could stand on top of them and get a better view of the proceedings.

There were quite a few family members on my mum's side who could be considered 'characters'. My grandad was pretty much a saint compared to his nephew, Anthony (my mum's cousin), who I only met a couple of times. He was a real-life East End gangster, straight out of a Guy Ritchie film. He had been implicated in some very shady business back in the 1980s, but somehow he avoided a prison sentence – only on the condition that he never set foot in London again. He had moved to Brighton and set up a chain of successful pubs and clubs along the seafront. When I moved to Brighton, unbeknown to me, I was a regular at one of his clubs. I met up with him at a funeral a few years later and we got chatting about Brighton. I was just talking about some of the bars I went to, and casually mentioned that I'd been thrown out of one for being too inebriated. He replied in cryptically Vinny Jones-esque fashion, 'If you ever want my boys to sort anything out for you down there, let me know.' That set alarm bells ringing, I pieced two and two together and avoided him for the rest of the day.

My mum's sister, confusingly also called Eileen, lived about ten minutes away from my Grandad, down a bustling market street called Church Street. She lived with her partner Anthony and my two cousins Claire and Jo McPhillips. She had a heart of gold, but would be turned down as an *EastEnders* character for being too gritty. She had a fear of the dentist, the result of which was a series of blackened teeth that caused her to be banned from various weddings, due to the risk of her ruining the wedding photos. Despite being eight years younger than my mum (the baby of the family), she looked about ten years older. Scary teeth aside, Matt and I loved going round there when we were kids, mainly because we could play with our cousins who were close to our ages and were able to breathe a bit easier. There was still a nicotine haze but at least the windows occasionally got opened.

However, the best thing about going there (to a ten-year-old child, anyway) was that they had a computer console called a NES (a Nintendo Entertainment System). The only computer game I'd played before was Trains, a basic signalling game on the Year 5 class computer (one of only three computers in the entire school). But this was something else entirely; they had 'Duck Hunt', a car racing game whose name eludes me, and best of all 'Super Mario Brothers'. We became obsessed with all the different levels and colourful graphics and begged our parents for one. I think if we'd got a console then it would have melted our brains, so rather sensibly it was another three years until our parents acquiesced and bought us one for Christmas.

The estate which my cousins lived on was pretty rough, even by inner city London standards. There were so many things I'd never experienced before, like bars across the lower ground windows. In spite of all the degradation, though, there was a real sense of community. Most of these people were just trying to survive the best way they could and although money was tight, people tried to do their very best for their kids. I remember going with our cousins to this huge swimming complex, complete with water slides and jacuzzis- that was so much more exciting than the bog-standard pools we had back in Canterbury.

Another thing we used to do semi-regularly was to go and feed the pigeons in Trafalgar Square. You would buy bags of pigeon food from various sellers around the square and turn yourself into a walking bird buffet. Your feathery friends would then flock around you in a twister-like formation, whilst you dodged the bird poo like a stealthy ninja. It was great fun. The pigeons actually began flocking to Trafalgar Square before it was even completed in 1844. Food sellers quickly cottoned onto the fact that they could make a living out of it by charging people for bird seed. (Tuppence a bag, if Walt Disney is to be believed.) This finally became illegal in 2003, when it was decided that the square was starting to look tatty and that the pigeons posed a health risk to visitors. There was a surprising number of people who were unhappy about this and there was a big campaign in the media around re-introducing small numbers of birds. There was even an action group called the STTSP (Save The Trafalgar Square Pigeons) set up. As far as I'm aware, this is no longer in existence, though driving past the other day on the bus, I began to feel nostalgic for feather and bird poo-encrusted shoes. Maybe I'll start a campaign to relaunch the STTSP.

A couple of years later, my auntie received a knock on her door from the police. They were investigating various flats on the estate, including the flat above, as they believed it to be housing a sophisticated drug factory. They wanted to use my auntie's flat as the base for their police operations and said that in return they would offer them another property anywhere in the country. That must have felt like hitting the jackpot. Imagine a stranger turning up on your doorstep and offering to buy you a house! They chose a small town just outside London called Potters Bar, and essentially upgraded to a larger house in a leafy commuter area. It wasn't glamorous by any means, but it was a huge step-up from that estate.

My mum had another sister, Norah, and two brothers, Jimmy and Charlie. It was a bit like the Spice Girls, in that I had nicknames for all of them when growing up. Jimmy was the fun one; Charlie the mad one; Norah the posh one; Eileen the baby one; and my mum (through closer association) the normal one. As a ten-year-old, I think I was pretty spot-on with my one-word character descriptions.

My dad's side of the family was based in Colchester. My grandad, Eric, had worked as a lorry driver as a younger man, whilst my grandmother was a well renowned accordion player. They lived in a 1940s' style house just up the road from the Colchester army barracks. Colchester, as a town, wasn't that dissimilar to Canterbury. It was a settlement of similar size, with a population that was slightly on the right of British politics. It once had an important role as the Roman capital of England, but was now better known for being the home of Dermot O'Leary and the band Blur. The best thing about visiting my grandparents was the hilarious cat they had, Fred, who was nicknamed 'Fat Fred'. A rescue cat from previous owners who had severely overfed him, he was gigantic, resembling a furry armadillo more than a house cat. When he walked downstairs, the landing would vibrate with a thud, thud, thud. He wasn't able to clean himself, if he turned over onto his back he wouldn't be able to get back up again. He would just lie there with his paws flailing in the air, like an upside-down turtle, until someone came to his rescue. He had such a lovely temperament and was affectionate to everyone he met. Most cats are wary of strangers, especially of toddlers and kids with their unpredictable movements, but not Fat Fred. The only issue was if he caught you unawares by jumping onto your lap, which was always a seismic shock. He was lovely and warm, though; better than a blanket in winter. My dad's brother, Howard, lived directly opposite his parents in Colchester. This meant it was just a quick dart across the road whenever we went up to see them. He lived there with his wife Sharon and three daughters, Leonie, Gemma, and Crystal. He worked all his life as a taxi driver in Colchester and the associated towns.

Here's a little bit of trivia. Now that (spoiler alert!) I have a daughter, I've been doing a bit of research into the origin of various nursery rhymes. The world's most famous nursery rhyme 'Twinkle Twinkle Little Star' was written in Colchester in 1806, in a street called Stockwell Street. Incidentally, 'Twinkle Twinkle' is just about the only nursery rhyme that doesn't have sinister undertones. All the rest are a 'who's who' of inappropriate topics for young children. 'Ring-a-ring-a-roses' is famously about the bubonic plague, but there's much worse. 'Oranges and lemons' is about child sacrifice; 'Georgie Porgie' is about sexual harassment; and 'Pop goes the weasel' is a tale of child destitution. 'Mary, Mary, quite contrary' just about wins the award for the most inappropriate, being a jolly old tale of the favoured torture practices of Queen Mary's court. The silver bells refers to thumbscrews, and cockleshells is a reference to a torture device you attach to the genitals. All good wholesome stuff for toddlers.

It was on one of these trips up to see my grandparents in Colchester that I had an accident involving a train door. Back then, almost all train doors had to be physically slammed shut by the passengers. There was usually a train guard on the platforms who would double check that the doors were closed, but basically passengers were responsible themselves. They became known as 'slam door trains' once electronically controlled doors became more common place. It sounds unbelievable now but as they could be opened from both the inside and outside, they could and would be opened when the train was in motion. When the locomotives would pull into busy stations, it was normal practice for eager commuters to open the doors before the train had stopped, jumping out whilst the engine was still slowing down to save a precious few seconds. When I was at secondary school, I recall running along the platform to catch a train that had already left and jumping on whilst half the carriage had left the platform. The guards would shout at you, but it was still a relatively normal thing to do. After a series of high-profile accidents they started to be withdrawn at the end of the 90s.

It was on one of these trains that I got my thumb slammed in one of the doors. I was sitting with my dad and brother when a lady got on and forcefully closed the door behind her. I must have somehow rested my hand in front of the locking mechanism without realising. I remember crying out and my thumb throbbing. Luckily, my hands were so small that they were sort of wedged into the mechanism without anything breaking. We got off at the next station, which I think was Dartford, and made our way to Darent Valley Hospital. Fortunately, there was no permanent damage – just a thumb that I could suck to make myself feel better.

Lansdown Road was a great street to grow up in. The summer months were heaven. We had a street where cars were rare, and a series of back alleys to play in. One of these ended behind my friend James' house, so we were continually charging around and climbing over fences, in a perpetual loop of giddy excitement. We played all the usual childhood games: catch, water pistols, football, constructing treehouses. There were about eight of us who would regularly play outside. Aside from me and my brother, there was James and Emily across the street, a pair of adopted brothers called Jason and Darren, and Sam and Warren who lived directly opposite.

I think we were pretty well-behaved kids, although some of the neighbours didn't seem to think so. Next door to us lived a really cranky man called John, who we christened Grumpy John, or GJ for short. He was miserable as sin, and forever complaining about the noise. He once wrote my parents a letter complaining about how often the door to our bedroom banged, and had even sat down with a watch to time it. One day, we were outside just having a kick around with a football when he came out absolutely livid about something, picked up the ball, and volleyed it about eighty yards. It flew down the street like a speeding bullet, dipped over some railings, and bounced onto the nearby railway track. We were gob-struck. One day, we found an abandoned pram down the back of the alley. We attempted to do it up, and christened it the Lansdown buggy. We got some paint off the neighbours, added some bike spoke beads (you used to always get them free in cereal packets), a horn, some reflectors, and greased it with oil to make it go faster. I don't know why we put so much effort in, we all had our own bikes to ride down the street with. Anyway, we were very proud of our buggy and had great fun pushing each other along in it. We would take it to the local park, pushing each other down the hill whilst we clung onto it for dear life, as if auditioning to become the perilous prodigies of Evel Knievel. Inevitably, we always came back carved up in a range of cuts and bruises.

Lansdown Road had quite an interesting history. Like most places, the area was originally fields and known as Nunnery Fields because of a nunnery that stood to the west of them. There was one nun in particular who gained notoriety – a lady called Elizabeth Barton, who was executed by Henry VIII for prophesising his death after his divorce to Catherine Aragon. The land was first developed into houses after the railway cut through the area, and the train station was built in 1860. They were built by a chap called Jon Lansdowne in 1874, as railway cottages for all the rail workers. The name of the street is a play on words, being his surname and also its location at the bottom of a hill. There used to be a pub that stood at the end of the road, called The Nunnery Tavern, that was built at the same time but closed down in 1968. When I was growing up there were two corner shops at the end of the street. One was a standard convenience store that was owned by an Indian family. The other was a really strange little shop that we nicknamed 'Aliens'. I can't remember the reason why we called it Aliens, but it was a really odd shop. It didn't sell very much and was hardly ever open. We came up with an advertising slogan for it which went: '*When other shops are open, we're closed, when other shops are closed, we're still closed.*'

I remember going in there – I must have been about ten or eleven – to buy some yoghurts. The lady behind the counter looked ancient; she probably wasn't, but she looked like she was knocking on 100. She couldn't reach the yoghurts from behind the counter, so we were told to come back the following day. No wonder it closed down a couple of years later. It's now been converted into flats. They did try to branch out once, by turning the back space into a little art gallery café. 'Be dazzled while you dine' was the slogan. I seem to recall some of the artwork having shards of glass sticking out of the wall, which was ill-advised in such a confined space. I think it got shut down due to health and safety; either that, or people gave up with the shop when they couldn't get their weekly fix of yoghurts.

In 1994, I went to my first football game when Richard's dad took me, Richard, and Chioma to watch our local-ish team, Gillingham. Tony Pullis, who would later go on to manage in the Premier League, had just taken over as manager. Although I wasn't aware of it at the time, this was a big deal and the start of them clawing their way back up the leagues. The general admission price for an adult was £1.50 and 90p for children. I remember seeing it on the ticket stub and thinking, 'Wow, that's the price of three Mars Bars!' The stadium was a bit of a wreck, with wooden benches and converted sheds covered in peeling green paint circling this muddy bog in the centre. It was a far cry from the gleaming stadia of today. I recollect seeing people clambering up these gangly beech trees which overlooked the ground, in order to get a free view of the action. That looked so much more exciting than these twenty-two men chasing a ball back and forth. It seemed to go on forever, so we spent most of the time playing hide and seek amongst the benches. I can't even remember if the super Gills triumphed.

Christmas was a massive deal when I was growing up. We always had a real Christmas tree with the smell of pine needles being something I still associate with snowy winter mornings and the excitement of the big day. Chocolates on the Christmas tree never seemed to last. There was this bizarre tradition (probably initiated by me) where we would replace the eaten chocolates with Lego bricks, re-wrap them, and hang them back on the tree so that people assumed there were more treats left than there actually were. It started off as a clever ploy for me to eat more chocolate than I was probably allowed but once my brother joined in, it became impossible to know what was real and what was fake. Inevitably, when my mum fancied a chocolate and took one off the tree, she would end up exclaiming, 'Not another Lego brick!'

My brother and I used to go wild with the decorations, pinning tinsel and cards over every surface we could: picture frames, the TV, the jukebox. It looked like Santa's grotto by the time we had finished. There were also the excessive Christmas cards. For many years my parents never threw away any cards; they would just be added to this festive pile which was expanding faster than Santa's waistline. When it came to getting the decorations down from the attic, we would find all these old Christmas cards stretching back years, which I would endeavour to put up in as many places as I could. When people came round, they would always comment, 'That's a huge amount of cards you've received this year.' It did make us look rather popular.

I remember waking up early on Christmas Day one year, and hearing my mum shouting at the dog. She was a German Shepherd and, rather like an obstreperous Labrador, had no sense of self-control when it came to eating. I don't think I ever witnessed her turning up her nose at food of any description. She had snuck into our living room during the night and eaten everything edible she could find: the selection boxes, the remaining chocolates on the tree (those that had survived the Lego reassignment), even the plasticine that had been beautifully wrapped as one of our presents. The tree was also upturned, and most of the gifts had been ripped to pieces. She was lying in the middle of it all, feeling sick, having gorged on everything she could sniff out. I think she had thrown up all over the floor, so the room looked and smelt like the aftermath of a teenage house party. Rather than the Grinch that stole Christmas, it was the dog that ate Christmas. Only one edible thing survived – a tin of biscuits which she had been unable to break into. They were a present from my friend's mum. I remember my mum saying that she had saved Christmas that year.

In the final year of primary school, I worked much harder. This was partly because we were preparing for the Kent Test, the outcome of which determined whether you were eligible to go to a grammar school. To this day, I am a big advocate of the grammar school system – a type of secondary school that is common in Kent, Buckinghamshire, and Lincolnshire. Some people consider them unfair, in that those who don't get selected lose out, and that standard secondary moderns have grammar streams anyway. I would have debates with my friends about this who would say, 'You're only pro-grammar school because you benefited from the system.' And I guess that's true, up to a point. I have always argued that children who are more academically able, but can't afford to pay for a higher quality of education, should have the opportunity to learn amongst equals. It is an imperfect system, certainly, but schools will never be equal, and in a world of financial disparities it's refreshing to have something that benefits certain children regardless of their parents' ability to pay. I had my heart set on going to Barton Court Grammar School, so put the extra hours in. The other reason for the upturn in my effort levels was me being terrified of our Year Six teacher. He was a brilliant man, but for some reason I was really scared of his moustache. He worked us hard but was very good at getting the best out of us. I was very rarely in trouble, but I got called in by him one lunch break and was told that my work was not up to standard. He made me re-do it over lunch and I remember the very words he said to me. 'Chris, not only is this badly presented, but most of it happens to be wrong.' I don't think I'd ever been told anything so candidly before. It was the kick up the posterior I needed.

In March that year, the whole class went on a weekend away to a children's adventure camp, called PGL. The rumour was that it stood for Parents Get Lost, but I never knew if that was true. It was one of those camps based in a small forest, where you would take part in a range of activities like go-karting, climbing, orienteering, and fencing. This was the first time I'd properly been away from my parents, so it felt like a real adventure. The coach journey down was the usual ordeal, where I would spend most of the time looking ghoulishly green and trying desperately to keep my eyes firmly planted on the horizon. But once we got there, it was great. We shared these dormitory rooms, so it was like having a big sleepover with your mates. One of the kids brought his Walkman and a pair of speakers along, but he only had one tape with him – a single version of Ace of Base's *All That She Wants*. He was very proud of it and played it endlessly every night. He had obviously 'borrowed' it from his parents, with no idea what tape was inside. So it was the same song and its hideous B-side on repeat until midnight every evening. By the third night and the 164th play, the tape had started to distort, making it even more irritating. To this day, I still cannot stand that song.

Looking back, the whole PGL experience was pretty basic. The go-karts went round this small dirt track which had turned into thick squidgy mud. I think we spent more time being winched out of the mud than actually driving round. The orienteering was a cheerfully cheap way for the teachers to get all the kids out from under their feet, by sending them into the forest with a barely decipherable map for three hours. This was years before anyone had mobile phones or GPS, so map-reading was quite a useful skill. We were always learning about scales, contour lines, and what all the various multi-coloured symbols represented. We spent most of the time arguing over who got to hold the sacred map, whilst others got bored and started jumping over streams and climbing up trees. It was hardly *Lord of the Flies*, but it was fascinating watching people quarrel and quibble as it became apparent that we were missing lunchtime and bellies started rumbling. Talking of food, I remember that the camp had this little tuck shop, and there was this strict rule that we were only allowed to buy three items of confectionery over the course of the three days. The teachers were savvy enough to realise that, given the opportunity, a bunch of twelve-year-olds would happily have eaten nothing but chocolate and crisps for three days straight. We must have spent a good couple of hours trying to work out the maximum amount of sugary grams that we could get with these three items. We got the brainiest kid to do some maths and work it all out for us. He deduced that the best value item were the packs of jammie dodgers so, decision made, we each bought three packs of jam-centred shortbread biscuits. Great practical use of maths there. The other thing I continually remember learning about at school was fire safety. Every year up until about the age of sixteen, we would go over the same stuff about how fire spreads, and the dangers of smoke inhalation. Stop, drop, and roll was such a big deal as a kid that I really thought I'd be much more on fire than I have been as an adult.

The day we found out whether or not we had passed the Kent Test was pretty nerve-wracking. No-one likes to be classed as a failure, and I had no idea if I'd passed or not. I was only twelve, and this was the first exam I'd ever sat. Less than half the class ended up taking the test, so about eleven of us were shuffled into attend a special assembly. We were told that we had all passed and there was a lot of whooping and cheering. One person wasn't there though – a guy called Josh, which I was sad about. Aside from a kid I didn't like called William, Josh was the only other person I knew that had applied for Barton Court. I found out later that he had only just scraped through and there was some level of debate as to whether he would be admitted. Josh and I got on at primary school, but weren't exactly close friends. My clearest memory was of a birthday party his mum threw, which was immense. They hired a bouncy castle and a bubble machine, and it seemed like the entire school turned up outside his house. I think it got announced at one of our assemblies. Anyway, I was pleased that I would be going to secondary school with at least one person I liked.

That summer was great. Every summer is great when you're a kid; it just seems to stretch out languorously in front of you like an infinity pool. I have a theory that the reason time goes so much slower when you're younger is that you have less to compare it to. So, for instance, a three-month summer when you're ten years old is 2.5% of your entire life. But as you don't remember anything until you are at least three, those glorious summer months feel like 11% of your entire life. That summer was particularly exciting, as my mum whisked us away to Butlin's holiday resort in Bognor Regis for a week. Butlin's were first founded in the 1930s and 1940s as a way of providing affordable holidays for ordinary families. They reached their peak in the 1960s, but a combination of package holidays, cheap flights, and a cultural shift towards hotter and more exotic destinations, meant that they declined substantially in the 1980s. By the mid-nineties there were only three left – the other two being Minehead and Skegness. We very rarely went on holidays as kids (my first proper holiday abroad was when I was fifteen), so this felt exhilarating. The main concept behind Butlin's was that you paid to stay on site in chalets, where you either went self-catered or all-inclusive. You then spent the day either splashing around in the swimming pool, whittling away your money in arcades, or making yourself feel ill on the fairground rides. In the evening, most people would indulge in the cabaret entertainment provided by the Butlins' staff, known as Redcoats. Occasionally, there would be special guests at weekends, who generally fell into two camps – washed-up D List celebrities, or acts who saw it as a bit of fun when they could squeeze an appearance into their schedule. My mum was quite excited that we had Bobby Davro on stage on the Saturday. He was a TV mainstay throughout the 1980s, with shows like *Copy Cats* and *Bobby Davro's TV Weekly*. I knew him from his appearances on Children's TV programmes like *Live & Kicking*, and I remember he dressed up in a giant kangaroo costume and hopped across the stage. Not exactly high-end comedy, but good fun.

The only issue with Butlin's (in those days, anyway) was that it was rather challenging for one to leave. Obviously, they wanted you on-site spending money in their arcades/food stalls, etc., so it was a bit of an ordeal trying to escape. We could hear the breaking waves upon the shore, the gentle crunching of pebbles underfoot and the cries of the circling gulls, but the beach was hidden from view behind a twenty-foot high fence. My mum described it as a bit like 'breaking out of prison'. Bognor Regis itself was a bit of a drab, depressing place. It was your classic neglected British seaside town – fine in the sun-soaked summer months, but in the winter it was a desolate ghost town, with all the tourist shops bordered up. Interestingly enough, my brother and I would go back to the same Butlin's twenty-two years later for my stag do. That was more of an ironic weekend away, but strip away the alcohol and the bunch of lads, and it was pretty much exactly the same.

CHAPTER 3

Barton Court

Getting ready for big school was quite daunting. My mum took me to a uniform shop in Canterbury called Deakins to get all measured up for the new year. St Peter's had a very loose uniform policy, but now I had to wear the individuality-sapping classic blazer, white shirt and tie combo. Just learning how to do up a tie properly was a challenge. One thing I learnt quite early on was the secret to avoid being 'peanutted'. Being peanutted basically meant someone yanking your tie really hard, causing it to become so oppressively tight that you couldn't remove it without cutting it off with a pair of scissors. The trick was to have a 2p coin within the knot itself, so that it could never be pulled too firmly. Anyway, I now had a smart new uniform, and of course my mum couldn't resist taking photos of me looking all grown up. I arrived in the assembly hall and me, Josh and William ended up grouped together like ducklings huddling around each other for safety. Within about five minutes, this cheerful smiling cartoon-like character with mad hair and glasses came bounding over to say hi. He was there with one other person from his primary school, Blean. He said his name was Bjorn and that he was slightly Swedish, which had me in hysterics. We hit it off straight away and we've been friends ever since.

Barton Court was quite an unusual school, being set around a picturesque pond, with a 17th Century Georgian Manor House as its reception area. It was originally the farm for a nearby abbey, with the name Barton meaning 'Barley Enclosure'. The pond was where the monks of the abbey farmed their fish, but when Henry VIII destroyed it, he gifted the farm to one of his supporters. It remained a privately owned farm up until 1945 when it was turned into a girls' technical school. From certain angles, the school looked incredibly serene, like the setting for a Jane Austen novel, though as far as I was aware, we never had a Mr Darcy lookalike emerging from the reeds. From other views, it looked more like a standard comprehensive, with a series of unsightly sixties-style blocks imposing themselves around the south side of the pond.

It took a while to get used to the intricacies of secondary school. I found it so confusing that you had to move around the building and navigate where you were supposed to be going by yourself. It was also complicated having four form groups in each year, so in some classes you were mixed up with other people whom you didn't necessarily know. On day two, Josh and I caused a bit of a stir by forgetting to go to afternoon registration. The teachers assumed we had 'bunked off', so a search party was called out when in fact we were just sitting in a history class learning what chronology meant. One of the biggest shocks of moving to a bigger school was literally seeing how much bigger everyone was. Josh and I must have been amongst the smallest in the entire place. Girls grow faster than boys at that age, so most of the girls in our year were taller than us, and the kids who were in sixth form seemed like proper towering adults.

We were in Form X (for some reason, our forms were called W, X, Y, & Z) and were sort of the midway form in terms of behaviour. Form W were the ones that we considered to be a bit out of control (relatively speaking), and form Z were the goody two-shoes. I was still very young, so I didn't really understand all that middle-class snobbery stuff that went on. There were simply people I got on with, and people I didn't.

The other guy from primary school, William, was turning into a horrible little kid. I had never particularly liked him anyway, but back then it hadn't really mattered. At Barton Court, you had a lot more independence, so there was always more opportunity for confrontation. He was always making snide remarks and picking on people. Kids can be cruel, and for some reason he used to pick on me during that first year. Nothing major, he just seemed to enjoy putting other people down. He always thought he was better than everyone; his older sister was an actress who was on TV quite a lot in those days. In fact she played one of the lead roles in a show I used to love called *The Queens Nose*. Maybe he had a feeling of superiority because his family were well off. Josh and I both disliked him intensely, because we could see how shallow he was. But like the old saying goes, 'what goes around comes around'. At some point during that first year he left, because it turned out he was being bullied by someone else. I'm sure he probably ended up taking the piss out of the wrong person.

That first year of school was really interesting. The curriculum had expanded to include more practical subjects like 'Food Technology' (or simply cooking, in layman's terms), and CDT (craft design technology). My very first project in FT was to design and make a challenging sandwich. Most people in the class just went for size, piling on as many different types of meat, veg, and condiments as they could. I, of course, had only remembered on the way to school that morning, and my leftover pocket money only amounted to about 60p.Whilst in Safeways (a now defunct supermarket chain), I came up with the disgusting idea of a Cucumber and Smarties Sandwich. I took it seriously, hollowing out the bits of cucumber and carefully planting individual Smarties into the holes that I'd chiselled out. I think I even tried to use matching colours on the individual pieces. The teacher very diplomatically said, 'Yes, Chris, that is definitely a challenging sandwich.' The upside was that I had half a tube of Smarties left over, so from my point of view it was a win-win.

By this time, I had taken over walking my brother to his school. We had this strange ritual where Bjorn would come down and meet us at my house, which was vaguely en route. There was an awful lot of hanging around though. He must have had the patience of a saint as I was forever running late. By this point, I had pretty much abandoned having any breakfast for ten minutes additional sleep. I used Del Boy's motto that 'breakfast is for wimps'. Bjorn would be there patiently waiting before I was anywhere near ready. Sometimes he was even my alarm clock. Many a time I would be lying in bed and I would hear this whisper in my dreams, 'Chris, Chris', and suddenly it got louder and more frantic, 'Get up, you lazy bastard!' It was then a mad dash to get ready, whilst Bjorn talked about the superiority of the Swedish football team with my parents. Taking my brother to school involved an additional twenty-minute detour, so I gradually began dropping him off further and further from the gates. I've no idea why Bjorn put up with my tardiness for so long, but I would always take the blame if we arrived late.

The teachers at Barton Court were generally excellent. I didn't really appreciate it at the time, but they put up with a lot. It's one thing to teach to students who want to learn a subject (as I intermittently do now), but it's quite another to teach kids who just want to mess around. We were also getting to that age where hormones start flying about, so concentrating could be difficult. We had this brilliant French teacher called Mr Adidas, who was an incredible ball of energy. During our first lesson, he asked if anyone knew any French, and someone shouted out, '*Bonjour.*' He started flailing his arms around going 'Yes, yes, yes!' He was great when he was happy, jumping up and down, injecting loads of energy and enthusiasm into pointless French directions that we never ended up using. But then there was the angry energy. He would go as red as a beef tomato, and we would brace ourselves for a tirade of shouting.

There was one particular class clown – a guy called John Hughes. He lived with his grandparents just a few streets up from Lansdown Road, so I used to walk to school with him sometimes. He had these ears that stuck out, making him look like a mischievous pixie. I liked him. He could be really funny, but he had no sense of when he had taken things too far. It seemed to be his mission in life to wind the teachers up as much as possible. He used to make giant versions of spit balls (basically phlegm and lots of tissues) and fling them around the class. The teachers always assumed it was him, but he only ever did it when their back was turned. One day, Mr Adidas warned us that he was in a bad mood and told us to behave ourselves. John took that as a personal challenge and threw this giant spitball (about the size of a tennis ball) onto the ceiling. We watched it slowly peeling off for a couple of minutes before it fell straight onto Mr Adidas' desk, with phlegm flying everywhere. He went ballistic. Turning his usual beetroot hue he kicked a chair over and then picked up a food tray which he smashed across his knee. All these shards of plastic pieces went flying across the classroom – it was like Jekyll & Hyde; we were totally stunned. A couple of years later I found out that the near identical looking man who worked alongside my dad at Rastro's was actually his older brother. If you wanted to buy or sell from him, it always felt like being interrogated by the Gestapo. I remember trying to sell him a couple of duplicate Beano Annuals once, and he would say things like, 'How much would you expect to get for it?' or 'If you were in my shoes, would you buy it?' It was hardly the *Antiques Roadshow*. It was a grotty little market stall, and I would have been happy with a couple of quid. But I digress...

There was another teacher who was a real eccentric. He never taught me personally, but he had a reputation for being a loveable misfit. He was called Mr Fox and somehow managed to both act and look like a fox. He had bright ginger hair that was combed back into a frizzy pony tail, with a bushy ginger beard to match. He was always just kind of 'hanging around' and would barely say a word. There was this strange rule at Barton Court where you had a one-way system when walking down corridors. I'm not sure why; it was never that busy, but this one-way system was enforced with an iron fist by Mr Fox. He used to literally hide behind lockers and doors to try and catch you out. He was in a relationship with the deputy headmistress so maybe he thought it was his duty to enforce it. I was always running late for school, despite living less than a fifteen-minute walk away. My classroom was inevitably the nearest to the entrance, but on the opposing side of the one-way system, if that makes sense. One day, I sauntered in and must have been no more than five metres away from my classroom door, when Mr Fox popped out of nowhere, smiled and twirled his fingers round in a circular motion (code for 'go back the way you came'). Maybe he wasn't a teacher at all, just a glorified hallway monitor. Trying to outfox him (ahem) was like trying to un-boil an egg – impossible. Sadly, he died in a strange scuba diving accident whilst we were still at school.

There was one major exception to the 'excellent teacher rule' – a guy who shall remain nameless, but was incredibly creepy and had this weird habit of massaging everyone's shoulders whilst they worked. You couldn't quite believe what you were watching and wondered if your eyes were playing tricks on you – a bit like seeing those mawkish photographs of small Victorian children dressed up as angels and realising after a few moments that they are in fact corpses. He would always let us watch things that weren't really age-appropriate. *Schindler's List,* for instance – a great film, but hardly suitable for thirteen-year-old kids. He had a bottle of something in his drawer that he would swig during class and genuinely believed he had been chosen by God for some greater purpose. This was after being in a car accident and apparently being told that he would never walk again. Clearly the religious education he'd been teaching had gone to his head. After taking a year or so off he came back to teaching even more crazy than before. He was eventually fired for some kind of inappropriate conduct but about five year's too late. There was one occasion much later on when he approached Josh in the middle of the high street and, whilst chatting, starting rubbing his finger in a circular motion in the middle of his chest, the whole time chatting away and maintaining eye contact. Up until that point, he had just been 'very weird', but now we were genuinely scared by him. From then on, we did our best to avoid him but he was always hanging around, waiting for the pubs to open at 11 a.m. We would often see him sitting in the window of Canterbury's only gay bar chatting to boys close to a third of his age. I realise I've made my teachers sound like a real rag-bag of bizarre characters but most of them were perfectly normal, just not these three.

It quickly became apparent that being one of the quieter kids in the class meant that I could get away with a lot more tomfoolery than some of the other pupils. I frequently forgot homework or was late for things, but I somehow always seemed to wriggle out of being in trouble. I think the amount of detentions I had at school could be counted on one hand. Having a reputation as a troublemaker seemed to be a self-fulfilling prophecy. There was an occasion when I was shouting something in French very loudly for a laugh (I can't remember why) and the teacher turned around and just assumed it was John Hughes. She gave him a detention, despite his protestations. Poor guy; I felt pretty guilty and considered buying him an Easter egg to make up for it, though I never got round to it. About eight years later, I was working as a temp in a glass factory (in-between university terms) when I turned around and saw John Hughes standing there grinning away. He was working there as some kind of foreman in this ill-fitting hard hat which made his ears protrude out even further.

'Mr Chris, how are you doing?'

'I'm fine,' I responded. 'How did you know I was working here?'

'I could ear you from over ear.' You could always rely on him for a low brow pun. I confessed there and then, but by that point it was probably water under the bridge, out to sea, and over the horizon. It's funny how something small like that can fester as guilt for years.

Starting IT lessons for the first time was like entering another world. You had to walk up two flights of steps to the top of this manor house, and lo and behold, there was the magic 'computer room'. There sat twenty-five or so shiny PCs with the Windows 3.1 operating system. I didn't have a clue what to do, and neither did our teacher really. She was this plump elderly woman called Mrs Baggerly who had no sense of her surroundings. Every time she turned round, she would hit one of our chairs and spin us around. She knew the absolute basics and not much else, in her words 'the internet would never catch on'. IT lessons basically consisted of her reading a set of instructions from a manual which we would then follow. If you asked for clarification or a bit more detail she would then look back through the index and search for another section, which would take up half the lesson. Whether she was incapable of reading the instructions online I don't know. In fairness, this was still years before Napster and Nupedia, never mind Spotify and Wikipedia. I recall one student asking her what was wrong with their computer.

'I think it's frozen,' she said.

'So, miss, how do I defrost it?' replied the student. These were not tech-savvy times. Everything was done at a snail's pace. It took about twenty minutes just to get the PCs up and running so IT lessons would frequently overrun. She would always say, make sure you practise at home, which was no good to me, we didn't get a PC with dial-up broadband for another four years. What we did get that year, however, was (drum roll, please...) a Nintendo Entertainment System. All that nagging had paid off and we were finally able to play computer games at home. We started off with Super Mario Brothers and over the next couple of years collected more games like Micro Machines, Jurassic Park, Gremlins, and this terribly primitive football game where they didn't have any naming rights, so Beckham was Deckham and Cantona was Dantona. It was basic and literally held in place by Blu Tack, but me and my brother loved it. Sometimes the wires would slip and we would get severe distortion, whereupon there was a mad dash to get the wire/Blue Tack support back into position. There was also the strange ritual of having to blow on the game cartridges when they obstinately refused to load properly. I think the thought process was that dust would congregate on the exposed nickel connector, causing interference which blowing would usually remedy. I repeat my earlier assertion, these were not tech-savvy times.

Whenever my school friends came over, they always found my parents' house to be slightly unusual. It was full of odd little touches, including my mum's mercurial swings in taste when it came to decorating. There was a small area above one of the doors that she was never quite sure what to do with. Sometimes it was painted, sometimes it was wallpapered, and once it was plastered in this aberrant design which seemed to resemble chocolate box packaging. We had two massive items of furniture which didn't really fit – a jukebox and a piano. It was pretty eccentric to have this bulky piano taking up space when none of us could actually play. I did briefly take some piano lessons, but for some reason I didn't keep them up. I learnt a few basic chord sequences and that was about it. My dad started using the area under the piano lid as a storage area for the post and his various receipts. The jukebox was great, though. It originated from Amsterdam, so it only played using Dutch gilders. Unsurprisingly, these became very difficult to come by once Holland started using the Euro. It was incredibly loud, with no real volume control, so it didn't get played that often, usually just for the novelty value.

The other unusual thing about my parents' house was the heating – or lack there of. We had an open coal fire downstairs and a small gas fire stationed in the front room, but that was all. The coal fire was lovely and cosy once it was lit, but of course, keeping it burning was a challenge if you needed to do other things. My dad would always get up in the height of winter, whatever the weather, to light it using a mixture of logs, coal, and anything else that was to hand. There was no heating at all upstairs. Until I was about sixteen, there wasn't even any double glazing. On those January and February nights, it was freezing; you would go to bed in a mound of blankets and hot water bottles, wrapped up as tightly as a bug in a spider's web. I recall my mum's houseplants getting frostbite during one particularly bitter winter. Once the windows got replaced, it was more bearable; you couldn't feel the breeze coming through, but it was still an Arctic ordeal in the height of winter. The hot water would always be turned off at night (due to an incident where the boiler once split open), so in the morning it would take a good half hour to heat up. My parents didn't have a shower installed until after I had left home, so you either washed in the sink, or if you were getting up early, you ran a bath and hoped that the water was toasty enough. There were often arguments between us about who had used up the last of the hot water. You would think that living in a house with no real heating would toughen you up, but it didn't; quite the reverse, actually. What it did make you do was appreciate proper central heating.

On 31st August, 1997, Princess Diana was killed in a car crash in Paris. She was one of the first major celebrities I recall passing away. She was always on the TV in those days, visiting orphanages and campaigning against land mines, so this felt like real event television. There seemed to be nothing else on the news for days afterwards. The outpouring of grief was pretty over the top, especially with a dreadful re-release of Elton John's *Candle In the Wind*, it was a bad enough song the first time round. This was also the first time I became aware how the media could manipulate people by burying certain pieces of news and keeping a story running longer than it needed to. Mother Teresa died a few days later (the day before Diana's funeral), and was barely mentioned in the press.

I was totally disinterested in politics as a kid, finding it all incredibly dull. John Major was the dreariest character imaginable – there was a good reason for his spitting image puppet being completely grey. Then in May 1997, politics became exciting when Tony Blair came to power, riding a wave of tremendous national enthusiasm. Here was someone who was young, charismatic, and close to being relatable. The whole 'Cool Britannia thing with the Spice Girls and union jack iconography was clearly false and manufactured, but it was fun nonetheless. I remember watching Noel Gallagher drinking champagne with the Prime Minister on the ITV news and it being a big deal. Previously youth culture and politics never mixed; they were polar opposites at either end of the spectrum. It seems incredible now, but from 1997-1999 Tony Blair was almost cool. There was a bit too much of the 'dad at the disco vibe' for anyone to have Blair posters or anything like that, but it did feel like the start of something fresh. All that early goodwill soon evaporated, but I personally always thought that he was one of the best Prime Ministers this country has ever had. His government could claim a huge list of accomplishments that I don't think will ever again be equalled. Years later, it became hard to separate him from the Iraq war debacle and the accusations of him being a war criminal, which I thought were blown way out of proportion. What the Labour government achieved across those three terms made a genuine difference to the lives of millions of ordinary people. Namely:

- The Good Friday Agreement and the peace in Northern Ireland that followed
- Real incomes growing by 18% between 1997 & 2006
- The national minimum wage being launched
- A significant expansion of the welfare state which led to poverty levels falling
- New rights for gay people, specifically the Civil Partnership Act
- Child poverty being halved in absolute terms as a result of increased maternity pay, increases to child benefit, and working tax credits.

I could go on and on, but there's only a finite amount of space in this book for me to labour the point (pun intended). I just wanted it recorded that there was once a time when Tony

Blair's pearly white smile didn't send shivers down the spine. It was more likely that he'd just caught sight of Geri Halliwell's bottom than secretly negotiated a carve-up of Iraq.

In Year 9, we were studying for what was then referred to as SATS tests, now known as Key Stage 3. Back then, that meant sitting a series of exams, but nowadays it's just part of ongoing teaching assessment. This was when I started to struggle with certain subjects, those that I simply wasn't interested in. Chemistry was one of them. I always found it to be a bit of a waste of time. It seemed to me that it was either about really obvious chemical reactions (i.e. water boiling/ toast burning) or really complex things that might be useful to a nuclear scientist, but not in general life. I hated learning about the periodic table, I found it so tediously dull. I'm pretty sure that I only learnt one practical thing from Chemistry that has helped me in my adult life – how to make a natural drain cleaner. Brace yourself. Drain cleaners from shops are a waste of time, expensive, and terrible for the environment. Also, a dangerous thing to have around the house if you have young children. Try this little trick instead:

You Will Need:

2 cups baking soda
4 cups boiling water
1 cup vinegar

Directions for Home-Made Drain Cleaner:

1. Remove all water from the sink or tub and pour about 1 cup of baking soda down the drain. Make sure that baking soda makes it down the drain.
2. Next, pour about 2 cups of boiling water down the drain. The baking soda mixed with boiling water

dissolves the sludge and gunk in the pipe, even if you don't see it happening. Wait a few minutes.

3. Now, pour another cup of baking soda down the drain then add 1 cup of white vinegar and plug the drain immediately. If you're unclogging a double sink, plug both drains. You'll hear sizzling coming up from the drain and see bubbles foaming up.
4. When the bubbles have died down, add the remaining boiling water down the drain.
5. Repeat this process if necessary. This can be used as a monthly treatment to help prevent future clogs, too; simply pour a cup of baking soda down the drains followed by boiling water.

It was around this time that I started cycling everywhere. I would get through bikes like I got through socks. I was forever puncturing them, crashing them, denting them, and just generally running them into the ground. My mum would sigh every time I came home with another hunk of metal dragging behind me. Our reliably friendly neighbour, GJ, once called the police because he said we were breaking the speed limit on our bikes. He wanted the council to install speed bumps down our road to stop us from going too fast. If anything, that would have done the reverse. We were always building ramps out of wood to jump over, and speed bumps would have resulted in a permanent obstacle we could launch ourselves off. We used to do challenges like having no-handed races where we would dare each other to go as fast as possible without holding on. Most of the time, when I fell off my bike it was just cuts and bruises. However, there was one occasion when I actually had quite a nasty accident. I was cycling with my mum and brother around the university at the top of one of Canterbury's hills. We headed back home down the main slope and, being my usual reckless self, I went down first, going much faster than was wise. I figured that it being a dedicated cycle lane meant it was bound to be safe. The gradient was about 30% and I was picking up more and more speed. I could see these shiny metal barriers at the bottom of the hill approaching, so I gently applied the brakes. Nothing happened. I squeezed again, slightly harder this time, but still no response. Whether it was the speed I was going at, the brakes being faulty, or most likely a combination of both, I couldn't slow down. I remember trying to be really rational about it as the bars got nearer and nearer whilst I was approaching them probably in excess of 30 mph. By this point, it was a straight path with fencing either side of me, so there was nowhere to turn off. I calmly figured that there were two options: either I jumped off the bike there and then or I attempted a near impossible manoeuvre of swerving around these metal beasts whilst careering down at the speed of a cheetah chasing its prey. I figured that if I jumped off the bike, there was 100% chance that I would hurt myself, but if I attempted to go round the barriers there was a 99% chance that I would hurt myself. I chose the latter. Of course, the manoeuvre didn't work. I crashed into the barriers full on in my chest, got spun round, and landed on my head. I lay there momentarily dazed and confused before my mum arrived thirty seconds later. I don't think she saw the crash (she was too far behind) but I saw her reaction; she went as white as a ghost and started panicking. I had well and truly cracked my head open so there was blood splattered everywhere. It was dripping down the sides of my head and cascading over my brow and obscuring my sight lines, rather like the pre-credits sequence of the James Bond films. My mum took my T-shirt off and wrapped it around my head like a turban. I could stand but I definitely felt dizzy. I turned around to get my bike which was completely mangled. I was adamant that we attempted to push it along with us, but try as I might, it couldn't be wheeled in a straight line. I think we abandoned it there and then. Another bike bites the dust. As I turned back, I noticed the metal barrier was physically dented from where I had slammed into it. It may have been a shallow victory but I remember thinking that at least this inanimate object had also sustained grievous bodily harm. We jumped in a taxi and raced up to hospital where one of the doctors carefully examined my scalp.

'Would you like stitches or glue?' he asked in a kind soothing voice.

'Glue,' I instantly replied; it somehow seemed less invasive than stitches.

I was incredibly lucky. I told the doctor what had happened, and he said I was very fortunate not to have punctured my liver. Or, for that matter, severely damaged my head. I didn't have a helmet on, no-one wore helmets in those days. As stupid as it sounds, it was something of a badge of honour to sustain cycling injuries. That wasn't the last time that I would crack my head open either...

The canteen at Barton Court was a dreadful soul-crushing space. Overcrowded, noisy, and featuring a permanent ice rink floor, where the danger of slipping on spilt mushy peas was always omnipresent. I only ate the canteen food on a few rare occasions, but it was always the same. The chips were hollowed-out husks, the meat always dry and served lukewarm, and the mixed vegetable medley straight out of a freezer and over-boiled to a soggy, flavourless death. The overriding ambition seemed to be to always set the Blandometer to 'Ready Salted' before dishing up. It was distinctly odd, therefore, that we spent so much time trying to sneak ourselves into the canteen. Barton Court had this peculiar rota system for gaining access. You weren't allowed to eat anywhere else on site, so on certain days of the week you could spend 45 minutes of the lunch break just queueing to get in. It was a ridiculous system and exactly the kind of petty bureaucracy that used to wind me up, especially on the days when there was plenty of table space, but they stuck to the schedule regardless. There were occasions when we would run out of time to eat our lunch and spend the afternoon hungry. I'm sure there was a human rights violation in there somewhere. Anyway, we would turn it into a game of trying to sneak into the canteen undetected on the days when we were supposed to be at the back of the queue. We got quite creative, hiding in the stairwell and trying to sneak past the dinner ladies when their backs were turned. Me, Josh, and another school friend called Rory, were the masters of it, using all kinds of stealthy distraction techniques to slip in without being spotted. We would send in decoys or go in disguise – clearly, our SAS incognito skills should have been put to a better use. Sometimes the dinner ladies would catch us out, but I think they got a bit of a kick out of it. They were all pretty similar – rotund, middle-aged women, with names like Doris, Mavis, and Margaret. They'd cooked more hot dinners than I've had, er, hot dinners, so any kind of distraction for them was probably welcome. I remember one time when we'd successfully crept in like three stealthy ninjas and were sitting down to enjoy our lunch. We all promised each other that we would never end up working in an environment with such petty bureaucracy and superfluous regulations. Me and Rory later ended up in international tourism and Higher Education.

It was around this time that I first started becoming interested in music. One of the first albums I remember coming out and being discussed at school was Blur's self-titled fifth album. I also remember Michael Jackson being like a god back then. Even though he was well past his prime, he was always being discussed by my classmates. I remember watching his video for *Earth Song* on *Top of The Pops* and it leaving a lasting impression on me. It was also the first song I remember racing up the charts to become a Christmas no.1. We would all gather round in the classroom at lunchtime and attempt to do the moonwalk – none of us could do it. He made it look so effortless, which is partly the illusion, because it is actually a very complicated step. The trick is not to concentrate so much on your feet. Whilst getting them right is key (and going back on your heel not your toes), it's actually the way the whole body moves – the hips, the arms, even the neck – which gives it that gravity-defying look. Years later, I learnt how to do it properly. The first album I ever owned was a compilation my dad gave me of slightly left-field early 90s hits. Things by Mansun, Electronic, and Joe Cocker. But the first album I ever bought with my own money was *Transformer* by Lou Reed. I bought it purely because I liked the cover, and also because it was on offer at Woolworths.

Properly discovering music for the first time was like exploring a whole new continent. I would spend many hours listening to scratchy tapes through headphones at night when I should have been sleeping, trying to join the dots with everything I was absorbing. Mostly, these tapes were from my dad, but I'd also borrow them from friends at school. Occasionally I would tape shows from the radio, trying desperately to edit out the adverts where some beautifully unplugged performance would be ruined by a car insurance advert. It was like piecing together the bits of a giant audio jigsaw. I would omnivorously read all my dad's magazines and spend hours listening to new releases at the listening posts at HMV. I'd spend so long on them without ever buying anything that they'd sometimes have to shut them down to get me out of the shop. When I was bored at school, I'd write huge lists of songs and albums in order to memorise huge swathes of information. In those days, you would go to people's houses purely to see what music they had, so you could borrow it and record onto tapes. CDs were too expensive, those that you had were something you treasured and properly looked after. Woe betide anyone who scratched or damaged them. It was the scarcity of content that made music so intriguing for me. Without proper research and reading music magazines, you had no idea how many albums an artist like say, Neil Young, had under their belt. We are so spoilt now with digital technology giving us instant answers and allowing us to listen to almost anything on a whim. Listening to music via streaming sites is great in many ways, but you don't get that joy of discovery or intriguing paraphernalia that used to come with physical music. You don't get the artwork, cryptic messages, strange photos, fold-out posters, and strange mailing list adverts that would sometimes tumble out. Occasionally, you would get additional artwork hidden inside the case itself. Records are cooler; there's an obvious nostalgia there, but CDs were great in their own right. I must have hundreds of titbits floating around in my brain. Those of us who grew up with them, all know about the hidden tracks (at the end of an album, after a few minutes of silence, to make you jump out of your skin if you're not expecting it), but did you know there used to be hidden tracks at the start of some albums? You had to manually rewind backwards after you'd pressed 'play' to find them, and unlike traditional hidden tracks, they are never found on streaming platforms.

In Year 10, we started doing our GCSE subjects. It was great being able to have some choice over what we studied, though I still had to do science and a modern language, which were my two least favourite subjects. Early in that year I used to take a penknife to school. It was a cheap standard one which lots of kids had, useful for things like the scissors and the toothpick. I got it confiscated and told by the headmaster that it was a dangerous weapon, which I thought was ridiculous. Besides the fact that the two knives in it were blunter than kitchen utensils (you were probably most likely to cause harm to someone by throwing it at them), there were much more dangerous things around the school – Bunsen burners, electric hobs, even the school cutlery. I could go into the design technology room and use Stanley knives and saws, but this £15 penknife was considered dangerous. I think I would have struggled to chop a carrot with it, never mind skin a rabbit. I thought it was unfair that they wouldn't give it back to me at the end of the day, especially as I had spent all my hard-earned pocket money on it. As you can tell, I'm not bitter all these years later.

Like any kid growing up, I was obsessed with sweets. The shop around the corner had stacks of confectionery piled up in colourful plastic tubs which me and Bjorn would often get on our way to school. Bon-bons and liquorice swirls were great, but the best value ones were the everlasting gobstoppers at three pence each. I'm sure they probably could have been sued under the Trades Descriptions Act, as we would always finish one by the time we got to school, but 15 minutes' worth of sucking for three pence wasn't bad. One of the things that I still miss today are 'Broken Biscuits'. These were big plastic packs that weighed about a kilogramme, containing biscuits discarded from the factories due to quality control – mainly the fact that they were crushed and splintered or slightly beyond their sell-by date. You used to get them in garages and corner shops. They were always a random assortment, so it was fascinating seeing what emerged upon opening. Usually it was a mixture of standard supermarket fare, like bourbons, custard creams, nice biscuits, and jammie dodgers. Quite often you would get branded bars mixed in as well – caramel wafers, penguin bars, and if you were really lucky, higher-end delights like Fox's. They were unbelievably good value – less than a £1, I seem to recall. They stopped doing them a few years later due to Health & Safety. Random biscuits were literally just bundled into bags at the factory, so no-one knew what was actually in them. There were never any ingredients' lists so there were all kinds of issues in regard to allergies and potential litigation. In recent years Iceland have brought them back but they're not the same. You always get exactly the same assortment, and they've been properly branded. Not like the good old days...

In the summer of 1999, I went on my first proper holiday abroad with my brother, my mum, her friend Rosemary, and her daughter, Florence. Rose was as mad as a box of frogs. She could be a total neurotic about some things but totally nonplussed about more serious matters. Her house for instance looked like a squat with mouldy food sitting around, peeling wallpaper and furniture that a homeless shelter would turn away for being too tatty. She had budgies which were just flying loose around the house, and being chased by her over excitable cats. But on the flip side, she loved going to the opera and would drink the finest wine. Even as a kid it felt like you needed a flu jab to enter that house and yet she was generous to a fault, an amazing cook and was really interesting company. Every time I would go over there with my mum, there would be some kind of non-existent drama. We were going round to plan our holiday, which they had decided would be a camping trip in the south of France. She opened the door in a panic, worried that it was going to rain and that she would be flooded. She was talking above moving all her possessions upstairs and calling in the army to get some sandbags delivered, but no extreme weather was forecast, just a couple of days of moderate rain. My mum tried to calm her down but she was adamant that the River Stour was going to flood and she'd be stranded. The holiday was nearly called off. Her house was three roads back from the river and hadn't actually being flooded since 1909 – 90 years ago! Even then, it was only about a foot deep, and there had been various flood prevention schemes put in place since. Her partner, David, was also an eccentric. He had never had a job- he just read Latin novels and drank copious amounts of Malbec every day. He would wander around Canterbury always carrying an umbrella no matter what the weather was. Come to think of it, they both seemed to have an irrational fear of water. Unsurprisingly Rosemary's daughter, Florence didn't grow up as a normal child- but like her mum, she was very smart. She was a year below me at St Peters and went to a very prestigious girl's school where she was something of a maths genius. She got 4 A-Levels, all A*'s and then went on to become a stripper. You couldn't make it up. Anyway David wasn't coming- he had a fear of the French (as well as water) so the five of us headed off to the south of France.

We took the Channel Tunnel from Ashford to Paris and then the TGV down the spine of France. I remember trying to wind my brother up, telling him he would need to hold his breath when we went under the sea. The South of France was absolutely beautiful. We stayed in this campsite called the Calagogo, about fifteen miles to the east of the Pyrenees- you could see them glistening in the distance from the beach. It was late July and the weather was gorgeous. I remember the date vividly, because of a teenage actor-turned-pop star named Adam Rickett. Florence had bought along an issue of *Smash Hits* and had this fold-out poster of him topless. He had just released this terrible single called *The Air That I Breathe,* which Florence loved. I found the poster incredibly creepy, and really enjoyed having a ceremonial burning of it on our bonfire one night. I had done day trips to France before – Calais, Boulogne, and Paris – but this was my first extended holiday abroad. I have always loved camping. There's something really satisfying about unzipping your tent in the morning, the fresh air rushing in, and then feeling the damp morning dew on your bare feet. When it was summer in

Canterbury, I would insist on getting our tent out at home and camping in the back garden. It just felt like an adventure to be sleeping somewhere other than one's bedroom.

The amazing thing about the South of France was being able to jump into an outdoor swimming pool before breakfast and spend the rest of the day beside miles of pristine sandy shore C'était fantastique. Kent had its fair share of nice beaches, but they were a world apart from the cultural laid-back vibe of the French Riviera. Here, it was Bouillabaisse and Fougasse; back home it was more likely to be candy floss and a kebab. I also remember briefly trying to windsurf and being absolutely terrible at it. It didn't matter, though, we were on holiday in the South of France – there was nothing Toulouse. We visited a nearby town called Argelés (or Argelés-Sur-Mer, to give it its full name), which had quite a dark history, being the location of a Spanish Republican concentration camp. This was established after the defeat of the Spanish Republic in 1939, and housed over 100,000 people from both civilian and military backgrounds. Apart from the memorials that dotted the town, there was very little indication that this pretty little town had such a dark history.

Later that year, my parents bought me and Matt a pet hamster. He was an albino hamster with snow white fur and piercing red eyes, so we named him 'Beano.' He was great fun, we would build little mazes for him out of various books and video cases. We started off treating him well and feeding him normal food, but after a while it became irresistible to see what we could get him to squeeze into his pouch. Chips were particularly funny. He would try and run into his little house and would get stuck in the entrance with his giant pouch – a bit like a dog trying to get through a narrow doorway with a long stick. Like most hamsters, he was always trying to escape. He disappeared for a couple of days once, and later turned up totally black. He had been hiding in our fireplace so was completely covered in soot. There was one dark day when he died and my mum decided to bury him in the back garden. We stood around this tiny little grave and just as we were about to shovel the soil on top, he started wriggling. It wasn't a divine miracle – the poor thing had just started hibernating because of the cold weather! He was very nearly buried alive.

I think it was when I was reached my teenage years that I developed my borderline phobia of umbrellas. Phobia might be too strong a word, but to this day I still get nervous around umbrellas – particularly if they are out in force during inclement weather. I can't walk alongside my wife, for instance, if she's holding an umbrella; I have to walk either behind or in front. My relationship with umbrella's is a bit like the one the Archbishop of Canterbury has with Satan; that is, I renounce them. It does sound crazy, but I guess lots of worries are irrational. Some people are scared of heights whilst others panic in confined spaces. For me, it's umbrellas. I would much rather get thoroughly drenched than have to use one. I thought that this book would be a good opportunity to state the practical reasons as to why I dislike them:

1. **Their selfish design** – To me, they seem like a really selfish upper-class design, the kind of thing I would have expected to die out back in the nineteenth century with palananquins and leeches. They just seem to scream, 'I'm dry, so screw the rest of you.' Particularly when one is in a crowded environment with these giant golf umbrellas.
2. **Their vicious design** – They are always held at a dangerous height, where there is the potential for someone to be blinded or injured. With the instant open ones, they shoot out like a speeding bullet. I've seen

people sustain all manner of injuries when the prongs have come loose. My work colleague, for instance, recently cut his hand quite badly when inspecting one. They often more resemble a torture weapon than a fashion accessory.

3. **They break easily** – The amount of umbrellas I've seen where the spokes have come loose, or they've developed a tear. Unless you spend a bit of money on them, they tend not to last too long.
4. **They're a pain to dry** – People insist on drying their umbrellas indoors, spread open and generally cluttering up the place, whilst making other things (i.e. the carpet) sodden. Some people are repulsed by the smell of wet dog; for me, umbrellas are in a similar ball park.

And my biggest bug bearer of all:

5. **They don't actually work** – They never keep you fully dry. If there are strong winds, there is always a danger that they blow inside out. Unless you own a colossal one that takes up the entire pavement (refer to reason 1 for my rationale for disliking them), they simply don't keep you that dry in heavy rain. You're much better off in a waterproof coat and/or hat.

It's important to remember that in that awkward stage between being a child and being old enough to go to the pub, there wasn't a huge amount to do in your social time. This was the pre-digital age, so there was no online entertainment. Nothing was instantaneous: you couldn't download a game, or easily find out what events were happening that weekend. The things that we did were probably the same that things that kids a hundred years ago used to do, play football in the park or get a bit creative with everyday objects. A particular favourite game was to see how far we could kick a vegetable (usually a potato) through the streets, avoiding the crowds, and dealing with obstacles like kerbs and drains. We could make a game involving a potato last for hours. Another game we used to play involved choosing a random member of the public and placing bets on the first shop that they would walk into. This wasn't as difficult as you would think. It was often quite easy to spot a McDonald's or a Marks & Spencer's customer, for instance. I do genuinely believe that us getting creative and making our own entertainment when we were kids put us in good stead for later life. I think as an adult I have quite a bit of patience and I never get bored. My mum's favourite saying used to be, 'A bored person is a boring person', a pithy aphorism if ever there was one. How anyone can be bored now with so much information and entertainment at their fingertips, is beyond me. Maybe the youth of today should try entertaining themselves with potatoes for a time.

I was never early for school. Most days, I would only just make it in on time, but I reckon I was late at least once a week. Living near to Barton Court didn't help in any way; if anything, it gave you a false sense of timekeeping. I would always leave it until the last minute, so if someone was in the bathroom or I couldn't find my PE kit, it would be a mad Usain Bolt-style dash down the street. Signing the lateness register, which sat in the reception area, was always a bit shameful. I never knew what to write for a reason. I mean, what reason is there for continual lateness? I couldn't write 'I wanted an extra ten minutes in bed' or 'I was enjoying my tea too much', so I always needed to invent something that wouldn't get me in trouble. One morning I left my homework on the sofa whilst I waltzed into the kitchen to make some toast. I came back five minutes later to find the dog chewing on it. She hadn't exactly eaten my homework, but she'd certainly made a mess of it. It was crumpled, with drool running down it, and a couple of muddy paw prints decorating the margins. It was still just about legible, but I had to write out the two sides of A4 all over again. When I inevitably arrived late at the school gates, I wrote in the lateness book 'Dog chewed my homework'. Our year lead was not impressed, even after I explained the situation to her. It was a bit like the boy who cried wolf in reverse; inventing excuses didn't get me into trouble, but telling the truth did.

By year 11, I was starting to get fed up of sharing a room with my brother. Although we got on well, we would have arguments and fights like all teenage boys do. I tried to split our bedroom up as best I could, with a makeshift barrier down the centre. A wardrobe, chest of drawers, and fold-out desk was the boundary, so he could do what he wanted on one side and I could be master of all I surveyed on the other. The bedroom was starting to look pretty unusual by now. My dad had an excess of film and music posters that I used to plaster over every inch of the wall and ceiling. The music posters weren't the traditional ones you would buy from shops, but advertising hoardings that you would see in window shop displays like Our Price. I choose ones for either bands that I liked or ones that I thought looked cool. The film posters I cared less about; they were a real mixed bag of major blockbusters (*Independence Day*), Indie films (*The Big Lebowski*) and truly terrible films (i.e. *Speed* 2). I also started hanging random things from the ceiling like paper clips and toothbrushes and experimenting with different coloured light bulbs. I was going through that odd stage.

December 31st, 1999 was rapidly approaching, and everyone around us seemed very on edge with regard to something called the 'Millennium bug'. This anxiety turned into panic in November and December that the bug was going to cause computers to malfunction and potentially endanger everything from shop tills to power stations. The bug was about the limitations of the clocks inside computers. Since the

1960s, computers denoted years such as 1998 as 98 to save memory. As a result, when the new millennium arrived it was expected many computer clocks would see 00 and understand that to mean 1900. People were worried that aeroplanes would fall out of the sky and power stations would explode. I remember the teachers telling us to take precautions, and made sure we all read the government advice leaflets. It sounds hilarious now, but at the time many commentators were expecting a doomsday scenario. In the end, nothing really happened. I remember watching the clock countdown to midnight in my parents' living room. The only explosions that happened were from the traditional New Year's Eve fireworks.

Canterbury had some great music shops when I was growing up. There were the established chains like Our Price and Woolworths, as well as the quirky independents like Richard Records and the Indoor Market. My favourite haunt at the time was a place called Parrot Records. The store was rather grey and dilapidated, with an unfinished soviet- chic type vibe. The chaps who ran it were massive music fans and would happily chat to you about anything. I remember me and Josh would spend hours in there, mostly browsing and occasionally buying. On one occasion, one of the guys was so excited about the new Primal Scream album (*Exterminator* in 2000) that he played us the whole thing in its entirety and told us, though it was only February, it was the forerunner for the album of the year.

Dave Radford was an interesting chap. He used to be the lead singer of a prog band called Gizmo back in the 1970s and 80s. Prog-rock is mostly pretty dreadful and the so-called 'Canterbury Prog Scene' was mainly a bunch of ageing hippies chasing after the one Canterbury band that ever made any real impact: Caravan. They had song titles like *Looking Through The Knothole In Granny's Wooden Leg* and *Gravity Brings You Down*. If I was being kind, I would say that they were mildly interesting. If I was being critical, I would say that the amusing song titles were the best thing about them. When I was younger, we used to go round Dave Radford's house and watch *Jaws* videos whilst he and my dad talked about records. He became my go-to for buying albums for about ten years, until his market eventually closed in 2011. We used to think it was hilarious that the most expensive albums in his shop were his own Gizmo ones which had pride of place on his wall. He had that market stall for about twenty-five years and had stood in the same spot for so long that he had worn the carpet away and developed gout. He could be hilarious though. He would sometimes lie on the floor and wave his feet in the air so anyone walking past would just see this pair of perplexing legs dangling over the top of the counter. He used to find the oddest things hysterical, like the album cover for Frank Zappa's *Ship Arriving Too Late To Save A Drowning Witch* (see crude drawing below) which, to be fair, was mildly amusing, but not on the eighth time of him showing it to me:

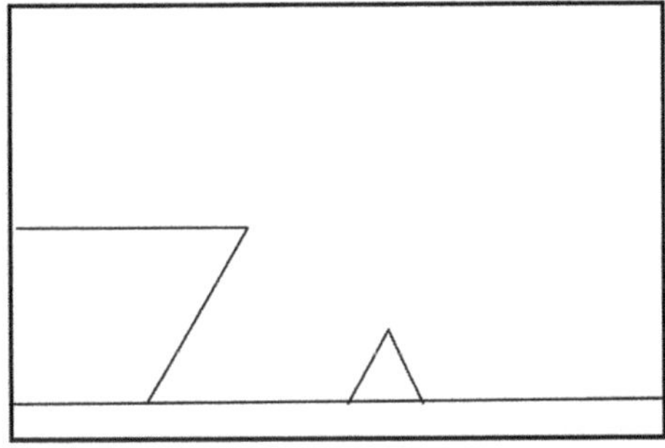

He would sell you anything and everything, which was good in some ways but could be rather irritating in others. For instance, I mentioned to him once that I was trying to find a particular out of print Iggy Pop album (this was before you could order things online), which he got for me a week or so later. However, he'd also ordered a load of other Iggy albums that I knew weren't that great. I ended up buying them all every time I went in there, out of some weird sense of duty. Many years later, whilst working at a university in London, I was speaking to a Japanese student doing MA Sound Arts, whose thesis was on 'The Canterbury Prog Scene' and she happened to mention Gizmo. 99.9% of people from Canterbury would have had no idea who they were, so I was very surprised when this young girl from Osaka seemed so interested. I casually mentioned that I used to know the lead singer and she was flabbergasted.

'What was it like knowing a legend?' she asked. I didn't know how to respond to that.

One day at lunchtime, Josh and I were messing about, kicking a plastic bottle around the classroom in a haphazard game of keepy uppies. Somehow, we ended up losing it. It probably ended up flying out of the window or getting trapped behind some lockers. I was looking for something else to kick around, and for some reason I thought a loose plastic window blind was a worthy substitute. It was barely hanging on, so I impetuously ripped it off and we started kicking it around, then other kids started joining in. Somehow that changed into throwing the window blind around, which then evolved into throwing multiple blinds around. Within ten minutes, we had upturned tables at either side of the classroom, and about eight of us launching window blinds at each other as hard as we could. Most of the other kids had left, so it started getting progressively more dangerous as we whittled ourselves down to the hardy elite. I then stood up, feeling something on my head. One of the girls on the other team shouted, 'Oh my God' and I suddenly felt blood trickling down my face. One of the sharper ends of the blind had embedded in my scalp, so once again I had managed to split the top of my head open. The funny thing was, it didn't really hurt that much. There was just an incredible amount of blood, so it probably looked a lot more dramatic than it actually was. The girl who launched it must have felt really worried. Assuming I was concussed, she dragged me down the corridor and into the boys' toilets to help me clean up. I held a pile of paper towels to my head to apply pressure to the wound, and came out to see a crowd of people waiting for me. They had followed the trail of blood like a pack of hungry foxhounds down the corridor and towards the toilet door. I was clearly the talk of the school. One of the teachers turned up and dragged me to the first aid room to patch me up whilst they called my mum. The classroom looked like a war zone with blood, broken plastic, upturned furniture, and a window barely hanging on. It felt a bit like waking up at a bacchanalian house party with a massive hangover, seeing all the destruction in broad daylight and wondering how everything had got so out of hand.

The deputy headmistress came to find out what had happened from me, so I tried to be as vague as possible. When she asked who the irresponsible miscreants were, I mumbled something about it being the entire class and that I couldn't name individual people. Unfortunately, someone else who was a bit of a tell-tale named us all, 'Chris, Neil, Josh, etc.' My mum wasn't impressed when she turned up in the middle of the day to see my head covered in bandages. 'You absolute berk,' was the first thing she said when she saw the state of me. And so, it was off to hospital to get checked out again.

We all loved playing practical jokes on the teachers and each other. There was always the usual stuff, like changing the times on the clocks to try and leave early, or wiping individual letters off the whiteboard to leave hilarious words behind. I've always been a fan of whiteboards; I find them quite re-markable. My personal favourite game was waiting for people to leave their bags unattended and then hiding all their textbooks. You would then fill the bag with something else, usually grass or mud, so that when they emptied it later, all the debris would go flying across the desk. All harmless fun. Another thing I used to do was graffiti my notebooks with all kinds of humorous anecdotes and word play. My school diary, for instance, had a details section at the front which I would embellish with things such as the following;

Name:	*Chris Bryant*
School:	*of fish*
Form:	*Solid*
Subject:	*It's all subjective*
Address:	*would look silly on me*

Both of my parents were really supportive when it came to my school work. It was that tricky parent juggling act of showing an interest and talking things through with me, whilst at the same time giving me the space to learn independently and make my own mistakes. A couple of years earlier, my mum had been furious with one of the teachers at Barton Court after she gave me a 'C' for a charcoal drawing of a shoe. I am not the world's best fine artist, not by a long chalk, but I really tried hard with this particular sketch. I fastidiously spent a great deal of time studying my shoes: making sure to get the shading right, capturing the proportions, and trying to bring across realistic three dimensionality. I was a little deflated with my mark, but my mum took it to heart. She was on the verge of complaining to the school and I'm sure she would have done if there had been a parents' evening coming up. Instead, she framed this particular drawing, and it hung up on her bedroom wall for the next fifteen years. I would often stare at that picture over the years thinking to myself, *That actually is a very life-like shoe.* I certainly couldn't do a better drawing now. But then again, I do work in an arts university – clearly the shoe is now on the other foot.

Parents' evenings are strange occasions for everyone. The teachers, the parents, and the kids are all trying to be on their best behaviour. You'd walk around and see all the 'cock of the walk kids' standing alongside their parents, like butter wouldn't melt. I didn't mind them for years, but once I started losing interest in certain subjects, they became a bit cringeworthy. I was perfectly happy talking about the things I enjoyed, but when it came to subjects like Chemistry, I would be dreading it for days building up to it. That year, it was my dad's turn to take me. From what I remember, you could go and see the various teachers in any order you wanted, so I deliberately went round all my stronger subjects first, saving the dreaded Chemistry until last. I was truly terrible; I couldn't even balance an equation, so had no idea what Mr Jefferies was going to say. We sat down and one of the first things my dad asked about was a guitar badge that was pinned to my teacher's lapel. It was an Eric Clapton badge, and they proceeded to spend most of the next ten minutes talking about Eric Clapton. I was watching the clock with one eye, thinking to myself, *Keep going, keep going*. They'd had such a nice chat that at the very end he didn't have the heart to tell my dad the truth. Words to the effect of, 'He does try and has remained fairly consistent' were said, and that was pretty much it. Bullet dodged.

In May of 2000, I sat my GCSE's. I did put quite a lot of effort into revising; Barton Court had drilled into us the importance of obtaining good grades if we wanted to do A-Levels and then go on to university. I read somewhere that listening to background music was good for helping one to retain knowledge, and so on went Dinosaur Junior and Nirvana whilst I studied the finer points of algebra and oxbow lakes in my bedroom. 'You call that revision,' my mum would shout up the stairs. I insisted that it helped, but later found out that it was actually background classical music that was a proven effective learning aid. I surprised myself with how well I did. Even the subjects that I disliked I did reasonably well at. I could barely speak a word of German and yet still came out of it with a C. Apart from German, Maths & Science, everything else was As and A*s. Listening to the warbling Seattle tones of Kurt Cobain had clearly paid off.

The last day of compulsory education felt momentous. It was the last day of wearing that ridiculously impractical school uniform that we all had great fun defacing. About half our year was leaving and moving onto pastures new. Apart from Josh, who left to go to college, most of my friends stayed on to do A-Levels. We celebrated by going to the local park and pouring detergent into the central fountain. It frothed up like a giant bubble bath and we all jumped in. We then scribbled goodbye messages all over each other's shirts.

'What a waste of a good shirt,' my mum said when I got home.

'It's tradition,' I retorted.

'What's the point? You'll be seeing most of them again after the summer.' That was certainly true, though things were very different upon our return. It was such a refreshing change of atmosphere being sixth formers. I was studying subjects I wanted to learn, there was no uniform, no registers, and you could come and go as you pleased. Having decided that I wanted to be a journalist, I had signed up to do four relevant A-levels – English, Geography, Media, and Sociology. Finally, a little taste of independence. The times were-a-changin'.

CHAPTER 4

Teenage Kicks

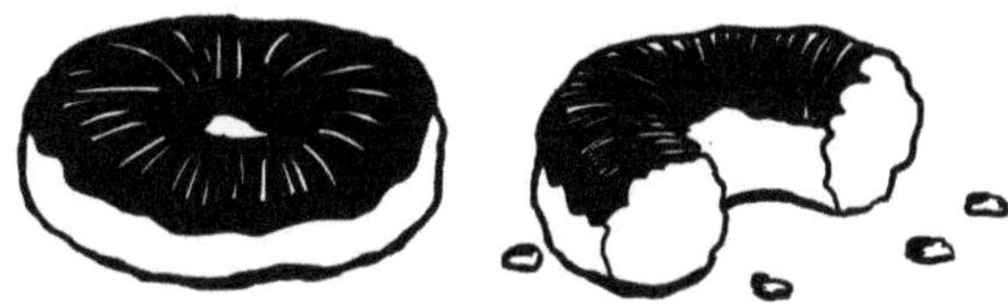

The first time I visited a pub, I was only sixteen. I have always looked young for my age and was regularly ID'd up until my mid-twenties, so God knows how young I must have looked back then. We chose our pub well, though, it was called the Black Dog which we had heard wasn't a strictly legit venue. Me and Josh went with two girls we had known back at primary school, and it may have supposed to have been a double date, I can't remember. It was a real grubby, grungy pub, packed to the rafters, incredibly noisy, and thick with smoke. Neither of us had any real money so we just settled for a couple of Coca-Colas. Never mind buying the girls a drink, we couldn't afford to get ourselves a drink. We just sat there trying to talk above the deafening noise until we got bored and started playing with the beer mats. After that good impression, the girls were off to talk to older men with beards that they could get a drink off. We just sat there not really sure what to do. The Black Dog got closed down not long afterwards, probably due to half its clientele being under-age.

Around this time, the vile rise of non-celebrities began when reality TV programmes started to gain popularity in the UK. There had always been programmes with a reality feel, but they were somewhat constricted by technological limitations. With advances in computer editing software, it suddenly became possible to film people stranded on an island or locked together in a house over a prolonged period of time. *Big Brother* launched in July 2000 and was a huge television landmark. It was all anyone could talk about at school for weeks. I hated it from the get-go. Even at my tender young age, I found it to be embarrassing and slightly demeaning. For the first couple of years, it was nothing more than tediously sad voyeurism. Once people became aware of the formula, it just got sillier and sillier, as people played up to the cameras and moved it further and further away from the concept of 'reality TV'. Imagine, if you will, being a sentient alien being on some far-flung planet and your job is to scan the deepest reaches of the universe for transmissions from alien civilizations to prove that there is intelligent life out there. And then imagine that after decades of searching, the first video transmission you come across is of one of our esteemed elected leaders. It is politician George Galloway, on all fours, purring and pretending to lap cream from the hands of actress Rula Lenska. You would wipe one green tentacle across your heavily perspiring forehead and deduce that there was nothing approaching intelligent life on this planet. I am proud to say I have never actually watched a full episode of the show. The bits I did see were painful; I could feel my intellect dissolving like Berocca.

Big Brother and the programmes that followed in its wake made fake celebrities out of ordinary people for basically doing nothing. Five years later, at a bar in Brighton, I experienced my only ever 'Do you know who I am?' moment. Some guy pushed past me whilst I was ordering some drinks, and when I challenged him, he gave that exact response. I think I retorted with 'I literally have no idea', he grunted and that was it. When I got back to my table, my housemate informed me who it was. It turned out to be one of the contestants off *Big Brother 3*. It reaffirmed my thoughts on the self-entitled type of people drawn to these shows who want to be famous for fame's sake. These kinds of people didn't really exist before 2000. It's hard to believe twenty years later with these kind of shows now ten a penny, that there was a time when everyone needed real talent in order to become famous. Don't get me wrong, like everyone else I have my guilty pleasures. I'm quite partial to *The Apprentice,* and me and my wife both enjoy passing the time with certain cooking competitions. Whilst they do come under the bracket of reality TV, the difference, I think, is that there is some level of skill involved and you, the viewer, are invested in a journey that isn't pure sensationalism. On a slight tangent, those TV shows that show such promise in their title but are just an exact replica of everything else out there, are a pet hate of mine. Just when I thought *Paul Hollywood Eats Japan* would be about the titular presenter gradually consuming the members of the 1980s pop group, I was subjected to yet another overpaid chef staying in luxury hotels and gorging on sushi.

By now, I was longing to start earning my own money. I had done a few odds and ends, like being paid to hold a golf sale sign in Canterbury High Street. Josh and I took turns holding it for a few quid, when a gust of wind blew it over and damaged it slightly. We then got deducted half our wages and came away with less than £15 each for an afternoon's work. On another occasion, my mum had the crazy idea of me, Josh, and his mate, Chris Kennard, joining the circus. We trundled up to this field in Kingsmead where she had told us they were hiring, but got turned away for being too young. It was probably a good thing in retrospect, it turned out they were actually looking for labourers. We weren't that desperate for money that we wanted to spend the summer shovelling elephant dung.

My first proper job was working as a kitchen porter in a Mexican restaurant in Canterbury. I worked two or three shifts a week in-between my studies: Tuesday evenings, Saturday daytimes, and sometimes on Sundays. It was physically quite hard work. Basically, I was washing up, loading and unloading an industry dishwasher, and putting equipment away. When it was busy, the heat in that place was intense and you would come away drenched in sweat by the end of a shift. It was also quite dangerous, as the chefs would just fling these giant carving knives in the sink without telling you. It was a high-pressured environment, so the chefs would often do crazy things to relieve the tension. They would lock each other in the walk-in fridge and see how long the person would last before panicking and banging on the door. Occasionally, I would do other jobs – a little bit of cooking, like frying the taco shells – or carrying out a bit of stock-taking. The worst job was cleaning the grease trap, which was basically a sewer that ran under the restaurant, where all the fat and oil would congregate. If you forgot to empty it (which happened on more than one occasion), it would overflow and flood the kitchen floor with a tsunami of sludge. You had to remove the drain lid and scoop out the pungent contents into black bin liners, which you would then dispose of. Once, when I was halfway through this delightful process and my back was turned, one of the chefs pushed his colleague into it. I don't think he meant to. I think it was supposed to be a light shove, but he ended up on the floor with his arms coated in all this gunk.

'Sorry,' the chef said. 'I didn't mean it. I was just trying to scare you.'

The guy sprawled out on the floor was furious. He rose up and grabbed one of the nearby kitchen knives and started waving it around, chasing the chef through the kitchen. It was a cross between Benny Hill and *Psycho*. After a couple of minutes, he threw this twelve-inch carving knife in the chef's direction and it narrowly missed his head when it pinged into the wall behind. It made that metallic vibrating noise like it was part of a sketch from a Tom & Jerry cartoon. The whole kitchen went deathly quiet.

'Sorry,' he said. 'I was just trying to scare you.' Just another day at the office for me.

The hygiene standards varied from adequate to illegal. Generally, the food was of good quality and stored correctly, but it was the temperament of the chefs that determined how likely you were to get salmonella. I remember once having to scrape mould off a seriously old piece of cheese. It looked like it hadn't left the safety of the fridge since the Napoleonic Wars.

'They'll never notice by the time it's grated and coated with sauce.' Since working in a restaurant, I've learnt never to order anything just before closing, that's what really makes a chef irate. On one occasion, we had already started clearing up and had discarded all our old meat into the bin. There was a gentleman who had been sitting at the bar upstairs and had come down to order some duck, just after the restaurant had officially closed. The chef on duty went ballistic, smashing a couple of plates and cursing the customer. The poor waitress who brought the order in looked terrified. He turned to me and solemnly said, 'Chris. We have five minutes to plate up. Fetch that duck out of the bin.' I rinsed it under a tap, and within four minutes and fifty seconds the dish was served with a side salad garnish, and a dollop of phlegm for good measure.

I had an additional duty on Sundays, which was acting as a 'look-out'. Sundays up until 1pm were the best shift, as the restaurant was much quieter and less stressful. There was usually only one chef on duty, and all of them (bar one, I think) smoked weed, so Sunday was the day that they would climb up onto the roof and have a cheeky toke in-between orders. If the General Manager or owner turned up unannounced, I would cover for them, 'Oh, they've just gone to the toilet' or 'they've just popped to another restaurant to get some CO2'. I was then allowed all the ice cream I wanted out of the freezer. Whilst the work generally was (pardon the pun) as dull as dishwater, there were some perks. I got free food and drink, and when there was a bit of downtime, the chefs would whip me up a burger. And the tips were generally pretty good, (so the food can't have seemed that inedible).

Going to collect my wages was always a great feeling. We weren't paid by BACS; it was all cash in hand. I would go down on a Monday after school every week at 4pm on the dot. For some reason, I always took Bjorn with me, and the owner, who counted all the wages himself, would always stare at him with the same quizzical expression.

'I see you've brought the cavalry again.'

I kept that job up for just over a year. Towards the end of my time there, they kept adding more and more shifts, so I left to spend more time studying for my A-levels. I did learn a valuable lesson from my stint there, though – I never wanted to work in a restaurant again.

It was around this time that a branch of HMV opened in Canterbury. Having a big music shop launch was a big deal back then. We all traipsed down after school to peruse the racks of shiny CD's and suck the helium out of all the promotional balloons they were giving away. I remember buying *Californication* by The Red Hot Chili Peppers. I already had it on tape, but it was such a massive album at the time that I really wanted it on CD. On 4th December, 2000, I attended my first gig. For some unfathomable reason, Josh and I went to see Status Quo at the Winter Gardens in Margate. It was a somewhat strange first gig, as neither of us are what you might call Status Quo fans. It was about £40 each, which was a lot of money back then. I think my mum was more excited than us.

'You get to see the legendary Quo.'

'Yeah, at that legendary price,' remarked Josh.

Status Quo were exactly how you would imagine them to be, good fun – nothing more, nothing less. However, I thought the support act, Steve Harley & The Cockney Rebels, were brilliant.

About three months later, me and my mate Mark made plans to go to Reading Festival. He had been the previous year with another of our friends, Andrew Dray and his sister. The year they went had boasted a great line-up but the band that Mark raved about most was this truly terrible hard rap-rock act called Limp Bizkit. Thankfully, they had vanished into obscurity a few years later. Anyway, we had decided that we would go in August that year and made arrangements to get tickets. You couldn't just casually order them online like you would do now. You had to read the record magazines and find out when they were going on general release, then go and queue up at the various stockists. I went down to a shop called Richards Records, and after twenty minutes of waiting managed to get hold of two precious tickets. I think they were something in the region of £80 each.

The festival took place over the August Bank Holiday weekend, so on the Thursday morning we took the train up to Reading. I had been warned to get there early, as the previous year Mark and Dray's tents had been trampled after getting there at night and pitching on a major thoroughfare. When we arrived, it was a fantastic atmosphere – the crowds, the noise, even the smell of the Portakabins had a weird allure. We found a spot amidst a circle of other tents, and made friends with a group of hippies who were maybe slightly older than us. I got Mark to sing Elvis songs to them in exchange for alcohol. We had a great evening, lighting a bonfire, swaying and slurring to power ballads, and drinking whatever concoction was being passed around. At one o'clock in the morning, when lots of people had passed out, Mark thought he would do some clearing up. We weren't exactly equipped with cleaning products, so Mark decided the best thing to do was just to stick all the rubbish on the fire and keep it burning. Two birds with one stone, right? Maybe it was the booze, maybe the tiredness, or maybe just a moment of unbridled madness, but whatever the reason, rather than select suitable items for the fire (i.e. cardboard) Mark just chucked everything on. Suddenly everyone woke up in a panic when a glass bottle exploded, and shards went flying everywhere. He had probably thought it was plastic, and in fairness, it may have been difficult to tell in the pitch black. After that came the plastic carrier bags that Mark had dumped on. There was a bit of a breeze and they got caught in a gust of wind and took flight, whilst still on fire. There was some frantic whizzing around as flaming pieces of Tesco carrier bags started raining down on reveller's tents, like a troop of kamikaze fireflies. We dashed around checking no tents had caught fire. Thankfully, there was no serious damage – just a few scorch marks and a handful of bemused bohemians emerging from their slumber to witness the impromptu firework show. The following year bonfires were banned.

The line-up in 2001 was pretty eclectic. There were a few acts that I was very excited to see – Mercury Rev, Iggy Pop, and PJ Harvey. I think on the first day Mark and I just stood by the main stage the entire time. I had a bottle of whisky in one pocket, and a bottle for urinating in the other. It was pretty intense at times. It was a very young crowd, so there was a lot of jumping around and fights breaking out (moshing basically), which I tried to avoid. There was a band called Staind, who were your typical American hard rock act of the time. They came on and the crowd went wild, but halfway through either their first or second song, there was some kind of power failure. There was a lot of cursing and sulking, both from the band and the crowd. They did the rest of the set sat on stalls with acoustic guitars. I thought it was great, but the majority of the crowd didn't know what to make of it. I don't know if Reading has become more mellow since, but back then the front of the main stage could be more like a riot than a gig. You needed to be careful of crowd-surfers who could unexpectedly fall on top of you, which happened to me on a couple of occasions. I actually saw Mark get squashed by this huge naked crowd-surfer, which was half disturbing/ half hilarious. After that first day, I made sure that I was further back from the main stage, and made more of an effort to go to the smaller performance areas where it was easier to enjoy the music. I saw some brilliant bands on some of those smaller stages, bands like the Drop Kick Murphy's and The Fun Lovin' Criminals.

A couple of weeks later, we were back to finish off our A-Levels. It was hard work taking four subjects (most people do three) and working three shifts a week – I didn't finish working at the restaurant until around Christmas time. We had to make our University UCAS choices not long after we came back for that final year. I had narrowed it down to two for Media & Journalism – Cardiff or Sussex. I went to open days at both with my mum, but funnily enough I can't remember anything about those trips. I do remember preferring the Sussex campus, though. It's actually the only university in the country where everything is all on one site. I thought it had a nicer vibe and it was further up the rankings table, so it became my no.1 choice.

Me and my mates had started regularly going to the pub by now. We were all seventeen but, despite me being the oldest of the group, I looked the youngest. Every Friday at school we would plan which pubs we would be frequenting and how we would get in. The plan was generally to go to the establishments that were struggling financially (as they were less likely to care) and make sure that only the two tallest (Dray & Bjorn) would order at the bar. The advantage of going to these places was that they would often have games like pool tables and darts to entice people in. We would write out these pool tournaments on Friday lunchtimes at school, and then spend all of the evening playing knockout competitions in these bars. The disadvantage of these places is that they were as lively as a leper colony. Usually there were just a couple of old men drinking ale at the bar. Sometimes they would waddle over and say hello, which would be the pinnacle of the evenings' social interaction with others. As well as gentlemen who looked like they'd been permanently glued to the bar stools since 1962, faded upholstery, surly landlords, an abundance of pork scratchings, and the absence of natural light were the other notable qualities of these places. Of course, once we had been served at these establishments, that meant staying for the duration of the night. Sometimes when there was a change of staff, we would be kicked out and have to re-strategise.

Generally, our watering holes were three grotty bars called The King William, The Tally Ho, and The Bat & Ball. The Bat & Ball was the best of these, very occasionally we would talk to a girl in there. None of us had much money, so it was usually only a couple of drinks and then some chips on the way home. If we had some spare change, we would play a few songs on the jukebox. We sometimes played this entertaining game where we would line up the songs in the most random order we possibly could, just to freak out the other people in the pub. So, for instance, we would play a heavy metal song (i.e. Marilyn Manson), followed by a 50s country song (i.e.

Hank Williams), followed by an *avant-garde* track like *Revolution 9#* by The Beatles. You could see people looking round thinking, *Who the hell put this crap on?* It was quite a challenging game as most pub jukeboxes are fairly conservative, but we had great fun trying.

The girls in our year had it so much easier than us. They would go to much plusher and more popular bars, being able to get served without any issues. Just applying make-up and wearing the right clothes would make you look older; that, and most people didn't care. Once when we were feeling brave, we turned up for one of the girls' birthdays at one of these 'trendier pubs'. We had heard that one of their uncles was working that night, so getting served wouldn't be an issue. We arrived in high spirits, but they were the only spirits we had that evening. No sooner had we arrived and said hello, than we were booted out. Talk about losing your street credibility.

Dray would turn round and say to me, 'Cheers for getting us kicked out again.'

'How is it my fault? I'm the bloody oldest.'

We would return to school on the Monday to much joshing from the girls.

September 11th, 2001 is one of those dates that is engrained in people's psyches. Afterwards, everyone said they'd never forget where they were when that happened. I remember vividly, because I was about the only person on the planet who didn't find out until the following day. The first plane hit the north tower of the World Trade Centre at 8.46am (US eastern seaboard time zone) which was 1.46pm UK time. The second plane hit 17 minutes later, so 2.03pm UK time. This was around the time that I was walking home from school as I had a free period on Tuesday afternoons, allowing me to start my evening shift at the restaurant a little earlier.

I had about an hour's turnaround time at home, so went to play some computer games before my shift started. My dad, who had been listening to the radio, came in and said, 'They're bombing America', which I took to mean there had been a mass shooting or a bomb in a shopping centre. I didn't think it was anything out of the ordinary for America. Plus, the details were a little sketchy at that point. There was no Twitter or 24-hour news back then, so you would usually need to wait for the next news bulletin to get any information. I left for work and didn't think anything of it.

The chefs at the restaurant weren't (to put it politely) an enlightened bunch. When I first started working there, they had a radio, but the chefs used to play a game of seeing how ear-splittingly loud they could play it before the Manager came in shouting. One day he came in, ripped it out of its socket, and threw it in the bin in a boiling rage. Henceforth, we were never allowed a radio again. That evening was the usual banal chatter about football transfers and tattoos before we started clearing up at around 11.30pm. We had a couple of drinks at the bar and then I left. I was always exhausted at the end of a Tuesday shift, it was a long day and I was feeling pretty fuzzy from the beer. I got home about 1am and briefly put the TV on. I thought it was some 1980s Bruce Willis action film, *Inferno*, or something. I realised the following day that this had been actual footage from the disaster, but at the time I was too tipsy/shattered to piece two and two together. I turned it off and went to bed.

Only the following morning did I actually find out what had happened, on the BBC News. Like everyone else, I couldn't believe it. America had always seemed invincible. The twin towers themselves were these giant monuments to capitalism that seemed to typify the American Dream – they were everywhere. In films, on the front covers of magazines like *Time*, the credits sequence to *Friends*; it seemed impossible that they were now gone. It also seemed impossible that a bunch of terrorists from a country like Afghanistan were responsible for causing so much destruction in a city like New York. Details were still a bit sketchy, and to this day are still shrouded in mystery. Why were 15 of the 19 terrorists from a supposed ally like Saudi Arabia? Why was there no wreckage from the third plane that crashed into the Pentagon? Were there any more attacks planned? Was London or Tokyo next? The whole thing seemed so well co-ordinated that many people thought this was just the tip of the iceberg. That there were all these sleeper cells all around the world just waiting to spring into action. People were also worried that it could escalate into a third world war. After all, this was the first time that America had been attacked on its own soil since Pearl Harbour in 1941.

There was a very strange atmosphere that day at school. Lots of people had friends and relatives who were in New York, and we knew of a couple of extended family members in our year who had been killed. Our tutor gave a speech about the importance of positive thinking and that 'life goes on'. I remember buying a newspaper at lunchtime. I knew that this would be history, and part of what my children might eventually learn about in school, so I wanted to keep a record of the news for posterity. I collected newspapers every day for about two weeks afterwards, until the September 11th attacks stopped being front page news. I kept those newspapers in a pile in my bedroom until my mum infuriatingly assumed they were rubbish and threw away the newspaper on top. I still have a collection of all the others, from September 13th onwards, but I am missing that elusive copy from the day afterwards. Our tutor was right, though, life did go on. Nothing really changed in Canterbury, but on my occasional trips up to London, I did notice an increased police presence. I don't remember guns being something that the police ever carried until post September 11th. A couple of months after September 11th, George Harrison died. I remember it vividly, as I found it strangely upsetting. Around that time, I was obsessed with collecting Beatles' albums and dissecting each and every track. Whilst everyone else at school was into Radiohead and the Manic Street Preachers, I was refusing to conform to 'cool teenage type'. There was always this vain hope in the back of my mind that Paul, Ringo, and George might get back together with Julian (Lennon's son) and perform a few gigs. In reality, it would probably have been a deflating and slightly sad spectacle if it had actually happened (ala the nineties Velvet Underground reunion), but still, there was always that hope to cling on to. That was now extinguished. Whilst on the subject of George Harrison, I can't resist a hilarious story involving my future father-in-law, Rob. He won't mind me saying this, but whilst he's a brilliant man in many ways, he's not always the most observant person. George Harrison's son, Dhani, was performing in the same concert as my future wife, Debs. She was playing the violin as part of this show when she was about ten years old. Jen and Rob went along to watch her and, unbeknown to Rob, he was seated next to George Harrison. At some point during the performance, he turned round to him and proceeded to tell him that he was learning to play the guitar and asked if the man himself was musical. I'm sure George Harrison probably found it quite refreshing being an anonymous dad for once.

Mark Phipps was a unique character. I'd known him for a few years, but we spent a lot more time together whilst studying for our A-Levels. He was, and still is, a great lad, but back then he would do anything to please you – he just couldn't say no. If you asked him to do something, he would always oblige, no matter how ridiculous. One day, we were discussing ways to raise money for Children in Need and he dropped into conversation his prowess at eating doughnuts. He claimed he could eat a hundred doughnuts over the lunch break, i.e. within an hour! Dray and I straight away saw the potential of this being comedy gold. So, we trundled off down to the supermarket to buy 100 doughnuts. We cleared the store out, but as they didn't have 100 of any particular flavour, we just got whatever we could: plain, jam, custard, chocolate-topped ones, iced ones. After all, Mark never specified the type. We also bought six litres of lemonade to wash it all down with.

We found the perfect spot for Mark to do his challenge, outside on the steps where the whole school could gather to watch the unfolding spectacle. He was eager to get going and started off at lightning pace, eating the first four within a minute. He very soon started to slow down after that, but was determined to keep on going. I think he got to about eighteen when he started feeling ill. Rather sensibly, he downed half a bottle of lemonade to quench his thirst and then carried on. The problems really started at around twenty doughnuts, when he started going, 'No more jam! No more jam!' We then tried to limit him to the other flavours, but it was hard to know precisely what we had. He started throwing up half digested doughnuts but, bless him, he wanted to carry on. We had to estimate what we were losing, so the count went down as well as up: 21, 21.5, 22, 21.75. We tried to be very precise in judging the quantities of doughnuts we were haemorrhaging. Despite the crowd that had gathered and the chanting of 'Mark, Mark, Mark', he eventually collapsed into a pile of remorse after 28 doughnuts. He'd not even got a third of the way through, but it was a herculean effort. To put it into context, 28 doughnuts equates to the following;

- 6160 calories*

---

* = *Medium UK doughnuts range from 198 calories (for a plain doughnut) to 240 for a glazed doughnut. For the purposes of the comparison above, I have taken the average calories of Mark's doughnut intake to be 219.*

- 364 grams of saturated fat (28 x recommended daily amount)
- 7 x average roast dinners
- 43.5 cans of Coke
- 24 McDonald's Big Mac burgers

Despite the money he raised, he wasn't happy that he hadn't reached his target, so we came up with a much more feasible challenge of drinking ten pints of Guinness over the course of a night out. Again, he couldn't say no. Now, obviously there are people that could do this, but we were only seventeen at the time, and Guinness is a notoriously difficult drink to consume in large quantities. Mark was a stocky guy, but he wasn't huge. So, a crowd of us went out, starting off in Wetherspoons as usual. Mark made the fatal error of starting off too fast; I think it was four pints within the first hour. One of our other friends, Chris Slater arrived with his girlfriend just as Mark was finishing off pint number seven. Within seconds of arriving into the arena of anarchy Mark threw up all the over the carpet, much to the disgust of Slater's girlfriend. In fact, I think all the girls who were reluctantly along for the ride, abandoned us at that point. He then got booted out by the staff and we had to find somewhere else to carry on the show. He managed the next two pints much slower, but was still just about conscious. The final pint was a challenge. He threw up again after about half of it, but this time rather than chucking him out of the pub, they got a mop and bucket from the storeroom and made him clear it up. Watching someone who can barely stand up trying to mop is like witnessing the aftermath of a car crash or a celebrity's plastic surgery procedure gone wrong. You don't want to watch but you can't help yourself. He tried in vain to clean up, the offending fluids, but just ended up spraying it everywhere. It was so grim. It was all over his clothes and was flying all over the other tables where people were trying to have romantic dates. We made him down the last of it and then just got out of there as fast as we could. We had to half drag/half carry him home. We left him in his conservatory and, despite his horrendous state, he was grinning like the cat that got the cream.

'When's the next challenge then, guys?' What a trouper!

In March 2002, I finally turned 18. It was a great feeling to suddenly have the world open up in front of you. We celebrated with a proper pub crawl, where there was no danger of not getting in. In fact, I made a point of deliberately going to pubs where they were much stricter.

'Do you have any ID, young man?'

'Well yes, sir, I do.' In reality, we couldn't go to half those pubs as a group anyway, as not all of us were 18 yet, but still it felt momentous.

We would usually start our nights in Wetherspoon's with a sticky toffee pudding, before commencing our quest into alcoholic oblivion. The cuisine in Wetherspoon's has definitely improved over the years, but back then it was pretty soul destroying. The peas always seemed to have a haunting back note of fag ash and the scampi resembled stiff orange coffins that emitted an ooze of vaguely fishy goo. We learnt pretty quickly just to skip these culinary feasts and go straight for dessert- you couldn't go wrong with a diabetic deluge of sugar to get a Friday night rolling. We also started going to nightclubs, although the selection in Canterbury was pretty terrible. There was The Bizz which played mostly rubbish music, and Churchill's which played exclusively rubbish music. Both were expensive and The Bizz had watered-down beer on tap. Nowadays, these kinds of establishments have about as much allure to me as a dentist's drill, but at the time that was our world.

When we first started going to pubs, I would just order what I knew I could pronounce (John Smiths was a favourite), but we'd all started experimenting with other drinks now. One of our chums, a guy called Alistair, would always order Vodka Red Bull, which we initially scoffed at before discovering you could order it in massive pitchers and it was a very economical way to get drunk. We would get through bucketloads of the stuff. It's actually really bad for the body as Red Bull is a stimulant and vodka is a depressant. You could actually feel your heart excessively pounding if you drank too much of the stuff. Another big favourite was turbo-shandies, where you would mix a lager with a Smirnoff ice to create this strange Frankenstein drink that would make you go a bit loopy. I'm not sure of the science behind it but it was certainly potent. The bar staff would always confiscate your drinks if they found out you were doing it, so it was always a stealthy under-the-table operation.

Mobile phones were only just starting to become mainstream at around this time. The first time I had seen anyone our age with a mobile was about eighteen months earlier at a house party for a girl in our year called Sonya. Her friend was so proud of it she carried it around in a separate bag. To be fair, she needed to, it was huge. As we didn't know anyone else with one, we couldn't make proper calls with this new-fangled device. Instead, we all took turns calling the house phone. It basically functioned as an expensive one-way walkie-talkie. By early 2002 a few people at Barton Court had phones but they were still uncommon. Going on a night out meant you had to be on time; if you were more than a few minutes late, there was a real danger of getting left behind. Luckily, we had a fairly set routine of pubs by then, but I remember coming out later and having to systematically go round a few places before I could find the lads.

We sat our A-Level exams in June that year. After the last exam we had a massive end-of-year ball to celebrate. It was a bit weird; a kind of American-style prom night where we all dressed up like we were attending a wedding. It felt pretty surreal drinking Orangeboom alongside the tutors. I remember Bjorn arm wrestling with our old P.E. teacher and realising that we were to all intents and purposes now adults, at least in body if not quite in mind. We got our A-Level results about six weeks later and all went down to the local Wetherspoon's to celebrate/ commiserate. It was a strange atmosphere as not everyone had achieved the grades they needed to go to their first-choice university. I had achieved 4 Bs, and although it would have been nice to have been awarded an A, it was still a high UCAS points tally.

I had about eight weeks off before starting university. I had planned to go to Reading again that summer, so needed money for that, as well as keeping up a hectic socialising schedule. I found a temping agency called Plan Personnel, where I got a job for a few weeks in an assembly factory called Amphenol. This was a company that manufactured various electrical components like connectors, sockets, and cables. Although much of it was automated, most of the assembly work was done by hand, so the company employed a huge number of staff. I ended up in one of the more interesting areas (relatively speaking), filing vials with various small bits of circuitry, and then taking them to the stock area to be processed. My other role there was making up the air pillows – basically industrial-sized bubble wrap. This involved pumping air into the plastic casing and then packing it into boxes. That was exciting for about 20 minutes. The area I worked in actually produced 20% of the UK's air pillows.

Most of the older staff had spent their whole lives working there and were just counting down the days until their retirement cheques to come through. There was one crabby woman who was in the classic middle management position of allowing the power go to her head. She was managing the temporary staff (not me fortunately) and was something of a slave driver. She was tiny, probably less than five foot and scurried around, so I nicknamed her 'the crab'. She would inspect the temps' work and throughout the day, above the din of the factory floor, you would hear her screeching 'not good enough! not good enough!' over and over again. The temps were all under 25 and were just hired in to help out during the busier manufacturing cycles. All of them towered above the crab, but that didn't make her any less scary. The work was repetitive, but the five of us in my area tried to swap jobs whenever we could, just to keep things interesting. Even then, you would hope for something to go wrong, like the packaging machine to break or a fire alarm to go off, just to keep work that little bit more stimulating. There was a guy called Stuart who was based in the area next to us. His role was to go round the whole factory floor with a clipboard and record the work that everyone had produced three times a day. I had a chat with him at lunch once and discovered he had also started off as a temporary contractor but twenty years later was still here.

'Chris,' he told me over a lukewarm canteen lasagne. 'If you keep your head down, in twenty years' time you could be doing my job.' I mean it was great he had such confidence in me, but it really wasn't where I was hoping to end up.

There was a lot of partying that summer. One week we even managed to do seven nights out in a row. We were also coming up with wilder and sillier challenges. The *crème de la crème* of these was known as the 'Dane John Challenge'. The Dane John is a park within the Canterbury City walls, with a tall burial mound based in the middle. The challenge involved drinking a certain number of pints (at least five, or the equivalent thereof) and then proceeding to run up and down the hill. Three things made this very difficult. The alcohol consumption was obviously one of these. The second factor was that the hill itself was very steep, and the rules stipulated that you had to run up and down it, touching the hedge at the top. It was also full of trip hazards – various holes and mounds. The third factor was that it levelled off really quickly onto a solid concrete path. Upon reaching this, you only had about four metres to slow yourself down before you reached a wall with a thirty-foot drop on the other side. Some of us were not so stupid as to try this challenge, but four of us were. Chioma and I completed it unscathed. However, Slater and Dray both came off a little worse for wear. Slater came away with a few cuts and bruises, but Dray was covered in blood after his attempt. He had managed to rip open his shirt, scraped his face, and chipped a tooth. Even in that state, we still attempted to carry on the night before he called his parents to take him up to hospital. The Dane John challenge takes no prisoners!

Going to Reading Festival for a second year in a row, I was a lot more clued up. Again, I went with Mark, but this time Josh and a girl called Amanda that he knew through college joined us. I came equipped with enough tinned peaches, toilet rolls, and torches for a small army. I even had the good sense to decorate our tent with a sellotape stencil of a pyjama man (my style of drawing has been christened 'pyjama style' for many years) so that we wouldn't fail to spot it in a sea of identical tents. It was a better line-up than the first year- it was particularly great to see Pulp. I remember Jarvis coming out on stage looking like a librarian in his tweed jacket and specs.

'I hope you've all brought your library books with you,' (queue puzzled looks) 'this is, after all, the reading festival.'

One of the joys of going to music festivals is discovering new bands, especially when they are totally unknown and then go on to become highly successful. That year at the very bottom of the bill on a tiny stage were The Libertines. They had only released one single at that point, and because of the strong use of profanity it had received next to no airplay. But they were dazzling in this really sweaty tent that had no more than sixty people inside. Three months later, they released one of the greatest albums of the decade.

CHAPTER 5

University Challenge

The road twists and turns through ancient boggy marshland across a landscape as flat as a millpond. I gaze out of the window across this windswept and desolate scene. Romney Marsh is 250 square km of reeds, salt marshes, and tidal flats in every direction. All the roads are narrow and winding, due to the hundreds of drain ditches that pepper the landscape. It's very sparsely populated for the south of England. Many small hamlets that once stood there had been abandoned over the centuries, with just the occasional ruined farmhouse or remains of a church arch the only clue as to their prior existence. Apparently, many of these settlements were decimated by the black death in the 1300s, whilst others were abandoned when they started sinking into the marsh. I notice Dungeness Power Station clinging to the horizon, which only adds to the general eeriness. I guess the sparseness of the location was why it was chosen as a site for a nuclear power station. I visited there on a school trip once, not that I remember much of it. The rare glimpses you would get of ruined structures made it seem as though the reactor core had exploded and all that had survived the ensuing apocalypse was wading birds and thousands of grazing sheep. This is the only south coast route that connects Kent with Brighton. The more well travelled route is the M2 up to Maidstone, skirting round London on the M20 and M25, before taking the M23 towards the South Downs. If you enjoy a bit of bleak scenery and like to avoid Europe's biggest car park, this is the only real alternative. The railway which serves this route is the woefully inadequate Marshlink Line. It's one of the few non-electrified lines in the South East. It's also single track for part of the route and before arriving at Eastbourne a mere two carriages long. Over the next three years, I would regularly take that rickety old train on my journeys to and from Brighton. It was always late, would frequently break down, and would groan and wheeze the whole way like an asthmatic man jogging for the bus. It wouldn't have surprised me if on one of my journeys the passengers had been asked to get out and push. I see the train chugging along as we sail by in my mum's friend Carol's car. It's the 21st September, 2002 and the three of us are wedged in among all my clutter. Almost all my worldly goods are crammed into the back of this VW. I didn't own much – a few bags of clothes, a stack of CDs, some stationery and a basic selection of toiletries. We can't be doing more than 35mph, but before long the train has faded to nothing in the rear-view mirror. We stop off in Rye for a quick cream tea before recommencing the journey. I was so excited to be going to university. I just wanted to get there and throw myself into student life. The one bit of advice I received from my mum on that journey was never to go to The New Amsterdam bar along the seafront. Strangely enough, I never did, so maybe that was sage advice. A few more hairpin bends later, and we're past Winchelsea and Iklesham. The landscape becomes less foreboding, and it's onto Hastings, Bexhill, and Lewes.

Finally, the bright lights of Brighton rear into view. We turn off the A27 and onto Sussex University campus.

After I'd registered I then had to lug all my bin bags and boxes up a steep hill to my student accommodation – East Slope. The clue was in the name; it was built into the east side of a valley which looked down upon the rest of the campus. The East Slope blocks had been built in the early 1970s as a temporary measure whilst they constructed the accommodation proper – that was finally completed 46 years later! At night when East Slope was lit up, it looked like a shanty town or a Brazilian favela clinging onto the sides of the hill for dear life. I don't think my mum was overly impressed when she saw where I'd be living – we later nicknamed it 'the prison cells'. It had claustrophobically narrow hallways, low hanging ceilings, this disgusting dark green carpet, and one toilet to share between eight official residents – ten unofficially. But I didn't care at all. Having my own room was exciting. I was lucky in that regard, four of my house mates had to share their bedrooms. I think I would have been crushed if I'd ended up sharing a room in Brighton after sixteen years with my brother. I was the first one to arrive, so got round to unpacking. Another five people arrived later on that day, including Nick, who was aghast to find that he was sharing a room. He had specifically written on his application form that he didn't mind where he stayed as long as it wasn't East Slope and it wasn't in a shared room. They must have taken one look at his application and had a good chuckle.

My rent for residing in the East Slope Palace was £260 a month – the prices were steep as well as the accommodation! To be honest, I didn't care. I wanted to live on campus and we were in the cheapest block. My total student loan came to just under £12,000, which felt like a fortune at the time. I was lucky in that my actual course was free; those were the days when not everyone paid tuition fees. The £12,000 was just for living costs, so £4000 to live off per year. The rent for nine months of the year took up more than half of that, so in spite of my excitingly large bank balance, it was only just enough to get by.

Brighton was a fantastic place to be a student. I thought it was the coolest place in the world – the jewel in the South Coast crown and a liberal mecca for music, art, theatre, and innovation. It had everything: great shops, a beach, a burgeoning art scene and a huge array of clubs and bars. My favourites were a Latin jazz bar called Casablanca's and an indie club called The Pav Tav. There were some brilliantly quirky pubs as well. There was England's only charity pub, appropriately enough called 'The Robin Hood'. The owners had made their money in banking and set it up as a not-for-profit pub, so all the money went to good causes. There was a lively seafront bar called 'the Bedford' which we re-christened as 'The Betty Ford', and a pub run by an eccentric couple who had no business acumen and hadn't bothered to name it, hence everyone called it 'The Pub With No Name'. The Lanes were a maze of quirky, independent stores, including a 'Vegetarian Shoe Shop' that you could spend hours in (the lanes, not the shoe shop). The beach was brilliant in the summer – a seemingly endless expanse of pebbles where you could barbecue and drink to your heart's content. One of my mates described Brighton as 'the terminus of gravity's rainbow'. I thought that was a great quote, but later discovered he'd pinched it from a novel by Thomas Pynchon. Sadly, I arrived just after Fatboy Slim had stopped doing his famous beach parties. Six months before, scores of people were injured when 250,000 people turned up to what was dubbed 'Glastonbury by the sea' so the council revoked his licence to hold them. I would later get to meet Norman Cook (aka Fatboy Slim) at other events, though.

The people I was cohabiting with were a great bunch. There was the aforementioned Nick, who wanted to be a theatre director and was doing the same course as me. He is now quite renowned in his field, with a number of successful productions in London venues like The Old Vic. Ritchie was from the island of Jersey and was studying to be a bio-chemist. He was unbelievably lazy though. He liked to profess how smart he was, but pretty much all I ever saw him do was smoke weed and play on the PlayStation. He also had this amazing ability, which I've never seen from anyone before or since, to hibernate. He would stay awake for three or four days straight and then sleep solidly for the next 2-3. When he awoke he reminded us of a bear coming out of hibernation. He would have a dark brown beard starting to form and would stumble around in a complete daze for about half an hour. Often when people wake up it takes a couple of minutes for them to get going, but Ritchie could hardly walk for the first hour. He would also be absolutely starving, and would cook up these massive feasts for breakfast that would resemble Sunday roasts. There was also Jesus. His real name was Sam, but because his middle name was the bearded one from Bethlehem, it was irresistible not to re-christen him as that. He didn't care; he said that people had always done that. There was Kate, a bubbly ginger girl whose ambition was to be a *Blue Peter* presenter, and Mary who had some tenuous connection to royalty. There was also Antonio, a borderline dwarf who looked about fourteen and skateboarded everywhere like Bart Simpson, just with added intellectual lucidity.

During that first year, there was a revolving door of people who came and went; some dropped out, whilst others just ended up living with us for some or all of the time. Smalley was one of them. For some reason he had enrolled a couple of weeks late so had ended up with a host family about four miles away. He hated living there, so we just let him crash at ours. Despite being called Smalley (which was his surname), he was a decent height and pretty well built.

I think it was literally on day one that I acquired my nickname, though it was never meant to be a nickname. For some reason, when I was introduced to Jesus, he thought my name was Dave and it stuck. Everyone else thought it was hilarious and started calling me it. For a couple of days I tried to shake it off, but no avail so I just gave in and started responding to it. Henceforth, to almost everyone I met at uni I introduced myself as Dave; it became second nature after a while. It reminded Nick of a character called Papa Lazoura in *League of Extraordinary Gentlemen,* who would go around saying creepy things like, 'You're my wife now, Dave.' The only time it got weird was during seminars when we did class registers. Some tutors ended up calling me Dave (usually if a couple of people I knew were in the class) and some just called me Chris. Outside of that, most people always assumed it was my actual name. Even now, when I get emails or Facebook messages from uni mates, they always start with 'Hi Dave'.

East Slope was definitely the social hub of Sussex campus. Every single night there would be parties. Our house was far too cramped to host them (some of the taller people would bang their heads on our ceilings), but we would often go elsewhere on campus. Ritchie was the only person in our house to have a laptop. We were amazed by it, particularly the fact that it didn't need to be plugged in the whole time – that was a revelation. Back in those days a portable laptop was as rare as rocking- horse shit. Using a dongle to access the internet was prohibitively expensive to do anything other than work, but we used it as a makeshift DVD player. The Libertines had suddenly got huge, and were always being played in our house, along with other garage revival bands like The Hives and The Datsuns. Radiohead was the band that everyone was obsessed with, though. They had played at our local

East Slope bar about six years earlier, and there was a frame around where Thom Yorke had scrawled his signature on the toilet wall. There was a club on campus called 'The Hot House' – aptly named, as there was no ventilation in there; it was like a sauna. We would frequently have showers at the end of the night after going there.

I really enjoyed my BA, I found delving into the world of print media fascinating. There's a simple technique in journalistic writing called the inverted pyramid structure. Basically, the most important information in an article is at the top, and as the pyramid goes down you get less crucial information with each successive paragraph. Sometimes this is called summary news lead style. What's really interesting is that certain papers, usually those of a more of an alarmist persuasion, flip this on its head, often called 'Burying the lead'. A paper like the *Daily Express,* for example, uses this technique perfectly to highlight whatever angle it wants a particular story to focus on. I learnt that if you're left wing and want to get the actual gist of a story in the *Express*, the best way to read it is backwards. The headline might scream 'Asylum seekers are eating our pets', but the last paragraph will say something more grounded in reality like, 'There have been three confirmed cases over the last twenty years.' News writing will always highlight the active over the passive to get to the story quicker. So, for instance, you will never see what at first glance appears to be a simple passive statement like 'The car was driven by her'. Instead, it will say the much punchier 'She drove the car', reducing the word count and freeing up space. I also found the concepts around subjective assessment fascinating. A reader will always accept a journalist's opinion if they don't understand the facts. Just by using the term 'terrorist' instead of, say, 'opponent', you've already made up the reader's mind. You can play on unconscious bias, gather sympathy, illicit fear, change a vote – the power of writing is incredible when one can peel away the layers and see what goes on behind the scenes. There are literally hundreds of little tricks that I learnt. Once you're aware of them, you can never read newspapers in quite the same way again.

For Christmas that year, I got my first ever mobile phone – a Nokia 3310. It was revolutionary at the time, one of the first phones to have an inbuilt calculator and a stop watch. It was also one of the first phones that exceeded the limit of 150 characters in a text. With the Nokia 3310, you could run three messages together containing nearly 450 characters! Although with messages that size, the data only allowed you to store a handful before you had to delete them. It also had a game called Snake II that came as standard. Unlike the regular version of Snake, though, this allowed you to go off one side of the screen and come back round again – incredible. The best thing about the phone, though, was its sheer durability. I had friends who would use it as a bottle opener. So hardy was the plastic construction that you could lever off beer bottle tops. I only really got the phone out of necessity. Although most people had them by now, they were still something of a novelty. Inevitably, people compared them to pay phones and home phones when they first came out. Beforehand, I might have made three or four calls a week, so the concept of paying hundreds of pounds for a bit more convenience seemed crazy at the time. People didn't realise how SMS messaging and later WhatsApp would catch on, even the designers thought of that as more of a 'bolt on' function. I got a phone simply because everyone else had them. It was easy enough to manage without in Canterbury, where everyone knew everyone else, but Brighton was a different story. It was a much larger place and keeping track of everyone proved impossible without one.

It was during my first year at university that I met one of the most bizarre characters I have ever known – Jack Proto. Everything about this guy was totally crazy. Even his name, which no-one could pronounce, was unusual. His full name was Jack Proto Papodakious, shortened to Proto for short, but more usually just referred to as 'Jack the Rapper'. His trademark was the wearing of two hats, one on top of the other – usually a Trilby balanced on top of a Beanie. He pretty much wore them everywhere, inside and outside, no matter the weather. When I asked him why he wore two hats, he replied that one was for warmth and other was so he could have a pillow wherever he went. At first, I thought he was joking, but would later get to see the portable pillow in action. Everyone assumed that he was at university studying, as he was always around campus. He had actually just followed his friend down from Fleet and never left. He had no student loan, no money, no reason to be at university, but never left for the three-and-a-bit years that I was there. He was here to rap. He would rap at anyone and everyone. His first question on meeting me and anyone else was, 'Do you like rap?' It didn't matter what you said, he would then proceed to rap to you for what felt like an eternity. He would rap at complete strangers in the street, at old ladies at the bus stop, at kids in the park – it didn't matter who. He had jobs that would last for a couple of days before he would inevitably be fired for rapping at the customers. One day in the second year, he had managed to get a job working on the supermarket checkouts at Somerfield. We went down to see him and, lo and behold, there he was rapping at this old lady who just wanted to buy her weekly grocery shop. A massive queue had formed behind her and everyone was just assuming this was some kind of TV prank (trigger-happy TV or something). By the end of the day he had been handed his P45. What made this whole situation even more hilarious was that he was as far removed looks-wise from a rapper as you could possibly get. He was tall and gangly with bright ginger hair and a face that was as pale as milk. He was very good at blagging, however. He never had a penny to his name, but was always able to blag meals at restaurants and entry into clubs. I think they would give in just to shut him up. He would say things like, 'I'm a little bit short this month. How about instead I give you an exclusive preview of my latest track?' and fifteen minutes later they would say, 'Just go.' One day, he even managed to get a record company executive (they were still a big thing in 2003) to pay for a day's studio time in the Lewes Road recording studios. I remember it really well because he was so excited, he was convinced this was going to be his big break. He got hundreds of CDs printed and gave them all away. He didn't even try and sell them. He didn't care about money, all he wanted to do was spread the message. I've still got my copy – I dug it out whilst writing this book just to refresh my memory. I know next to nothing about rap music, but I'll let you be the judge:

> Yo,Yo,Yo. The ginger man's back in town so you know when you've been tango'd.
> Best expect the unexpected, I'll put you six feet under like Jill Dando.
> I cruise with my crew through the mean streets of Worthing
> But I'm in the wrong gear so it feels like I'm reversing
> Living the dream with my Sussex Homies, I'm yearning
> To get back to the Hood so I can go surf and turfing
> There goes Cliff Richard in a convertible he's gurning,
> Some bitch cut him up, so reluctantly he's cursing
> Like Gordon Ramsey in a kitchen that's close to burstin'
> There goes his profiteroles, all the cream is dispersing.

Essentially, Jack the rapper was homeless. He would sleep literally anywhere – friends' sofa's, broom cupboards, park benches, wherever he laid his hat. His personal hygiene was non- existent. One day he came round to my house for some pre-drinking, and retrieved some discarded chips from the bin that I had finished a couple of hours' earlier. He was nomadic, so you wouldn't see him for a few days until he would just turn up in some random place. On a night out once, I went to use some public toilets down on Brighton seafront. There was someone sleeping on the floor opposite the urinals that I assumed was someone who had just passed out. I didn't notice a Trilby being used as a pillow. I turned around to 'Alright, Dave, how's it going?' It turned out he was sleeping on a urine-soaked floor because he didn't have any bus money to get anywhere else. I paid for him to come back to my place on the other side of town, and he spent the night on my sofa. The next morning, I was awoken by a loud banging on my door – it was my housemate Mike.

'Dave, why is there a fucking smelly tramp on our living room sofa?'

'Oh, that's just Jack,' I replied, and rolled over to go back to sleep.

I remember him turning up to a house party once, all covered in red marks; they were plastered all over his face and running down his back. When we asked what happened, he said he'd managed to get a bed at the local homeless shelter but had been warned about an infestation of bed bugs. 'So why did you stay then?' we asked. He said that he didn't believe they were real and thought they were a made-up story to scare kids, like the bogeyman or something. We all found that hilarious. He was always getting into scrapes like that and always being arrested when he wouldn't shut up. People would call the police, saying that he was scaring the customers. A policeman would turn up and he would then start rapping at them.

'Officer, Officer – I was only rapping about blowing up the shopping centre, I didn't mean it. Check this lyric out..." He was totally naïve, but totally fearless at the same time. A group of us went down to the police station once to bail him out after one of us received a phone call. We heard him before we'd even told the reception why we were there. The other prisoners were complaining about the strange rapping noises reverberating from the cells. After we left, he then had the audacity to go back and ask for a copy of his interview tape, as it was a rare example of his 'spoken word artistry' being recorded. I often wonder what happened to that guy.

Sussex campus was swarming with badgers. The grounds were pretty leafy and, amongst all the foliage, dens were to be found everywhere. The college newspaper was called 'The Badger' because of the large number that lived in the surrounding areas. They could be really vicious, especially late at night when you were strolling along and would hear growling noises behind you. Sometimes they would jump out of bushes at you or you'd turn round to find one lumbering after you. I know badgers are supposed to be shy, peaceful creatures, but these ones were about as docile as the killer rabbit from *Monty Python and The Holy Grail*. Sometimes when we were royally sloshed, we would go badger hunting with water pistols. Another of our ridiculously stupid games was 'bush diving'. There weren't many rules to this; it basically involved jumping into a large bush or hedge and seeing what happened. It was sort of a game of chicken, whereby you would all aim to jump into a bush over the course of a night. This could be incredibly dangerous, as you could never be certain what was behind or even inside it. Sometimes there were thorn bushes or railings hidden within. After a couple of injuries, we grew out of this game pretty quickly.

We used to spend many of our evenings drinking on Brighton's West Pier. It had been closed for years, but in 2002 it was still just about standing. It was nothing more than a skeleton of what it had once been, but still retained a sense of Edwardian elegance. We would jump over the padlocked gate and sit on the crumbling structure, watching the world go by. You would see really beautiful sunsets, when the sun would dip below the cliffs and the last rays of light would cling to the surface of the water. Then, when it was dusk, you could watch the starlings who nested in the top of the structure, swoop round the pier in their hundreds. There was always talk of restoring it, but later that year there were two massive fires that pretty much destroyed what was left. I remember watching it burning from the beach – really tragic and really beautiful at the same time. The council decided at that point that it was beyond saving. We must have been amongst the last people to ever set foot on it.

During my second term in that first year, I started hosting the university radio show with my mate Mike. I did a five-hour radio show every Friday afternoon, and then would occasionally cover other slots when people weren't available. It was fun, but much harder work than I initially thought. Silence is golden but radio silence (anything longer than two seconds) is a death sentence. Even with 3-5-minute intervals for music, my voice would feel incredibly hoarse by the end of the show, though after the first five or six recordings my vocal chords started getting used to it. You had *carte blanche* to do what you wanted, so we would talk about everything and anything from politics to our badger infestation. Getting guests to come on was surprisingly tricky. Once we'd gotten through all our friends, we started asking people from the nearby Falmer village. In retrospect, that was a mistake. There was a small village pub there which we thought could use our show as a sure-fire way of publicising it to all the students. The village was less than a ten-minute stroll from the campus, but being hidden away over the crest of a hill, most people didn't know it was there. The landlord agreed to come on, and we assumed he would talk about beer, what he had on tap, what breweries he used, etc... When he arrived, we all introduced ourselves. He was polite if a little terse. He then proceeded to spend the whole twenty-minute slot complaining about the Sussex students, how noisy they were, how disrespectful they were of village life, and how, if he had more custom, he would ban them all. It was painfully awkward. We would try and steer him off topic, but he would keep coming back to the disrespectful youth of today.

'So, Mr Adams, what changes have you noticed in the industry over the last ten years?'

'More and more bloody students getting too drunk and not appreciating beer – bloody layabouts. They all need a good spell in the army.'

Mr Adams was never invited back after that.

As well as being a local issues station, we would invite up and coming bands on the show to talk about music, play their tracks, and promote their gigs. These were mostly bands around East Sussex but some came from further afield. Some of them would do tours around all the student unions to try and acquire a fan base and get a kick start to their careers. We must have interviewed maybe twelve bands in that first year, and maybe twenty or so in the second year. Most of them went nowhere, but there were two big exceptions. One was Kasabian – a band from Leicester who'd been steadily touring for years but hadn't officially released anything. I don't remember too much about them, but they gave me a signed record (which I've still got) and provided with us free tickets to their gig that evening. For some reason, I never went.

The other band which I remember much more clearly were The Killers. They were a hilarious bunch of guys who hailed from Nevada. They were so excited to be in the UK for the first time and had decided that Brighton would be the first place they visited. Their agent had emailed me and Mike a couple of weeks earlier, but told us nothing about them. They'd sent us a promo of the songs *Mr Brightside* and *Smile*

Like You Mean It and we just assumed they were English. The songs, the lyrics, the artwork, all sounded so English. They were great; they reminded me of a cross between New Order and The Cure, so it was a bit of a shock when these four spindly American guys sauntered in. We played some more of their first album and I asked them why they used so much rain imagery. They said they were fascinated by it as it so rarely rained in Las Vegas. I thought about that quote many years later when me and Debs were on our honeymoon and just missed some flash flooding in Vegas by a couple of days. My claim to fame was that I was the first person to play The Killers on UK radio. We ended up hanging around with them for a couple of days. I remember teaching Brandon Flowers (the lead singer) the rules to English pool, but he still thrashed me anyway. We went to their gig at a famous venue along Brighton seafront called 'The Concorde 2', where they played to a crowd of no more than a 100 people – and that included about 10 of us who hadn't paid. I don't know why the agent had booked them there. It was better known as a dance music venue, there were much more obvious places. We interviewed them in June of 2003, and their debut single *Mr Brightside* was released three months later in September. I remember Mike rushing into the living room all excited.

'Dave, our band is on *Top of The Pops*!'

They weren't actually an instant hit. The single quickly fell down the charts, which delayed the release of their debut album *Hot Fuss*, which finally came out the following year. I like to think I played a small part in their rise to fame.

Towards the end of that year I got into the only proper physical fight I've ever had. Looking back, it was entirely my fault, but a night of heavy drinking had clouded my judgement. It was a warm night so a few of us were out messing around with water pistols. One guy, whose name now escapes me, kept on soaking me and was really starting to wind me up. I kept telling him to desist but he carried on, oblivious to my annoyance. I gave up and just walked home, we were ambling back that way anyway. I got back a few minutes before him, and had the bright idea of ambushing him with a bucket of water. We didn't have a bucket in the house, so I found the next best thing I could – the vegetable drawer at the bottom of our fridge. I filled it up with water and then hid behind a bush just outside our front door. When he arrived back, I launched the whole thing at him. There were two big issues with this that I didn't foresee. One, we were students, so the vegetable drawer had never been cleaned. It was full of decomposing peppers, rotting tomatoes, and furry cucumbers. He must have felt like a medieval prisoner in the stocks, being bombarded with all this putrefying veg. Two, it was incredibly heavy when filled with water. I was too good an aim, the whole thing hit him square on the head, with the water and side salad thoroughly drenching him. I think I knew I'd gone too far, but by then it was too late. We ended up in a fight on the floor and our housemates had to prise us apart. There was lots of shouting and screaming, it was all very dramatic, but by the following morning we had all calmed down. We both apologised and moved on.

During the summer of 2003, I went to Reading for a third time. This time, I camped with Ritchie, Nick, and a mutual friend called Adam. Mark made the journey up, too, and brought his girlfriend, Lorraine along. On the very first night, Lorraine had a panic attack after she witnessed the delightful state of festival toilets. (She had never been camping before, never mind a muddy music festival, so she had no idea what to expect.) We all tried to calm her down but she was inconsolable, so someone ended up calling an ambulance. Manoeuvring an ambulance through rows and rows of tightly-packed tents in a field is quite an ordeal. We heard the sirens after five minutes, but it must have taken a good half hour to travel the last 100 metres. It was around midnight, so some people were asleep, others were off their heads, and some were trying in vain to pull out their tent pegs so the ambulance could pass through. It was a bizarre scene. Ritchie was stoned as usual and thought the whole thing wasn't real. He later described it as like the scene from *ET* when all the agents with flashlights descend upon the alien. Eventually it got through and Lorraine was whisked off to hospital, with Mark beside her. I called him up the following day; after her ordeal they had both gone back to Canterbury. In order to convince her to come, Mark had bought her ticket. He'd spent all that money and travelled all that way only to leave on the first night without seeing a single band.

In our second year, we moved out of university accommodation and into a proper house. We found a four-bedroom property on a road called Seville Street, which was adjacent to another road called Coronation Street. Later that year, the soap opera *Coronation Street* featured various real Coronation Streets from around the country in its opening and closing title sequences. Because our house was close to the end of the street, you could see it in the titles for a week or so. Me, Ritchie, and Nick moved in with an American girl whose named eludes me. She left after three months and Mike replaced her as the fourth housemate. Nick insisted on getting the largest room – fair enough, he had been sharing with someone else for a whole year. It wasn't The Ritz by any means, but it was a sizeable step-up from our last abode. Three times the size with half as many people. Although rent-wise the house was cheaper, the bills (which we didn't pay on campus) and extra money spent travelling to and from the Uni, meant I was paying slightly more than before. Money was always a struggle. I would do odd jobs outside of term time, but during study periods that wasn't really practical. My monthly budget during my stint at Uni was roughly as follows:

Rent & Bills:	£300
Alcohol:	£60
Food:	£40
Travel:	£25
Phone:	£10
Extra's:	£15
Total Money:	£450

I got pretty good at eating for less than £10 a week. You would always find coupons in newspapers for free meals at selected stores like Tesco or the Co-Op, usually pizzas or microwave dishes. We used to walk down to Brighton train station, collect all the discarded newspapers, and cut the coupons out. That would usually get us two or three solid meals a week. We also knew at what times the supermarkets would start reducing their produce – it was always the more expensive shops like M&S and Waitrose that would have the biggest discounts. You would be able to get things like steak & kidney pies for 10p. I never really found food an issue when I was a student; I might eat a couple of big meals a week, but other than that it was mostly toast and cereal. We would sometimes go to the house parties of some of the more 'well off' students, purely so we could indulge in a spot of party food. We would chow on jammie dodgers and cheese straws like we were hyenas gorging on prime wildebeest.

Making alcohol stretch further was always a bigger conundrum. One of the cheapest ways to get drunk would be to visit the local corner shop which would sell two bottles of wine for £5. I remember on one occasion signing up to do a psychology experiment on campus, where they were testing participants' cognitive abilities after drinking ethanol. Obviously, it wasn't pure ethanol; it was diluted with tonic water. Still, ten shots of diluted ethanol was a great way to start a night out. And as a bonus, you would get paid £20 for participating.

One day, Smalley bought a bottle of Russian vodka round to our house. He had gone on a trip with his parents and was very excited to have bought back this limited-edition premium drink. This was Belvedere Vodka – I can't remember how much he paid for it, but it was three figures, maybe around £200. It was a huge amount of money for students like us. We were going to have a few shots to celebrate his birthday and then head out into town.

He put it on the table and we all studied the label, admiring the way the bottle sparkled in the sunlight. Truly a thing of beauty.

'Right, where are the shot glasses?' asked Smalley.

Someone told him which shelf they resided on, and as he got up to fetch them, he knocked the bottle off the table with the corner of his elbow. The bottle shattered as it hit the floor and the contents began dripping through the cracks in our wooden flooring. I think Smalley actually screamed. What happened next was one of the saddest things I've ever seen.

Smalley got the mop out and started desperately mopping the vodka and squeezing it through the ringer and into the bucket. He then got onto his hands and knees and started trying to save as much as he possibly could by ringing out kitchen towels and sponges. After this began the process of sieving out all the small pieces of glass. By the end, he had retrieved about a pint's worth, which then sat upon the table in a grotty glass – a slightly murkier colour than before, with bits of dust floating in it. It was a forlorn sight.

'Shall we do it then?' he asked.

As it was his birthday, we let him keep the vodka to himself.

It's funny how much our lives were centred round alcohol. We used to play this rather amusing drinking game in Canterbury called 'Drink your name' where each drink had to start with one of the letters in your name. So for instance 'Chris Bryant' is 11 letters worth of drinks, starting with perhaps C for Carlsberg, followed by H for Heineken, etc. We all had roughly the same number of letters in our Christian and surnames, so it was a good group challenge that you could get creative with. The letter 'n' was always a notoriously fiendish one. This was a game that you had to see through to the bitter end (or lager end).

Another game which we used to do in Brighton was centre a whole night around one drink, with as many different mixers as you could creatively think of. I remember a few of us doing a pub crawl where Malibu was my drink of choice. It would start off relatively simple in that I would have a Malibu and Coke, and then a Malibu and Pepsi, before getting progressively weirder. I had it with lemonade, cranberry juice, lime cordial, tonic, milk, even water when I had run out of ideas. This was done to the tune of the famous Black Lace song, with Malibu replacing the 'Agadoo' refrain. We must have looked like complete morons.

The drinking culture of university has now changed beyond all recognition compared to twenty years ago. I read a report recently which suggested that now 36% of 18-24-year-olds in full-time education in the UK now abstain from drinking. I don't recall meeting one person during my time as a student who didn't drink something. Looking back, I wouldn't say that it was a golden era, but there were certainly far less of the worries that students now tell me about in my counselling sessions. Now, students seem to take their studies more seriously, with alcohol some way down the pecking order. I meet plenty of students in their second or third year who don't even know we have a bar on site! When I was at Uni it was pre-2008 recession so there were no worries about the job market, no worries about career paths, no sky-high tuition fees, no housing crisis, very little about climate change, and of course, this was many year's before all the Brexit and Covid-19 drama. Simpler times, I guess.

Blockbusters was still a relatively large chain in 2003. They would display all these life-size cardboard cut-outs in their shop windows to promote various new releases. These would be big stars like Tom Cruise or Keanu Reeves, but they never stayed that long – maybe a couple of months or so until the next big film got released on DVD. One day Ritchie and I were walking past when we saw one of the staff moving a cardboard figure of Sylvester Stallone outside. We asked if they were throwing it out and they said yes, it was ours if we wanted it. We were never guys to turn down a freebie, so we rolled up our sleeves and carried this life-sized Sylvester Stallone back home with us. We decided that it would be a great way to freak people out, by simply moving it around the house and hiding it behind various doors. All four of us did this for weeks and it never got any less funny. When you open a door, the last thing you expect to see is Sylvester Stallone staring at you, especially at night when it's dark; it's the jump scare you get from something totally unexpected. We would put it in the kitchen, the bathroom, inside people's bedrooms, everywhere. When other people came round, they would often get traumatised by their harrowing encounter with Rambo. Sometimes they would actually scream. I think it was Nick's girlfriend who finally said enough is enough and burnt the bloody thing after the tenth time it happened to her.

It used to be common for bands to do launch nights for new album releases. These were usually events at bars and clubs, where the venue would theme a night around a particular band. They'd play new tracks as well as a few classics, with a handful of freebies and occasionally a mystery guest thrown in to DJ or do some kind of performance. I went to a handful of these events, but the one that sticks in my mind is the launch night for Blur's *Think Tank* album. We all loved Blur at Uni; they had been going for thirteen years by this point, and a new album from them was very exciting. The mystery guest was Fatboy Slim who had produced the album, though apart from a couple of the more up-tempo tracks, you couldn't really tell. That was the first of three occasions when I met Norman Cook (aka Fatboy Slim). The artwork was done by Banksy – it was a really clever cover that symbolised the barriers that exist between relationships. It was a fun night, with Blur song-themed cocktails – the only one I recall is 'Irish Coffee +TV', and we all got given posters of the artwork. We ended up trashing most of these by having sword fights with all the rolled-up posters on the beach. I managed to keep one which hung on my wall for a few years. It's a shame that these promotional music events don't really exist any more; nowadays it's more about horrendously expensive VIP experiences and gala dinners before gigs.

One of the modules on my course was based around war propaganda in the mass media. In March 2004, our seminar group went on a field trip to Northern France and Belgium, where the allied front line stood in the First World War. This would be the first time I ever went on a plane. Nick and I had just mentioned this to Jack Proto in passing when he came round to our house a couple of days before the trip very excited.

'Hey, guys, guess what? Proto's coming with you.' Aside from the fact he didn't have any money and wasn't a student, he didn't own a passport.

'Why?' we asked.

It turned out he had Googled 'Belgium and rap' together and thought there was a burgeoning scene there. Of course, you could Google anything and make that connection. He had no idea where Belgium was and no idea what language they spoke, but that was fine. By now, we were so used to him we didn't bother trying to explain things. Nick, Proto and I got the train down to Gatwick Airport early in the morning and left him to it whilst we checked our bags in. I'm sure before September 11th when security was a bit less stringent, you might have been able to sneak onto a plane if you planned it well and were stealthy, quiet, and conspicuous. Jack Proto was none of those things. He was strolling around Gatwick wearing two hats, trying to rap his way past the immigration officials. That was the last we saw of him for a couple of weeks.

There were about twenty of us in our cohort. I think I was probably the only one who had never been on a plane before. People thought I was nervous, but I wasn't. I was trying very hard to distract myself in case I started feeling ill, as I didn't know what the sensation would be like. I was actually fine, and to this day I don't mind planes at all. Turbulence, I struggle a bit with, but then so do most people.

It was a fascinating trip seeing the war graves and the reconstructed trenches. There was an area of no man's land we visited that looked like a scene from a fantasy film. The ground was heavily undulating (from where all the bombs and mines had exploded) so it was difficult to walk in a straight line. Trees had sprouted up in these peculiar angles which made it seem as though the branches were reaching out to grab you. The floor was covered in this thick green moss – an almost radioactive shade of bright green. There were so many nutrients in the soil from all the thousands of decayed bodies that life was flourishing. There was also an eerie feeling of calm that made it all seem slightly surreal. Walking out across the surrounding farmland you would see shrapnel everywhere. Every three or four paces you would glimpse things half buried in the soil. Apparently, every year when the fields are ploughed, more shrapnel and bones get churned up. We were literally walking through history.

The war graves themselves were huge. We visited the British, French, German and Canadian graves whilst there. Ten million military personnel (plus many millions more civilians) died in this tiny slither of land that stretched across France. As shocking as that sounds, it's hard to comprehend such a large number. Seeing all the graves stretch out in front of you like an infinite white carpet was really humbling. The highlight of the trip was meeting a survivor. He was a French soldier who had signed up when he was fifteen, and was now living his last days in Ypres, aged 103. He was obviously very frail but mentally he was all there, spoke perfect English, and was very eloquent. He talked to us about why he signed up, the excitement of leaving his village with his friends, and the slow, dawning realisation that the war wasn't going to last just a few weeks. I felt very privileged to meet him – the last surviving veteran from France died five years later, in 2009.

By now I was doing less of my radio show and spending more time writing for the university paper. It wasn't a real newspaper in the sense that there was very little quality control; basically, whoever wanted to work on it would inevitably get something published. I wrote a small article on some of Brighton's lesser known music venues, which wasn't great journalism. I think I knocked it together in about 45 minutes, but they stuck it on the front page. To pad it out, the editors just slotted in some massive photos that weren't really necessary. In one sense it was great that I had something on the front page, but on the flip side I was a little embarrassed. If I had known it was going on the front cover, I would have put a bit more effort in. I went to talk to the photographer about some of the photos he'd used – he was a really quiet, shy Indian guy called Feraz. He would go on to have a complete personality change over the next ten years.

Smalley, Jesus, and co. lived about fifteen minutes away from us. Whenever I went round there, I could never remember which was their house. It was situated in a line of identical looking terraced properties, all with small patio front gardens. For some reason there was no house number on the front door. Their landlord lived abroad and didn't have the inclination to attend to trivial aesthetic matters like house numbers. On top of that, all the doors were painted the same shade of red. It turned out that I wasn't the only one who couldn't find their house. Everyone else had the same problem and would often end up knocking on the wrong door, much to the chagrin of the neighbours if it was past bedtime. One evening, on a typically sozzled night out, we decided that we needed some form of identifying landmark in their front garden. As students, we would often steal things like road signs and traffic cones; it seemed like every house we went to had a street sign propped up in the living room. However, we wanted something a bit different, something unique. One day whilst walking down the street, we saw a battered old red phone box. There was a notice from the council pinned on it, saying it was due to be taken away and scrapped. It was leaning slightly, looked rather unstable, and the telephone itself wasn't working. So we thought, *Why don't we save them the trouble?* The twelve of us managed to prise the phone box free from its concrete base and carry it all the way back to their house. I learnt how heavy an old phone box was that day – back-breakingly so! This wasn't one of those flimsy modern boxes, this was a 1950s cast iron phone box. Eight of us carried it a time, any more and there would have been a danger of tripping each other up. Every five minutes or so, we all swapped over, with the other four carrying the lighter bits, the phone itself, the stand, etc... It was such slow progress. After ten minutes, we started asking ourselves if it was worth it, but decided to carry on anyway. We got some very strange looks on that journey, meandering through the dimly lit back streets of Brighton. With regular breaks it took us about three hours to get it all the way back to its new home. One of their friends knew a bit about setting concrete, so within a couple of days it was standing proudly in their front garden. It was a great landmark, we never missed their house again after that. The last time I was in Brighton (for a funeral in 2019), I went back and it was still there. Clearly, the landlord didn't mind it residing there amongst the shrubbery and garden gnomes – either that or it wasn't worth the hassle to move it. It proudly stands as a monument to student creativity, endurance, and sheer bloody mindedness.

The European football championships started in June 2004. We were quite fortunate in that we had a reasonably sized back yard. The weather was getting warmer and we thought it would lend the tournament a nice ambience if we could watch the games outside. However, we only had one small TV between us, and thought maybe we could find something more fitting for a grandiose sporting occasion such as this. There was a nearby pub that was being refurbished and selling loads of bits that the previous owner had left, like old chairs and tables. The main possession he was selling, however, was a giant TV screen. I think the new landlord was hoping to sell it to another pub because it wasn't cheap – he was selling it for about £400. Nowadays, pubs just use digital projectors, but then huge TV screens were really common for screening live sports. It was gargantuan – the screen was about 2.5 metres across. We could just about stretch to £100 between us, but that was about it. For once, Jack Proto was actually useful; he did his usual 'I'm a big-name rapper' shtick, and amazingly it worked. The landlord agreed to sell it to us for £100 on the proviso that Jack performed at an open mic night for the pub's relaunch. That was all fine and dandy with us. Hands were shaken, terms agreed, and then we proceeded to haul this giant beast of a TV up the hill. I seemed to spend my entire time as a student hauling stuff up hills, but once again it was worth the sweaty effort. We set it up in our garden alongside a couple of sofas and a bin full of ice and beers. We felt like kings. We had the perfect set-up, gorgeous sunny weather, and the largest screen in the whole of Brighton & Hove. We invited everyone over for the first England game, which was against France. We lost on penalties (of course), but apart from that it was great.

Our house had become something of a party house for those two weeks over June. England reached the quarter finals on the 24th June, when we went out to Portugal on penalties. We were all crushed, we all thought we had a very strong team that year. The so-called 'Golden Generation' were just hitting their stride. There were established players like Stephen Gerrard, Frank Lampard, David Beckham, and Michael Owen, alongside younger players like Wayne Rooney, who seemed to have the world at their twirling little feet. I'm not sure how we got rid of the giant TV after that. I think we probably just left it outside and somebody decided to rehouse it. In the meantime, we had Jack Proto's headline performance to cheer us all up. It was on a Friday night, and the pub was on our way into town, so we stopped by for a quick drink there first. It wasn't quite the relaunch the landlord was hoping for. Apart from us, there was just a handful of old men smoking pipes and drinking stout. This was their established local and no amount of glitzy rebranding was going to turf them out. The hordes of trendy young punters had failed to materialise. We arrived to see the last fifteen minutes of the previous act – a middle-aged man on acoustic guitar singing things by John Denver, James Taylor, people like that. It was charming, but low key – the kind of thing you might enjoy as background music on a Sunday afternoon. He got a small but polite round of applause after his set. Five minutes later, Proto walked on stage with a 'What's up, bitches!' It was his usual mix of offensive and bizarre lyrics. A couple of guys walked out, a couple turned their backs and carried on chatting, and after two numbers we left to go somewhere a bit more entertaining.

For my final year at Sussex, I moved into a house at the top of the tallest hill in Brighton, called Elm Grove. It was a ridiculously steep hill; I swear the air felt thinner up there. Opposite my new house was a hospital, so if you had a heart attack on the way up, it was just a short hop across the road to A&E. I moved in with a guy I knew called Robert Boot, who was usually known as 'Boot Man' – I'm not sure why. When I told Nick, he couldn't keep a straight face. 'Who's that? Batman's arch nemesis?'

Ritchie had failed his second year so was spending twelve months back in Jersey, before coming back to repeat the second year in 2005, but everyone else was still there. Mike had acquired a new nickname which he despised – 'Millionaire Mike'. During the summer, he had worked in Tesco's and been part of a lottery syndicate with eight other people. He had seriously debated taking a year out from university and carrying on with the job, to save some money. He decided against this, but three weeks after leaving, the syndicate won £18.2 million. At that time, it was the biggest lottery win in Yorkshire. He had tried to keep it quiet but it proved impossible. It was in the newspapers and on the radio, and once one person knew, everyone did. Henceforth, for the rest of Uni, he became known as 'Millionaire Mike.'

That winter was especially bitter, and the house wasn't very well insulated. On top of that, the boiler would frequently break down, so we would never have heating in all of our rooms. You would feel the icy grip of winter coming in through the windows, so we were frequently wrapped in dressing gowns and blankets over the top of our clothes. Elm Grove became really treacherous to walk up when it was icy. In fact, it was borderline impossible. Walking on ice when the ground is flat is difficult enough, but schlepping up a hill with a gradient of twenty degrees means you put more pressure on the balls of your feet. You would be sliding around with all the grace and poise of a drunk uncle at a wedding. It wasn't unusual for me to wait twenty minutes just for a bus to go that extra 400 metres to my door.

We would spend more of our time at the nearby pub than in the house itself, a slightly ramshackle establishment called The Hanover. It was always nice and cosy, with an open fire and a vast selection of board games attracting a crowd who passed through in various states of dishevelment. Dog walkers brought in sodden dogs from their walks along the South Downs, whilst exhausted junior doctors shambled in after shifts at the nearby hospital, with their sleeves pushed up. There were scarved and suited old men, frail as antique hatstands, and bearded, beer-bellied ale drinkers who seemed permanently glued to the bar. In short, a quirky, non-pretentious place where everyone mingled – it became our second home, as we became adept at making a couple of rounds of Doom Bar last all afternoon and into the evening.

A good pub quiz question which will often stump the most hardened quizzer is: Where is the world's oldest, still operating electric railway? Based on this chapter, you may have already guessed that the answer is Brighton. The Volks Electric Railway (VER) has been in continuous operation since 1883. Whilst the London Underground was still using creaky steam locomotives, the British inventor Magnus Volk had pioneered the use of electric motors to pull carriages along Brighton seafront years before it was commonplace. Although it's a very narrow gauge of two feet and eight inches, and only runs for 1.6km, it is to all intents and purposes a fully functioning electric railway. I've only ever ridden it once. It doesn't really go anywhere useful, but retains a simple Edwardian charm that attracts thousands of tourists over the summer months. However, much more interesting and pretty much unknown even to long standing Brighton residents, was Magnus Volk's second attempt at a pioneering railway. Officially called the 'Brighton & Rottingdean Seashore Electric Railway', but generally referred to as The Daddy Long Legs due to its unique design, this was probably the craziest railway ever built. It was fully electric and partly submerged under the sea, standing at more than double the height of a conventional train, at nearly thirty-five feet. As geography had constricted his original railway from going any further, Volks designed a railway that could function at both high and low tide; nineteenth century ingenuity triumphing over nature. It resembled one of those alien invaders from *War of the Worlds,* wading through the choppy waters of the English Channel. It was incredibly popular but woefully inefficient. At high tide, the train slowed to a crawl where it became quicker to actually walk the journey. If you pardon the pun, Volks was way out of his depth. It only lasted for six years, after a combination of storm damage, erosion, and sedimentary shift caused by the construction of groynes, eventually condemned it to a watery grave. When I found out about it, I convinced my housemates that we should go for a walk along the beach at Rottingdean to see the remnants of this bizarre railway. They were somewhat sceptical to say the least, but we made a day out of it with a cool bag of beers and sausage rolls aplenty.

The beach beneath the cliffs at Rottingdean is a strange place – barely two miles from the bustling shores of Brighton but always virtually deserted. A couple of metal detector enthusiasts and the odd naked sunbather (nearby, there's an official nudist beach), and that was it in terms of frequenters. Its inaccessibility, crumbling cliffs, and seedy reputation made it a bit of a no-go area. We had to wait for low tide for the tracks to become visible. Whilst we sat there, letting the moon perform its magic, we skimmed stones and drank Newcastle Brown Ale. After an hour or so, the concrete sleepers became visible. With an eighteen feet span, this was the widest rail gauge of any train ever built. The four of us were able to lie head-to-toe and only just cover the width of the barnacle-encrusted tracks. I don't know if any of the sleepers still exist – they were pretty weather-beaten in 2005 – but it did give you a sense of the scale of the thing. Whilst we were sitting there, something slightly surreal happened. There was this loud engine roar and we all jumped up, instinctively getting off the tracks. A hundred railway safety films from primary school were still etched in the back of our minds. Clearly, a ghost train from a hundred-year-old defunct railway wasn't going to plough into us, but we were all slightly shaken. It was some boy racer revving his car engine on the cliff tops above, which had disturbed the peace. The noise had reverberated across the deserted beach, sounding uncomfortably like a blaring train horn. After we laughed this off and I'd had my quota of historical train geekery, we packed our bags and headed home. If you ever get the chance, I would heartily recommend looking this up on YouTube – there's some great grainy black and white footage of this bizarre sea train in action.

A student rite of passage back then was the concept of library all-nighters. People who had previously been incredibly chilled about the looming deadlines would suddenly swing into academic action. You would typically start during daylight hours, carry on all through the night, and then stagger out blinking into the sunlight the following morning, hopefully with a Pulitzer prize piece of literature residing in your hands. I would estimate that by the time I was finishing up at Uni, maybe 40% of students had their own laptop or a PC/Mac. Those that did were lucky in that they didn't have to suffer the indignity of the mad library scramble. When a deadline was approaching, particularly for the third-year students, one had to either get to the library computer room insanely early, or spend a good couple of hours queuing up. Once you'd claimed your spot, you couldn't leave for any length of time as the PC would shut down after about fifteen minutes of inaction. Hence, you would tend to stay until your work was done, kept alive by a combination of Red Bull energy drinks and the tooth-dissolving confectionery that rested in the nearby vending machine. Any trip further afield risked exceeding your precious fifteen-minute leeway and having to queue up all over again.

Although I envied people who could work from home, there were drawbacks. You would see people at the beginning of each term lugging these cumbersome machines around – hard drives, monitors, printers, speakers, and keyboards, with all manner of wires and assorted bits dangling behind them. Forgot dumbbells; carrying these back-breaking machines was a sweat-inducing workout all by itself. Those lucky few that had portable laptops, like the IBM ThinkPad or the Dell Inspiron, were truly living the dream. Anyway, I'd pulled two all-nighters in a row to finish off my final dissertation. It wasn't that I was particularly disorganised, it was more that I'd underestimated the amount of time it took to edit a 25,000-word essay. I proudly handed it in on deadline day with a comfortable four or so hours to spare. I then sat down on the grass alongside the 'gauntlet'.

Running the gauntlet was another tradition – a 200-metre stretch of pathway that led straight to the hand-in room. Those that were in a position to relax or be smug about it, lined the grassy banks, feasting and drinking whilst cheering on those who literally needed a sprint finish to get their assignments submitted in time. With the clock ticking down to midnight, you would see more and more flustered students running the gauntlet. With about fifteen minutes to go, you would see the light joggers show-boating and soaking up all the applause of the hundreds of people reclining on the grass. Some people would be giving each other piggybacks, whilst others would jog it backwards, initiating thunderous cheering. With five to ten minutes to go, you would get the proper runners who might wave to the masses but would be visibly perspiring. When there was a minute or so left, you were down to the desperate sprinters clutching their work and pelting it down the gauntlet like they were in training for an Olympic sprinting event. Finally, you got the people who knew they were late but were rather *laissez faire* about the whole situation and were just enjoying the attention. Those glorious gauntlet days are all in the past now. With almost everything now submitted online, I can't imagine there are many similar traditions left.

On 15th July, 2005, we had our graduation ceremony at the Brighton Dome. The dome is a famous arts venue that dates back to 1803, originally housing a riding school and stables for the Prince Regent. It was later turned into a concert hall and was where Abba won the Eurovision Song Contest in 1974 with *Waterloo*. The university would hire it on an annual basis for its graduation ceremonies. My mum came down, along with Matt and his girlfriend, Katy. I was to receive my degree from the Chancellor, Richard Attenborough, who had a long association with Sussex University. His various children had attended the university and he had used our students during the filming of *Oh! What A Lovely War*. We all loved Attenborough, but still wanted to do something light-hearted on stage to cut through all the pomp and circumstance. We discussed in advance things that we could do. Nick decided that he would make dinosaur shapes on stage as a tribute to Attenborough's role in *Jurassic Park*. I came up with the idea of doing a Bruce Forsyth pose. When my name was called out,

I went up onto the stage and shook his hand. We had a few brief words, I said he was a legend, and then turned around to do my Bruce Forsyth 'thinking pose'. (For those who don't know, this basically involves putting your left hand behind your back and your right hand towards your chin with a clenched fist, originally adapted from the strong men at the Victorian circus.) However, as I was doing this, my mortar board fell off and skidded across the stage. I then fumbled around on the platform while trying to retrieve it. I must have looked like a right wally. My mum was mortified (or should that be mortar-fied), especially as the whole thing was captured on video. Afterwards, we did the obligatory throwing our hats in the air, and that was it. University was finished. Now what?

CHAPTER 6

Living in a Shed

I stayed in Brighton for a few months after graduating, as I figured that Brighton was as good a place as any to get a job in journalism. I moved into yet another house, but this time I was sub-letting. I moved back in with Mike, and I took Ritchie's room before he came back for the start of the new academic year. I fired off various cv's to local newspapers, but the only people that came back to me were *The Argus* and they would only offer me an unpaid position. As tempting as that was, I couldn't afford it, so I signed up for a temporary role whilst I waited. This was based at a small company in Hove that produced circuit boards. I was in a team of five whose job it was to test them and make sure the current was successfully going through. I always found the people that you would meet through these temping agencies to be interesting characters. The guy who sat next to me, Sam, was a bit of a chav. He wore a baseball cap and cheap gold jewellery, but was a massive fan of Syd Barrett (out of Pink Floyd). I thought that was a really interesting juxtaposition.

Another chap I remember was a very angry Scottish guy, who had two fingers missing. He had apparently lost them in an industrial machine when he had stuck his hand in to retrieve his watch. I don't know if his missing fingers were what made him so angry with the world, but he radiated bellicose bravado. The smallest thing would wind him up, so you had to be very careful with everything you uttered. Someone once made him a cup of tea and he was absolutely livid when it arrived with merely one spoonful of sugar, after he had requested two. I remember him telling me that the Scottish League was the best football competition in the world. Absolute codswallop, but I was too scared to argue, I just nodded my head and agreed with him. A grotesquely grumpy Glaswegian who should be in anger management therapy is what everyone looks for in a work colleague. He could be unintentionally hilarious, though you were just never sure if it was safe to laugh or not. I remember him talking to a couple of us about the Paralympic World Cup (this started in Manchester earlier that year), with his missing fingers seemingly his conduit for being an expert in all things disability related. He was convinced that many of the competitors didn't have real disabilities. He was scanning the paper, all the while getting angrier and angrier.

'What's wrong with him? And him? OCD, bloody OCD! That actually helps with synchronised swimming!'

After a while, I decided that in order to save money, I should move back to Canterbury; there were far too many distractions in Brighton. If I saved enough, I could do an unpaid internship or go travelling. I wasn't entirely sure yet. One thing that I was sure about, however, was that I didn't want to share a room with my brother. He was now in his second year of university in Canterbury, besides which he had a long-term girlfriend, which made things trickier. About six months earlier, I had come up with the idea of living in the shed at the bottom of my parents' garden. They had recently bought it to replace the old one which had been falling to bits, and I road-tested sleeping in there when I came back for the Easter holidays. It was fine and reminded me of camping when I was younger. My mum would refer to it as the chalet, or the summerhouse. It sounded very Enid Blyton, but in reality it was just a decent quality shed. The deal was that I would pay reduced rent and look after it, in terms of maintenance. This was relatively easy; it just required a couple of weatherproof coats of paint over the next eighteen months. The first job was insulating it and getting electricity to it through a cable that ran from the main house and through the garden. My parents had some old carpet tiles stored in the attic, so I used these on top of some underlay to create an insulated floor on top of the concrete base. The shed wasn't huge, but it was big enough to get a single bed, sofa, clothes rail, chest of drawers, and a TV stand wedged in there. I turned it into quite a cosy man cave, complete with a beer fridge and a footrest made out of a discarded builder's pallet (initially used for copper coil). I loved being able to hear the cats walking on the roof at night, and when it rained, it sounded like someone was tipping hundreds of packets of frozen peas over the shed. Looking back, it was probably quite an eccentric thing to do, but I loved it at the time. There were occasions, particularly over the summer, when I would get odd glances from the neighbours or people that my parents would invite round. It was very easy for them to forget that I was in there, particularly if it was the weekend and they assumed that I'd already ventured out. I remember one occasion when my mum and her friend Bernie were drinking in the garden, and I came out in my dressing gown at around midday. Bernie saw me and did a double-take, like I was a ghostly apparition gliding past.

The single biggest issue with living in a shed was heating. I bought a portable radiator, but it was very expensive to run as it was just plugged into the mains. It would also eat quite heavily into the house electricity consumption. My parents were still using an electric meter, so it meant more frequent trips to the shop to keep it topped up. That heater on its own was probably burning through about £100 a month in the winter. Trying to regulate the temperature was also quite difficult. Even though the shed was insulated, it would still magnify the outside temperature – so in summer it could get ridiculously warm, and in winter ridiculously cold; the greenhouse effect in microcosm. The other issue was going to the bathroom. This involved putting shoes on, traipsing through the garden, unlocking the back door of the house, walking upstairs, and then coming all the way back, which could be a soggy ordeal if it was raining. But heating and bathroom practicalities aside, it was a swanky little den.

I went back to working at Amphenol whilst I searched for something better. It wasn't what I would have chosen to do, it was just straightforward. I'd signed back up with the agency and within two hours I had a contract starting the following day. It was a bit of an unhappy reunion. All the permanent staff were still there, but this time I was being managed by the crab (shudder). She wore these appalling wide-rimmed wooden glasses whenever she was inspecting work. She would always have them pulled down slightly so she could give you a disdainful stare whilst looking down her nose at you, even though she was the height of a twelve-year-old child. She was also impossible to have a normal conversation with. I would try and strike up a bit of banter in the mornings, 'How was your weekend?', things about the weather and suchlike, but I never got anything other than a grunt or a one-word response. She had all the wit and warmth of a crash test dummy. She also didn't like us chatting to each other, which was hardly cohesive to a good working atmosphere. It made me long for the days when I was working in the bubble wrap team.

In this section, I was assembling and soldering a series of electrical components together. It was that terrible combination of being dull and repetitive, but also fiddly and precise. There were obviously quotas to meet, so you needed to have a certain amount completed by the end of each day. If you didn't they would make you stay later to finish, without additional pay of course. That probably wasn't strictly legal but with temporary contracts it's easy enough just to terminate someone's employment if they complain. There were rumours that we were making parts that were being shipped abroad to be used for missile guidance systems. I'm not sure if that was actually true or not, but it's hard to take a moral stand when you need the money. I think I lasted about six weeks there.

That summer, we decided to go on a lads' holiday. We were all in the same boat, having finished university and now adrift on a sea of uncertainty. Something cheap and cheerful was called for. We hit upon the idea of going on a caravan holiday in Newquay. We found a campsite called Sunnyside, and by booking slightly out of season in early September, we were able to afford a decent-sized caravan for the five of us. The only issue with it were the beds, which were absolutely tiny. It was clearly a caravan designed for a family with kids, so sleeping was more like an endurance test than a restful night's kip. I'm sure there have been comfier beds in Russian prisoner of war camps. There were various arguments about who got to sleep where, particularly in regard to the one relatively luxurious double bed. We all agreed just to leave the double bed, though we discovered by the end of the holiday that Josh had secretly been sleeping in it. His fold-out kitchen couch sleeping arrangements had proved too unbearable. The only sensible thing for everyone else to do was drink to excess in order to numb the pain of sleeping in these coffin-sized beds.

It was a classic British caravan holiday where the weather doesn't quite live up to expectations. Despite the name Sunnyside, sunshine itself was in short supply. It spent most of the time raining and blowing a gale. I would subtitle our Newquay jaunt as 'existential angst in the rain'. The Newquay nightspots like Corkers and Sailors (for some reason these tacky seaside clubs were always pluralised) were pretty dismal. Somehow, Bjorn managed to burn through £60 at a club's £1-a-drink night. We made friends with a group of girls who were in the caravan next door to us. They were a fun bunch and we spent much of the time trying to impress them – Slater with his barbecuing, and me with my dancing skills. Josh came up with the bright idea of trying to serenade one of the girls with a toy plastic guitar he got free with a comic. I think it was the *Beano* or *Dandy*. It was about five inches long, bright yellow, and had three strings attached, so was about as tuneful as Tom Waits with a heavy cold. One evening, Josh sat outside the window to their caravan and played this ridiculous instrument to the tune of a five-line song he wrote. Safe to say, there was no reaction from the girls inside. Other than drinking and questionable serenading, we spent the rest of the time barbecuing in inclement weather, and playing air hockey at the local arcade. The campsite closed down about five years later.

When we came back to Canterbury, Dray and I got a new job working for a design company start-up. It was quite a clever, well thought-out business. Local schools would sign up to this scheme where the children would do arts and crafts-type designs for Christmas cards, using things like felt and glitter. They also did designs for T-shirts and mugs, though the Christmas cards were the main source of revenue. We would print off multiple copies of them as gifts in time for the festive holidays. Nowadays, these businesses are quite common, but fifteen years ago they were much scarcer. It wasn't a bad little job. We would get to do a little bit of design work, removing shadows and smartening up rough edges, but the margins were tight. We couldn't spend too long on the individual designs as it was more about the volumes that we produced.

After a few days working there, some of the team started to complain about an unusual fishy smell. It turned out it was actually one of the new members of staff who had a very rare disease called Trimethylaminuria. This is when a person lacks a particular enzyme, which means the body is unable to metabolize nitrogen, sulphur and phosphorous. Essentially, this means that a person's body odour is so strong that it can't be masked by deodorant, and the resulting smell is akin to rotting fish. Because the condition can be managed to a degree by a person's diet, it would vary on a daily basis. Sometimes you would smell it as soon as you walked in the building, other times it was barely detectable. We all felt sorry for the guy but there wasn't much that could be done. I think we ended up keeping the windows open and strategically positioning him in a certain part of the room. It was a very difficult situation, especially when new people would start and they would need to be discreetly informed. The general manager was great fun. She was in her mid-fifties and was a bit of a flirt with the younger boys (in a harmless kind of way). We got on really well, I think because we would chat about various eighties bands she listened to- she was really into *Squeeze* I seem to recall. I came back to the company the following year and she promoted me to the office supervisor.

I was taking regular trips to Brighton throughout 2006. I started a relationship with a girl I'd known from university, but the inevitable problems of having a long-distance relationship surfaced pretty early on. Add to this the practicalities of living in a shed, which made her occasional trips to Canterbury more of an endurance test than anything else, and it was pretty obvious why it didn't last very long.

It was around this time that I remember the fears around the potential reach of the internet first surfacing. The catalyst for this was the execution of Saddam Hussein. He was found guilty of crimes against humanity and sentenced to death by hanging. His execution was recorded on mobile phones by various people in the crowd, and was leaked on the internet within hours. I remember watching it and thinking that we had entered a new age. We were now a 24-hour news society. Up until that point, everyone had assumed (with a few obvious exceptions) that the internet was a tool that could be controlled. Now, anyone could post anything they wanted, whenever they wanted. Was that a good thing? I wondered if this would mean the end of traditional journalism.

It's always a shock to realise that current and future generations may never know the joy and frustrations of certain sounds – the noise of a cash register, a rotary phone, or the music that accompanied the strange test card girl that was on BBC television every night when there was no on-air programming. Of all the noises that future generations will not understand, the one that resonates most with me is not from a television show or a jaunty nineties jingle. It's the sound of a modem connecting with another modem across our re-purposed telephone infrastructure. The metallic hiss and shrill tones were irritating and grating like an electronic representation of a cow in labour. But equally, it was exciting and futuristic – the noise of an electronic door creaking open to a digital world that was beaming into your home. Having undertaken a bit of research on the subject, I found out that this was a choreographed sequence that allowed these digital devices to piggyback on an analogue telephone network. A phone line carries only the small range of frequencies in which most human conversation takes place, roughly 300 to 3,300 hertz. Modems had to work within these limits in creating sound waves to carry data across phone lines. Basically, what you were hearing was twentieth century technology being tunnelled through a nineteenth century network. The narrow bandwidth of a dial-up connection meant that the internet was a slow, ponderous place in which it was almost impossible to be swamped with information. I recall on many occasions going to make beans on toast or brushing my teeth whilst I was waiting for a site to upload. It could be incredibly frustrating, but on the positive side, many of today's online problems simply didn't exist. It's safe to say that children weren't watching self-harm videos on a 14kbps internet connection, cyber-bullying (if it were even taking place) would have been rudimentary, and it was impossible to troll with the speed or aggression that it is now. Hours went past when nobody would call, because the only telephone line in the house was busy. We waded in a shallow stream of information, rather than drowned in an ocean.

Sometimes in life you have these strange realisation moments when, out of the blue, you realise that something has changed beyond all recognition. It can be the most mundane of things, but it leaves a lasting impression. This happened to me with budget supermarkets. The first of these, Netto and Aldi, had been in the UK since 1990, with Lidl joining them in 1994. I had been going to them for years, particularly when I was a student, but there was a real social stigma involved in admitting it. People would scoff at you and make jokes about 'poverty produce' and so forth. Even though none of us were exactly living the life of Riley, where you shopped was still a bit of a taboo subject. I remember that people (and I include myself in this) would take branded bags from better known supermarkets along, and hide their budget shopping within them. The quality was always at least as good as Tesco's or Morrison's, but for some reason people didn't seem to believe that it could be. Once I started earning a bit of money I stopped going, and almost as soon as I did, low and behold, they suddenly became in vogue. Post-credit crunch, they exploded in popularity amongst the middle classes. They transformed into an acceptable dinner party conversation topic, with people discussing the merits of their superb cheese and wine ranges. Now I think they're actually a trendier (as far as supermarkets go) alternative to the bigger brand names. I think this change happened over the course of four or so years, but I remember the overnight realisation that my ten years of previous non-street cred had finally been verified.

That year me and my mates decided to take a trip to the emerald isle, specifically Dublin. We had been told that the Guinness over there was out of this world. None of us much liked it – we would have the occasional half pint but that was about it. It took me a few years to fully embrace the Stouts' unique flavour of old socks mixed with burnt cheese. It used to irritate me that it was always the drink at university that was heavily promoted with free merchandise, like pens/hats, etc. I always felt slightly bitter about never claiming my novelty Guinness hat. Going over to Ireland to check out the quality of a particular drink seemed as good as excuse as any to choose a holiday destination. Our trip to Dublin basically consisted of going out in the Temple Bar area, looking round tourist shops, and of course visiting the Guinness brewery. The Guinness itself was delicious; it's something to do with the mineral water they use that just doesn't travel well. All the Guinness that's sold in the rest of Ireland and the UK is brewed in Dublin, so it's never as fresh once it has spent hours or days being transported. It's also more likely that in Dublin you're drinking from a fresh keg with clean draft lines. We were all Guinness converts by the end of the trip, but upon returning to Canterbury, it just wasn't the same.

In early 2007, a new law was introduced, prohibiting smoking in all public places. A few businesses such as Wetherspoons had started banning smoking a few months earlier, but now there was a nationwide blanket ban. It made a big difference to having a night out. Beforehand, your clothes would always stink of tobacco smoke the following morning. It didn't matter where you went or what you did, second-hand smoke would always linger like an annoying acquaintance at a party that you couldn't quite shake off. You accepted that part of a weekend ritual would involve washing your garments (or at least dumping them in a washing bag) and aerating your bedroom (or shed) on a Saturday morning. There was also the danger, which happened to me on numerous occasions, of getting cigarette burns, if you were in a drunk, crowded environment. The ban was certainly a positive change. However, people quickly realised that the smell of tobacco masked all the other unpleasant smells in bars and pubs. Suddenly you could smell the toilets, and it became obvious if the carpets hadn't been cleaned for months. The smell of nicotine was swiftly replaced by the smells of stale vomit and cheap air freshener. It was funny to think that beforehand it was common to smoke in restaurants, where two sides of the establishment would be divided into 'smoking' and 'non smoking.' When you called up a restaurant to make a booking, you would always have to specify whether you preferred to be seated in the smoking area or not. That idea that it was socially acceptable to smoke around other people eating now seems as distant as the corn laws.

I remember as a child that you used to be able to buy candy sticks that looked just like cigarettes, with a white end and a darker brown end. They came wrapped in plastic and card that were exact replicas of cigarette packaging- Marlboro is the brand that clearly sticks out in my memory. Obviously, the kids would then stroll around pretending they were smoking like they were posing in some Audrey Hepburn photo shoot. I do not know how these companies got away with such blatant cigarette advertising aimed at children for so long. I also recall people smoking on trains, back when the armrests of the seats would have ashtrays built into them. Friends of mine recall smoking on planes and my grandad used to tell me how it was once common practice to smoke in hospitals. One of the nurses' roles was to come round the wards and change all the bedside ashtrays. All gone, in a puff of smoke.

A few weeks after the ban, I started working as a journalist for Trinity Mirror on two local papers based in Margate, *The Thanet Times* and *The Isle of Thanet Gazette*. It was something of a shame that the papers happened to be based in Margate. It's hard to put into words how depressing a place Margate was back then. In 2021 it has a slightly retro-trendy vibe, with celebrities like Pete Doherty, but back then it was a tomb. A boarded-up, windswept tomb of a town. However, I couldn't complain. It was great to finally have a job that I was excited about. I was both researching potential stories and writing articles, but being 'local issues' papers, the stories themselves could range from mildly interesting to incredibly dull. The most mildly interesting story I researched (that my editor later turned down) was about a gentleman who was convinced there was treasure submerged in Margate harbour. When I dropped by his house to interview him, I found the walls covered in maps, diagrams, and newspaper clippings on the subject. He had devoted his life to a shipwreck that happened just outside Margate harbour in 1895. It was a Swedish schooner called the *Valkyr* which was sailing back home from Portugal when it got caught in a storm and decided to take shelter in the Thames Estuary. Unfortunately, it never made it that far, and ended up blown off course, whereby it struck the rocks just outside of Margate. It was known to be carrying sardines, salt, and cork – some of which was retrieved by divers decades later. However, this gentleman insisted he had proof that there was also priceless treasure on board, which the divers never recovered. His evidence was woolly at best; one of the crew had a name similar to a renowned thief from Lisbon, and some gold from a church disappeared a couple of years before the ship set sale. He was really passionate about the subject, spending a good two hours talking to me and filling me in on all his various conspiracy theories, all the while serving me a conveyor belt of tea and biscuits. His general demeanour suggested a man who didn't quite have all his marbles and whom was enjoying my company a bit too much. It later transpired that he had spent many years contacting all the various papers in Kent, some of which had run small segments on it. He was never satisfied with this though, and felt that it should have been the scoop of the century.

I really enjoyed going out onto the streets of Margate and doing vox pops. These are basically a way of ascertaining general opinion from members of the public through a series of informal chats. It was fascinating to see how people could get so passionate about the smallest of things. I remember on one such occasion my colleague and I were gathering public opinion on the council's plan to reduce the number of spaces in a small car park, from forty down to thirty-six. Some of the locals were absolutely livid about the proposal. We would get comments like 'these people are ruining Margate' or 'this town is going to hell in a handcart'. Most of the articles that I had published were of the 'vandals graffiti bus shelter' ilk. It wasn't award-winning journalism by any means. However, my colleagues quickly realised that I had something of a talent for coming up with puns. I would frequently suggest mildly amusing headlines for various stories. 'Sex shop goes bust' was one of mine, which I used on a piece about an adult entertainment shop closing down. I loved playing with language and would use any opportunity I could to include mixed metaphors. For instance, there was a snowman competition which took place on the beach one day. Obviously, it wouldn't last once the weather changed and the tide came in. I came up with 'Time and tide melts the snowman' rather than the more traditional 'waits for no man'.

The novelty of working on a paper started to wear off quite quickly. I had always wanted to be a journalist, because I thought it would enable me to be creative in my writing. I found it irritating frequently being challenged by my editor for using too many 'big words'. There was a general rule in the office that if you used any words longer than eight letters you had to get it signed off first. There was also the issue of it being a high-pressured environment which wasn't conducive to creating thinking. I was fully aware that this was an industry in which you needed to work your way up, but the thought of many years struggling on low pay doing sub-standard journalism wasn't appealing. I didn't want to stop enjoying something that I loved. Additionally, I found out that one of my colleagues from school (who shall remain nameless) had managed to get a head of features role on a major London magazine, purely because one of her family members happened to work there. I knew her relatively well, because we took two A-Levels together. She wasn't the sharpest tool in the box, in fact she would struggle to string a cohesive sentence together. I knew that nepotism was a big issue in the arts industry but it still felt really galling knowing that someone with barely a journalistic bone in their body was in role that it could take me many years to achieve.

I had also become aware of what I felt was a slight undercurrent of xenophobia permeating the newsroom. This was subtle but it was definitely present and would make me feel uncomfortable when it started seeping through into some of our stories. I understood that part of journalism involved dumbing down for your audience, but at the same time, our role was to educate and inform. It's fine for certain national newspapers dumb down because the reader is making an informed choice to purchase the paper, but with local news that choice often isn't there. This started making me feel uneasy, particularly when it came to perpetuating stereotypes based on race. (i.e. the classic all immigrants are here to sponge off the state angle). It became apparent years later that the disillusionment that festered in these small towns definitely played a part in the rise of UKIP and later the circumstances that led towards Brexit.

For all these reasons, I decided that I needed a change in career and started applying for university jobs. I thought that Higher Education would be an interesting industry to get involved with – I was fascinated by the size and complexity of educational establishments and all the different roles housed within them. Additionally, I was missing my old life in Brighton, and so spent a couple of weeks travelling up for interviews at the two universities located there. On my third interview, I got offered an administrator role in a Student Services team at Brighton University. On my last day at the newspaper, I gave my colleagues a parting joke.

'Want to hear something terrible?' I asked.

'Er, sure,' they responded with a slight hesitation.

'Paper,' I replied, followed by a pause. 'I told you it was tear-able.' The man-in-a-shed years had come to an end.

CHAPTER 7

Return to Brighton

It was a breath of fresh salty air being back in Brighton again. My new office was housed in an old manor house, appropriately enough referred to as 'The Manor House'. This was an eighteenth-century building, but the barn which connected to the building at the back was much older. It was, in fact, the oldest existing building in Brighton & Hove, dating back to 1500. George IV used to stay there on his frequent trips to the coast before construction began on the Brighton Pavilion. The timbers that held up the roof to the barn are said to have come from the Spanish Armada. It had many uses throughout the years; as well as a private house, it was used by the council and was briefly a social club before the University of Brighton purchased it in 1993. As you can imagine, it was a fascinating building to work in, full of history and secret, poky little rooms. It was said to be haunted by the ghost of a lady who fell down a well and got trapped there. That added a touch of the supernatural to the evenings when I stayed later in the winter and could hear all the creaking floorboards and rattling windows accompanying my typing.

The Manor House was the central Student Services hub for the whole university. Essentially these were services based around Careers, Student Finance, Disability & Dyslexia, and Counselling. My role was in the counselling team, booking appointments, maintaining records, sending out letters, invoicing – basic administration duties. My starting salary was £16,000 and my office was on the first floor, overlooking the grounds of the estate. It was a great little job to have as an entry point into Higher Education. The flip side to working in a historic building was that it was totally impractical for the needs of a Student Services department. Confidentiality was difficult because the walls were paper thin, the hallways were too narrow for more than one person to walk down side by side, and most ridiculously of all, the steps leading up to the Manor House were grade 1 listed – so we weren't allowed a ramp. Considering that one of our services was disability, it wasn't exactly disability friendly.

I moved into a shared house a ten-minute walk away with three other flatmates. I became good friends with one of them – a Greek guy called Stelios, who I managed to horrify with my diet of chips, fish fingers, and pizza. He loved his cooking and had spent time as a chef in the Greek army. He would frequently end up preparing meals for me, especially if I was feeling lazy and would just rattle up something like beans on toast for dinner. His motto was 'no-one goes hungry in my house'. He was a brilliant flatmate to have, especially if you woke up hungover, where upon he would come to the rescue with a spread of Mediterranean delicacies. It wasn't until I started living in London that I began properly cooking meals for myself. My repertoire when I lived in Brighton was pretty limited. My signature dish was something my mum used to cook, which I later adapted, called cheese pie. Very tasty but incredibly calorific. Here's my recipe for Bryant's cheese pie:

Ingredients

For the pastry

- 450g Flour
- 2 tsp baking powder
- ½ tsp salt
- 120g unsalted butter
- 1 egg yolk
- 50g grated parmesan cheese
- 120ml water
- 1 egg for glazing

For the Filling

- 2 medium potatoes, peeled and cut into cubes
- 2 onions
- 1 tbsp flour
- 50ml whole milk
- 50 ml double cream
- 150g mature cheddar cheese, grated
- ½ tsp mustard
- ½ tsp cayenne pepper

Method

1. For the pastry, mix the flour, baking powder, salt, butter, and egg yolk in a food processor until the mixture resembles breadcrumbs. Add the grated parmesan and stir together.
2. Gradually add the water, mixing continuously until the mixture comes together as a dough. Roll the dough into a ball, then wrap it in cling film and chill in the fridge for an hour.
3. For the filling, bring a saucepan of salted water to the boil. Add the potato pieces to the pan and cook for 10-15 minutes, or until tender, then drain and set aside.
4. Bring a separate large saucepan of water to the boil, add the sliced onions, and cook for 2-3 minutes. Drain well and return the cooked onions to the saucepan.

5. Sprinkle the onions with the flour and stir well to coat. Add the milk and cream, and heat the mixture over a medium heat for 3-4 minutes, stirring continuously, until the liquid is smooth and has thickened. Add the cooked potato pieces, grated cheese, mustard, and cayenne pepper, and stir well. Season to taste with salt and freshly ground black pepper, stir well, then set the filling mixture aside.
6. Preheat the oven to 180C/Gas 4. Grease a deep pie tin with butter. Add a small amount of flour, turn the tin to coat the base and sides of the tin, then shake out any excess.
7. When the pastry has chilled, roll out two-thirds of it onto a clean, floured work surface, until it is almost twice as wide as the diameter of the pie tin. Using the rolling pin, lift the pastry and lay it over the pie tin to line the base and sides. Gently press the pastry into the corners of the tin, trimming off any excess, then prick the base of the pastry case several times with a fork.
8. Cover the pastry with a sheet of greaseproof paper and fill it with rice or dried beans. Bake in the oven for 10-15 minutes, or until the pastry is pale golden-brown. Remove from the oven, discard the beans and greaseproof paper, and set the pastry aside to cool. When cool, pour the pie filling into the pastry case.
9. Roll the remaining one-third of the pastry out onto a floured work surface until it is slightly larger than the diameter of the pie tin. Brush the rim of the cooked pastry case with some of the beaten egg, and place the pastry lid on top of the pie. Trim off any excess pastry. Seal the pastry lid to the pastry case by crimping the edges of the pastry lid with a fork.
10. With a knife, make two small holes in the centre of the pastry lid to allow steam to escape. Brush the pastry lid

with the remaining beaten egg, then transfer to the oven and bake for 25-30 mins, or until golden-brown. Grate extra cheese on top if desired.

Later that year I started attending martial arts classes. Stelios had bumped into a lady in the street who started chatting to him about this great new class she had been going to, called Wing Tsun. After a couple of weeks he convinced me to go along. It was nothing like I expected it to be. It was a real mish-mash of people – different ages, heights, and abilities, with no egos whatsoever. I'd always wanted to do some form of self-defence class but had always been put off by the people they tended to attract. This class had a really fun crowd who were there to socialise, grow in confidence and learn a beneficial skill.

Wing Tsun is basically a southern Chinese style of Kung Fu, with the key attribute being softness and the performance of techniques in a relaxed manner. The beauty of Wing Tsun (compared to a lot of other martial arts) is that you don't need to be the strongest, fastest, or largest to succeed against your opponent. The goal is to maintain one's flexibility and softness, all the while keeping in the strength to fight back. If one were to use an analogy, it's much like the flexible nature of bamboo.

We learned a series of set move pieces called the 'Siu Nim Tau' which were the basics of all the techniques we would later learn, equipping us with the key rules of balance and body structure. Each term we would focus on a particular fighting style or scenario with which to defend against – things like ground fighting, multiple opponents, fighting out of a corner, boxing, attacks with knives, and so forth. Defending against knife attacks was really interesting. I had never considered it before, but because the range of a knife is so limited (compared to, say, the length of someone's arm) there are really only two motions any assailant can do. Slashing from right to left, or lurching forward with a stabbing motion. This is the kind of predictability that Wing Tsun seeks to exploit. We would practise with rubber knifes with lipstick smeared on the end. If we got said lipstick smudged upon our T-shirts, we would know we had been stabbed. After six weeks or so, it became almost impossible for any of us to land that killer greasepaint blow. Boxing was also a really fun thing to practise. I never appreciated before how much it hurts to be punched in the head, even when wearing a fully padded boxing helmet. You'd think with my previous head injuries I would have been accustomed to it. When someone would land an occasional direct blow, you could almost feel your brain rattling around inside your skull, like an ice cube being vigorously swirled around a glass of whisky. No wonder so many professional boxers end up with brain injuries by the time they retire.

Stelios and I would go to Wing Tsun twice a week, on Tuesday and Thursday evenings. Our tutor, Ben, was a great guy. He had been studying Wing Tsun for about twenty years, so was pretty tough. We would all take turns going up for demonstrations. It was amazing how the softest, most effortless movement from him would send you staggering back. He was able to do that trick in the movies of smashing through solid wood with his bare hands. He only demonstrated it a handful of times to us as a class, but it was amazing to witness. The secret is the relaxation of your muscles. It's the tension in your arms that causes the pain. If you can relax the muscles in your arms (which is incredibly hard to do), suddenly your range is an extra inch or so, and that will enable you to force your way through a range of materials. Of course, in a fighting situation, that extra inch is an incredible advantage over an opponent, hence why it is practised. It took me over two years of training to learn how to relax my muscles in such a way. It's a really hard sensation to describe; making your limbs go as floppy as possible is surprisingly tough – no-one does it in their normal day-to-day routines. Then being able to focus that floppiness solely in your upper arm and move it at speed requires a huge amount of discipline and repetition. I had many months of bloodied and bruised knuckles, and that was just through experimenting with mdf. Eventually, I managed to break through wood with no pain or bruising whatsoever. It was still a long way from breaking bricks, but it was a great achievement. I can still relax my arm muscles now, but nowhere near to the degree I could when I was training.

Occasionally my Wing Tsun class would do weekend trips to other schools, to meet and practise with other students. On one visit to Tunbridge Wells, we got to meet and spar with the head of the European Association of Wing Tsun – Grand Master Koenspect. His tutor had been a famous Hong Kong martial artist called Leung Ting, who trained alongside Bruce Lee. Koenspect had also sparred with Bruce Lee on a few occasions, so we all knew he was going to be one tough cookie. He was more than tough; he seemed to defy the laws of physics. He was in his sixties, but had the strength, flexibility, and stamina of a man forty years younger. We took turns sparring one-on-one in front of the class, to see if any of us could land a decisive blow. The first couple of people who went up were really tentative; after all, this guy was nearly triple the age of many of us. Gradually, though, people started trying to attack him with more vigour, but he sent all of them flying. When it was my turn, I just went for it. It was a lose-lose situation, really. Either you went easy on him, he defeated you, and you looked like a bit of a wally, or you gave it everything you had, he still defeated you, and you ended up looking like an overconfident wally. Trying to hold your own against someone who has sparred with Bruce Lee is a bit of a nugatory endeavour. It's rather like using a frozen halibut as a hammer. Theoretically, it could work, but it's grossly inept at the job. The technique for sparring in Wing Tsun is something called 'sticky hands', where you mirror your opponent with your hands, keeping contact for the first 10-20 seconds, and then trying to break out of it with fighting techniques. I lasted less than ten seconds – he landed a blow to my upper chest and I flew about four metres backwards. I was winded for the next hour. Supposedly, that was a great honour.

Chioma came down to visit me in Brighton around this time. He's a great guy, but him and alcohol were never a sensible combination, he was wired enough as it was when he got excited. Even just a couple of drinks would tip him over the edge and make him think he was invincible. I mentioned that I was going out in Croydon the following week for Dray's sister, Laura's birthday, and asked if he wanted to come along. He had recently qualified from his medical training, so was now a bona-fide doctor. It was a fairly non-descript evening. We were in some glitzy pretentious bar that was not really to my taste, but it was fine. A girl called Alexia, who was Dray and Laura's neighbour back in Canterbury, was getting very merry on the dance floor when she suddenly decided to do the limbo. She was rather inebriated, wasn't the most nimble and attempting to do a manoeuvre that required balance, poise, and finesse. To the surprise of no-one but herself, she didn't succeed, and fell backwards on the floor in some discomfort. I remember turning round to Chioma and catching his eye; this was his turn to shine.

'Don't panic!' he announced, arms aloft like some Christ-like figure. 'I am a doctor.' All the rounds of shots had given him that extra air of confident authority. Everyone breathed a collective sigh of relief as Chioma examined her ankle. He deduced it was fine, just a sprain, and after a strategically placed pack of frozen peas, it would be as right as rain. She was hobbling around for a while before we all decided to call it a night. I found out later from Dray that she had woken up the following day in even more pain and was eventually advised to go to A&E. It turned out she had broken her ankle in three separate places and I think ended up in a cast for the next few weeks. Chioma's first medical diagnosis as a qualified doctor was somewhat wide of the mark. We joked that the shame was so great that he hot-footed it out of the country to New Zealand, and never came back.

By the end of the year, I had joined Facebook. By now, lots of aspects of people's lives were beginning to move online (things like music and online banking), and Facebook was the culmination of all the old social media channels like myspace. Having a digital archive of one's life has been very useful for me in the writing of this book (at least from 2007 onwards), but at the time no-one was quite sure how big it was going to become. Certainly, no-one envisaged that older generations like our parents would eventually have profiles on there. It started off as a 'cool youth movement' but gradually morphed into something much more encompassing. I remember how precious people used to be over their profiles, un-tagging pictures of themselves that they didn't like, or getting really upset when there was an upgrade or design change. It's now so intertwined with people's lives that we almost forget it's there.

I think it was also around this time that it finally dawned on me that the days of certain physical things as genuinely useful objects were now numbered. Everything was by now slowly moving into the digital realm. There was a lady who worked at Brighton bus station who used to come into Student Services and drop off stacks of bus timetables. She was a sweet old lady who genuinely had the students' best interests at heart. I remember the slightly bemused look on her face when we told her one day that they weren't really needed any more. When we informed her that students could just look up the times at home she didn't quite get it, bless her. She continued to come back over the next two years and the pile of precariously balancing bus timetables just grew bigger and bigger until, in the end, we just had to dump them.

There are so many reference guides like that which have vanished over the years. The Yellow Pages was another – this was a huge book which listed all the various services/tradesmen in the local area. It was very distinctive due to its yellow tinted pages. This was a happy accident when the company printer ran out of cream paper and accidentally printed onto yellow. It was a serendipitously effective branding strategy. No home was complete without one in the 1990s – it was a bible, particularly for people like electricians and plumbers. As a kid, I used to spend hours flicking through it, looking for the most random listings – the animal rescue ones were particularly funny: '*Need help with an escaped alligator? Call Fred, the man who puts the croc back in the lock.*' They always had these memorable names as well – lots of handy Andys and Ruth Tyler, the roof tiler – things like that. Nowadays you can filter search results by star ratings and cost, but back then you needed a good professional name to get noticed. Another thing that I was sad to see disappear from high street shelves were computer game magazines. These were owned by Sega and Nintendo and had huge circulation figures before the internet came along. If you were stuck on a particular game, they were a godsend. I would occasionally read them in WH Smith if I was looking for tips/advice on a certain computer game level. There was one game in particular, 'Teenage Mutant Hero Turtles', that try as we might, my brother and I could not complete. We spent one summer trying everything we could to finish it whilst we waited for that special month when Nintendo Magazine would enlighten us. I think we found out about a year later that the game had a glitch and couldn't actually be completed! Something that took us twelve months to discover would now take just a twenty second Google search – incredible when you think about it. These physical reference things still exist, but now just have a kitsch novelty value – at least for anyone under 50. I mean, an encyclopaedia is still a great thing to have displayed upon a bookshelf, but who would now actually spend the time using one? As with all these previously useful things, the rarer they become, the more value they accumulate over time. Unused BT phone cards, for instance, are now worth a huge amount of money to collectors. Though I haven't yet heard of a collector of old issues of the Yellow Pages.

That year, I was part of a small team that was organising our staff Christmas party. One of the ladies in the team was this eccentric Irish nun called Blanaid who really enjoyed a drink. She was part of the chaplaincy team and must have been in her late seventies. She was always slightly tipsy and liked to keep a bottle of brandy or gin on her person at all times. Anyway, we were going round Brighton looking for suitable venues to host this seasonal soiree. This one particular bar had a sign in the window: 'Free wi-fi'. We wandered in and had a quick chat with the bar manager about numbers and logistical bits and pieces. When we had finished, Blanaid turned around and said, 'Can I get that shot of free wi-fi now, please?' (She pronounced it wee-fee.)

The barman looked really confused, and we explained to her that it meant a wireless internet connection.

'Oh,' she said, 'I thought wee-fee was a drink.' For years afterwards we would always refer to it as wee-fee in a slurred Irish accent.

In April 2008 me and the Canterbury boys went on a holiday to Munich. We had planned to go there six months earlier for the famous beer drinking festival, Oktoberfest, which we had logically assumed took place in October. The two-and-a-half week festival actually takes place mostly in September, with only a couple of days at the start of the following month. I think we'd all planned for October and then, having realised we would miss all the frothy festivities, decided to postpone until Easter. It was probably a good thing. The year before, we had gone to Brussels and experienced the strength of Belgium beers for the first time. Bjorn had got so drunk he ended up eating the aluminium foil off his kebab. We then managed to overload and break a lift in the hostel we stayed in, and had to crawl out when the cleaner found us stuck between floors of the building. We decided that in light of missing the beer festival and the previous year's shenanigans, this would be more of a cultural trip. Apart from visiting Munich Zoo, which is continually voted as one of the best zoos in Europe, I can't remember any other cultural activities we did. We were very excited to go to the Hofbräuhaus – the city's famous beer hall. Dating back to 1589, it has an incredibly rich history. For instance, in 1919 the Munich communist government used it as a base for their headquarters, and in February 1920 Adolf Hitler and the National Socialists held their first meeting there. Other famous visitors over the years have included Mozart (who at one point lived round the corner), Louis Armstrong, Vladimir Lenin (another regular), and John F Kennedy. The building was stunning, with these beautifully ornate frescoes decorating the ceiling, and cathedral-like stone pillars that rose up to meet it. There's something so much more civilized about drinking establishments on the continent – the Hofbräuhaus even had drinks lockers where regular patrons could store their own steins. That would be a recipe for disaster if it were ever tried in the UK.

One night after some pre-drinking, we ordered a taxi and asked the driver to take us 'where the action was'; I think those were our exact words. He drove us to a lively bar where we had a really fun evening. The beer was flowing, we were chatting to the locals, people were offering to buy us rounds, it was a mirthful old time. We keep commenting on how friendly and hospitable everyone was. After an hour or so, when we were decidedly merry, we raised a toast to David Hasselhoff. Everyone joined in with our ironic toasting.

'Ja, we love the hoff, he is our idol,' said one of the guys.

I was chatting about the England football team to another bloke who seemed a bit too interested on my thoughts on Fabio Capello's team selection. It suddenly started to dawn on us all that we were surrounded by men, and that we were quite possibly in a gay bar. Nothing wrong with that, of course, it just wasn't the kind of evening that we had planned. Our suspicions were later confirmed when we were propositioned on the stairwell. Quite why our taxi driver suggested we go there, I don't know.

Back in the UK, things were going well. For the first time in my life, I had managed to accumulate some savings. I had started saving one-third of everything I earned, my intention being to pay off my student loan as quickly as I could. Over the next five years, I would regularly send off cheques to the Student Loan Company, on top of the deductions which were coming out of my salary. Most people thought I was mad. 'Why pay more than you have to?' was most people's response. I look upon financial management as a bit like a bobsleigh run – the more effort you put in at the beginning, the faster you go overall. I didn't feel comfortable having that level of debt hanging over me, even though it was relatively manageable compared to the average student debt today. I have definitely noticed a shift in mindsets since then. Maybe it's because student debt is now so high in this country (as of 2020, roughly £50,000) that people shift it to the back of their minds. Essentially, it is just an additional tax on higher earners, but my worry would always be a future government shifting the goalposts and moving us more towards an American model. Anyway, I managed to clear it by 2013, and by then, as I was earning more, it gave me an extra £250 in my monthly pay packet. I thought it was worth a bit of frugality.

I was progressing well in Wing Tsun, having moved up a couple of grades, and was planning to start some counselling courses through a company called Grassroots. Work had agreed to give me some paid leave for these, as it was forming part of my CPD (continuing professional development). I thought that this would be an interesting route to go down and was just a couple of weeks away from starting, when out of the blue my manager, Sue, suddenly passed away.

When someone who appears healthy and well unexpectedly passes away, it's a massive shock. Sue sat next to me in the office, she was on my interview panel, and essentially was the person who gave me the job. We always got on really well, I couldn't have asked for a better colleague to share an office with. She had been in her role for about fifteen years, essentially managing the whole team. She knew everything and acted as the glue that bound the whole department. We were in the office together when she told me she was having some mild pains in her stomach and decided to leave early. She didn't want an ambulance called and said she was fine getting the bus home. She died later that evening from a Ventricular Septal Defect, basically a hole in her heart. As you can imagine, everyone in the department was very upset. There wasn't really a nice way of telling people, either. Over the next few days, people were constantly coming into the office and asking me where she was. It can be quite harrowing telling people bad news over and over again, especially as you're never sure of the reaction. Work colleagues are people you don't choose to spend time with, so your emotional responses are different to a family member or close friend passing away. Some people were in floods of tears, whilst others acted quite blasé about it. There is nothing wrong with being on either end of the spectrum, it just made being at work tricky, especially as I was surrounded by her belongings and family photos. A few days later, I packed these away for her son who came in to collect them.

The funeral took place at Woodvale Crematorium and was the traditional sombre affair. Funerals are strange things. They are supposed to be a celebration of a person's life, at the same time as being deeply sad. I also felt rather out of place, I'd only known her fourteen months, whereas everyone else seemed to have known her forever. The drinks reception took place in the beer garden of a pub called The Gladstone. It was there I met a guy called Ben Dew for the first time; he was good friends with one of my work colleagues. He had met Sue on a couple of occasions but didn't really know her. Essentially he had gate crashed a funeral. We became close friends soon after, but when people asked where we met and we said 'at a funeral', it always raised a few eyebrows. As one door closes, another one opens.

On Monday morning, I was called into the Head of Department's office and told that I would be taking over Sue's job as Departmental Manager. I didn't really have a choice; the work was piling up and I was the only person who had a detailed enough understanding of her role, as well as having access to all her documents, projects, etc. I hadn't entertained the notion that having worked in a Student Services team for a year, I'd end up in a management role. It was mixed emotions. Everything was awkward for a while, changing the office layout, re-organising her files; it all felt a bit wrong. Stepping into the role of a person that everyone depended on was odd, especially as I hadn't planned on it happening. I had deferred my place on the counselling course, as it would have been impossible to do both at the same time. I contacted a recruitment agency to get someone to help out with the office, and as chance would have it, it was someone I knew from when I was a student – Feraz.

We worked quite well together and it was nice to have some male company in the office, even though he was nothing like he had been when we worked on the Sussex newspaper. He was a lot chattier and spent much of the time flirting with the various students that came in. He only lasted a couple of months before he was offered a job in a bank. Luckily, I had another replacement already lined up. Ben had recently quit his job, and came in looking to speak to someone in our careers team. I bumped into him in the corridor and said half-jokingly, 'There's going to be a vacancy in my office in a couple of weeks.'

Before I knew it, he'd signed up with our in-house temping agency. His friend, Anita, had vouched for him, and as it saved me the job of doing interviews, I hired him on the spot.

Ben and I got on like a house on fire. We worked hard on restructuring things, our motto was that this was now 'a no bullshit office'. Because Sue had been such a kind and accommodating person, some unscrupulous people had taken advantage of her. One person in particular did everything she could to avoid doing her job, including hardly ever being at the office. She was continually off sick with 'general malaise' and would refuse to fill in sickness notes. She would say things like 'no-one needs to know' or 'it's just a couple of extra days, no need to bother HR with it', which was ludicrous, especially as she was leading a team. Sue was always chasing her to do paperwork, which she might reluctantly complete weeks later. We implemented a one-strike-and-you're-out rule for people who were being deliberately obtuse. After a couple of calls to HR she started being much nicer to us. We also banned the excuse of 'general malaise', and added it to a list which we pinned to our wall, alongside other military-based excuses, including Sergeant Sniffle, Colonel Contagion, and Brigadier Bullshit. The nature of management in the public sector inevitably means that half your job is chasing other people to do theirs correctly. The only confidential spaces in the building were for 1-1 student counselling, so we ended up talking in code a lot of the time. We referred to the department as the SS (the initials of Student Services), so anyone we didn't like got a Third Reich nickname – Goring, Goebbels, Himmler, etc.

I would quite often mosey around the building and chat to the various teams, especially in the afternoons to see if there were any stray biscuits floating around. Ben mentioned that one of the teams in the building behind us thought I was spying on them for the Head of Department. Unbeknown to me, I apparently used to always head over there at 4pm on a Friday afternoon. They obviously thought that I was checking on them to see if anyone had snuck off early for the weekend. That wasn't the kind of thing I was ever asked to do, but we thought we'd have some fun with the rumour anyway. We concocted a scheme with some walkie-talkies to mess with their heads. After one of my (this time deliberate) 4pm visits, I walked out the door and loudly spoke into the walkie-talkie; 'The eagles are in the nest. I repeat, the eagles are in the nest.'

Ben, in his best 'Head of Department voice' then answered, 'Roger that, over and out.'

We confessed our joke a couple of weeks later. It had actually worked, they had all thought it was genuine.

The financial crisis of 2007/2008 was a huge event in the UK. It was given many names by the press – the credit crunch, the great recession, the liquidity crisis. It began at the end of 2007, with the collapse of the investment bank Lehman Brothers creating a domino effect around the world. In the UK, there was a run on the bank Northern Rock, and when it was nationalised in 2008 it became clear to everyone that we were going through a severe economic downturn. The austerity measures that were put in place weren't officially abandoned by the government until the end of 2019. It seems strange now, but up until that point, I had naively assumed that recessions were things that didn't happen to rich industrialised nations. No-one predicted that interest rates would plummet from 6% to near zero and twelve years later would still be there. It seemed so abstract, especially down in Brighton where people would make light of it. I remember lots of cafés promoting a 'credit crunch brunch'. The amount of big high street names that closed down within a five-year period was scary. As well as my beloved Woolworths, there were a plethora of others – MFI, Zavvi, Focus, Jane Norman, C&A, Borders, Comet, Barratts, Blockbusters, JJB Sports, Athena, and BHS, all bit the dust. Of course, thousands of small independent businesses also folded, but the closure of these big giants was a striking representation of this new merciless world.

Now that I was back on track with work, I commenced my counselling course. The counselling offered at the university was standard humanistic counselling – basically, a way for students to explore personal growth and self-development, hopefully leading to greater self-awareness and self-realisation. My course dealt with this as a basic model, alongside key areas such as confidentiality, boundaries, and more specific behavioural challenges. It was fascinating to learn, but I wasn't sure yet if it would take me anywhere.

I was really interested to learn that far more women than men have traditionally sought counselling. Men have emotional needs in exactly the same way as women. They feel emotions such as anger, grief, shame, and anxiety, in precisely the same way. The difference is that women have traditionally been 'allowed' to name these feelings and to seek support for them. Men, meanwhile, have been silenced through male gender roles, and have felt the need to keep their emotions secret, adding feelings of shame and isolation to the emotional mix. I was thinking that there must be a massive gap in the market for men seeking help, support, and even just friendship. Ben had been having similar thoughts. He had been seeking support after a failed relationship, but had found it difficult for people to take him seriously. It was a bit of a 'man up and get on with it' attitude. So, we decided to try and set up our own charity with the goal of raising money for local men's support groups.

Setting up a charity is notoriously difficult. We had no idea what we were doing, so we enlisted the help of a mutual friend called Glenn, who had set up charities in the past. The first thing we needed to do was decide upon a name. We had lots of ideas and initially settled on the 'Brighton Men's Project'. Very quickly, we realised that there were two major issues with this as a name. Firstly, if the charity was to get bigger, it might exclude people from other nearby towns, particularly Hove, which is Brighton in all but name. Secondly, once we had mocked up some flyers and abbreviated our name, the BMP could easily be mistaken for the BNP – not the kind of message we were hoping to get across! So, after a while, we changed it to the much simpler 'Men's Network'. At the start, we encountered quite a lot of resistance and criticism from people. 'It's sexist! It's not inclusive' – things like that. As I pointed out at the time, there are literally thousands of women's charities, but most people would be hard pressed to name one male charity. (At least back in 2008.) We would also point out the massive funding discrepancies that essentially meant vastly more men died of preventable diseases than women. For instance, breast cancer gets more than three times the funding of testicular cancer. In addition, men are more likely to be excluded from school, more likely to become alcoholics, more likely to spend time in prison, more likely to be homeless, and more likely to commit suicide. There was a whole raft of issues that disproportionately affected men but weren't being addressed. So, our aim became to raise awareness and hopefully make a bit of money that could be used for good causes.

Ben and his partner Darren weren't having their lease renewed on their accommodation but had found a flat in an art deco style building along the seafront, called Embassy Court. They couldn't afford the rent on their own, but asked if I wanted to sub-let so we would all save some money. After going round to see the flat and the sweeping views with a balcony overlooking the beach, I instantly said yes. It was a beautiful building, constructed in the 1930s and designed to look like an ocean liner. It was (and possibly still is) the tallest building directly on the UK seafront, at eleven storeys. It used to be known as Brighton's most luxurious address, with many famous people having resided there, including Max Miller and Rex Harrison. For many years, there was even a rooftop swimming pool, though sadly that had long since been abandoned by the time we moved in. Although the glamour had faded, it was still an impressive building that people wanted to live in. (A little bit of trivia – the building featured heavily in the music video to the James single *Just like Fred Astaire.*) There were a few minor celebrities who lived in the block. In fact, our next-door neighbour but one was the actor James Lance, who had appeared in numerous British TV shows (Alan Partridge, Teachers). Although work was now much further away, requiring a bus ride to get there, I was directly on the beach and only a ten-minute walk away from my Wing Tsun class.

I put the money that I saved through sub-letting, into the Men's Network, so the three of us put in a total of £4000 to get the charity off the ground. The living room became the HQ, which over time developed into a store room of leaflets, collection buckets, and props. Our first event was a fund-raising DJ night at a local bar. We had a raffle with various free drink prizes, but I don't think we made more than £60 that night. Something bigger and more imaginative was clearly required.

We came up with the idea of a charity fun run, which we called 'Tash Dash.' We kind of stole the name from the charity Movember (the idea that men grow moustaches in November to raise money for men's health issues), although at that time most people in the UK weren't aware of it. It was nowhere near as ubiquitous as it later became. Besides, as the ultimate goal was the same, it didn't really matter. The idea was that people would dress up as moustached idols and then do a 5k fun run along Brighton seafront. Organising a simple fun run was incredibly time-consuming. We had to get various things relating to health and safety signed off before the council would allow us to do it. We had to plan for all types of weather, employ first-aiders, make sure we had enough bottled water in order for our insurance to be valid – it was an endless list.

We were running everything on a shoestring budget. The signage, for instance, was a combination of arrows in plastic wallets and chalk arrows that I drew along the route in the morning. In terms of promotional materials, we set up a website and got some flyers produced with photos of various moustached men, everyone from Yosemite Sam to Freddie Mercury. Then the three of us blitzed all the pubs, social clubs, and supermarkets in the days leading up to it. I dressed up as a Sergeant Pepper era Ringo Starr for the day. We had invited the local paper to come down and run a story on us, but as our numbers were relatively low, I came up with the ingenious idea (if I do say so myself) of starting all the race numbers at 100. We had roughly 50 people signed up, but displaying a race number that was, say, 146 rather than 46 gave the impression of a bigger event in the photos. In the end, the day was a success, the weather was half decent, and with all the sponsorship pledges we received, we made something in the region of £2500. Once deductions were accounted for, we had over £1800 going directly to charities. The following week we saw our event in the paper as a half page spread- we were really chuffed. That was the moment when we realised that this was going to work.

January 2009 was the last time that I recall seeing CD singles in the shops. I remember the date because it was the launch single of U2's twelfth album *No Line on The Horizon*. Physical media was still a big thing, but CD singles had been on a downward slope for years. I remember when you would see entire aisles of singles in shops like Our Price and Tower Records. I actually thought CD singles had been gone for a while, so seeing them on the counter in a small box actually looked a bit odd and slightly sad.

Later that month, history was made when Barack Obama was inaugurated as the 44th President of the United States, the first time that someone from a non-white background had held that esteemed position. There was a real sense of euphoria in that America had finally entered the twenty-first century and we were now entering a more liberal and tolerant world. Most of the people I knew were so relieved that the embarrassment of the George Bush years had finally ended. It's easy to forget now just how crucified George Bush was in the British media back then. He became the brunt of stupidity jokes for years. There was a political cartoon sketch show I used to watch called 2DTV, which always showed Bush having to have concepts explained to him by a general crouching under a desk and using a sock puppet. The thinking at the time was that never again could someone so woefully inept be able to ascend to the highest office in the land. If we had been told back then that Bush would be usurped in the stupidity stakes by an orangeade spray-tanned imbecile with the reading level of a ten year old child, we might have counted our blessings. The bizarre arrival of Donald Trump in 2017 made George Bush look like Einstein in comparison. My mum was delighted when she later discovered that she shared a birthday (14th June) with the Donald. But for now at least, the US of A had the relative normality of the Obama years to look forward to.

America had always fascinated me as a child- this huge lumbering beast of a nation where anything could happen. From giant gorillas in New York to dinosaurs in San Diego, it just seemed to instil a sense of wonder in me. So much American cultural heritage is sucked into you through TV and films that it becomes a part of you. I'm sure there are many English children that would be able to name more American states than they could English counties. That year, my mum and I decided to take a holiday to New York – the first time that either of us had ever left Europe. I managed to get quite a good deal on a room at what I thought was the Chelsea Hotel. This was a famous historic block that had had many notable residents over the years, people like Dylan Thomas, Bob Dylan (who chose his stage name in homage to the aforementioned poet), and Allen Ginsberg. However, when we arrived, we discovered that it actually wasn't the Chelsea Hotel where we would be frequenting, rather the Chelsea Hostel. Someone had snuck an 'S' in there. It didn't really matter. Apart from the occasional cockroach (which we were informed by the staff was perfectly normal), it was clean and comfortable. Much to my mum's irritation, I had written out an itinerary for the week. There was just so much to see and do that I wanted to make sure we squeezed in as much as we could. We did all the normal touristy things that a first-time visitor would do: a boat cruise, the Empire State Building, Central Park, Greenwich Village. The beauty of New York, and pretty much any American city, is that it's almost impossible to get lost. The street layouts are so simple and logical that you hardly need a map. Walking round and seeing all these famous places that you instantly recognised was amazing. We went to visit the Dakota apartment (former home to John Lennon) where Yoko Ono still lived. As we were walking past, my mum saw an elderly Asian lady carrying her groceries, and shouted out, 'Yoko.' Of course, it wasn't her. I'm sure she was rich enough to have someone else carrying her groceries, but that didn't stop a number of other passers-by from turning round and pointing their cameras in her direction. There was almost a tsunami of excitable paparazzi chasing after this poor woman.

Back in Brighton, I started my Master's degree. I had acquired a taste for events organisation and promotion from all my charity work, so decided to undertake an MA in Practical Business Marketing. One of the big perks of working at a university was that they would allow me to do the course for free, as long as I was still employed there and it bore some relation to my role. At the time, we were discussing restructuring the university's nursery provision (it was common for universities to have their own subsidised nurseries for staff then), so my final major project was a business plan that would enable our nurseries to become more profitable. I did the MA as a part-time course over a two-year period, alongside my full-time job and my charity work. It became a very hectic two years.

That summer, we went on a Wing Tsun camping trip. One of the instructors at another branch, Warren, had a fruit farmer for a father (bit of a tongue-twister there), so owned a fair bit of land near Horsham. He owned one particular field that wasn't being cultivated that year, so we decided to host a Wing Tsun camping festival there. This took place over a Bank Holiday weekend, where we all rocked up with our tents, barbecues, sound systems and a ton of beers. During the day we would spend a few hours practising Kung Fu, and then in the evening drink and light bonfires. Warren had hired a truck, and drove into the field with this colossal amount of wood to get the bonfire started. It looked like a whole forest's worth wedged in there, with whole tree trunks that needed fifteen of us to lift off the truck. The bonfire we actually got going must have been ten feet tall, with flames stretching another ten feet in the air. The dad didn't know we were camping in his field, but we were assured that as long as we tidied up afterwards, he would never find out.

There were three different schools, so we were quite a large crowd – maybe around eighty. It was our Woodstock. The Friday and Saturday passed by without incident. They were perfect summer evenings so some of us didn't even bother sleeping in our tents. There is nothing quite like sleeping under the stars, especially in the middle of the countryside with no light pollution. On the Sunday evening, a few of us were sitting around our main bonfire telling stories and exchanging camping-related jokes. My joke of choice was 'Why can't you run through a campsite?' You can only ran, because it's past tents.' One of the guys just wasn't getting it, no matter how many times I tried to explain it to him. Then out of nowhere, one of the girls from our class, Stephanie, started running towards the fire. A few of us saw her and assumed she was just jogging over. She got nearer and nearer without slowing down, before launching herself straight into the middle of the fire. It was surreal. It took everyone a couple of seconds to work out what was happening. A couple of us jumped in and pulled her out. There was a real panic then. Someone had the good sense to grab some of our jerry cans and pour water over her. She was incredibly lucky. She was burnt all over, but amazingly, her face looked untouched. Her trousers had melted into her skin but she was strangely calm. We talked about this for days afterwards, but I imagine what had happened was she had wolfed down some drugs, woken up in a blackened field in a panic and then run towards the only light source she could see (i.e. our bonfire). I joined in with taking it in turns to do water runs whilst other people attempted to call an ambulance. That took a while, we were in the middle of nowhere and none of us could get a signal. In the end, someone had to trek across some wheat fields before they could achieve a strong enough reception.*

Warren was clearly worried about what was going to happen. This was unlicensed, there was no insurance, and it could have had big implications for the school. The ambulance was going to be a while and we were running out of water. It was 1am in the morning, no-one could drive because everyone was over the limit, and besides, the nearest 24-hour shops were probably over an hour away. We reverted to using beer to try and keep her wounds cool. She started coming around to the pain as the drugs were wearing off. The screaming was horrible; it was a dreadful situation to be in, as none of us were medically trained. She wanted to take her clothes off, but we didn't think that was a good idea – most of them were probably stuck to her. Eventually, the ambulance arrived. Me and four others had to stand in the middle of a country lane and flag it down. It almost crashed into us. It was the middle of the night in a winding country road, and the vehicle was racing down at 60 mph. It was a relief when she was stretchered onto it and they left for the nearest hospital. A couple of the guys who had pulled her out had also sustained minor burns to their hands, so they got treated as well. We sat around for a short while, chatting about what had happened, though no-one was in the mood to drink any more. We put the fire out with the rest of our beer and went to bed. Stephanie was okay in the end. A few of us went to visit her about a week later in hospital. She had permanent burns to her legs and arms, which would need skin grafts, but at least it could

---

* *(It wasn't until the following year that all network providers introduced the ability to make cross-network emergency calls with little or no signal.)*

all be covered up. Considering the ferocity of the fire, the fact that her face and neck were untouched was a minor miracle. She never came back to Wing Tsun after that.

After about eighteen months, we moved out of Embassy Court. We'd had a pretty sweet deal for a while (especially with me sub-letting), but the landlord had realised he was sitting on something of a goldmine and jacked the rent up too much for us to afford. The infuriating thing about renting wasn't really the wasted money or the sometimes living with strangers, but that vexatious feeling of never being truly settled. I lived in eight different houses during my two stints in Brighton, and a further five in London, before finally buying somewhere. During those years, I could never purchase furniture or nice ornaments to make those lodgings feel more homely. I never knew what the next space would be like, whether it would be furnished/unfurnished or have a garden. It was irritating, because I just was starting to feel somewhat settled. We had the added problem with this particular move of needing a spare room for all our Men's Network paraphernalia. Ben had also split up with his partner, so we started looking for new housemates as well as a new place to call home. We had one guy lined up that we knew through our charity work – a chap called Dan. The funny thing about Dan was that, despite being in his twenties (I think about 26 at the time), he was completely grey – eyebrows, hair, the lot. He used to call himself the 'Silver Fox' and, being a bit of a ladies' man, liked to introduce himself as this. We were clearly never going to call him that. All he ever seemed to eat was nuts – peanuts, almonds, mixed nuts; he never seemed to eat a proper meal. As a result, we started calling him 'the grey squirrel' instead of his pompous self- christened nickname. He hated that nickname, but the more he protested, the more we used it. We put an advert on Spare-Room and found a fourth housemate, a guy called Hassan Sajid – or Hass for short. He was a massive music fan, so we got on really well. He was really into his funk and psychedelic stuff and got me interested in a lot of different things, bands like Parliament that I would have never thought to listen to. We went to see the Red Hot Chili Peppers later that year, solely so Hass could deduce how 'funky' the new rhythm guitarist's playing was.

The new house was just a stone's throw from Embassy Court and only a five-minute stroll from the pebbled shoreline. As part of the rental agreement we also secured a garage, which became the perfect storage space for all our charity bits. I always seemed to live in places with posh-sounding names. Embassy Court sounded reasonably posh, but I also rented in 'Deauvelle Mansions', and the new abode was the regal-sounding 'Queensbury Mews.' It was a quiet little street, with Brighton's smallest pub tucked away at the end – The Queensbury Arms. Not only was it Brighton's smallest, but also one of the smallest in the country; I think it came in at number three or four. That sounded lovely and quaint but in reality it was too poky to be practical. It had two tiny tables with a maximum of six seats, and the bar itself was no more than two metres from the entrance. You couldn't swing a gerbil in there, never mind a cat. I remember going in for a pint and it was pretty embarrassing, even if you whispered like Bob Harris, the barman could decipher your entire conversation. The pavement outside was very narrow, so only a couple of plastic tables would be squeezed outside in the summer months. Most people who went there would just stand outside and drink. Even with the selling point of being one of the UK's smallest pubs, I don't know how they made any money.

Around this time, I started training for my first half marathon. I had always been a decent runner but had never really pushed myself in an endurance event before. Me, Ben, and a chap from work called Daniel decided to enter a half marathon in

Greenwich, called 'Run to the Beat'. It was a slightly unusual run, in that various bands performed live music along the route, usually beside hairpin bends, to give you more of a chance to hear some adrenaline-inspiring tunes. Brighton seafront was the perfect place to train; it was flat and wide, with a boulevard that ran for about four miles in one direction. The other route was a twisting road that followed the undulating cliff edge where the South Downs petered out into the English Channel. Being our first event, Ben and I took it quite seriously, with two training sessions a week – one focusing on distance, and a shorter one focusing on speed. In spite of the training, Ben refused to give up smoking. In fact, on occasions he would run whilst puffing away – he called it altitude training.

Most of the training for a half marathon, or indeed a full marathon, is mental. It's particularly difficult to force oneself out of bed when it's pouring with rain to go and schlep eight soggy miles along some cliff-tops (which I did on a fair few occasions). One morning, whilst returning from a particularly exhausting solo cliff-top run in the pounding rain, I was relieved to have reached Brighton promenade with less than a mile to go when I spotted something odd. It was early on a Sunday, around 9am, and incessantly drizzly so there was no-one around. In the distance I saw a huge camera dolly, about fifteen feet high, careering towards me. As it loomed nearer I saw a figure jogging underneath it, and as I approached him, I saw who it was- David Cameron. The Tory Party conference was taking place at The Grand Hotel that weekend, so this was obviously a bit of publicity footage for his leadership campaign that they were shooting. The hotel clearly had a gym inside, so he wasn't running in the rain for the sheer joy of it. I ran right past him and, feeling absolutely exhausted, all I could manage was an 'Alright Dave?'. He nodded and just carried on. I wish I could have thought of something cleverer to say.

It's often said that training for an endurance event is much harder than actually running it. I was surprised at how (relatively) easy I found my first half marathon. I had only trained up to 11 miles, but still managed to do the 13.1 (never forget the 0.1– that's the hardest part) without any major difficulties. I was quite chuffed with my time as well, one hour and forty-eight minutes. Ben also got a respectable time but didn't want to sign up for another. Almost straight away I put my name down for a full marathon that was taking place in Brighton eight months later. That was a different kettle of fish, though. I made the crucial mistake of thinking that with a half marathon under my belt, I could do a full marathon without much training. I can't remember the distance I trained to, I think it was about 15 or 16 miles, which wasn't enough.

The Brighton Marathon happened to be on one of the hottest days of the year. On top of that, I found out the week before that competitors wouldn't be allowed to run with headphones. This was a health and safety requirement so that the runners could hear approaching ambulances. I always trained to music, as it helped take my focus away from the pain, and I had prepared a specific distraction play-list for the day. There was no question of me running without it, so I ended up wearing a woolly hat to conceal my earphones, which then surreptitiously ran down my back. Unfortunately, 30-degree weather, a woolly hat, and running 27.2 miles, do not mix. Running that race was probably the hardest thing I have ever done but by hook or by crook I was going to emerge victorious. I was dead on my feet at the halfway mark. My pace slowed to a crawl, and although I finished, it was not a pretty sight. People say that running can add years to your life, and I think they're right; by the time I finished, I felt twenty years older. I had pulled a tendon in my leg, which meant I collapsed like a deflated jelly at the end. I was probably running on a damaged tendon for over half the race, so was in quite a lot of pain. Walking was gruelling for a few days afterwards. I had a big problem with stairs which I could only take one step at a time. After some physio, I was fine, but it probably took me a month to fully recover. I'd also injured my lower back slightly, so one of my Wing Tsun colleagues suggested a chiropractor. I was slightly dubious about how good he would be, but I was wrong to be sceptical. I stand corrected! I have run a couple of half marathons since then, but that remains my only full marathon experience.

In 2010, all the drama at work began. I had been in the department for three years and my current role for about two years at that point. To my mind, I had proved myself and done a good job under difficult circumstances. I was line-managing staff on five different sites and had reorganised the department, so everything was functioning smoother and with greater efficiency. I was told by the Head of Department that I would need to be re-interviewed for the role, which was fine. I later found out – the day before, in fact – that I was being interviewed alongside other candidates. Now, obviously I wasn't happy about this, but there was nothing I could do about it by this point. I found out a couple of days later that they had offered the job to someone else, and to rub further salt in the wound, they were being paid more than I was. To say I was livid, was an understatement. Not only would I be losing a job that I enjoyed (and initially been forced to do), but I would be going back down to a lower salary, and Ben – with only a week's notice – was being made unemployed. There were multiple meetings and visits to HR. They said I was only 'acting up' but I argued that doing a role for two years could never be considered 'acting up'. Their own guidelines stated that acting up could only be for twelve months' maximum, but they had got round this by changing the job title (hence a higher salary). Ben was obviously very upset as well, and him losing the role might ultimately have meant him moving out of our house. I thought I was being treated shoddily, especially in the light of Sue's death, so I told them I was resigning. I was then told that if I quit, I would have to pay back the money for my MA which still had one year to go. So, I was in a lose-lose situation: take the moral high ground and end up with a bill for £10,000, or stay in a job that felt demeaning considering the circumstances. It was sad, because I had given my all to the university. In one sense, I had learnt a valuable lesson. It was, however, a ridiculous moral to take away: don't get too attached to a role, because ultimately hard work and dedication is secondary to procedure and bureaucracy.

When my replacement, Emily started, I was at a low point. I was essentially working sixteen-hour days with my MA and charity work, so I was feeling burnt out as it was. I was told I had to induct her into doing my role, as well as re-learning my old job. Ben was now unemployed, so going off the rails a bit and drinking heavily at home. Throw into the mix an old girlfriend who I had fallen out with, deciding to join the same team as me and now working down the corridor, and it felt like the world was out to get me. It would have been comical if it wasn't so stressful. There was also the problem that me and the new boss didn't get along. There was a lot of resentment on my side, which was immature of me, but I couldn't let it go. Emily thought I was being obtuse, because I was by now refusing to do beyond the bare minimum. I thought she was incompetent, because there were parts of the role which she struggled to do as efficiently as me. I ended up doing a lot of her work anyway. Resentful reluctance floated around the office like ectoplasm in the hostile air. It was a pretty horrible time. What I really wanted was a fresh start, but I would have to wait another twelve months to finish my MA. That whole period was unrelenting, I felt like a salmon struggling against the cascading currents whilst trying valiantly to make it upstream.

I had a bit of a reprieve from all the stress that summer. I took a two-week unpaid sabbatical alongside some annual leave, in order to take a good chunk of time off work. They didn't want to give me unpaid leave, but I said I needed it to avoid having a stress-induced breakdown. It was a slight exaggeration, but it wasn't far off the mark; for the first time in my life, I was having trouble sleeping. Ben had managed to find another job so that had worked out okay. The guilt regarding me being responsible for him losing his role had started to fade. I planned a couple of holidays and some time back home in Canterbury. The first of these holidays was to Gibraltar, where I went that July with my mum. When you're caught between a rock and a hard place, it takes the edge off when the rock is a sun-kissed Mediterranean paradise.

Gibraltar is a fascinating place. Perched on the edge of the Iberian Peninsula, the rock, made of out Jurassic limestone, guards over a major shipping lane like some giant stone lighthouse. It stands 1400 feet high, so tall compared to the surrounding landscape that clouds congregate around the peak, forming a unique micro-climate. Gibraltar is a British Overseas Territory with a long and bloody history. Being so strategically important, it has changed hands several times over the centuries. with the Italians, the Vandals, the Dutch, and the Spanish all claiming it at various points. The rock has been British since 1713. It felt so strange to be walking down a high street with shops like WH Smith's and Marks & Spencer's in a humid Mediterranean climate, with this giant rock towering over you. It was almost like an Austin Powers parody version of an English town, with Union Jacks, red telephone boxes, and greasy spoons everywhere. The airport is also unique in the world, containing the only runway that has a major road intersecting it. That road, called Winston Churchill Avenue, is the main north-south thoroughfare which requires movable barricades to close when aircraft land or depart. It's an odd sight watching heavy traffic, cyclists, and pedestrians, going about their daily business whilst crossing a runway. The thing I loved most about Gibraltar was the monkeys, though technically they are Barbary apes – the only wild ones in Europe. They are incredibly clever creatures, sneaky, and capable of stealing anything and everything. You would witness them ganging up in these little monkey clans, distracting tourists and making off with their food. I saw one jump on someone's back, unzip his rucksack, and scamper off with his cheese and ham baguette. Totally brazen, they would even wander into some of the smaller tourist shops and hassle the staff. The baby ones were particularly adorable, though you needed to make sure you kept your distance. The last thing you wanted was a maddened monkey mum chasing you down the path.

The rock itself is gargantuan. Despite all the technology that exists, all the tunnels and caves still haven't been comprehensively mapped – some of them stretch for miles underneath the Alboran Sea. There was a rumour that some of the tunnels stretched all the way to Africa, which is how homo sapiens first arrived in Europe. Plainly untrue, but a good story nonetheless. Walking inside the rock is like venturing into a massive, calcified cathedral. The giant stalagmites almost resemble pillars, and the tiny cracks in the rock allow beams of light to penetrate into the upper chambers, as if illuminating some divine altar. There was seating in one of the larger chambers, called St Michael's Cave, which has been used as a theatre and occasional music venue since the 1960s. Various classical, jazz, and pop bands have played in there over the years due to the amazing acoustics. We took part in a caving expedition, along with a handful of other people, where we were led underground. We signed a disclaimer, which was our first indication that it would be quite treacherous in parts. We crawled and squeezed our way through these tiny passages that led us deeper and deeper into the rock. At times, we were in total darkness, when the torchlight wouldn't reach us. At one point, we clambered across this cavern on ropes, past what our guide described as 'an uncharted bottomless pit'. I was quite surprised that my mum agreed to do it, though once you were down there you didn't have much choice but to carry on. Luckily, no-one in our group suffered from claustrophobia. It was wonderfully tranquil down there, with just the occasional burbling noise from underground streams and the gentle dripping of water. Where these tributaries met, they had formed lakes and eroded gorges, which seemed to stretch for miles. I felt like a character from a Jules Verne novel, exploring all these secret caverns and passageways. You would glimpse all these strange shapes in the darkness, where your eyes would play tricks on you, making you think you were seeing gargoyles or monsters. When the torchlight fully illuminated them, it looked like they had been frozen in time by some great cataclysm, doomed to remain underground for all eternity. It's funny how the subconscious works. In dark, spooky places, it's never pretty flowers or a fluffy bunny rabbit that you think you are seeing, or if it is, it's more likely to be the creepy rabbit from Donnie Darko. I remember the guide telling us that the water down there had taken over ten years to seep down through 1500 feet of limestone. It was incredible to think that the water I was now drinking had fallen on the top of the rock whilst I was still at school and the World Trade Centre still dominated the New York skyline. I think they stopped doing these caving tours not long after our trip, due to health and safety concerns. Now, only professional cavers are allowed to go exploring inside. Maybe someone had stumbled into the bottomless pit and was still falling.

The proximity of Gibraltar to Morocco meant it was pretty convenient to do a day trip across the strait. The northernmost section of Morocco around the port is actually a Spanish enclave called Ceuta. As a territorial claim, it's probably equally as controversial as that of Gibraltar, although essentially having a buffer between Africa and Europe at its nearest point is politically convenient for the EU. We took the inevitable guided tour to Tangier, which was an interesting, if rather restrictive, experience. I've had my eyes broadened by visiting more places over the years, but travelling to an impoverished country for the first time is a real baptism of fire. Being such an obvious group of tourists, people would swarm around you, hassling for money. We were in a relatively touristy area, so we knew there were police nearby, but you were still very aware of being surrounded by a crowd that saw you as a walking dollar sign. Not realising the notes she had in her pocket, my mum gave this young child a huge sum of money for some chewing gum. We worked out later over lunch that it was the equivalent of about £200 in Morocco. When we arrived at our restaurant, our guides physically pushed all these people away from us and locked us inside this courtyard, behind an imposing metal gate. There was no chance of any real integration on this trip; it was very much us and them. I have got used to bartering over the years, but being such an alien concept to Westerners, it doesn't always come naturally. It's much harder to look in shops and peruse items when you are constantly being hassled to buy them. Even when you have no intention of purchasing something, it doesn't stop the traders from bartering and following you out of the shop. It didn't make for a relaxing trip, but then again, that was Moroccan culture. And if one is not willing to be accepting of other people's culture, then there isn't really any point in travelling. Seeing real poverty for the first time can be distressing, but simply by being there you are helping the local economy in a small way. Of course, it inevitably leads to comparisons with your own life, making you realise how lucky you are. It's an old saying, but it's as true today as ever: travel really does broaden the mind.

A couple of weeks after Gibraltar, I went to Bestival – an annual music festival that takes place on the Isle of Wight. I went with Josh and his girlfriend Emma, this being my first time properly meeting her. I had spoken with her briefly on a drunken night out when they first bumped into each other, but my memories are pretty hazy. I liaised with them in Portsmouth, and within about half an hour, Josh realised that he had left his ticket back home in Ross-on-Wye – an eight hour round trip. The tent they happened to bring was this huge family-sized thing that weighed a ton. So, whilst Josh trudged all the way back home, me and a girl I barely knew lugged two massive tents all the way up to the campsite. Josh finally turned up the following day, after spending hours trying to locate us in a sea of guy ropes, rainbow flags, and primary coloured nylon. The music itself was a mixed bag that weekend, with some tediously dull acts like Level 42. (I still have one of their branded whistles that they threw into the crowd.). The Flaming Lips, The Prodigy, and Echo & the Bunnymen, however, were all great. We were somewhat disappointed to have missed Rolf Harris (we were in the supermarket buying drink at that point), but the gods must have been telling us something, as a couple of years later he was imprisoned for sex offences. One of the highlights that year was meeting Mr Motivator. He was a mainstay on TV during the nineties when he would do exercise classes on Breakfast TV. Mr Motivator mostly wore tight-fitting and very colourful Spandex outfits for his fitness sessions, which he would narrate with incredible enthusiasm. He named all his exercises after everyday activities, so would shout out an array of catchphrases like, 'You're driving a car, you're driving a car', all the while bopping to a big beat gym soundtrack. Despite not having been on TV for over a decade, he looked exactly the same, still dressed in gaudy Lycra, and grinning away. A group of us did a workout there and then in the middle of the field. It wasn't the easiest thing to do, I was wearing cumbersome wellies and kept getting stuck in the boggy mud. Bestival was a much more relaxed festival than Reading, and I managed to add a number of bands to my ever-growing list of performers that I'd seen. For posterity, I thought I would list all the music acts that I've seen to date. Many of these I have seen multiple times. This list is by no means exhaustive. I haven't included cover acts or bands that I've seen but have no memory of (either through intoxication or boredom), but otherwise here is my artist inventory:

Marc Almond
Ash
Richard Ashcroft
Austel
Bad Manners
Bill Wyman & The Rhythm Kings
Billy Bragg
Blondie
British Sea Power
Jo Brown
Nick Cave & The Bad Seeds
Charlotte Church
Eric Clapton
Gaz Coombes
Elvis Costello
The Cult
Beck
Blur
Boy George
Phil Collins
The Courteeners
The Crystal Fighters
The Dandy Warhols
The Darkness
Dinosaur Junior
Dizzy Rascal
The Doves
The Duke Spirit
Bob Dylan
Echo & The Bunnymen
The Editors
The Eels
Electric Six
Eminem
Brian Eno
Fatboy Slim
Fear Factory
Feeder
The Flaming Lips
Florence & The Machines
Fleet Foxes
The Foals
Foo Fighters
Fun Lovin' Criminals
Liam Gallagher
The Gaslight Anthem
Glasvegas
Green Day
Harpo Smith
Heaven 17
The Hives
The Horrors
Hot Chip
The Jacksons
James
Janes Addiction
Jay Z
Elton John
Grace Jones
Tom Jones
Kaiser Chiefs
KC & The Sunshine Band
Kool & The Gang
The Killers
Level 42
The Libertines
Linkin Park
The Living End
The Lost Prophets
Manic Street Preachers
Marilyn Manson
Johnny Marr
Shane McGowan
Mike & The Mechanics
Laura Mvula
Mercury Rev
Metallica

Paul McCartney
The Moons
Chrissy Moore
Muse
The Offspring
PJ Harvey
Placebo
Robert Plant
The Polyphonic Spree
Iggy Pop
The Pretenders
Primal Scream
Pulp
The Prodigy
Queens Of The Stone Age
The Red Hot Chili Peppers
Nile Rodgers & Chic
The Rolling Stones
Roxy Music
Run DMC
Scritti Politti
Seasick Steve
Simian Mobile Disco
Staind
The Strokes
Slipknot
Smashing Pumpkins
Spiritualized
Starsailor
Status Quo
Steve Harley & The Cockney Rebels
The Stone Roses
The Strokes
Suede
Supergrass
System Of A Down
U2
The Undertones
The Wailers
Rufus Wainwright
The Waterboys
Weezer
Paul Weller
The White Stripes
The Who
Toyah Wilcox
Will I-Am
Bobby Womack
Neil Young

Back in Brighton, I started job hunting. I figured that if I got another job with a different team but still within the university, I wouldn't have to pay back the money for my Masters. After a couple of months, I got offered an International Retention role, which I thought would be a good springboard for what I wanted to do – counselling and advising students in Higher Education. After a few more tedious meetings with HR, it was agreed that I could leave the SS and not have to pay back the fees. However, as my project was on the university's Nursery Provision, I would still be based in that team one day a week.

One of the things I always loved about Brighton was the melange of unusual characters you would bump into. There were the celebrities that you would occasionally see, people like Chris Eubank, who walked around with a cane and a monocle like some Edwardian landowner. Then there were the random bohemian people you would just come across in the streets. One guy who I would regularly see in The Lanes had a skateboarding dog. It was this cute little Jack Russell that would jump onto his board and push himself along down a short incline. When he got to the bottom, he would carry the board in his mouth back up to the top of the slope and perform the same trick over again. He would always gather quite a crowd of excited people.

One day, Ben's new partner, Markus, was rhapsodising about his friend, a hilarious comedian called Lee Tracey and told me that I had to come round for dinner to meet him. When someone in Brighton invites you to dinner with an acquaintance that they have described to you as 'hilarious', you usually know you're in for a good time. We trekked across town to see this guy on a blustery Thursday evening. When we arrived, a miserable-looking old man opened the door. I assumed that this was someone else, his father perhaps. But no, this was the man we had journeyed to see. Markus introduced me, and this dour face simply said, 'You better come in then.' What followed was an incredibly monotonous two hours with a guy who was as miserable as sin. He seemed to have a permanent grey cloud over his head and a full portion of chips on his shoulder. I mentioned to him that I worked at a university. 'It's a waste of bloody time, if you ask me' was his blunt response. He looked and acted a bit like Victor Meldrew, just much more docile. Even his dog looked depressed. I asked him what he did, and he said that he was a comedian, but didn't do so much of it these days. In-between courses, I went to the bathroom and saw all these A6-sized picture frames dotted on the wall; there must have been about forty or so. They all had celebrity photos in them, people like Cilla Black, Bruce Forsyth, Paul McCartney, Freddie Starr, Michael Barrymore – a real who's who of British entertainers. Upon closer inspection, I noticed that Lee was in every single photo, posing or shaking their hands. We had a chat about it when I got back, and it turned out he had been doing the comedy and vaudeville circuit for about 40 years. In addition, he used to write catchphrases and punchlines for other people. I found this fascinating; pretty much any British light entertainment show had him in the credits – things like *The Generation Game* and *Celebrity Squares*. He had even come up with the catchphrases that other comedians had built their careers around, like Bruce Forsyth's 'nice to see you, to see you nice.' He answered a mystery that had been bugging me and my dad for 20 years, namely what the audience repeated back to Michael Barrymore every week on *Strike it Lucky*. It turns out that Lee had written all the scripts for that show, and told me that the audience responded with, 'Not a good spot.' [This won't make any sense unless you've watched the programme]. On the TV show it was always muffled, so you could never quite make it out. At least I had learned something that evening.

Lee had given us some free tickets to his upcoming gig but I wasn't planning on going. Markus eventually talked me into it and I went with four others – Markus, Ben, and two girls I worked with at the university, Jen and Oda. I was aware that lots of comedians took their work seriously and in private could be dour and a complete inversion of their on-stage personalities – people like Rowan Atkinson, for instance. However, I wasn't prepared for this guy's transformation. This frail, grumpy old man, who could hardly walk properly when I last saw him, came bounding on stage in a pink dress and Harpo Marx wig, and had the audience in hysterics for the next hour. I couldn't believe it was the same person. It was part comedy, part drag, and part dance act. It was an old-fashioned routine, but it didn't stop it from being hilarious. Afterwards, a few of us went backstage, and he was back to his usual grumpy self.

'Don't know why I bother, total waste of time. You'd get more appreciation from a bailiff. ' You couldn't figure out if it was genuine or he was just being deadpan. His USP was that he was Brighton's oldest drag queen. I don't know how old he was; on stage, he could have been in his 40s, but without make-up he was definitely seventy-plus. Lesson learnt – never judge a book by its cover, and I guess the drag show must go on.

Mark was the first of my friends to get married that year, to his long-term girlfriend, Flora. That year was also the first ever stag do I attended, up in Blackpool. Stags are renowned for featuring a random assortment of characters who would never normally hang out together, but this one was particularly weird. His best man was a guy called John Elmer, who was a mathematics genius – he was a contestant on the Channel 4 show, *Countdown,* and stayed unbeaten for a few weeks. There was also a chap who looked like a miniature David Cameron – he was a walking parody of a posh person, insisting on wearing a blazer and matching handkerchief for the duration of the weekend. We nicknamed him Mr Hanky. At the opposite end of the scale was a guy called Paddy, who was, without putting too fine a point on it, incredibly irritating. Josh had arrived late so ended up sharing a room with Paddy. I think it was on the first night that Josh had already had enough of him and locked him out, forcing him to sleep in the corridor. I had one in-depth conversation with Paddy that weekend that I've never forgotten. We were discussing potentially useful items that hadn't been invented yet. His idea was inflatable ladder chairs for music festivals and sporting events. A bit like those high chairs that lifeguards sit in around swimming pools, but inflatable, blow-up versions. He thought it was a brilliant idea whilst I was pointing out some of the many flaws with the concept. (They would annoy people, take forever to blow up, be a dangerous height, could potentially burst in a tightly packed crowd, would pretty quickly be banned, etc.). Anyway, when I pointed these out, he retorted that people didn't think the invention of the light bulb was a good idea at the time.

I remember thinking to myself, *You literally couldn't have thought of a worse example:*

a) The light bulb was a useful and life-changing invention that everyone agrees with
b) It was, in fact, such a good idea that the visual metaphor for a good idea is a light bulb!

I've no idea if he ever got around to designing and marketing his concept, but I certainly haven't seen him on *Dragon's Den* yet. Mark's brother, Tom, was something of a character as well. He seemed to have inherited Mark's old trait of inappropriate drinking. We came down for breakfast one morning and found him doing shots of Jägermeister – on his own! At 10am! We stayed in a pretty basic B&B on the edge of Blackpool. The owners thought we were incredibly well-to-do, one look at Mr Hanky would give anyone that impression. They told us that they had procured some southern cereal just for us. I wasn't entirely sure what southern cereal actually was, but it tasted fine. We didn't manage to do very much other than drink that weekend. The Pleasure Beach was closed due to high winds, and we never made it to Blackpool Tower. We did stay sober long enough to steal Mark's clothes and dress him up in a leather corset, though.

The wedding itself took place at St Mary Bredin Church in Canterbury. The church is located at the end of my parents' road, so my mum saw it as the perfect opportunity to gate-crash. It's always been hard to keep her away from a wedding, though in fairness it was only the gathering for the photos after the ceremony. It was all done on an extremely tight budget, but I think Mark had only just finished his PHD. It was the first, and I think only wedding I've been to without alcohol, not that it really mattered. I was one of four ushers, which was a pretty easy role. There wasn't really anywhere to usher people to – the ceremony and reception were all in the same place. Nevertheless, it was nice to see one of us finally tying the knot.

Later in 2011, I started seeing a girl who worked as an air stewardess for British Airways. She did a mixture of short and long-haul trips, so was often away for long periods. I didn't mind, it meant an uncomplicated relationship where I still had lots of weekends to myself. We were still organising various Men's Network events and that, alongside my MA, was keeping me busy. The big advantage was that, as cabin crew, she was allowed a certain percentage of what are commonly known as 'cling-ons'. This meant that I got to take free flights whenever she went on certain trips, often in Business and First Class. These trips were no longer than four or five days, but it was still amazing getting to see so much of the world without having to pay for flights or accommodation. Often the food and drink would be included, too.

Over the next three years, I got to travel to destinations that I would never have gone to, places like Mauritius and Mexico. Going First Class on British Airways really felt like living the high life (no pun intended). On one trip, I was reclining in one of the flat beds, chatting to the lady next to me. She had been saving for three years to go on this particular trip and had spent a small fortune on her ticket. I didn't have the heart to tell her that I was travelling for free. I was actually under explicit instructions not to tell anyone that, but having to make up a story would be equally as awkward. On another trip, I was seated opposite someone I vaguely recognised but I couldn't quite put my finger on it. My ex managed to get hold of the passenger list for me and it turned out to be Mark Owen from Take That. He was really friendly, and I think appreciated being sat near to someone who wasn't a star-struck female fan.

The flight deck crew on these trips could be hilarious. They would often try and sneak little messages over the tannoy to confuse the passengers. There were always debates about what they could get away with, and if it was something borderline inappropriate, they might mumble it instead. If you're ever on a BA flight and there's a passenger announcement that you can't quite decipher, that's probably the reason. I guess they needed to do something to release the tension on a twelve-hour flight.

'Hold on, I've just entered the Red Bull challenge,' was one I heard.

'That's the first cloud I've ever seen with a ski lift on it,' was another.

In the evenings, when we would be sitting around drinking in a Marriott, the more *risqué* stuff would come out. The things they wanted to try out but would probably get them fired if they dared.

'Ladies and gentlemen, if you look out of the port side window in a minute or two, you'll see me. Bye!'

Of all the BA trips I went on, I think the Yucatan peninsula in South East Mexico was probably my favourite. It's a stunning part of the world and, outside of the big resorts like Cancun, relatively unknown. The beaches were virtually deserted in terms of people, but swarming with sea turtles. The Hawksbill and Loggerhead Turtles had come ashore a few weeks before to lay their eggs. We happened to be there during the hatching season, so were able to witness one of the world's great natural wonders right in front of us. These were the turtles you always see on wildlife programmes, the ones that scurry down the beach in their thousands, hoping to make it to the safety of the waves. Vultures and other predatory birds were swooning overhead, trying to pick out the weak and the vulnerable. The noise of these lumbering creatures nonchalantly dragging themselves across the baking sand in unison was extraordinary, rather like a broom going back and forth very slowly over a scraper mat. I watched them for hours, it was an almost hypnotising experience. My other memory of that trip was wearing a comically oversized sombrero along the beach one day. It was a classic impulse buy from a tacky tourist shop, harmless enough until I happened to walk straight past a funeral that was taking place by the water's edge. Someone must have thought I'd misread the dress code. Sombre, whilst being only two letters away from sombrero, is a world apart in tone.

In August that year, I said an emotional goodbye to my first record player. My dad had given it to me ten years earlier – it was an original HMV listening post from the 1960s, and was pretty special. It had an incredible depth of sound, was attached to an in-built carry case, and still had the original dog insignia logo that became HMV's trademark. The logo is a small dog, head cocked, curiously looking into an early cylinder phonograph player. Here's an interesting story; This logo was based on a painting by a Liverpudlian artist called Francis Barraud. He painted it in the late 1800s after his brother, Mark, died. He noticed that his dog, a small fox terrier, would run over and listen intently to the phonograph whenever he played records of his deceased brother's voice. It was a sad but charming little story, which captured the public's imagination. It became HMV's corporate logo in 1900. The initials HMV stand for 'His Master's Voice' because of this. Anyway, I loved that record player. One day, it just stopped working, so I lugged it all the way to a musical repair shop in the North Lanes. The guy behind the counter examined it before pensively stroking his goatee beard in a downward motion, as if willing it to grow. He then drew a sharp intake of breath, the classic tell-tale sign that this wasn't going to be a straightforward job. After a few minutes, he deduced that it was the belt drive and damper plate that had finally worn out. Unfortunately, he said, nowhere in this country made spare parts for it any more. He could order them from abroad, but it would cost a fair whack – substantially more than a new record player would. I asked him if he could order the parts anyway, and two weeks later they were flown in from somewhere in Eastern Europe – I think it might have been Bulgaria. It was a huge expense, but I thought it was worth it. Then about six months later, the same thing happened, it suddenly stopped working again. I made a decision there and then not to keep paying for expensive repairs. I bought a new record player and binned the old one. Maybe, in retrospect, that was a mistake. Now I would probably have kept it, but I was trying to build up some savings and antique record repairs weren't within my budget. Still, I got a great ten years out of it.

My MA was finally coming to an end now. I had put together a business plan for our university nurseries, which suggested using our spare capacity to promote our services to the general public, thus allowing a subsidised rate to stay in place for staff and students. The Deputy Head of Nursery Services was a lady called Sarah, who seemed quite impressed. (She had some real rock 'n' roll connections, being Marc Almond's sister and also married to the lead singer of Gomez.) It seems crazy now, but even a few years ago, there was no sense of universities wanting to make a profit. Higher Education was considered to be a public service. As long as there was a bit of money to re-invest, no-one particularly cared. The profit margin was something like 2%, and I demonstrated how some simple restructuring of the business model could easily lead to a gross profit nearer to 10%. There were only two other nurseries within a three-mile radius, so the number of potential customers within the catchment area was huge. It felt a bit odd submitting a business plan to a department that I no longer wanted anything to do with, but at least I was leaving on a high note. After seven years of living the Brighton dream, I was more than ready to fly the coop. It was now on to bigger and better things.

CHAPTER 8

London Calling

In November of 2011, I went for an interview at the London College of Communication, one of six art colleges that made up the University of the Arts London (UAL). This was based in Elephant & Castle, creatively nicknamed Effluent & Castle by one of my mates. I always get asked by students where the name Elephant & Castle came from. It's such an exotic-sounding name (for South London anyway) that everyone assumes there is a fascinating story behind it. For many years it was assumed that the name is a translation of the Spanish phrase – *Infanta de Castile*, usually said to be a reference to Eleanor of Castile, the wife of Edward I (an infanta is the eldest child of the monarch without a claim to the throne). In actual fact, the name appears in English a hundred or so years before this. It's related to a 15th century craft guild who produced various implements like knives and scissors. The knife handles were made from Indian elephant ivory. A blacksmith, who set up his business in the local area, came up with an elephant and castle logo to denote the quality of the products he was producing. The castle refers to a howdah on the back of the elephant (in India, a seat traditionally used by hunters), connoting the idea that people had travelled to the furthest corners of the globe to produce these finely crafted implements. When the blacksmith's closed down, a public house opened in the same building and retained the name and sign. It became the Elephant & Castle public tavern, which is actually referenced in Shakespeare's *Twelfth Night*. (Interestingly, although the play isn't set in England, it was cheekily inserted for advertising purposes, being a short, drunken stagger from the Globe Theatre.) The name was so eye-catching that people started referring to the area as Elephant & Castle rather than just the pub. Over time, it replaced the official name of the area which was Newington Butts. So, the name is basically an early example of a clever advertising slogan entering the English lexicon.

Elephant & Castle is now virtually unrecognisable from a decade ago, before gentrification kicked in. The notorious Highgate Estate was still in existence back then. This was the setting for any British film or crime drama that wanted to shoot on a council estate, to show inner city urban decay. Pretty much every episode of *The Bill* had scenes shot there. It was also widely used for various music videos as a grimy urban background, Madonna's 'Hung up' video, for instance. I remember walking round the estate when I turned up early for my interview, just to get some sense of the surroundings. It was pretty foreboding. Lots of residents had moved out by then, with only a handful of dodgy characters remaining which gave it a real post-apocalyptic vibe. Afterwards, I went to the equally infamous Elephant & Castle shopping centre. The name was somewhat erroneous – when you think of shopping centres, you think of big-name stores and shiny retail outlets. This was mainly a maze of fried chicken shops, Western Unions, and dodgy herb stalls, in the middle of a huge traffic gyratory. It was opened in 1965 as the first covered shopping centre in Europe, and was ground-breaking at the time. The initial enthusiasm quickly subsided and it soon became a building of derision – it was once voted the ugliest building in Britain. There was a brief period in the 1990s when they decided that the best way to inject some vibrancy into the building was to paint it bright pink. One of my work colleagues later described the shopping centre as being like the Star Wars cantina from *A New Hope*, 'a wretched hive of scum and villainy'. Certainly, many of the patrons in there didn't look human.

You could buy some very strange things in that place. I remember once when I was warding off a cold, I popped over there to buy some echinacea. I'd only recently discovered how effective echinacea was, but having only pronounced it a handful of times, it was never on the tip of my tongue. In my slightly fatigued state I went up to the counter and spoke with the shop assistant.

'Excuse me, do you have any euthanasia?'

The shop counter assistant looked a bit confused and asked me to repeat myself.

'Euthanasia pills.'

'I think so,' she replied. 'I just need to go in the back and check.'

I stood there whilst she went off to the stock room, and quickly realised what I had said. When she came back, I corrected myself – much to her relief, I imagine. It honestly wouldn't have surprised me if there were such a thing floating around somewhere in the shopping centre. There was always talk of knocking it down and redeveloping the site, but it somehow managed to cling on to life. Eventually, the land became too valuable for an oddball 1960s relic to survive, and the wrecking balls finally turned up in September 2020 to condemn it to an ignominious grave.

The interview itself was in a 60s tower block overlooking these two glamorous locations. It looked very precarious, like an overambitious giant had made it by playing a game of Jenga out of enormous metal blocks. Walking inside was like entering an oasis of calm after my initial experience of the local area. My interview was on the twelfth floor of the tower block, so I had pretty impressive views stretching out to Canary Wharf and the docklands in the east. The job was a role that wasn't widely known across the sector – International Student Experience. Simply put, this was a mixture of pastoral support, 1-1 counselling, events organisation, and academic development for International and EU students. One of the things that tipped the scales in my favour (apparently) was my insistence on doing a pre-prepared presentation. This wasn't an official part of the process, but my enthusiasm seemed to win them over. By the end of the day, they had offered me the role.

I quickly realised how difficult it was to find accommodation in London, compared to Brighton. Anything decent would get snapped up incredibly quickly. I spent a few days over Christmas searching in areas around Clapham, one of the few districts that I vaguely knew. Dray had spent some time living there before sharing a flat with his sister, so I'd had a few nights out there over the previous couple of years. It was also a convenient location, being only five or so tube stops away from Elephant & Castle. After a while, I gave up trying to find anywhere nice, and just settled on whatever I stumbled across as a temporary measure. I ended up renting a room in a grotty little apartment block just off Cavendish Road.

I had my Brighton leaving do in February 2012 at one of our local cocktail bars. It was a good turnout – about thirty people came along to say goodbye (or to make sure I actually left). One of my mates was working as the bartender, so there were a lot of free drinks flowing. I even jumped behind the bar and had a go at making cocktails/pulling pints for the first, and so far, only time in my life. Some interesting cocktails got served up that evening. I gave up following a recipe and just bunged it whatever I thought would work. I seem to recall Ribena, whisky, and a chocolate liqueur with raspberries on top – safe to say it was not my forte. It was quite hard saying goodbye to my Wing Tsun class. I was just about to reach technician level, with my final grading being only a few weeks away. The start of the lease on the flat didn't quite tie in with the start of my new job, so for a week or so I was doing the Brighton-London commute. That helped to ease the big smoke transition somewhat.

The new flat was very basic. The two guys I was sharing with were decent enough blokes, but they lived like complete animals. It was more like a squat than a flat, with piles of washing-up that never moved during the six weeks I lived there. There was a constant buzzing of flies permanently circling around the accumulating filth. It was too much for me – it was like the house in *The Young Ones*. Everything these guys ate came from either a packet or the singular plate that they kept in their rooms. I did attempt to clean up part of the kitchen when I arrived, but no sooner were a few things scrubbed and cleansed than they would straight away get used and be back on the towering pile again. After that, I just gave up with the cleaning. One of the guys whose name eludes me was a bit of a nutcase. He would keep stacks of chocolate in his room. It was approaching Easter, and he'd come back from the shop with all these Easter eggs which he would then proceed to scoff in one marathon session. He would then be throwing up for the next few hours and then start all over again. I know bulimia is a serious illness, but he did himself no favours with his diet of Easter Eggs and Carling. We only had one bathroom, with no real lock on the door. You would be in the shower having a nice relaxing scrub, when all of a sudden he'd rush in and start throwing up in the toilet. You'd never see that on a Head & Shoulders advert. It certainly wasn't the most serene of experiences. I didn't even bother to unpack most of my boxes. I knew I wouldn't be staying long.

The first day of my new job was interesting. No sooner had I walked in the entrance than a middle-aged woman barged past me and started running out of the door with a trail of papers falling at the wayside. My new manager then came over to me looking very worried.

'I'm sorry, Chris, things are a bit hectic this morning. My boss has just run off.'

Her boss, the lady who had just barged past me, was the (now ex) head of the college. By all accounts she was a crazy character. She had been accused of embezzling money, and had hired a famous public relations man called Max Clifford to find out which members of staff were responsible for leaking this to the press. Her last day was my first day at the college during which the police came round interviewing various people. It was a big story at the time, making several newspapers, and it meant that the building was in a state of chaos when I arrived. She had fired numerous people over the preceding three years and various KPIs had taken a tumble as a result. Part of my role, I discovered, was to try and address this from an International Students' perspective.

It was an odd first day, because it was all anyone could talk about. Once all the drama with the media settled down, I started to relax into my new job. I had a great team around me. I was part of an International Development office that included people working on recruitment, exchanges and student funding. It was a complete mixture of ages, with people from 25 all the way up to 65. Annette, one of the older ladies, had been working at the college since the early 70s. When she had first joined as a photography tutor, she taught

Johnny Rotten and Sid Vicious (from the Sex Pistols) for a term. Another of my colleagues, Cath, was friends with the band The Undertones, and did a photo-shoot for them which became the front cover of their Best of album, *All Wrapped Up*. For this, she wore a dress made out of meat – mostly streaky bacon and sausages. She told me that these were leftovers from a full English breakfast that she once cooked up for the band when they briefly shared a flat in Camberwell. It gained further notoriety when Lady GaGa wore a similar dress in 2010. The London College of Communication (LCC) had so many interesting connections like these.

Being part of the world's second largest arts university meant thousands of famous people had studied there. People like Pierce Brosnan, Jarvis Cocker, John Rankin, Stella McCartney, John Hurt – the list is endless. Incredibly, 40% of all Turner Prize winners have been UAL alumni. It was such a joy to be working in such a creative environment, with exhibitions and private views happening at regular intervals throughout the year. It was a refreshing change of pace from the dusty corridors of Brighton University. During those first few weeks, I got to take part in some really interesting projects. It was great finally having my own budget and being able to spend it however I saw fit. One of the things I was most proud of was an International Skype booth that I designed. This was a confidential space where students could Skype family back in their home country. I designed the space, hired some builders to construct it and decorated it with a time zone map and some incredibly funky light bulbs.

Considering that the London College of Communication had 'communication' in its title, it was incredible how much miscommunication went on. Usually, it was just irritating little things, but occasionally there would be a massive blunder that made us all look ridiculous. I recall a document that we had published which was relatively straightforward, just a list of our courses that we could hand to International visitors. The document had been proofread, sent to print, and delivered in large numbers. When it arrived my colleague straight away noticed that rather than 'Post Graduate Courses' it read 'Pot Graduate Courses' in the main title. We really didn't need to advertise the fact that there were pot graduates in an art college. We all thought this was hilarious, and it resulted in various druggy puns flying around the building. *Which dopey person did this? Why do they have such a high opinion of themselves?* And such like.

A few years later, I attended a talk by an info-graphic designer called Matt Cooper. He was one of the people responsible for designing the monolith maps that you see peppered all over London, usually around tube and rail interchanges to help tourists get their bearings. He was the keynote speaker at our annual conference that year, and it was he who made me realise that Elephant & Castle (and, by definition, the building I work in) is the exact geographical centre of London. Conventional wisdom has always dictated that the area around Charing Cross is the beating heart of the capital, but if you look at a map, that isn't strictly accurate. Elephant & Castle is the convergence of five major roads which meet there. If you travel in a straight line from the five key bridges in Central London (Westminster Bridge, Waterloo Bridge, Blackfriars Bridge, Southwark Bridge, and London Bridge) you end up in Elephant & Castle. A further two bridges (Lambeth & Tower Bridge) take you to within the area, if not the roundabout itself. Within 1000 metres of the Elephant, there are two major train termini (Waterloo and London Bridge) and seven tube stations. Charing Cross, by comparison, has five tube stations and only 1.5 train stations (Waterloo and Charing Cross) within the same distance. The tube map suggests that Elephant & Castle is on the fringes of Zone 1, when in actual fact it's horizontally parallel to

Belgravia and Buckingham Palace. The winding Thames distorts the map in such a way that most people don't realise its further north than, say, Earl's Court or Kensington. Quite why the area remained unloved for so long is a mystery, considering its prime location and amazing transport links. I am always reminded of this whenever I hear the noise outside from some major event, whether that be Donald Trump's visit in 2018 or the London Bridge terror attacks. Often, I will hear the commotion from the sirens or the roar of helicopters before anything appears on Twitter or the BBC news. It's the unglamorous equivalent of being in Times Square during some major international incident.

One of the many things I love about working in such a diverse environment is the knowledge you gain from different cultures. Whenever I run workshops with students or external overseas visitors, I inevitably learn something new. I've probably learned thousands of interesting titbits over the years. For instance, in South Korea a tick on a form or exam paper means that an answer is wrong; in Bulgaria shaking your head from side to side means yes (the opposite to everywhere else); and in Iran giving someone the thumbs-up is equivalent to giving them the middle finger. That last one in particular was a seriously embarrassing *faux pas* on my part. I was conducting a tour for a delegation from Iran in advance of a meeting later that day. I asked them to wait in the corridor whilst I popped into one of our photographic darkrooms to check that it was safe. When I came back out again, I gave them a big thumbs-up gesture, assuming that they knew it meant it was now okay for them to follow me. There was a bit of muttering and nervous laughter. Only later on in the boardroom did one of the Iranian professors explain to me what it meant. He had taken it in good humour, but I was pretty mortified for the rest of the afternoon. There was another incident when I was teaching a CTS class and there was a bit of a slanging match going on between a UK and a Russian student. After trying to calm the situation down, it turned out that the UK student had thought that the other girl was deliberately insulting her. They had used a Russian expression, 'Don't blame the mirror for your ugly face.' The British girl had taken it as a personal insult, when in actual fact it's Russia's blunt version of the British idiom, 'A bad workman always blames his tools.'

Later that year, the UK finally said goodbye to Teletext. Teletext, also known as Ceefax, was basically a real-time information service that was available on televisions before the digital switch-over, when most signals were analogue. During the 1990s, this was an information mecca, with TV listings, news, weather, and sports, all available at the touch of a button. We didn't have it at Lansdown Road, but whenever I visited friend's houses I was always transfixed by it. The font and format were incredibly primitive. There were no photos, images or interactivity, just pages and pages of primary colour text against a jet-black background. On many TVs you couldn't even skip pages, but had to wait for the relevant content to roll back round on its perpetual loop. It was basically how an early version of the internet might have looked in North Korea – one without interactivity, speed, or choice. Despite its painful limitations, though, it was a great way to pass the time, particularly the quiz page 'Bamboozled', which was strangely addictive. Growing up, most kids I knew watched it for the football scores, whereas I enjoyed flicking through the Foreign & Commonwealth Office travel advice pages, telling you which countries to avoid for what reasons and where various infectious diseases had been identified. The best thing about Ceefax was the simplistic impartiality of it; it was a voice of quiet authority, with no angle or spin whatsoever. It was entirely straight, irreproachably trustworthy, even its name 'see facts' was devoid of all frippery. There was no right wing/left wing ironic angle – you knew exactly where you were with it. In April, the signal was finally switched off in the South East. I was down in Brighton on the day it ceased broadcasting, so we had a little party to mourn its passing. We sipped gin and tonic as the screen faded to an eternal blackness.

By now I had moved out of the 'Young Ones' flat and into a period Edwardian house. Dray had also been looking to come back to Clapham, so we recruited two of his friends that he met travelling, and we all moved in together. It was the nicest place that I had lived in up until that point. It was spacious, had a nice sized garden, and was only a five-minute stroll from Clapham Common. Again, I had a semi-famous actor for a neighbour – Alex McQueen, who had starred in programmes like *The Inbetweeners, Peep Show* and *The Thick of It.* Clapham was quite a posh area – the kind of place where you could only dream of owning the kind of house we were renting. To give you a sense of how posh it was, I recall going to the local fish and chip shop with some orders from my housemates. It was all pretty normal stuff like battered sausages, cod, and of course chips. However, when I got there, I was informed that they didn't have any chips. I assumed they were joking at first, but no, the manager assured me that chips were not on the menu. I came back with three smoked salmon salads instead. Hardly a fitting substitute for a Friday night takeaway.

The two big London events that year were the Queen's Diamond Jubilee and the London Olympics. The jubilee marked sixty years since Elizabeth II's accession to the throne, which was celebrated with a parade of boats down the Thames. I went down to watch from Vauxhall Bridge, where 670 boats took part in a procession which I believe was a world record for the number of vessels at a singular event. It was a grey, windswept day, and the crowds were probably twenty deep along the banks of the Thames. Me and my then girlfriend appeared to be the only British people down there in the trenches. Everyone else was from the far-flung corners of the globe, with predictably very excitable Americans and Australians standing out from the pack with their cheering and waving of union jacks. The balconies of the penthouses that lined the banks were packed to the rafters with barbecues and beer bellies – the more muted British response. The royal barge itself was in sight for no more than two minutes, though it was surprisingly easy to spot everyone. I remember being impressed that the Duke of Edinburgh, at the grand old age of 92, was standing and waving for two hours' straight. That was the last time I remember a real euphoria and national pride in the institution of the monarchy. Six or so years later, the media were much more cynical, particularly in light of the scandals that surrounded Prince Andrew, and to a lesser extent Harry and Meghan.

The 2012 London Olympics almost completely passed me by. For some reason, everyone in Brighton had been so negative about it during the build-up. Everyone I spoke to thought it was going to be an embarrassing failure, with most of my friends and colleagues not bothering to try and secure tickets. The allocation system was also a bit odd. I personally was put off by having to buy bundles of tickets and not knowing which events you would get. In retrospect, not going to the 2012 Olympics (which was by now pretty much on my doorstep) was a big mistake. Me and my housemates watched it on TV with a dawning realisation that it was actually pretty special. In terms of heart and creativity, it seemed to eclipse the 2008 Olympics in Beijing, and there was a real euphoria in London for weeks afterwards. Suddenly everyone seemed proud to be part of a modern, multicultural Britain (this was still four years before the Brexit vote). Oh well, I guess I'll end up going in 2048.

One of the things I always found strange were people's attitudes towards my living in London. Katy's family, for instance, would always ask me if I felt safe or if I was worried about terrorism. Those thoughts had barely crossed my mind. People who have never lived here have this strange notion of it being a busy, dangerous, polluted hellhole. It's pretty much like any global city, in that it has nice parts and not so nice parts, but that's bound to happen if you put eight million people together. People also cling to the idea that places don't evolve and change over time. Even now (in 2021), people from Kent say to me, 'Isn't Brixton scary as hell?' They still associate it with the Brixton riots and the race wars from decades ago. If I tell them that houses there are easily in excess of a million pounds, they look at me like I'm from another planet. The benefits of London far outweigh the negatives. You have everything you could possibly want in abundance. I have been to countless exhibitions and shows that I would never have gone to if I hadn't have moved here. Ai Wai Wai, for instance – an exiled Chinese artist – put on this amazing show at The Royal Academy of Arts that I saw in 2015. There was David Bowie's retrospective at the V&A in 2016, and this amazing glass sculpture collection at Kew Gardens in 2019. These are all things that people travel from all corners of the globe to visit, yet they were all just here, sitting on my doorstep. I remember after me and my wife bought our house, Katy was very excited for us.

'I can't believe you're within a twenty-minute drive of Ikea,' she said. 'That's amazing!'

'We're not,' I replied. 'We're within a twenty-minute drive of two Ikeas!'

I had been taking regular trips back to Brighton to attend Men's Network meetings over the course of 2012. The charity was growing bigger, with an excess of thirty volunteers and an annual turnover in the tens of thousands. That year, we organised a Father's Day event. We hired out some volleyball courts on Brighton Beach and held a tournament for dads who, for whatever reason, couldn't be with their children. It was really successful and we even managed to get a small piece on the local ITV news. Not only were we holding events almost every weekend, but there were now programmes that Ben and Glenn were running throughout the week. For instance, they organised a work experience programme with the city council where they would visit disadvantaged kids on housing estates and help them find volunteering opportunities. Rather than simply raising money for other charities, we had almost become a fully-fledged charity in our own right – albeit one led entirely by volunteers. However, it was becoming increasingly difficult for me to commit. Inevitably, living sixty miles away meant that I was becoming a bit-player and was starting to feel left out of certain decisions. So, after four years, I made the difficult decision to step down.

Buckets are contradictory objects. On the one hand, they are the most mundane of everyday items. On the other, they have acquired a semi-mystical alternative existence, first as a door marked Exit between this world and the next, and secondly as a receptacle for all dreams and must-do life experiences. My 'bucket list' had around twenty or so things that I endeavoured to do before I turned forty. As of 2020, I have managed to tick around half of these off. That year, it was the turn of Glastonbury, which I had been wanting to go to for years. Every time it rolled round, I seemed to miss the opportunity. I either couldn't get a group of committed people together, or I'd find out that it was a fallow year (in order for the ground to recover, every four years the festival takes a break). Unlike other festivals, it required military-style organisation. Tickets would sell out in less than half an hour, so you needed to have a group of dedicated people, preferably eight of you (the most number of tickets you could purchase), in order to maximise your chances. In 2013, I finally had seven other people who wanted to go, including Feraz and my house-mate Claire. All of us were online at 7am on a Sunday morning, frantically refreshing the pages. With just two minutes before they sold out, I managed to secure the eight precious tickets.

It was worth all the effort. It was easily the most impressive festival I'd ever been to – a sizzling symphony of sights, smells, and sounds. Nothing prepares you for the sheer size of the place. The outer fence forms an eight-mile radius, making it the size of a large town. Inside, there are nearly a hundred different stages, including everything from comedy sets to politics debates. In fact, Glastonbury is unique in that you could go there, not see a single music act, and still have an amazing time. There were massage tents, cooking classes, writing clubs, trapeze artists – you name it, it was there. You needed to plan who you wanted to see, as it could easily take up to an hour to walk anywhere. I learnt that on the first day, when I missed Brian Cox running an astronomy lecture. The weather that year was, by and large, pretty good, although I made the crucial error of only bringing one pair of shoes. There was a small amount of rain on the Wednesday we arrived and, of course, sharing a campsite with 200,000 other revellers meant that the major thoroughfares would very quickly turn to mud. My shoes were pretty much destroyed within two hours of arriving – caked in two inches' worth of organic Somerset mud. I quickly binned them and bought a pair of (predictably expensive) Hunter wellies. The second I did, the sun came out in all its blazing glory, and we had sweltering weather for the following four days. Although you can pretty much get away with wearing whatever you want at festivals, wearing wellies in 35-degree heat definitely drew some strange looks.

Seeing Bruce Forsyth was a definite highlight, and I was surprised at how entertaining he was. His show was a mixture of singing standards, some comedy, a bit of magic, and some tap dancing. The tap dancing was great; he did about ten seconds before he said he needed a rest, pulled out a ladderback chair, and then carried on whilst sitting down. On the Saturday, I got to the front of the Pyramid Stage at 11am and stayed there for the whole day. It meant I was in the front row for Elvis Costello, Primal Scream, and the headliners, The Rolling Stones. It took a lot of discipline to stand in the sun for twelve hours, but I had a bottle of Glenlivet to keep me going. There were so many great acts that weekend. I saw Bobby Womack in one of his last performances before he passed away, and during the Smashing Pumpkins, I saw the one and only crowd-surfer of the weekend, surfing on a full-sized mattress. Funnily enough, my future wife, Debs, was also at Glastonbury that weekend. Who knows, I may have bumped into her at some point? Maybe it was sunny Somerset synchronicity?

Festival crowds can often be as entertaining as the acts you go to see. The smaller festivals, in particular, will often attract a rag-bag assortment of interesting characters. A couple of years earlier, I went to an Irish music festival, and in true rock 'n' roll spirit, I took my mum. I didn't want to presume that a music festival where over 90% of the audience were Irish would be an inebriated mess, but let's just say the crowd lived up to their notoriously boozy reputation. Shane McGowan was stumbling around on stage completely sozzled not even sure what he was supposed to be singing. Meanwhile, half the audience was facing the wrong way and bumping into each other, singing *Fairytale of New York* to every song. Someone else was hugging my mum, thinking that we knew Bob Dylan because we had backstage passes. My favourite quote of that day was when we were waiting to see a folk singer called Christy Moore. My Mum and I had no idea who he was but everyone around us couldn't contain their excitement. Then, in the most stereotypically slurred North Dublin accent you could think of, a guy turned to us and said, 'They say Jesus Christ could walk on water, but he couldn't play the guitar like Christy Moore.'

I love the fact that that quote, rather than being applied to a Hendrix or Clapton-type figure, was reserved for an inauspicious man from County Kildare.

Back in London, I was regularly being 'bribed' by students (and their parents) at work. Although I had no sway over assessed work and degree classifications, it didn't stop them from trying. However, one thing I was responsible for was investigating students who weren't attending classes, or had issues that were affecting their academic performance. That would usually involve me having a 1-1 with the student in question and trying to root out what the problem might be. Sometimes they would bring a friend along, and in extreme cases, family members would be present. In some of their cultures, failure is simply not an option. Sometimes they were terrified of being withdrawn or their parents finding out, and would do anything they could to avoid that 'shame'. Higher education isn't cheap in this country, and whilst there is a perception that all our international students come from rich families, that obviously isn't the case. I know of many instances where the family has scraped and saved for over twenty years so that their only child can go to a prestigious British university. The guilt of that student then failing, or being withdrawn in the first year, was too much for some of them to bear. I've had all manner of things bought for me – chocolates, bottles of wine, theatre tickets – none of which we are officially supposed to accept. I've even had two marriage proposals from mothers offering me their daughters! They said, in all seriousness, if I allowed their daughter to pass, I could marry her and come and live in their family abode. I had to politely decline and explain that the decision ultimately didn't rest with me. Sometimes students would buy me gifts as a thank you, with no strings attached. These were okay to accept. I remember one student brought me a bottle of champagne to say thank you for helping her out with her progression statement. I know next to nothing about champagne, so I brought it home where one of my housemates exclaimed, 'Wow! That's an £800 bottle of champagne!' I checked and indeed it was; a rare 'Moet & Chandon Nebuchadnezzar Brut Imperial'. I saved it for the following night, when I suggested that we make Champagaboms. These are champagne mixed with Jägermeister and then drunk as shots – the kind of thing that city boys with too much money might drink to show off. I'm not a particular fan of champagne, so I thought why not use it as a mixer? Downing the kind of drink that should be savoured with my housemates, made us feel like rock stars. Good times.

In 2014, I turned thirty. Apart from eighteen, it's probably the most significant birthday to make you reflect on things. My life was pretty positive: I had a job that I loved, had finished paying off my student loan and most of my mates were now living in London. I had also started learning Tai Chi. I had wanted to carry on with Wing Tsun, but the particular style that I learnt was only taught in two places in London, both quite far away from Clapham. I went to a class nearby to try out another form of Wing Tsun, but I found learning something that was familiar yet subtly different to be quite irritating. I opted to try Tai Chi because I knew how well it complimented other martial arts, whilst being an interesting and more relaxing art form in its own right. I attended Tai Chi regularly for about four years once I'd started training. For my birthday I decided to go on a trip to Edinburgh for a long weekend. Accompanying me were Josh, Bjorn, Hass, Slater, and his girlfriend at the time, Kat. We had an interesting time visiting Edinburgh Castle, doing ghost tours, and generally just larking about. We also discovered the delights of deep-fried Mars bars. Interestingly, the deep fried Mars Bar was one outcome factor on research done on the 'Glasgow effect', whereby the city had a notably higher mortality rate than other British cities of a similar size and scale. Having sampled the offending snack, I can honestly say that I believe it.

My dad, aged 10

My mum in the early 70's

Little old me - 1985

Little old me with my mum

Outside our record shop - 1986

With my dad in the Turner Street flat

Ramsgate in winter- 1987

Brothers in Arms

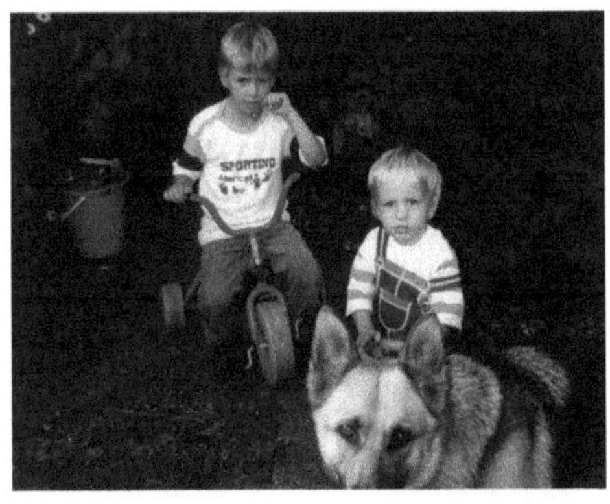

With my brother and our dog, Sally - 1990

Colchester- 1993

Year 6 School photo - 1995

Canterbury East train station, with Bjorn and Matt- 1996

Geography field trip - 1999

Last day of school- 2002

Halloween at Sussex University

Celebrating Euro 2004

Graduation - 2005

Brighton seafront with
Matt & Katy

Lad's holiday in Newquay - 2006

Tash Dash - 2010

Drink driving on the Norfolk Broads - 2011

Working the bar at my own leaving do - 2012

Glastonbury: Front row of the pyramid stage - 2013

Selection of gig tickets

Blending in with the locals- Bangkok -2014

Me and Debs- Halloween - 2015

Valentine's Day - 2016

First day in our new house-
December - 2017

Real life Mario Kart

Butlin's Stag do - July 2018

Debs on her Hen Do

Santa Monica Pier - California

Cutting of the wedding cake

Wedding day bliss - September - 2018

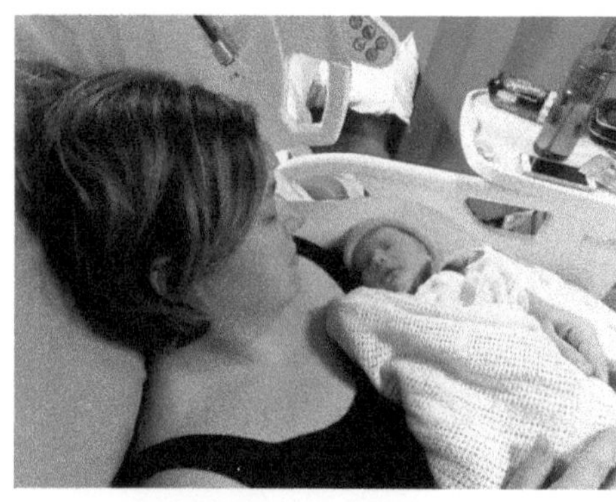

Amber - a few hours old - February 2020

Tummy time at two months

Lockdown baby - May 2020

The Bryant's on holiday - August 2020

CHAPTER 9

Travelling

I had always wanted to undertake some form of solo travelling but had never really found an appropriate time. Now that I had turned thirty, I thought this could be my last opportunity before relationships and mortgages inevitably got in the way. Work were very accommodating and let me take an unpaid sabbatical for a few months. Once that was all agreed and I had some cover in place, I started planning where I wanted to go, narrowing it down to two options: South America and South East Asia. After some deliberation, I thought South East Asia would be a bit more varied, and being more compact, would allow me to visit a greater number of countries. I planned to do a mix of guided tours, group trips, and parts of it solo. Glenn, my brother's gambling-obsessed friend, was living in Bangkok at the time, so I planned on visiting him whilst I was out there. It was more work organising that trip than one might expect. I had to move out of my house and put everything into storage, get various vaccinations, plan my route, and book places to stay in-between all the various tours. Getting money out of the *bureau de change* was a strange experience, with the cashier counting out these seemingly gargantuan sums. One Vietnamese dong was equivalent to 0.00003 British pounds then, so the denominations I was receiving were like something out of a gangster film. As she was counting aloud, 'Eight million, nine million, ten million,' I did instinctively glance behind me. I didn't want to get mugged walking down the Strand, only to have the disappointed assailant return the money to me.

Vietnam was my first destination. The journey took about twenty hours, over two connecting flights. By then, I was a much better traveller than I used to be; the sickness had got a lot less severe over the years, but I still had to watch what I ate. Sleep was also out of the question. If there was one thing guaranteed to make me nauseous, it was suddenly waking up on something that was in motion. Even when I travelled as a 'cling-on' in a flat bed, I never actually went to sleep. Clearly, the benefits of First Class travel were wasted on me. I remember flying over Crimea, mainly because the shape of it reminded me of the Isle of Wight. Russia had annexed Crimea in March that year, so it had been featured in the news quite a bit. As I gazed down upon it, I wondered how safe it actually was and had that nagging presage at the back of my mind that something might go awry. *Was there anyway that the fighting going on down there could potentially reach any aircraft?* Those thoughts later proved to be spookily prophetic.

Landing in Ho Chi Ming City was a real baptism of fire. No matter how prepared you think you are, you still end up stumbling around in a jet-lagged stupor whilst being bombarded with an array of new sights, smells, and sounds. Somehow, being in a humid tropical climate just makes everything that much more intense. Even on the short two-minute walk to the taxi rank, I was surrounded by ten or so people bartering for my custom.

Vietnam has changed a lot since I was there. There was only one real motorway in the country then and cars were not very common, at least amongst the general population. Car prices were kept high by import and sales taxes, which made Vietnam one of the most expensive countries in the world to buy a vehicle. Instead, everyone rode motorbikes, with 45 million of them registered in the country – the highest per head ownership in the world. As soon as you stepped out of the airport, you were surrounded by them. People would transport anything and everything on the back of them – children, sofas, pets, cages of chickens. They were often piled precariously high, sometimes two or three times the height of the bike itself. Whilst I was there, we had a little competition to take a photo of the most ridiculous thing we witnessed on the back of a motorbike. I won it when I saw another motorbike haphazardly perched on the back of one.

Crossing the road was a perspiration-raising ordeal. Traffic lights were pretty much non-existent. My guide later told me that the secret was just not to look; you simply had to walk in a straight line and the motorbikes would swerve around you like a stampede of wildebeest avoiding an obstacle. It was a difficult thing to master. Instinctively, you wanted to try and dodge them, but that was far more dangerous. Eventually, it became second nature, but it was a weird sensation, almost like feeling invincible. (There's a scene in the Film *World War Z* where Brad Pit injects himself with a virus whilst rampaging zombies charge around him like he's invisible. It felt like a similar experience to that.)

I met up with the rest of my tour group the following day. I was the only British person amongst them, the others being American, Canadian, Japanese, and Australian. We would spend a few days in Ho Chi Ming before travelling up the coast of the country. It was a fascinating city, for many years called Saigon (a Westernised name given by the French in the 1860s), that sits on the edge of the Mekong Delta. During the Vietnam War, it was the capital of South Vietnam, the area that sat below the 17th Parallel. It was a capitalist and anti-communist state which fought against the communist North Vietnamese and their allies during the Vietnam War, with the assistance of the United States. The Viet Cong (the Northern soldiers) were supported by the Soviet Union. When Ho Chi Ming fell in April of 1975, it ended the Vietnam War with a victory for the North. In spite of this, the city seemed to have escaped relatively intact, with a large amount of French colonial architecture and wide Parisian-style boulevards within the centre. I visited gorgeous buildings like the Reunification Palace and the Notre Dame Cathedral, built by French colonists in a very similar style to the one in Paris. At night, the city would start to take on a new identity. Once the sun was setting and the humidity had begun to lift, the traffic would be replaced by people. The streets would come alive with buzzing neon signs, fairy lights and that particular inebriated evening ambience you only get in humid climates.

Visiting the Chụ Chi tunnels was an eye-opening experience. The section we visited was just a tiny part of an immense network of connecting passages located in the Củ Chi District of Ho Chi Minh City, which link up to a network of tunnels that underlie much of the country. They were the location of several military campaigns during the Vietnam War, used by Viet Cong soldiers as hiding spots during combat, as well as serving as supply routes, hospitals, and food and weapon stores for numerous fighters. The tunnel systems were of great importance to the Viet Cong in their resistance to American forces. We entered them through a series of hidden trap doors that led down these incredibly narrow passageways, no more than three feet wide. Occasionally, they would come out into a slightly larger cavern, but there was always a feeling of intense claustrophobia. The most difficult thing to deal with was the unbearable stuffiness. It was hotter than Satan chowing down on a bucket of Carolina Reaper peppers. It was at least seven or eight degrees hotter than the surface, so somewhere between 45 and 50 degrees. I was only down there for about twenty minutes, and came out completely drenched in sweat. Soldiers would have spent the entire day in the tunnels, working or resting, and only coming out at night to scavenge for supplies or engage the enemy in battle. Sometimes, during periods of heavy bombing, they would be forced to remain underground for days at a time. Sickness was rampant among the people living in the tunnels, especially malaria, which was the second largest cause of death next to battle wounds. No wonder the Americans couldn't beat them; they must have had Terminator levels of resilience. We also saw some of the booby-trapped tunnel entrances. The Americans were aware that the tunnels existed and would try and locate the entrances, so the Viet Cong would wire up explosives or construct trap doors that led into spike pits. Some of these traps that have since been preserved looked really vicious, like something out of an Indiana Jones film. By helping to secretly move supplies and house troops, the tunnels allowed North Vietnamese fighters to prolong the war and increase American casualties until their eventual withdrawal in 1972.

I always have mixed emotions when it comes to war sites being turned into something of a tourist attraction. The idea that something that is responsible for so much suffering and has claimed thousands of lives now exists as a profit-seeking enterprise sits a bit uneasily with me. At least in the case of the Chu Chi tunnels, the money raised is being used to preserve and restore them. The section around Ho Chi Ming alone is 75 miles long, and requires constant upkeep. (They stretch to many hundreds of miles across the country.) I thought some of the other things nearby were in really poor taste. For instance, there was a shooting range where you could pay to fire weapons that were used during the war, like assault rifles and machine guns, with targets dressed up to look like soldiers within the woods. I didn't agree with that. One of the guys I was travelling was an ex-Canadian soldier so I was a bit perplexed why he wanted to try. It was hardly a once-in-a-lifetime experience for him. It wasn't as if it were particularly challenging either, with the guns fully mounted and the sights already trained. It wasn't so much shooting fish in a barrel, as it were firing a nuclear warhead at a dozing haddock.

The area around the Mekong Delta is absolutely beautiful. Much of it is very low-lying so the ground is mostly swampy mangroves interspersed with dense jungle. I was there during the monsoon season, when many of the roads became impassable, so we went by boat. The majority of the houses and villages were elevated above the ground, resting on flimsy-looking bamboo stilts. They reminded me of giant insects (i.e. water striders) that gracefully skim the surface of ponds. It was in one of these hovering dwellings that I tried Durian fruit for the first time. I approached it with some trepidation. The smell is horrific, something like a cross between rotten onions and raw sewage. Other people suggest that it smells like stale vomit, so as you can imagine, not exactly pleasant. In fact, the smell was so off-putting for the original Western explorers that it remained unknown to the outside world for centuries. The irony, of course, is that it's delicious. It tastes rich and creamy, a bit like a raspberry pudding. Some people need to hold their nose in order to eat it, but once you get past that, it's worth it. The other issue with Durian is that the odour persists and can linger for days. The fruit is forbidden in most hotels and public places, like train stations and airports, for this very reason. Some people are more sensitive to it than others. I couldn't smell it after we left the village, but one of the girls in our group insisted she could smell it on us for days afterwards. There are hilarious signs all over Vietnam that will often list it in their forbidden items, e.g., no firearms, no animals, no Durian!

We travelled through various Vietnamese towns and villages over the next few weeks with all manner of delectable nourishments accompanying our every port of call. I loved the Banh mi rolls – basically the Vietnamese equivalent of a baguette – and the Goi Cuon (cold spring rolls) were always wholesome local delicacies. Most of the time we ate street food, which generally consisted of noodles and veg. Occasionally, we would be a bit more adventurous. I tried rat, which was surprisingly tasty, apart from all the little bones. One thing that I couldn't stomach was snake soup. This was another local delicacy that some of us tried in a town called Nha Trang. It was too chewy; that and the fact that that you could see the skin floating in the broth, really put me off. No-one seemed to know exactly what it was we were eating either. Traditionally, it's Water Snake, Python, or Indo-Chinese Rat Snake, but it could have been anything. Apparently, it's becoming rarer and rarer. Less people are cooking it for a living because of the hardship, danger, and difficulty involved in the process which requires frequent contact with venomous snakes.

After Nha Trang, we headed north to the middle part of Vietnam, which is much more remote than the southern and northern regions. We were getting more and more strange glances from local people. In one village, there was a gentleman who was totally astonished that I and one of the girls had blond hair. He wanted to take a picture of us to show his family. We expected to have to wait a short while whilst he got his camera out, which he claimed with some measure of pride was a Kodak. It turned out to be a 130-year-old Kodak mounted upon a cumbersome tripod. It was the full works, with a curtain and plate holders – the kind of thing I'd never seen in real life, only in a museum. I think we were there for a good fifteen minutes whilst he fiddled around with his prize possession. He offered to show us the final result once he'd processed it, but we politely declined. I had torturous visions of multiple fifteen-minute photo shoots if he wasn't satisfied with the finished article.

We visited an ancient trading settlement called Hoi An. The town is famous for its tailors, which grew from its history as a trading port on the silk route. Many people travel there in order to get high-quality, tailor-made garments that are a fraction of the price elsewhere. I didn't really fancy getting a suit made. I owned a couple and wanted to get something more elaborate created instead. Me and one of the guys I was travelling with tried to get the garish blue and orange suits from *Dumb & Dumber* made for us. Unfortunately, they didn't quite have the colour and material match. Instead, I got a purple velvet jacket produced, which they then shipped back to my parents in the UK. It's a great source of pride to me that the only tailor-made item I own is a novelty purple party jacket. I still wear it occasionally; I call it Willy Wonka chic.

Halong Bay was a contender for the most beautiful place I have ever visited. The bay itself is about 600 square miles (though when combined with the other bays to the North, it is far larger), with thousands of limestone rocks and islands jutting out in unusual and gravity-defying formations. Very few of these islands are inhabited; those that are, form small self-sufficient fishing communities. Most are unreachable and have their own micro-ecosystems. We hired a boat and went sailing through various rock channels which would tower above you encasing you in a canyon of petrological splendour. Cliffs of lush tropical rainforest would gaze down upon you, as you sailed through like Jason of Iolcus on some voyage to the edge of the world. We would occasionally see rare animals curiously peering out at us from high above. One that our guide pointed out was a Serow – a cross species of goat-antelope that was found nowhere else in the world apart from the remote mountains of Sumatra. We moored for the night in a cove and woke up in the morning to a deafening racket. A troop of monkeys (macaques) were running around on the deck above. They had come down from the cliffs to investigate the boat and were creating havoc. They were running around with people's clothes, opening packets of crisps, and just generally creating an almighty mess. They didn't seem that fazed by us, so it took a while to clear the deck of these pestiferous primates. It's one of those strange sights that lends itself well to Benny Hill music, people trying to retrieve their jumpers and hats, whilst others are chasing monkeys around in circles with brooms.

Our final stop in Vietnam was Hanoi – the capital city, though a much smaller and quieter place than Ho Chi Ming. The old quarter had this amazing street formation that I've never seen anywhere else, where each street only had one type of trade. For instance, there would be a whole street of nothing but shoe shops; next to that, one which just sold pipes and plumbing; and on from that, a street that just sold china. Because it was more developed than any other part of Vietnam, it was the only place where I saw a scattering of Western shops, like KFC and River Island. I also managed to get a cup of tea for the first time in three weeks. I said goodbye to the group that I had travelled with, and hung around in Hanoi for a couple of days before catching a flight on to Laos. There wasn't really any other way of getting there. There were barely any roads that went across the border, and those there were, were little more than mud tracks. It was either 48 hours wedged in the back of a van with no guarantee of getting there, or a one-hour flight. I chose the flight.

Laos was a total contrast to Vietnam – much more wild and mountainous. Its infrastructure was very basic, being one of the few countries outside of Africa to have no railways. Many towns and villages had no real roads, so goods were mostly transported on boats down the various rivers. My first stop was Vientiane, the capital city, which in reality felt more like a French market town. Vietnam made up for its lack of cars with motorbikes, but here it was mostly pedal bikes and tuk-tuks. I checked into my accommodation and met up with my guide. I was sharing a room with a Laotian man, who was himself training to be a tour guide. This was his first trip, so he was tagging along to learn the ropes. He was fascinated to learn that I was from London. He had been reading about it in one of his guide books, and kept asking me questions about Westminster Abbey and Chelsea Football Club that I couldn't answer. He was eager to learn, so I told him about some of the things in London I did know about – the Houses of Parliament, the South Bank, and the glamorous world of Elephant & Castle. He couldn't quite comprehend the size of London, with it having a larger population than the whole of Laos. He wondered how we didn't bump into each other the whole time. This trip, which went down into Thailand, was his first time leaving the country, so he was very excited. He was as straight as a die in comparison to our actual tour guide, who spent the next two weeks drinking, smoking, downing Valium, and partying. We would all be drinking in a bar and my room mate would just be sitting there in silence, waiting for us to finish. We offered to buy him beverages, but he never accepted. I think he was just so grateful to have a job that he didn't want to jeopardise his position in any way. He would be awake every morning at 6am, studying his guides' handbook, and scrupulously scrawling notes into his journal. He was actually a really great room mate to have, as he would always cheerily wake me up if I was running late or feeling hungover.

The drive to the next stop, Luang Prabang, was a big undertaking. Distance-wise, it wasn't that far, but the roads went along these fairly treacherous mountain passes. We spent the best part of a day going up and down these towering peaks on mud tracks with continuous hairpin bends. We had been warned that these roads often made people feel ill, so I made sure I sat in the front of the jeep. On route, we stopped off at a local factory that made wheelchairs and various walking aids for landmine and bomb victims. During the Vietnam War, more than two million tonnes of cluster bombs were dropped by the US, making Laos the world's most heavily bombed country by capita. The air-strikes were mostly aimed at disrupting movement along the Ho Chi Minh trail – a key logistical supply route used by the North Vietnamese. Many of the bombs were blown miles off course and now cover a huge area across the country. It's estimated that between twenty and thirty percent of these bombs didn't detonate on impact, meaning that there are still up to forty million undetonated bombs across Laos. There were reminders of this everywhere we went, with signs warning us not to wander off the paths when we were in rural areas. Every year these unexploded bombs cause injuries and fatalities, particularly with farmers ploughing the land and children who inquisitively pick them up. The factory we visited produced physical aids, but also acted as an education centre to raise awareness. In addition, it offered employment opportunities for people injured by landmines in the surrounding areas. It was a really thought-provoking place to visit, though the fact that some of these charities were being funded by the same country that bombed them in the first place, was a strange concept to grasp.

After another three hours of riding up and down ludicrous mountains roads, we finally made it to Luang Prabang. It stood at the confluence of two major rivers, the Mekong and Nam Khan. It was a picturesque town known for its numerous Buddhist temples and monasteries that seemed to have been lifted straight out of a holiday brochure. It was an amazing sight waking up in the morning to see hundreds of monks swarming down the street towards their various monasteries. They shuffled along in total silence, in flowing orange saffron-clad gowns. They had nothing else on their person – no hats, no shoes, not even any pockets. I wondered if they even needed to store things like keys. I guess their equivalent would have been monkeys.

We spent the next few days hiking, cycling, and kayaking. Even in the Laotian towns, everything was unbelievably cheap. In Vietnam, the average price of a beer was around 40p, here it was more like 20p. Even then, when you went to the really local places, you could get good quality beer even cheaper than that. We always tried to go to establishments where we saw the locals gathering, knowing there would be considerably less chance of the beer being watered down. Many of these places didn't even have seating, just wooden crates stacked up which you would then perch on top of like some drunken Cornish pirate. The difficulty was usually finding your way back in an intoxicated state, especially when electricity was so irregular. Off the main streets there was next to no street lighting, so you had to be very careful. One of the things that I always miss when I go abroad is, strangely enough, pavements. Other countries don't seem to have them in quite the same way that the UK does. Even in highly developed nations, pavements will often just stop, or be located around tourist spots like hotels, and then disappear. I've always found that odd. The other danger in South East Asia is the terrifying spectacle of open drains. These aren't small channels either, but often huge trenches that can require a leap of faith to launch yourself across. The combination of limited electricity, non-existent pavements, and open drains, mixed with alcohol was the perfect recipe for sustaining injuries. One of my fellow travellers managed to fall into one of these Death Star-like trenches and sprain her ankle. She was pretty lucky though, it could have been a lot worse. Again, my room mate was invaluable in these situations, as he was always sober as a judge. Like a mother duck solicitously guarding her chicks, he would always manage to guide us home.

The next part of our journey was twenty-two hours on a boat. The border on the western side of the country was similar to that on the eastern side, pretty much non-existent, hidden amongst dense jungle, and impassable mud tracks. The boat would sail down the meandering Mekong river and into Northern Thailand. It was a lovely relaxing journey after days cramped into a jeep, we spent most of the time playing chess and watching the world go by. One amazing site I witnessed was seeing a herd of wild elephants coming down to drink at the water's edge. We spent one night in this tiny village which sat alongside the river. It felt more like the settlement of an Amazonian tribe than anywhere you'd associate with Asia. The villagers were very hospitable, although only a couple of them could speak any English. I had learnt a few phrases in Vietnamese but I just got blank looks. My room mate pointed out that even he couldn't fully understand them. Apparently, there are around 80 different languages spoken in Laos, most of them closer related to Thai than Vietnamese. The village was pretty much as basic as you could get – no electricity, no windows, no toilets and they'd only recently got a tap installed. They did have a football, though, so I spent a bit of time having a kickaround with the children. Sleeping that night was difficult. We were basically lying on solid ground with only our clothes as any kind of cushion. There's nothing like sleeping on a floor in a mud hut to make you realise how privileged and spoilt we are as Westerners.

The following day, we crossed the border into Thailand. Being a much richer and more tourist-friendly destination, the change was stark. There was much more of an abundance of things – people, electricity, shops, etc. We visited towns like Chiang Khong and Chiang Main, where we stopped off at various religious sites. One of the more fascinating temples we saw was Wat Rong Khun, generally just referred to as 'The White Temple'. It had an extraordinary look that resembled a giant ice-carving sparkling underneath the midday sun. It was constructed from white plaster and glass pieces. From a distance, it really could have been a sculpture made entirely out of ice, looking like something straight out of a Narnia story. It was also packed full of interesting quirks. Whilst it does honour Buddha, it was also full of carvings from across the popular culture spectrum. There was sculptures and models from Predator, Harry Potter, Hello Kitty, and Star Wars, dotted all around the temple like it was a theme park attraction. To get into the temple itself, you needed to walk over a bridge, with moats on either side featuring carvings depicting scenes from hell with all these hands reaching up to grab you. It was the kind of building that you would never witness anywhere else in the world; subtle architecture wasn't really a thing in Thailand. So many of the buildings that we might consider tacky or garish were part of the fabric of their towns. This was definitely on the tacky, Vegas-style spectrum, but at the same time was wonderfully ethereal and other-worldly.

Bangkok was a real assault upon the senses. It was the first proper city I'd been to since Ho Chi Ming, so it was a refreshing change of scenery. I met up with my brother's mate, Glenn, who was working at various bars along Khao San Road. Glenn is a great lad although he has a borderline gambling addiction. Whenever we would see him back in the Canterbury pubs, he would be permanently glued to the fruit machines. I've never known anyone else who could happily spend an entire evening transfixed by the colourful lights, twitching away as the numbers whirled round, slowly draining his bank balance. We had learnt a few weeks earlier that my brother was marrying his long-term girlfriend, Katy, and Glenn was going to be the best man. He showed me around some of the best bars, and I gave him a few pointers and ideas to include in his speech. I had ended one of my tours, so it was a nice change to do some things at my own pace. I visited a few famous temples, including Wat Pho, which houses the largest collection of Buddha images in Thailand. Its most famous one is a 46-metre horizontal sculpture known as the 'reclining Buddha'. As well as being incredibly long, it was 15 metres high at its tallest point. This was the first reclining Buddha to be constructed, and although a handful have been built since then (particularly in Burma), they are still relatively rare.

Whilst I was hauled up in the Thai capital I visited Bangkok International University. We discussed various international exchange ideas over a massive five-course meal which they insisted on paying for. I wasn't complaining. It was nice getting something for free and not having to worry about being scammed. I've always found that to be the most stressful part of travelling, that feeling of being on edge because you don't know if people are being genuine or if certain things are tourist traps. Bangkok was notorious for it, especially when it came to taking taxis. I'd done my research, so I knew what a fair price was, and that I had to negotiate before getting a ride (the meters were often rigged). I would always pay them a bit more than the local prices, but even then, some of the drivers would huff and puff and sulk despite getting paid a more than fair sum. It was irritating as it would create an atmosphere that would then mar the journey. You wanted to say, 'Let's not play games. I may be a tourist but I'm not an idiot. I don't have time for all this chicanery.' But of course, you never did. You just sat there making small talk and hoping they wouldn't drop you off in some dreary backwater miles away from your destination, out of spite.

Bangkok was full of market vendors trying to sell you anything and everything, especially when it came to food. Basically, anything presented on a stick passed for a tasty snack. It didn't matter what it was – cockroaches, beetles, scorpions – as long as it was on a stick, it automatically became a delicacy.

Most of them tasted okay to me, although I found eating the stinger of a scorpion a step too far. Sometimes you would see buckets of wriggling creatures outside shops, and you would struggle to identify what they actually were. I think chicken foetuses were amongst the most stomach-churning items I saw. I also recall these battered stoneflies that one vendor sold as 'prawns of the sky'. They tasted as opulent as they sounded. Of course, being in the city, most of these were sold as novelty items for the tourists. The food in general was delicious- Panang Curry and Tom Kha Gai were my two favourites. I've tried them since in London, but they can never quite replicate the flavours in the same way. I think it's the mixture of seasonings that makes our equivalents seem bland. Every day my taste buds were inundated with garlic, ginger, lemongrass, and chilli, and it was always a perfect blend of sweet, spicy, salty, and sour flavours. One thing that I didn't initially realise was that lots of famous Thai dishes are region-specific. I remember, for instance, having an amazing Khao Soi (a rice noodle soup served with pork) in Chiang Mai, but in the south it was almost impossible to find. One thing that Thailand and South East Asia in general were quite bad at doing (outside of the big cities, anyway) was replicating Western food. That's fair enough, items like flour, cheese, and decent bread are pretty scarce, and ovens in normal Thai houses are pretty much unheard of. Nothing is really baked. Still, we would take it in turns to order the most ridiculous attempts at making Western food. I had a hilarious hamburger once, where the burger was literally two slices of bread placed around some nondescript meat.

The next part of my journey involved taking a train from Bangkok Station down the spine of Southern Thailand and into Malaysia. I booked my tickets for a sleeper train, which was reasonably comfortable. The beds were basically large shelves, with a curtain that you pulled across for privacy. I think the journey took about twenty-four hours, with a couple of brief stops en route. Whilst staring out of that train window with the Malaysian countryside whizzing by, I pulled out a notepad and wrote some off-the-cuff poetry. It was literally poetry in motion. I've probably written hundreds of poems in my life, but I've rarely been confident enough to show them to anybody. Writing good poetry is incredibly difficult. It's probably the most subjective art form there is. How does one avoid lapsing into pretentiousness and clichés? Even poets that are universally admired, I often find to be rather overrated. I am quite partial to Rudyard Kipling, though. He does write exceedingly good poetry, or is that the wrong Kipling? Anyway, here's a small sample that I wrote on that journey that I don't think is too shabby:

Speeding through lands to destinations unknown.
The wheels, the track, the clickety-clack all un-shown.
A glass bubble of nature laid out in gallery formation,
Exhibits fly by, squeezed between intermittent stations.
Luscious and verdant but tamed into subservience,
Where nature is free to breathe, it is deemed worthless.
Palm oil, tea, and the fruits of labour prized
beyond description
Plough, sow, and reap the earth within jurisdiction.
A bounty of plenty remoulded into mere commodity.
The glimpses and gaze from passengers dressed in sobriety,
Symmetry and lines fade into natural order. A threshold
is passed.
The forests emerge, the mangroves swell, life emerges
amongst the tall grass.
The land is untamed, unrefined, and beset with imperfection
A passing phase, an echo of dream, and we change direction.
The habitation of man is now back with a vengeance,
Uniformity and stability sailing in ascendance.
Progress arrives to reclaim its throne,

And we ride restlessly onwards to destinations unknown.

My first port of call in Malaysia was George Town. It was established as a shipping port by the East India Company in 1786, making it the first British settlement in South East Asia. Together with Singapore and Malacca, George Town formed part of the Straits Settlements, which became a British crown colony in 1867. George Town is unique in Malaysia in that it retains most of its English street names. (Names like Victoria Street and Love Lane.) Even though some roads have been renamed, locals generally prefer to use the road's former colonial name – partly because the new names are often unwieldy, but also due to much of the population viewing their colonial history as part of their identity. One of the most distinctive things about George Town is its street art scene. Everywhere I went, I saw murals and Muslim-style pop art, which was always spectacularly vibrant and colourful. I was shocked to discover that not only was this scene really recent (it only dates from 2012), but it was actually a Lithuanian artist who kickstarted it with wall murals depicting local culture as part of the annual George Town festival. Since then, it has expanded immeasurably and is now world famous. We actually teach it as one of the units on our Graphic Branding & Identity BA course.

One of the fascinating things about travelling is how quickly one adapts to the environment. By now, I was completely used to the humid temperatures and wasn't even bothering to use sun creams most days. When I first arrived, it was factor 50 every day without fail, but now my skin had developed a bit of a tolerance. I also wasn't missing tea at all, which really surprised me. However, visiting the Cameron Highlands on my next stop, brought all the memories flooding back. The Cameron Highlands are an area of Malaysia between 800 and 1600 metres above sea level, and as such are considerably cooler than the rest of South East Asia. The daily mean temperature is between 17 and 19 degrees all year round. It's these cooler and stable temperatures that made the British explorer William Cameron conclude that the area would be productive farmland for tea, coffee, and vegetables. In the 1920s and 1930s, huge tea plantations were built across a large area, initially to grow tea leaves for the British. Once Malaysia established its own tea culture, these started to be sold across the country. We stayed on one of the plantations and tried a variety of Malaysian teas whilst we were there. I tried Sabah Tea and Boh Tea (both popular brands in Malaysia), as well as varieties grown for Europe that I was more familiar with.

After this, we caught a plane to the capital, Kuala Lumpur. The flight was uneventful. It was at a low altitude so a little bumpy, but otherwise completely normal. When we touched down, we were expecting the usual tedious trawl through the airport, but instead were greeted by swarms of people. There were men shouting and families crying, whilst journalists were trying to take photographs of us. It was chaotic, we had no idea what was going on. We fought our way through the airport which must have taken us nearly an hour. One guy asked if I spoke English and then thrust a microphone in front of me.

'What are your thoughts regarding the plane crash?'

I didn't have a smartphone at that time, so had no way of knowing what he was talking about. I muttered something about not knowing about any plane crash and walked off. After a while, when I found someone I knew in the crowd, we had a bit of a chat. It turned out that the flight due to touch down an hour or so before us, had vanished in mid-air. We later found out that this was Malaysia Airlines flight MH17, which was flying from Amsterdam and was shot down over Ukraine on 14th July, 2014. This was part of the Ukraine and

Crimea conflict with Russia, where pro-Russian rebels had fired on the aircraft with surface-to-air missiles, thinking it was a military aircraft. Reports were still sketchy whilst we were in the airport, so no-one really knew what was happening. I didn't see this personally, but some of my fellow travellers were being grabbed by strangers, asking them about their loved ones. Some people were assuming that our aircraft was the missing one, and were desperate for any kind of reassurance from anyone to hand. I wouldn't say it was foresight exactly, but the fact that I recall being worried about flying so low to Crimea a couple of months earlier, did send a bit of a chill through my bones. After this incident flight paths were diverted to avoid the entire area.

After weeks of relatively humble surroundings, Kuala Lumpur was a revelation – a gleaming metropolis of steel and glass towers. It was Canary Wharf on steroids, with all manner of unusually shaped buildings sprouting up across the landscape like shiny urban mushrooms. The famous Petronas Towers dominated the skyline for miles around. They were the tallest buildings in the world from 1998-2004, and even today remain the tallest twin towers on the planet. The view from the top was incredible. The thing I remember most about Kuala Lumpur was our doomed mission to go swimming. After the relative coolness in the Highlands, we were back to the usual tropical climate of the region. Me and a Belgium guy I was travelling with, called Wim, had a spare afternoon so we decided to go swimming somewhere in the city. We went to a sky bar that we had frequented the previous evening, knowing that they had a pool on the upper floors. No sooner had I lowered myself into the water than one of the security guards chucked us out for not being guests at the attached hotel. (Apparently it was okay to drink there as a non-guest, but not to swim.) We then hailed a taxi and asked the driver if he could take us to the nearest alternative pool. He seemed somewhat perplexed, unsure of where any pools actually were. Eventually, after forty-five minutes of aimlessly driving around, we thought we had found what we were looking for. We walked up to the reception and saw that it was indeed an outdoor pool. We were very hot and sweaty by this point, so very much looking forward to having a refreshing dip. The gentleman behind the counter then told us 'no beach wear'. We were a bit confused, but he kept repeating himself and gave us a copy of the pool rules. It turned out that the swim shorts that both of us were carrying were not allowed in the pool. It was a pool for Olympic training athletes, so there were strict rules about what you could and couldn't wear. If we wanted to use the pool, we would have to use the second-hand Speedos provided. There was an overflowing bucket next to the reception desk full of warm, moist Speedos, so we had to confer about what to do. Clearly, we didn't want to be wearing someone else's Speedos – they were just sitting there in the afternoon sun, so we were very much doubting that they'd been washed recently. We wondered what the chances were of catching something unpleasant. On the other hand, we had come all this way and were exceptionally hot and sticky by this point. The water looked so inviting, glistening behind us like a serene oasis from a Bounty advert. All that stood in our way was this smelly bucket of used swim gear. Luckily, I had a small amount of shower gel and shampoo on me, so we decided that we would just go for it, washing the second hand garments as best we could in the sink with my toiletries. To top it all off, we had to pay extra for the privilege of wearing someone else's swim shorts! I got them as clean as I could, but they were so tight on us it felt ridiculous. All the other swimmers in the pool were big and powerful, six foot plus with bulging biceps... and then there was us – two skinny, pale guys just splashing around. The entire pool was divided into lanes, and even in the slow lane people were going at three times my speed. We gave up trying to compete in the end and just sat on the edge, bobbing up and down. Apart from the Speedos and the fact that we stood out like two wallies amongst these elite swimmers, it was a very invigorating dip.

Our final stop in Malaysia was Melaka, another pretty town that was incredibly vibrant and colourful. The place looked like it was in a permanent pride carnival, with flags and painted buildings that seemed to be oozing every shade of a Dulux paint chart. Even the taxis and rickshaws were decorated with exotic red, purple, and pink feathers and flowers, forming a cavalcade of colour. Whilst we were here, we found out that one of our group, a guy called Matteo, wouldn't be allowed to cross the border into Singapore with us. He was Columbian, and there was a law at the time that Columbians had to fly into Singapore instead of using the land border. Singapore is very strict on a number of rules, so presumably this had something to do with controls around drug trafficking. He asked if one of us would carry his luggage over with us, to save him the cost of having to check it in on a flight. It was a massive, bulging rucksack, so it made perfect sense. I can't remember the name of the guy who offered to carry it across, but he was absolutely fine with it. Some people in the group started teasing him, 'You're carrying loads of cocaine' and 'You've become a drug mule' and so on. He started off by simply ignoring them, but as we got nearer and nearer to the border, you could see he was becoming visibly worried. When people keep repeating things over and over again, it's quite common for you to come around to their way of thinking and start doubting yourself. Although everyone was joking, I could see that he was starting to regret agreeing to this. We arrived at the border and started handing over our passports, when suddenly the guy had what can only be described as a panic-stricken breakdown. He threw the rucksack on the floor and started chucking everything out. All

Matteo's possessions went flying as he took a penknife out of his pocket and started ripping out the lining whilst shouting at himself, 'Where are they? Where are they! I know they're in here somewhere!'

A couple of the border guards ran over and dragged him away, whilst picking up the ruined contents and remains of the bag. Clearly, the joke had backfired. He was questioned and then released an hour later, whilst we were having a drink on the other side of the border. He'd had some kind of panic attack and convinced himself there were hidden drugs in there. When we met up with Matteo later and presented him with his shredded rucksack and ripped clothes, he was gobsmacked. 'What the hell happened?' We told him the story, but he didn't see the funny side.

I was in Singapore for a couple of days, but I can't remember much about my time there. One thing that does stick out is how clean the streets were. Graffiti was incredibly rare, with large fines and jail sentences for anyone found guilty of using spray paint in public. Chewing gum had also been banned since 1992, so the pavements were spotless. When a BBC reporter suggested that such draconian laws would stifle the people's creativity, former Prime Minister Lee Kuan Yew said, 'If you can't think because you can't chew, try a banana.' I thought that was a great response.

My next destination was Sumatra, the largest and most western island in Indonesia. When I was planning my trip, I wanted to go somewhere really off-the-beaten track, and I thought that Sumatra (rather than somewhere more obvious like Bali) would be really interesting. My first port of call was the city of Medan, which was once voted the worst city in the world to visit. Even today, if you type into Google 'worst cities to visit', it inevitably comes out near the top. It was certainly a depressing place – busy, dirty, and dangerous, with barely a tree in sight. It looked a bit like how I would imagine the outskirts of a polluted Indian city to look. It was the polar opposite of Melaka – a grey, disfigured world of concrete and traffic fumes. There was only one place that in anyway resembled a hotel in the whole of the city. Luckily, this was where I was staying. It was also conveniently located round the corner from a giant mosque, which basically served as the city's only tourist attraction. I wasn't particularly shocked or surprised. I'd read various reviews about the city before I arrived. I didn't want to be one of those visitors that only went to the pretty 'touristy' places, so I thought Medan would be a good place to see some of the real Indonesia. Unlike the majority of South East Asia which is Buddhist, the primary religion in Sumatra was Islam. It was a nice change of scene to be visiting mosques rather than temples. The food markets were a massive step down from the rest of Asia, but on the plus side, everything was incredibly cheap. Apart from my group of six, I didn't see a single tourist there for the duration of my stay. There was beauty in this dystopian nightmare of a city; you just had to look for it. Whether it was the beer-bellied labourers taking midday siestas or the occasional flower bed that added a bit of colour to the otherwise grey environment – you could find it, you just had to work extra hard to get that charming photo.

The major thing that Medan had in its favour was its close proximity to the rainforests of Northern Sumatra. As soon as we left the city, the countryside turned into rolling mountain ranges and dense jungle as far as the eye could see. I had booked on an excursion to go and visit the wild orangutans that only lived in the rainforests of Borneo and Sumatra. The place I was visiting was a national park called Gunung Leuser, where we stayed in this isolated log cabin alongside one of the major rivers that meandered through the park. The following day we trekked for about five hours through thick vegetation to try and locate the orangutans. Our guide told us how difficult they were to spot, and that in order to find them we had to look for clues to their whereabouts. This involved spotting the signs of disturbed undergrowth and looking for fresh droppings. Because orangutans are the most arboreal of the great apes, they spend most of their time high up in the canopy. We spent much of that trek craning our necks upwards to try and spot them whenever we heard rustling noises from far above. When we did eventually find a small tribe, it was really amazing to see them swinging on the vines high up in the trees. We even saw a couple of baby orangutans clinging onto their mothers. Although initially very elusive, once we had found them, their distinctive reddish-brown hair meant it was easy to keep track of them. We watched and followed them for about five or so minutes. It was a brief encounter, but totally worth it.

Indonesia is a huge country. Because it's made up of (incredibly) seventeen thousand islands, it's easy to overlook it as a single entity when scanning a map of the world. It's the world's fourth most populous country, with 260 million people, and size-wise is as large as the continental United States. There are also vast areas of the country that are almost completely unknown. Even up until the 1980s, there existed tribes residing in remote areas who didn't know that other people even existed. We trekked to an isolated village to meet a tribe who had only recently (less than 10 years before) given up cannibalism. We had been warned that we needed to be respectful and understanding of their previous way of life. Their village still had shrines and totem poles that had been dedicated to this practice, which was fascinating and creepy in equal measure. Part Indiana Jones and part Hannibal Lecter. We had an interpreter with us, which was probably a good thing, as he was able to censor any potentially awkward questions. I mean what do you say to a man that ten years ago was probably eating human flesh? Do you miss the flavour?

How does it feel now being a vegetarian? Once we left the village, our interpreter went into great detail about the process of cannibalism. Without going into the full gory details, they basically used to steam everything in an oven made from leaves and rocks. They would treat it like they would the flesh of a pig. They would cut off the legs separately and wrap them in banana leaves. They cut off the head, which goes to the person who found the victim. The brains are apparently the tastiest bit, but once devoured, they then keep the skull. They then cut off the right arm and the right ribs as one piece, and the left as another. Apparently, there's a common misconception that human flesh tastes like pig, but they say it tastes more like cassowary – a New Guinea and Northern Australian bird that resembles an ostrich or an emu. After that delightful little lesson we stopped off for lunch.

I ticked another thing off my bucket list whilst in Indonesia, by climbing up a semi-active volcano. Mount Sibayak hadn't had a full-scale eruption in over a century, but was considered semi-active because of all the geothermal activity. There were various steam vents and small trickles of lava visible on the climb up. You could feel the soles of your feet heating as if you were raising them to an open fire. With every step you took on this inclining pyramid of rock you were slowly starting to cook, rather like a frog in a saucepan of warming water. As is common in most of Asia, health and safety was pretty much non-existent. We got a warning about going up in a straight line and not deviating too far from the guide, but that was about it. It was over seven thousand feet high, but at least it was a relatively easy climb –sweaty certainly, but not particularly challenging. The smell with all the sulphuric gases escaping was intense, like the aroma of rotting eggs. It took us the best part of the day to climb to the top and trundle back down again. We treated ourselves to a dip in the hot springs which had formed at the foothills of the volcano after we descended. Usually hot springs are lovely, but the fact that they smelt so strongly of sulphur was a bit off-putting. It was like taking a bath in a giant jar of warmed up pickled eggs.

The final leg of my trip was visiting the Thai islands of Ko Samui, Ko Pha-Ngan, and Ko Tao. This was more of a beach holiday than the more arduous parts of my trip. Ko Samui was pretty much party central – the main beach in the early evening was packed with revellers and ravers, interspersed with local traders all jostling for attention. There were monkeys, parrots, and lizards all being paraded up and down the beach. You would turn round and just find one sitting on your shoulder and a vendor asking you to pay for a photo. Most nights there were fire limbos taking place – basically normal limbo but with a flaming stick to contend with. I didn't see any accidents, but I imagine they weren't exactly rare. There were beach raves, dance competitions, and DJ sets that would go on until 5am. As well as the beach itself, there were rooftop bars and clubs that backed onto the coastline. In addition, there was a sea of party boats moored up about 100 metres from the beach that people would swim between; rather than a pub crawl, it was a boat crawl. It was all incredibly fun, but again a health and safety nightmare. There were basically no rules, so you needed to be on your guard in the evening. You would get these huge six-pint pitchers of alcohol being passed around with no idea what it was you were drinking. One night, one of the girls I was travelling with got her drink spiked by someone, and we had to carry her back to our accommodation in an uncontrollably delirious state.

Away from the party resorts, Ko Samui wasn't that different to the mainland. I visited a Buddhist temple called Khunaram, which was famous for its 'mummified monk'. This was the shrine of a monk called Luang Pho Daeng, who died in 1973 in a seated meditative position. Just before his death, he had directed that his body be put on display as a reminder of the transience of human existence. His body was just sitting there in a glass cage, looking like a cross between a zombie and a skeleton. Having a dead man in full view is a pretty shocking sight for Westerners. Far from being frightened by death, most Buddhist Thais are highly accepting of the end of life as the natural order of things. They view death simply as an opportunity to be reborn into a better place. The only real effort to make the monk slightly less gruesome was a pair of shades strategically placed to cover up his eye sockets (though when the ears eventually rot away, I'm not sure how they'll stay up).

The other islands in the region were smaller but geographically more stunning. One day when we were on Ko Pha-Ngan, we were taken on a tour up a mountain by a local dog. There are packs of wild and semi wild dogs all across Thailand, some of them having learnt very clever ways of attaining food. This dog would follow travellers up this particular trail and then scamper to the front to take over. He would bark whenever the track split in two, to indicate the correct route to the viewpoint at the top. It was amazing to watch, and once we all got to the summit, he got his inevitable treats and then wandered back down again. There was this one particular rock formation at the top that jutted out over the sea. It was incredibly beautiful, but no more than five or six feet wide with a sheer drop on either side. Some people went out to take selfies, but I just watched from the edge. I'm not at all scared of heights, but this did feel borderline dangerous to me. Just as we were leaving, one of the guys said there was a quicker way down which avoided having to scramble over the rocks. Most of the group went the same way down that they had come up, but three of us went this alternate route. I don't know how he knew about this other path, but we didn't question him on it. It was the only time in my life that I was genuinely worried about dying. We walked along a ledge which formed a narrow but distinguishable pathway around the top of the mountain. However, it got progressively narrower and narrower. We turned a corner on the cliff face and it was ridiculous, about seven or eight inches wide. There was a sheer drop of maybe 200 feet down to the jungle below. We had to shuffle along a sheer rock face, just grabbing at small cracks in the stone and plants that were sprouting out of the various fissures. The wind was picking up as this side was directly exposed to the sea, and on top of that I just had my normal holiday shoes on, which had no grip whatsoever. I gingerly shuffled along, hearing the gentle whoosh of disintegrating granite underneath my feet. Trying to imitate a cat on a window ledge, I probably bore a closer resemblance to a helpless Janet Leigh or Grace Kelly clinging on for dear life. I remember thinking, *how on earth did I get in this position?*

I could see the point where the ledge widened again, so it was easier to carry on than to go back. After a couple more minutes of shuffling along, we made it to the other side. I was really pissed off with the guy who suggested going that way, it was totally unnecessary and incredibly perilous. If any of us had slipped, it would have been game over. I don't think I talked to him again for the last few days of the trip.

On our second to last night, we went to a Black Moon party – a version of the famous Full Moon Party. This basically originated from the idea that Ko Pha-Ngan had the most beautiful moon in the whole of Asia. To celebrate this, a lunar party was organised along a crescent-shaped bay, and now occurs annually. It's basically an excuse for lots of people to get drunk and listen to techno and house music in a beautiful setting, whilst dressed up in psychedelic clothes and face paint. It was good fun and a great way to end my travels.

The following day, I said my goodbyes and hopped on a plane back to London. It may be a cliché but travel really does broaden the mind. I wouldn't be as pretentious as to say it was life-changing, but it definitely gave me a lot of respect for other cultures and helped me to understand more about the world. It also brought into sharp focus the idea that democracy and the system of government that allows us in the West to have a good quality of life is a fragile thing that too many of us take for granted. Of course, I didn't have to go all the way to Asia to find that out, but by visiting countries with military dictatorships or that had controlled media or religious persecution, it did put things into perspective. I like to think that on one hand I came back financially poorer, but spiritually richer on the other.

CHAPTER 10

Tooting Bec(koning)

It's a big shock to the system coming back from travelling. Some things, like being able to browse in a shop without being hassled are like a nice warm comfort blanket, whilst others, like the dreary English autumn weather feel depressingly mundane. In fact, the monotony of everyday life is something that you tend to forget about when you're gallivanting around like a peripatetic Phileas Fogg. The first order of business upon returning to the UK was finding a new place to live. Purely by chance, I ended up back in the same area of South London, though this time the slightly grittier area of Tooting. One of my mates had secured a lease on a house where he and his girlfriend had planned to rent the top floor and was looking to fill the other rooms. It ticked all the boxes, had a small garden, and was only a five-minute stroll from the tube. Then about a week before we were due to move in, they pulled out, deciding that they couldn't afford the rent. Out of desperation, the landlord said if I took the top floor, he would give me a large discount. I snapped it up straight away. It was great, I had a whole floor and an en-suite to myself; it was a bit like having my own little studio up there.

The people I was living with were a convivial bunch. They were all younger than me, so I became the surrogate dad of the house, sorting out all the bills/broadband, etc. There were six of us, the others being Tom, Laura, Ami, Kelly, and Charlie. Charlie was nicknamed 'Jam Jar Charlie' by Emma, due to his propensity for drinking everything out of jam jars – water, squash, beer, anything liquid-based. 2014 was around the time when it suddenly became trendy to drink alcohol out of retro jam jars. Cafes and restaurants started to realise they could whack a 20% mark up on any drink if it came in a jam jar, preferably with a slightly retro straw (for added plushness). There was a bar not far from us simply called 'the jam jar' where no other glasses were allowed. As you can imagine, Charlie loved it there. He had a fair old collection at home as well, which must have numbered fifteen or so.

One of the best practical jokes I ever pulled involved Jam Jar Charlie. He was a big fan of a rather tacky TV game show called *Take Me Out*. The premise involved a guy trying to impress a group of unnervingly attractive women standing behind podiums, and convince them to go out on a date with him. We were chatting one day and he said it would be great to be in the live studio audience. At the time, I was signed up to a website which gave out batches of free tickets to game shows which needed a studio audience. Over the course of a couple of years, I had been to see various shows being filmed, including *Catchphrase*, *Mock The Week*, and *Jonathan Ross*. I gave Charlie the details and it turned out they were looking for people for the *Take Me Out* studio audience in a few weeks' time. He filled in a very quick application and that was it. My cunning plan was to send him a letter saying that he'd been invited to star on the show as one of the contestants. I constructed a letter on headed paper with various ITV and *Take Me Out* graphics, and signed it from the show's commissioning editor. The letter basically said that they were impressed with his application and wanted to invite him to an audition at the ITV studios on 14th February. I specified the time and that he needed to wear a dapper outfit for the interview. I had discussed it with my other housemates who thought there was very little chance of him falling for it, but it was a hilarious bit of japery nonetheless. When the letter arrived, he was over the moon. 'Guys, can you believe this? I'm going to be on TV! This will be the best Valentine's Day ever!' He talked about nothing else for the next two weeks; it was really hard to keep a straight face, but somehow we all did. He even did a rehearsal with me and Tom in the living room. On the day of the 'audition', he wore his best suit, bought some high-quality cologne, got a suave new haircut, and off he strolled. We all waited with bated breath to see what would happen. When he came back later that evening, he suspected that something was up, and I confessed. Turns out, he had gone all the way to ITV studios with the letter and the lady behind the reception had thought it was genuine. He waited for a couple of hours all suited and booted, until one of the runners from the show said that there must have been some kind of mix-up and they'd look into it. He took it really well but was a little deflated, so we took him out for consolation drinks (in jam jars, of course). But that wasn't the end of the story. It turned out that one of Charlie's cousins worked on the show, and news had reached Paddy McGuiness (the show's presenter) of my escapades. He thought it was a great story and it got mentioned on a subsequent episode of the show. He also sent Charlie a personalised video message saying that he was 'too good for the show'. Charlie was well chuffed with that, so he got a happy ending of sorts.

We were all obsessed with a poor quality fast food 'restaurant' called Chicken Cottage. Its close proximity, basically at the end of our road, meant it was always our first port of call whenever we were hungry and feeling too lazy to knock something up. We used to say we were 'going Cottaging' whenever we popped down to Chicken Cottage. Laura was Scottish, and she loved it because they had Irn Bru on tap – a relative rarity in London. I liked it because I would occasionally see Sadiq Khan (Tooting MP for eleven years) in there and we would briefly talk politics whilst we were waiting for our chicken wraps. Its claim to fame was that it was the first major fast-food chain to serve halal chicken, and the branch at the end of our road was the largest in the UK. It really helped put Tooting on the map. The food was never actually that good. I always left disappointed when my chicken burger looked nothing like the proud succulent specimen displayed in the picture. It was always a sad, deflated spectacle when it arrived - undercooked meat, limp lettuce and sickly synthetic sauce. The bun itself was always soggy as if someone had been washing the counter with it two hours previous. I don't think I'd ever been mis-sold anything quite so blatantly since I finished watching *The NeverEnding Story* on VHS.

I've always been attracted to slightly seedier places- there's something about life on the margins that I find fascinating. I think it's the notion of these being real living and breathing urban environments where all manner of people mingle. The students, the tradesmen, the market vendors, the unemployed, all sharing in the local hustle and bustle, radiates such a joyous community vibe. A kind of real *EastEnders* , just without the pub brawls and make-believe swearing. I used to always pick up a bagel from this local shop after my morning runs around Tooting Common, inevitably ending up chatting to the owner about how our weeks were going. He was an interesting character – a budding nature photographer who had hundreds of polaroids of foxes plastered all over the shop walls. He used to feed the foxes in the backyard with all his leftover bagel fillings. He'd proudly scrawled on the pictures the various fillings that they were in the process of digesting, like it was some kind of quality endorsement. 'Smoke salmon & cream cheese – refer to polaroid 24; salt beef and horseradish – that's those delightfully mangy cubs on number 38.' You'd never see something like that in say, Muswell Hill. So many urban areas that we choose to spend time in are false. All those touristy high streets, shiny shopping complexes and perfectly manicured parks- all lovely but not in essence, real life. I think that's why when areas get too trendy, I lose interest. Tooting was eventually dubbed the world's coolest neighbourhood by Lonely Planet five years after I left. Something of an exaggeration, but it's basically code for gentrified enough to exclude real locals but edgy enough for the hipsters.

One thing that I wanted to record in this book for posterity was the strange phenomenon that were internet cafés. In a world where we carry the internet in our pockets on phones, and lounge around in bed with our iPads, the idea of going to a dedicated location to access the worldwide web now seems quaint. However, once upon a time, the idea of the 'internet café' was both modern and exciting. I remember using them regularly in the early noughties. They were like digital caves of connectivity and excitement, where people would drink coffee and hang out to use this new-fangled technology to book a flight or do some research together. It made sense that when people didn't have access to their email or instantaneous communication via a mobile phone as we do now, they needed a way to connect on-the-go. By 2004, it was reported that there were 20,000 internet cafés dotted all over the globe. However, just as quickly as it started up, the phenomenon started to slip into decline. With home internet connections being more widely available, there was now no need to go down to a café in order to check an email or make an Amazon order. Once mobile devices became prominent – especially with the launch of the iPhone in 2007/8 – the cafés became even more redundant, as the need for a 'digital pit stop' became increasingly irrelevant. The last time I went to an internet café in the UK was in 2014 when our house wi-fi went down and I needed to check some last-minute holiday preparations. I was stunned at how much they had changed, transforming from these gleaming digital hubs into seedy little run-down spaces. They now had a bit of a reputation as being used for nefarious purposes, like illegal downloading, fraud, and the internet phenomenon of 'cat-fishing'. I felt rather awkward sitting there, and did my work as quickly as possible so I could get out of there pronto. I don't know if in another five years' any internet cafés will exist at all. If anything, their brief lifespan is testament to the shockingly fast way that technology changes and progresses.

It was whilst living in Tooting Bec that I visited a food bank for the first time. Prior to 2011, I had never really heard of the term 'food bank'; it sounded like the kind of thing that would be set up in a disaster zone after a civil war or earthquake. After the financial crisis, they started popping up all over the country, as a fall in living standards started impacting on the lives of people who were on the lower rungs of society's economic ladder. In one of the world's richest societies, people should be mortified by the presence of Dickensian-style food centres, but over the last ten years the general public seems to have become desensitised to the idea. Charlie and I had joined this running club called 'Good Gym' where you would run a set distance with a group of people, undertake some kind of charity endeavour, and then run the same route back. This was a great initiative that helped you to get fit and do some rewarding charity work at the same time. The second of our good gym runs involved helping with unloading at a food bank. Our job basically involved the twelve of us carrying in boxes, sorting through the food, and unpacking it onto the various shelves. The most shocking thing was seeing the queue that had already formed when we arrived. Twenty or so people waited patiently in line in the autumn chill – mothers, fathers, and children, standing there with their dignity and pride stripped from them. It really made your blood boil that austerity and all its associated policies (i.e. Universal Credit) were a calculated political choice designed to shrink the state. It was all very well for privileged people like David Cameron to bang on about tough choices, when a tough choice for them would be which vintage bottle of red to crack open.

I had been following politics quite closely for years, but in 2015 I started getting more seriously involved by joining the Labour Party. Meeting Sadiq Khan had inspired me, and I thought I could do some good by doing my small bit to rally against Tory austerity policies. I genuinely thought that this was a chance to help mould our politics into something better. For most of my life, British politics has basically been about choosing the least shit of two terrible options. It's a bit like knowing you're going to get waterboarded, but you have the choice between sparkling or still. My new-found enthusiasm was poorly timed, as this was the beginning of the fragmentation of British politics. Dray and I attended a few events in 2015, including Sadiq's rallies where he was campaigning to succeed Boris Johnson as the Mayor of London. I was surprised by how poorly organised the events were. I recall one in a school where the hall was strewn with rubbish and cardboard boxes, which we had to clear up before Sadiq arrived. He was also a terribly dull speaker. I liked him as a person, and I liked most of his policies, but I felt he did not present himself well. He had very little charisma, was just reading off cue cards, and would endlessly repeat the same lines, particularly his 'as the son of a bus driver' spiel. In person and on TV, he came across quite well, but when it came to public speaking, I thought he was really lacking that certain spark. However, I was glad when he became London Mayor, as he was a principled guy and there are far too few of them in British politics. As a Labour member, I took part in the leadership vote in September of 2015. I remember how non-credible Jeremy Corbyn was at the time. He was drafted in at the very last moment to 'broaden the scope of the leadership election'. Most people didn't know who he was and just assumed that he would go out during the first round. I personally voted for Andy Burnham, who would later go on to become the Mayor of Manchester. I was always uneasy with Corbyn's election as leader. I just didn't see him as a credible politician – decent and principled, yes, but his views weren't broad enough to be accepted by the wider population. I also thought at the time (correctly as it turned out) that having a hard-left leader was dangerous for democracy. My view has always been that if you have a hard-left leader, the party over time becomes more and more hard-left, with moderates resigning or gradually being replaced. The flip side to that is that you need a far-right party to challenge them, which the Conservative Party finally morphed into in late 2019. This pattern has been repeated throughout history, where the main political parties don't operate in the centre ground and there is a massive void. In reality, very few people are on the far left, and very few people are on the extreme right. Human principles are much more nuanced and complex than that. In ignoring the views of the majority of the country, you create anger, distrust, and a hardening of views. The direction of the Labour Party started worrying me more and more, so in the end I cancelled my membership.

By now I was meeting quite a large number of famous people through my work. Sometimes they would be visiting a private view, or sometimes they would come in and do talks or guest lectures for various groups of students. I met everyone from Boris Becker, to Ridley Scott, to Arsene Wenger. For a while I was working directly with Arsene Wenger's cousin, who was head of a European Language School that used our building in the summer. One of the most interesting people I saw was the Channel 4 newsreader John Snow. He came in to give a talk to our journalism students, arriving at Elephant & Castle by bike, and told us the story of how he came to be a journalist. I learned that he had no formal journalism training and only managed to become successful due to his prowess at cycling. When he was in his twenties, he used to beat the London traffic by bike and get to the scene of any incident faster than anyone else – that was how he made his name, and how he got the BBC to originally employ him. It just goes to show how dogged determination is always the key to success. He was really engaging and looked exactly as he did on TV, with his colourful socks and matching tie. I told my female Australian housemate at the time that I was going to meet John Snow that day and she was really excited, asking me if I could acquire a photo/autograph for her. That confused me slightly. She had only been in the country for about nine months, so I was surprised that she knew who this seventy-year-old news presenter was. She then told me that she really fancied him and thought he was incredibly handsome. *Each to her own*, I thought. I came back in the evening with said photo, and she looked rather befuddled. It turned out that she thought I was referring to the character of 'John Snow' played by Kit Harrington in the HBO adaptation of *Game of Thrones*. I had never seen *Game of Thrones* at this point, so didn't initially make the connection. As far as I was concerned, there was only one John Snow.

My job didn't involve that much travelling. People would often assume that because I worked in an international office, travelling would be an essential component to my role. There were people in my team who did regularly travel, but their role was international recruitment. My role, on the other hand, was academic and pastoral support post enrolment. I knew how monotonous and tiring travelling could be. There were people in my team that only ever seemed to see hotel lobbies and conference halls when abroad. If they were lucky, they might get half a day to explore, but even then, they would usually choose to spend the time in bed, recovering from jet lag. There were, however, a couple of occasions when I did travel abroad as part of my role. I was very lucky in that I could pick and choose the projects that I wanted to do, so very rarely did I work on a project that I wasn't happy with. 99% of the time I loved my job precisely because I managed my own workload. One of these self-initiated projects was a trip to Iceland to visit the 'Icelandic Academy of the Arts' based in Reykjavik. I was looking at the support mechanisms they had in place, to see if there were areas of good practice that we could duplicate. The college was tiny; I think they had about 150 students, compared to UAL's 20,000. For such a small college, they had quite a large variety of equipment, including screen presses, laser cutters, and plastic moulding devices. My audit took less than two days, so the rest of the time I spent seeing the sights and going out eating and drinking with the college staff.

Iceland was a fascinating place – a small, frozen island shivering in the North Atlantic, which reminded me of being on top of a giant Fox's glacier mint. The population of the country was about 300,000 – roughly the same as Brighton & Hove – which makes it the most sparsely populated country in Europe. I was staying in the capital city, but even that felt strangely deserted, like an early morning Sunday high street coated in snow and ice. The houses were beautiful, with these brightly coloured roofs careering over the streets in impossibly steep angles. I learnt that it was tradition in Iceland that when you bought a new house, rather than painting the front door a new colour, you painted the roof instead. It was quite a juxtaposition having all these plain-looking facades with variegated roof tiles that resembled all the colours of the rainbow. I also found out that the American martial arts actor, Chuck Norris, is bizarrely a big deal over there. Rather like David Hasselhoff in Germany, he is almost revered as a god. I went to the official 'Chuck Norris Bar & Grill' which had quotes and images of him plastered all over the wall. Considering that there are only three steak restaurants in the whole of the country, it's distinctly odd that one of them is devoted entirely to Chuck Norris. I also had time to do a couple of the more traditional touristy things, including visiting the Blue Lagoon. This is a geothermal spa located in a lava field, with a high silica content causing the water to turn a milky shade of blue. It's a magical feeling bathing in naturally heated water whilst the sides of the lagoon are encrusted with thick ice. It was large enough that you could swim around and find natural temperature variants, with the water feeling like a scalding bath in places. There are thousands of these naturally occurring spas all over the country, and all the locals knew where the best ones were located. The Blue Lagoon was obviously a bit of a tourist trap, but it was such a lovely sensation that it didn't really matter.

The countryside is breathtaking, with so much ice and water everywhere you turn. Steaming out of the ground, falling from the sky, and sitting in these huge, crystal clear lakes. Standing on top of the Vatnajokull Glacier, the ice itself goes on forever, but its the immeasurable silence of the place that is most liberating. There's no distant hum of traffic, no birdsong, no trees rustling in the breeze; just pure unadulterated nothingness. If you were so inclined, you could walk for days and barely hear a twig snap, never mind converse with another person. An empty, icy land, as if the whole of Narnia had exited backwards through the wardrobe.

I have always been a bit of a hoarder and really have to force myself to throw anything away. I have all my school reports stretching back to 1989, for instance. One day, when I was rummaging around in the Tooting pad, I came across some tea classifications which I came up with when I was at university. It was just hidden amongst a pile of papers, and I thought to myself that might be interesting to include in a book one day. These days, my wife would describe my tea drinking as something of an obsession (the various teapots that decorate our kitchen shelf are testament to this), but back in the day, I took it much more seriously. I would spend hours trying to investigate how to make the perfect brew. The tea classifications that I came up with back then were as follows:

Milk It: A watery anaemic beverage that has no business being classed as tea. Everything is lacking, apart from an excess of milk, in a vain attempt to hide the beverage's many failings. Best thrown over the person who made it for you. As 60% of the drink is milk, the stone-cold nature of it will cause no permanent damage. Usually made by someone who has never drunk a cup of tea in their life. 0/5

Dip & Dash: The lazy man's cup of tea. The water is poured first (possibly to mimic continental sophistication), and the teabag is plopped in as an afterthought. It may skim the surface, or it may just float for a few seconds. Usually the 'dip and dash' is the most thoughtless cup of tea, and as such could be any own brand of poor-quality teabag. Often the person who made it is in a rush, and as such, enjoyment is not really on the agenda. 1/5

Cause A Stir: The most common cup of tea. Everything is done in the correct order and the bag is given a good stir. The person making it may drink tea infrequently, but has opinions on the best way to go about it. They may 'cause a stir' with their thoughts on milk, sugar, lemon, or decaf varieties. They may need a bit of educating, but they are making a fair effort. 2/5

Stew The Brew: Often the most controversial cup of tea. When done well, a stewed brew is fantastic, but when done to excess it can ruin the balance. It should always be stewed between two and five minutes. Do not exceed this, even if you want the tea stronger. Unless it's herbal tea, stewing beyond five minutes won't make it stronger but it will make it more bitter. This is because the tannins (basically the protein molecules found in plants) will react the longer they are in contact with the water. Add extra teabags to the pot or cup if you want it stronger. Seasoned tea-brewers like grandparents have this technique down to a fine art. 3/5

Tight Squeeze: My personal favourite type of tea. Allow the brew to infuse for between 1 and 1.5 minutes. Then give the teabag a good squeeze, followed by a stir. By brewing, you allow a small amount of tannins to mix with the water and infuse. When squeezing the bag, you release more tannins, which allows you to control the strength. A dash of semi-skimmed milk to finish off the ensemble. 5/5

The Slam Dunk: This is basically the lucky dip of teas. The teabag or teabags are slammed in and squeezed to oblivion. Sometimes the bags will split, and sometimes they won't. The milk cascades in like the Niagara Falls, sometimes overflowing the rim – this is a called a 'brimmer'. Sometimes the water and milk will have been so misjudged that you only end up with half a cup, also known as a tidal contraflow. Basically, there is no way of scoring the finished article. Sometimes it's delicious and sometimes infuriating. ?/5

Earlier that year, my brother Matt and his (then) girlfriend Katy announced that they were getting married. It's an odd sensation when your younger brother starts ticking off the various life stages before you do. He'd already bought his first house in this tiny little hamlet called Beltinge, and now my baby brother was getting married. I was very happy for him. He had been together with Katy for twelve years by then, so it was probably about time. The stag do took place in Brighton and was the usual random mixture of characters. His best man, Glenn, had organised all the activities, but as the resident Brighton local, I had plotted out all the various pubs we were going to visit. I did my best to avoid what the Brightonian's commonly refer to as the 'Croydon Straight'. This is basically the only tacky street in Brighton where all the cheesy bars and clubs are – the kind of place that gets rammed at weekends when people come down to visit. It was called the Croydon Straight as it was basically a straight walk down from the main station where all the people from London would stagger to after a heavy session of binge drinking on the train. It was the complete antithesis of what most of the nightlife in Brighton was like.

The pub crawl was going fine, and everyone was having a jolly old time. We went to some interesting cocktail places which I knew Matt would like, as well as some quirkier places I knew, like the Robin Hood charity pub. But then we got to the section where we had to cut across the Croydon Straight. One of the guys spotted a Walkabout bar and that was that. Much like my childhood budgies, my carefully thought-through plan then went out the window, which was fine; it was a stag do after all. It was inevitable that we would end up in the cheesiest of cheesy clubs.

Josh had a torrid time that weekend, it was an absolute disaster for him from start to finish. He paid for everything, but didn't end up doing any of the activities or even staying in the B&B. We did an inflatable obstacle challenge based on the 1980's TV game-show *It's A Knock-out* and go-karting on the Sunday. Josh arrived incredibly late and missed the obstacle course. Having commenced drinking, Josh started chatting to a guy who Matt worked with. He was a bit self absorbed in a thuggish male posturing type way. He was obsessed with body building and kept talking about his pecs, so Josh started calling him 'pecky'. However, after a couple of hours, when people started slurring their words he thought Josh was racially insulting him by calling him 'Paki'. (I think he was Pakistani on his dad's side). Anyway, he went ballistic and punched Josh square in the face, sending him staggering backwards. It was totally out of the blue and no-one was quite sure what had happened. After a while, everyone calmed down, though there was a definite dampener on the evening. Josh was bleeding from his lip, but everyone thought he was basically fine. However, when he looked in the mirror in this club toilet, it looked nastier than we all thought. He disappeared off to hospital and spent the rest of the night in A&E. He had seven or eight stitches on his lip, and as the alcohol slowly began wearing off, he realised at 1am that he was supposed to be working up in Scotland the following day. He then had to bribe his way back into the B&B (he didn't have a key) and catch the first train, which was at about 4.30 in the morning. By some miracle, he managed to get to Scotland for his job at 11am, in spite of the raging hangover and busted lip. The rest of us had a merry old time. Glenn spent most of the weekend gambling, a couple of guys got lost and slept on the beach, and we dressed Matt up as a pink fairy. All good clean fun.

The wedding itself took place in east Kent, in a venue called 'The Old Barn'. Early on in the day, the boys had what was described as the 'real wedding breakfast', basically a morning fry-up in the local branch of Harvesters. Even on Matt's wedding day, Glenn couldn't resist a few cheeky spins on the one solitary fruit machine in the establishment. He was the best man, so it was his job to get my brother to the church on time. We were the ones saying, 'Come on Glenn, you've had enough. Time to go.' The weather was perfect, so Matt and Katy got married outdoors, surrounded by lovely rolling countryside. I was an usher, and briefly managed to screw up my most important job by reading the seating plan backwards. I forgot (having indulged in a couple of beers) that when standing at the altar, everything is reversed, so there was a bit of shuffling around whilst I attempted to work out who was supposed to be on the groom's side and who was on the bride's. Glenn had broken his arm some weeks earlier and so was in a sling for the majority of the time. However, he was determined that he wouldn't let this stop him from enjoying himself. It's quite a sight to watch a man with his arm in a sling attempt to do the Macarena.

CHAPTER 11

Brexit

When I first started writing this book, I thought that I would try my best to ignore the subject of Brexit. I thought it was best avoided, as I could talk about it until the cows came home and didn't want to bore the reader. I also thought that I might struggle to bring an argument that, if not impartial, at least looked at the opposing viewpoint. To be clear, I see Brexit as the biggest, self-inflicted danger that this country has faced in modern times, and I knew it would be difficult to avoid a situation where I just got angry and ranted my thoughts away. However, the more I dwelt on it, the more I realised that it was a defining moment in our country's history. The Covid-19 crisis would later put this in its proper context, but at the time, Brexit was the all-consuming number one subject of conversation. Ultimately, I decided that avoiding a social and political event of such significance was tantamount to rewriting history. I therefore decided to limit my thoughts to one short chapter. So, here goes...

First of all, a bit of background. What makes Britain different? Why do we have such an awkward relationship with Europe? Other countries in Europe have their fair share of euro-sceptics but not to the degree that we have. I think it's a misplaced sense of superiority that goes back centuries. This manifests itself in two forms, which have been festering in the background ever since we joined the European community in 1973. One is our historical achievements, and the other our present cultural hegemony. Historically, we have always thought of ourselves as being superior, through our status as an island nation, trading all over the world, and creating an empire. Other European countries (most notably France) also created empires, but not to the same degree. Culturally, I think the British still see themselves as a world power. This so-called 'soft power' is present in our arts, our music, and our television. The fact that English is the number one spoken language in the world also helps perpetuate this myth.

I remember when I was very young, thinking that the Queen was the queen of the world. I didn't know any other countries had monarchies. Everywhere else that I was vaguely familiar with was a republic – America, France, Germany, etc. Others like Australia and Canada were part of the Commonwealth. So, I just assumed that the Queen ruled everywhere. I think if you asked the average British fifteen-year-old today who were the more important people who ever lived, you would get very different answers to the average fifteen-year-old from the continent. I think most teenagers would mention people like Churchill, Queen Victoria, Charles Darwin, and Shakespeare (all taught in the British curriculum, of course). I suspect the average student from, say, Belgium would give a much more inter-cultural list, people like Gandhi, Julia Caesar, Dostoyevsky, and Sigmund Freud. I don't have any evidence for this, it's just my personal opinion, dear reader. I do remember reading an article a couple of years back where the results of a survey revealed that 80% of British adults (not kids) couldn't name one famous person from Austria. When I read stats like that, I'm inclined to think that with that level of ignorance no wonder people voted for Brexit.

So much of our soft power is smoke and mirrors. Our film industry may be in the top four or five in the world, but so many of those films are co-funded by America and the EU. The BFI classes a British film as something that can be perceived as 'culturally British'. That means it can be shot and financed elsewhere, such as *Mandela: Long Road to Freedom*, and still be considered a British film. Without international funding, massively successful franchises like James Bond and Harry Potter would probably never have gotten off the ground. Wholly British films are actually quite rare, which is something to bear in mind if EU funding ever runs out. It's not just films, either. People think of the UK as having one of the world's biggest music scenes, but in terms of worldwide consumption, it hovers between 10 & 13% of all global music sold. Not bad, but lower than most people assume. Our global military presence is another illusion. Every time a ship gets launched, it's front page news. In terms of total naval strength (including aircraft carriers, frigates, destroyer, and torpedo boats), we are only at number 32 in the world, with seventy-six ships. Countries like Egypt, Finland, Mexico, and Morocco, individually have more than us. In many cases, they are not as technologically advanced, but still I think most people would be surprised to see us so low down the list. The fact that we are one of the permanent members of the UN Security Council is totally ludicrous when you actually think about it. There is, of course, nothing wrong with being a medium-sized power; it would just seem that people haven't quite caught up with the reality of our situation. It's frequently said in the media that we punch above our weight, and that's true, but to a much greater extent than most people realise. I think if you combine our empire-building past with our present sense of entitlement, then you have the perfect recipe for a population that feels disengaged from its European neighbours.

There had always been dissenting voices on the back benches of parliament, saying that the UK would be better off outside the EU. However, for decades they were a very small group that were thought of as a bit odd. It wasn't until the formation of UKIP (the UK Independence Party) in 1993 that those dissenting voices started to grow that little bit louder. David Cameron famously referred to UKIP as a bunch of 'fruitcakes, loonies, and closet racists'. The paradox of UKIP was that they promoted a British nationalist agenda that encouraged a unitary British identity (in opposition to Scottish nationalism), but at the same time tapped into a sense of English nationalism which hadn't really existed before. Their main goals were to lower immigration and reject multiculturalism, alongside a right-wing conservative agenda. I remember when I was a teenager, they were pretty reviled, and I couldn't see much difference between them and the BNP. In the 1999 European elections (the first UK election for the European Parliament using proportional representation), they secured 6.5% of the votes. In 2004, this increased to 16% and twelve seats. I remember the outrage in the media at the time. TV show host Robert Kilroy Silk and, later, Nigel Farage, became household names with their fake 'men of the people Schick'. The 2007 financial crash and the subsequent recession that followed was a gift from God for the party; it was like someone delivering them a winning lottery ticket on a silver platter.

All populists do two things: they act like they are anti-establishment, and they try to deceive and confuse their target audience. The ultimate goal is to mix truth with fiction to confuse and scare the electorate still further. UKIP started to equate falling leaving standards with multiculturalism. To blame a global financial shock that had its roots in the American housing crash on immigration was ludicrous. If there was one group that wasn't over-leveraged in the UK, it was probably EU nationals who were here to earn money (and pay UK tax) for their families back home. But as the old saying goes 'never let the truth get in the way of a good story'. It was no surprise, therefore, when their performance in the 2013 local elections exceeded all expectations by increasing its number of elected councillors to 147. This was actually the best result for a party outside of the big three since the Second World War. In 2015, it secured 3.8 million votes, and briefly became the third most popular party in the country. This was when the then Prime Minister, David Cameron, made the historical mistake of promising a referendum on the UK's continued membership of the EU. The idea made political sense, in that a hardening stance on immigration would enable the Tories to take back some of the seats it had lost to UKIP. I remember when the referendum was announced in February of 2016, Tom and I turned to each other and both said, 'That's a bit risky, isn't it?' We never seriously thought that the government would lose the referendum – in fact, I didn't know anyone that did – but there was a sense of 'What's the ultimate goal here?' David Cameron said at the time that the referendum was designed to 'stop people banging on about Europe'. Oh, the irony of ironies.

There were various issues with the referendum campaign and the referendum itself. I could write an entire book on why I thought it was ill-judged. The biggest issue was that unbelievably no-one thought through the implications if the government were to lose. No-one considered the wording of the question, or specified if it was legally binding (it wasn't; it was technically an advisory vote). There was no referendum threshold specified, or indeed a turnout threshold discussed

– both of which are common practices across the world. The arrogance from the Conservatives was breath-taking. There was no effective positive messaging campaign, there was just a God-given assumption that people would vote the 'right' way. To this day, I still can't believe that a responsible democratic country wouldn't seriously think through the implications of what was essentially the biggest constitutional change for the country in almost 100 years.

When the referendum result was announced, everyone I knew was in total shock. Lots of people at work were crying, and we had various emergency meetings to discuss what we were going to do. It was a double whammy for us; nearly one-third of our staff were EU nationals, and on top of that we had roughly six thousand students from EU countries. We assumed that we would get some clarity from the government, but that never came. Over four years later, and we still have no clarity. It was equally upsetting for my Tai Chi class, about half of whom were EU nationals, and some of whom I had become good friends with. Some people I knew, like Stelios, who was now also living in London, bit the bullet and applied for settled status. Most people I knew just refused, not wanting to be treated like second class citizens when they came here perfectly legally. I could empathise with both points of view. The whole Brexit fiasco turned us into a laughing stock in the eyes of the world. Part of my job involved doing tours for various schools from abroad, but it became difficult to talk about how international and open-minded our institution was in the face of such division. I remember doing a tour for a school from Marseille, when they asked to go to the top of our tower block to see the view over London. At the time, Big Ben was covered in scaffolding whilst they repainted and cleaned up the clock tower. One of the guys likened it to Brexit, laughing and saying it was 'a clean break from the past'.

'The will of the people' is a statement I've heard numerous times over the last four years. It's something I've heard from politicians, commentators, and various broadcasters, when trying to justify Brexit. It is in fact nonsense. The phrase 'will of the people' is a total misdemeanour, with more holes in it than a wheel of Swiss cheese. There are literally thousands of things that are more clearly 'the will of the people'. To name just one, let's assume the question 'Do you want to breathe cleaner air?' was put to the people of this country. How many people do you think would answer 'no' to that question? 1%, 2%? You don't need a referendum to tell you that the number would be incredibly small. The only people that I think might answer 'no' either haven't understood the question, own a polluting business, or are perhaps shareholders in said enterprise. (Even then, they would want to breathe cleaner air; capitalism just dictates a conflict of interest.) If we assume a conservative estimate that 95% of people in this country do want to breathe cleaner air, isn't that more clearly the will of the people? Why aren't people shouting in the streets about air quality wanting a referendum? This is something that affects everyone, has been proven to shorten lives, and costs the NHS – and as a consequence, the taxpayer – millions every year. Why isn't that the will of the people? The answer is very simply – complexity. There are financial and legal implications, international supply chains across various industries, and a whole raft of technical and political challenges. This isn't to say it's impossible. I don't doubt that our air quality in the West will greatly improve over the next few decades, but it's complex and it takes time. It isn't a binary choice, and that's the reason that we don't have referendums that frequently. Brexit is exactly the same (well, apart from the fact that the majority of people in this country don't actually support it, but that's a different kettle of fish). It's a very complicated issue that cannot be resolved with a yes/no question. Even the term 'Brexit' is completely inaccurate and gives no indication as to the complexity. The name implies that Britain is exiting, which just isn't the case. Firstly, it's not Britain, but the UK exiting. Quick geography lesson: Britain refers to the mainland of England, Scotland, and Wales. The UK adds Northern Ireland and a couple of smaller islands. Part of the complexity is that it's the whole of the UK leaving, including the incredibly problematic area of Northern Ireland.

Secondly, we are not leaving. One does not leave one's geographic entity. It's also impossible not to have a close trading relationship, and thus a set of legal parameters, with our biggest trading partner. The idea is that we are withdrawing from an agreed common international framework of nations. A more accurate term might be a 'UK withdrawal from a European Union framework'. Doesn't Brexit roll off the tongue much easier? Isn't that much easier to digest for the average uneducated *Daily Mail* reader. 'The will of the people' and 'Brexit' simply act as easy soundbites for an audience that won't question their definitions or grounding in accuracy. That's the power of language.

So, why did people vote for Brexit? In my opinion, for the vast majority of people in this country there were only two reasons to vote in favour of leaving the EU – Racism, ignorance, or a combination of both. There was obviously an advantage for the extremely wealthy, the 0.1% who might benefit from looser regulation in terms of taxation and environmental standards. But for the other 99.9%, racism and ignorance are the only reasons I can think of. There were vague wishy-washy notions of 'taking back control' – a meaningless statement that I think refers to trivial matters like fishing grounds. One of the many lies of the Vote Leave campaign was that we would be taking back control from non-elected bureaucrats. Most of them are actually elected, and of course there was a deep irony that this was coming from a country that has the second largest non-democratically elected chamber in the world, otherwise known as the House of Lords (second only to the Chinese government). To this day, I find it bizarre how Nigel Farage conned so many people. Here was a man who was a multi-millionaire, ex-city banker, with a German wife, and two children with German citizenship, working in Belgium, and receiving a generous pension from the EU. Here he was, pretending to be a man of the people, grinning away whilst posing for photos with a pint of John Smiths bitter. It was enough to make your blood boil!

Reason 1– Racism and the fear of immigration came about not necessarily from strongly held racist beliefs or migrants themselves, but from the fear of migration. In country after country, the ghosts of the fascists have re-materialised and are sitting in parliaments such as Germany, Austria, and Italy. They have successfully convinced their populations that the greatest threat to their nations isn't government tyranny or inequality or climate change, but immigration. It is a successful strategy for the fear-mongers. Driven by this fear, in country after country voters are electing leaders who are doing incalculable long-term damage. It was fear of migrants principally that led to Brexit. A You-Gov poll in the days before the result found that 56% of Britons named 'immigration and asylum' as the biggest issue facing the country. I remember reading this and being absolutely flummoxed. I guess I was part of the twin liberal bubbles of Brighton and London, so pretty much never met anyone who voiced their concern over this. I suspect this fear was made worse by the mass media's refusal to clarify any immigration terms. I am convinced that over 90% of the people in this country couldn't tell you the difference between an asylum seeker, a refugee, or an economic migrant. They were being used interchangeably to prove whatever point the newspapers were trying to make. The people who were camped at the Sangatte refugee camp near Calais were somehow thrown into the Brexit debate. They weren't EU nationals, and in reality were actually an argument against leaving for people who were worried about them coming over. The only reason they were being held by French authorities was because of European law. If the UK left on a no-deal basis, France would be within their rights to wave them through and let Dover deal with the problem of undocumented migrants.

There were so many scare stories I read in the press that had no basis in fact. My newspaper of choice is *The Times*, because I think it gives the best overall balance in its reporting. However, I do try and occasionally read other papers just to get a sense of the nation's mood. Reading certain tabloids can be both heart-breaking and hilarious at the same time. The story about people pretending to be students by coming over to the UK on Tier 4 visas and then disappearing, was a classic. For one thing, this has nothing to do with the EU; anyone on a student visa is from much further afield. Part of my role, which I have been doing for eight years now, involves chasing up students who aren't progressing academically. In that time, I have only come across two students who were trying to stay, neither of whom were European (both were Chinese) or wanted to remain indefinitely. In spite of what the mass media thinks, it is actually very difficult for students from abroad to bluff their way in. There are all kinds of checks, language tests, and in our case, portfolio reviews. Considering all the upfront costs, using HE to remain in the UK illegally is not a sagacious strategy.

Tabloids with headlines such as 'Migrants Rob Young Britons of Jobs' and 'Britain's 40% Surge in Ethnic Numbers' stoked fear of outsiders, day after day. The fear of migrants is magnified by lies about their numbers; politicians and racists train minds to think of them as a horde. In all the rich countries, people – especially those who are poorly educated or right wingers – think immigrants are a much bigger share of the population than they really are. A recent study found that Americans, as an overall average, think that foreign-born nationals make up around 37% of the population; it is really 13.7%. In other words, in the American imagination, immigrants are three times larger than they are in reality. The French think that one-in-three people in their country is Muslim. The actual number is one in 13. British respondents to the poll predicted that 22% of the population will be Muslim by 2020; the actual projection is 6%. Stats like these are repeated again and again across the Western world. There are also counter-trends and counter-examples. Multiple studies have found that people who have direct contact with immigrants have much more positive views about them and are much more open to increased immigration. In a city like London, it doesn't even factor as a major political issue. Then there are leaders who welcome migrants, however embattled they may be. Look at France, which elected the unapologetically pro-immigrant Emmanuel Macron, or Germany under Angela Merkel, which welcomed a million refugees in 2015. Canada is an interesting case study. After the government declared its intention to increase the flow of immigrants, the economy had the strongest growth in the G7 in 2017 – 3% a year. Hate crimes against Muslims actually went down in Canada in 2017, whereas in its southern neighbour, they jumped by 5% (the true 'Trump effect'). This shows that when countries safeguard the rights of their minorities, they also safeguard, as a happy side effect, the rights and economic well-being of everyone else. If a court forbids discrimination against, say, Muslims, it is also much more likely to forbid discrimination against, say, gay people. The obverse is also true; when they don't safeguard the rights of their minorities, every other citizen's rights are in peril.

I often wonder where this fear and loathing of migrants came from. It didn't start with skinheads on the street or torch-bearing white supremacists. I think the hatred has been manufactured, an extension of an old-world idea. While the colonisers ruled over the colonies – and the slave owners in the New World over the slaves – they began to find it essential to distinguish themselves from their subjects, to hold themselves morally and intellectually superior to them. Flash forward a hundred or so years, and fear of migrants earns politicians votes. Fear of migrants sells. *The Sun* and *Daily Mail* newspapers are flourishing, feeding their readers a daily diet of xenophobia.

The not-so-secret secret at the heart of the UK immigration debate is that we desperately need more immigrants. Whilst immigration controls may be a populist vote-winner, the population replacement rate of the UK is only 1.6, far short of the 2.1 needed to simply maintain a steady workforce. The economy is mostly a numbers game, with our society entirely dependent on inward migration at all levels, from top engineers and scientists all the way through to fruit pickers. Without this, our economy would rapidly slide down the pecking order, with pensions and our tax system all at risk of collapse – something all politicians know. I knew someone who studied this whilst working at Whitehall for six years. He used to refer to his superiors as uncivil servants, but that's another story. He confirmed my suspicions that, like many developed countries, we are entirely dependent on this process. It could come to the stage in the next few decades where countries start to fight to attract immigrants. The reason Boris lifted the £30,000 earnings cap in 2020 was because he was well aware of these dangers. So, on the one hand we are restricting freedom of movement from the EU, but on the other we are balancing this out by trying to attract people from other parts of the world. It does make you wonder what the whole point of this torrid Brexit process was.

The second reason, ignorance, had its roots in a complex web of misinformation. A fake enemy was created out of the EU which, in the classic populists' playbook, diverted attention away from the real enemy and the real issues. As ever, those with the wealth tell those who are poor that they are poor, not because they have the wealth, but because of outsiders (i.e. we are forced to pay x-million into the EU coffers every year). Not only that, but those with wealth on the whole control the media, so that is the message that people hear. It's a win-win for the ambitions of profiteers like Boris Johnson – an abundance of cheap labour to drive down costs and break unions, while harnessing the rage of the poor and disenfranchised to bring about their own unregulated American dumping ground satellite state on the edge of Europe.

The principles and logic behind the EU position are clear, logical, and calculable. The EU is an organisation that works for the benefit of its members, and to that effect applies rules that follow international law and are the same for everybody. The reason why we have some of the highest food standards in the UK is because of the EU. In much the same vein, environmental standards, workers' rights, maternity and paternity rights, and a whole raft of other things we take for granted, are not there out of the goodness of Tory hearts. Far from it; they would love to cut much of this if they could. The European Court of Justice protects us from the prospect of a tinpot dictator (aka Boris Johnson) trying to tear up the rulebook. Equally, it protects us from people on the far-left who may go too far the other way, for example, in an unsustainable public spending splurge. No matter what your political persuasion, unless you're a tax-dodging billionaire the EU protects everyone by upholding common values. These are the kinds of things that should have been part of a positive messaging campaign in relation to the EU. When David Cameron said he wanted 'people to stop banging on about the

EU', what he should have said was, 'I want people to stop banging on about the EU in a negative way. Look at all the amazing things the EU brings to this country.'

I'm not sure who I blame more for Brexit – Nigel Farage, David Cameron, Theresa May, or Boris Johnson. All four have a large part to play in sowing the seeds of division across this country. Nigel Farage is my contender for one of the worst human beings who has ever lived, a deceitful self-absorbed character, a bit like an evil version of Toad of Toad Hall. David Cameron seems almost a liberal character compared to some of the charlatans that sit in government now (in 2020). His crucial mistake, of course, was calling the referendum in the first place, doing it for the wrong reasons (i.e. party political gain), and not bothering to think through the consequences. His successor, Theresa May made a series of catastrophic mistakes during her time as Prime Minister, like starting the firing gun on the Article 50 process before she had a plan, or refusing to negotiate with the other parties until it was too late. She was totally ineffectual, and up to that point one of the worst Prime Ministers we've ever had.

Boris Johnson started off as a joke, before morphing into a knock-off pound shop version of Donald Trump. He came to LCC once and managed to offend almost everyone he met. My colleague made him a cup of coffee and he complained about the quality of it, before starting off his meeting with the Head of College by saying, 'So why am I here then?' It was clearly a PR exercise, but he had no intention of reading up on what we taught or why he was there. The Head of College walked into my office after her meeting ended and just said aloud, 'What an absolute wanker!'

Any feelgood factor he may have had evaporated as soon as he suspended parliament. I think that was the last straw for many people. Here was a man who wasn't elected, asking someone else who wasn't elected (i.e. the Queen) to close down the very thing where people are elected to make very important decisions. What must the outside world have thought? The EU must have looked at us and asked themselves, 'Are they all on drugs?' It was inevitable that the proroguing of parliament would be overturned, but it wasn't so much the proroguing itself that angered people. Rather, it was the Prime Minister treating democracy like it was some kind of nuisance, something that could be disregarded if it got in his way. The other scary thing was how quickly the Brexit arguments changed Boris' character, or as I suspect, peeled away the fabricated cuddly image to reveal the real man beneath. Once the proroguing of Parliament was overturned and Boris Johnson had to eat humble pie, we no longer saw the zip-wiring, flag-waving, whiff-whaffing, hair-ruffling jester. Instead, he resembled more of a mean sarcastic bully.

Every populist is a walking contradiction. Their policies are so ridiculous that they have to be. Nigel Farage says he hates the EU, but his children have German passports. Boris Johnson proposes tough immigration policies, but was a liberal mayor who speaks multiple languages. Donald Trump's ex-wife is from the Czech Republic and his current wife is Slovakian. Adolf Hitler hated animal cruelty, etc, etc. They certainly don't practise what they preach. What they rail against also sustains them. There's a reason that Nigel Farage returns again and again to politics. You would think that having failed to become an MP on seven (!) occasions (five general elections and two by-elections), he would try and retire with some dignity. But no, like Noel Edmond's endless TV career, he continues to stick around. I'm sure that he secretly wants us to remain in the EU as long as possible (or until he receives his EU-funded pension) so he has a mass platform from which to express his vile views. Without the EU, he's surplus to requirements. Farage and people like him have benefited from the very system that they want to tear down. Why don't people see through this charade?

Is it because they're looking for what they want to see? Is it simply a case of 'I like to laugh, but I don't like black people, so I'll vote for someone who looks funny and is racist'? Sometimes, as in Boris Johnson's comment that 'Muslim women look like letterboxes' (yes, he really said that), you tick both boxes in one fell swoop. It's interesting that people on the right-wing side of British politics can get away with this type of duplicity, but people on the left can't. Imagine, for example, if Keir Starmer had an offshore bank account in the Cayman Islands. There would be outrage, accusations flying all over the House of Commons, and in time he'd probably have to resign. Why is it okay for Boris Johnson to talk about democracy and taking back control, and then act like a tin pot dictator of some banana republic by shutting down parliament? It's hypocrisy on steroids. I guess either his voter base don't care enough, or just don't make the connection.

In 2020, someone thought that the best way to bring the country together was to produce a new fifty-pence piece to commemorate our new-found freedom. On one hand, I thought that having legal tender that vast swathes of the population would refuse to use was lunacy. On the other, I chuckled quite a bit when I heard it was a fifty-pence piece that was getting the dubious honour. Really important and unquestionably positive celebrations that we're all on the same side about (like the London Olympics, or big 100-year anniversaries) get a big shiny special issue £5 coin. Smaller, feel good events usually get a £2 coin. But for Brexit, this miserable undignified shuffling out the back door, we get a blunt nickel thing that won't even stretch to a packet of crisps.

Perhaps the biggest fundamental flaw with Brexit is that it doesn't address the causes of itself. It is the implementation of a solution before we have identified the problem, and as any Project or Events Manager will tell you, that can often lead to disaster. What caused people to vote in racist, stupid, and ignorant ways? What were the fundamental problems behind this? I believe they were poverty and inequality. These were greatly exacerbated by the 2007/8 recession, when public spending and social services began to be cut to the bone. I am very lucky in that I lead a privileged life, but you don't need to go too far to see poverty and inequality in action. One of the projects I was involved in with the Men's Network was taking kids on some of Brighton's poorest estates to the beach for the first time. I was shocked to discover that over 50% of the under-18s in Brighton's outlying estates (places like Moulsecoomb & Withdean) had never once been to the beach. That was jaw-dropping. In many cases, you could actually see the beach from their houses, when they were perched high up on the hills at the edge of the South Downs. Brighton & Hove Council had cut the shuttle bus that served these routes, and without a car it was borderline impossible for them to leave, making it even harder for them to break out of the poverty cycle. These are the types of issues that need to be addressed in towns and cities up and down the country. A whole raft of measures around education, the role of public services, transport – this is where our energies should be going. Not only does Brexit distract from these, but it makes it worse by the removal of European funding. Areas like Cornwall and the Welsh Valleys have received huge EU subsidies over the past thirty years, which are unlikely to be replaced by the UK government. This then leads to the very real risk of civil disorder when people realise that leaving the EU has made their lives that much harder. If farmers can't export without tariffs, or if that one annual trip that a family makes to Spain becomes more expensive, people will not turn a blind eye. What happens if our food (which is incredibly cheap by international standards) comes to be more in line with other countries that import (i.e. Canada/Australia).

I remember going with an Australian girl to a London supermarket for the first time and she couldn't believe how cheap it was. '15p for a banana!' she exclaimed. 'That's amazing. It's five times the price of that in Oz.' We don't realise how lucky we are as an island nation to have imported food that is so cheap. As a country, are we really daft enough to disrupt crucial supply chains, shrink our country's GDP, and increase the hardship of millions of our citizens in the name of some ill thought-through, right wing, ideological crusade? Quite possibly, yes. Sadly, we are.

In 2019, I went to a debating festival (at a time when the whole Brexit question still wasn't resolved) and went to a talk by Vince Cable, the ex-leader of the Liberal Democrats. He was a brilliant speaker and it was really interesting to hear first hand the perspective of someone who was a sitting MP. He made some interesting points, one of which was that most pro-Brexit people don't actually care all that much. The debate was centred around the question of whether there would be civil unrest if Brexit didn't happen, and the consensus was that the reverse would happen – civil unrest was only a realistic prospect if Brexit (certainly in its hardest form) were to happen. The people likely to riot would be younger people, angry that their futures were being stolen from them. Vince Cable described the vast majority of hardcore supporters of Brexit as '*Daily Express*-waving old age pensioners in Cornwall and the New Forest'. For most people, he said, Brexit was a relatively minor issue, further down the pecking order than, say, the NHS or job security. It was something that had been hijacked by a small bunch of right-wing extremists. In other words, the amount of people truly opposed to the EU is incredibly small, the debate has just been re-shaped and remoulded into something else entirely. Apathy + bubbling anger = a void to be exploited. And a void can be filled with anything, no matter how contradictory.'Take back our sovereignty', for instance, really meant 'Let's put our (already) sovereign country into the hands of empire-yearning Little Englander xenophobes and fascists'. Vince Cable also said (and I wholeheartedly agreed with him) that pro- EU people hadn't cared enough either. Most people simply took the EU for granted for years. It's that old adage that 'you never truly miss something until its gone', whether it's relationships or one's health, it's all too easy to overlook it. Only now, with the real danger of losing something as precious as EU membership, have people suddenly woken up to the fact that the EU, and in fact democracy more generally, is under threat.

By the end of 2019, there was a creeping suspicion that perhaps the UK electorate had made a mistake and that public opinion was starting to shift. Can 17.4 million people be wrong? Absolutely, just look at the viewing figures Jimmy Saville used to get in the eighties. In 2019/2020, we were being presented with Boris'll fix it and another blond-haired egoist. It's also worth bearing in mind that 17.4 million people was only 26% of the population back in 2016. Boris Johnson really was the ultimate charlatan. His 'Get Brexit Done' tagline was a very effective slogan – a clear, simple, and easy message to implant into people's brains. It was irritating, because anyone with half a brain knew that it was a meaningless statement; it could mean whatever you wanted it to mean. All three-word slogans are basically nonsense. Rather like the McDonald's 'I'm lovin' it' jingle – no-one knows what they're supposed to love. Is it the sickly sauce? The smell that lingers on your clothes for days afterwards? All this talk of his Brexit deal being oven-ready and just needing to be popped in the microwave. What a load of steaming horse manure. A better analogy would be Boris as a microwave prime minister – fake, unpalatable, and likely to make you sick if over-consumed. A man who's been 'oven ready' for high office even since he was burning £50 notes in front of the homeless in his Bullingdon club days in Oxford. A microwave meal full of crap with no nutritional value at all. If you looked past his hilarious quips and amusing use of Latin, you could see Boris for what he really was – an egotist with no discernible talent, describing himself as a one-nation Tory after getting rid of every one-nation Tory the party had. He threw out members of his own party that voted for Brexit more times than he did. Johnson had such a lack of moral backbone I was surprised that he could still stand up by the end of the year. Anyway, because of the deadlock in parliament, he ended up calling the first winter election that the UK had held in nearly 100 years.

I remember all the talk at work around how woeful the Labour campaign was. Labour should have walked this election, what with allegations of bumbling Boris threatening to sell the NHS to Donald Trump – a man who probably thinks statesmanship is a luxury yacht! It was a bad omen that the result would be announced on Friday 13th. I wasn't particularly hopeful, but I thought with the country so split the result would at least be close.

In December of 2019, the Tories won the Christmas election with a thumping majority, much to the horror and surprise of almost everyone I knew. Many of my work colleagues went campaigning for Labour around London, though the election was lost in the traditional Labour-voting Northern heartlands. It was billed as a 'Brexit election' but the majority of people (both in terms of number of seats and the popular vote) actually voted for parties campaigning to remain in the EU. Not that Boris Johnson cared about that. Brexit was the wicked weapon that he had used to dethrone the last two leaders in order to lever himself into their place. Reckless in everything but personal ambition, he had now essentially trapped us outside of the EU.

The dawning realisation that we now had five more years of this horror show was too much for most of us to bear. To quote Stephen Morrissey, 'This joke isn't funny anymore.' The only positive to the whole sorry state of affairs was that because he now had a solid majority, he didn't need the right-wing ERG (European Research Group) votes, so whatever kind of Brexit happens, it should be softer than it might otherwise have been. Being one-quarter Turkish himself, this Turkish proverb is a good analogy for the situation we found ourselves in by 2020:

'The forest was shrinking but the trees kept voting for the axe, for the axe was clever and convinced the trees that because his handle was made of wood he was one of them.'

By 2020, I had come to acknowledge that Brexit was now inevitable. It's incredibly sad, but I've begrudgingly accepted it. I just feel incredibly sorry for young people who will be growing up in an age of such division. I have 150 'I told you so's' all lined up for when reality comes crashing down with a thud. The disastrous global events of 2020 would later throw into sharp focus what really mattered in life and where we, as a country, should have been focusing our energies. In spite of all the doom and gloom, I remain optimistic that there are enough open-minded and liberal people in this country to see us through this ugly period of our history. The greatest trick the devil ever pulled off, they say, was convincing the world he didn't exist. They say also that the devil is in the detail. There tends to be quite evil connotations when it comes to deceiving people, or confusing them, or essentially conning them into believing they are getting one thing, when in fact, they are getting something much worse. I suspect there will be a point in the not too distant future when the chickens really do come home to roost for Johnson, Farage, and their ilk.

Ultimately, the UK can never be entirely separated from the EU, because all our systems and processes are totally intertwined. That sense of people across the Channel being 'the other' is a total myth. We are as integral to the EU as anyone else. I like to think we are not actually leaving the EU, but rather the EU is leaving us.

CHAPTER 12

Shepherd's Bush

I hadn't felt truly settled in a long time. In early 2016, I moved again, to bring the total up to thirteen different houses since I moved out of my parents' home when I was 18. Some of them were brief stays and weren't even mentioned in the earlier chapters of this book. I guess it was a fairly bohemian lifestyle that I led for fourteen years. I was a bit of an eternal student, working alongside other students and still using an NUS card. I suppose living in a shed for eighteen months was probably peak-bohemian. It wasn't long before I was on the move again. I had begun to get tired of all this uprooting by now. When you own a lot of stuff (and by now, I had accumulated quite a large collection of various bits), it's an ordeal being continually nomadic. Just packing/unpacking and dealing with landlords and estate agents can be exhausting work, not to mention incredibly expensive. I've lost count of the number of deposits that I have lost over the years. I had started putting money aside for my own place, but only had a rough plan at this point, namely to buy a place back in Brighton. However, this particular move was much more exciting because I was moving in with my girlfriend and future wife.

I first met Debs on 23rd August, 2015. We started talking to each other online a few weeks before. For our first date, I took her to a pub quiz at The Elgin in Ladbroke Grove. I've always thought that pub quizzes are a great activity for a first date: it involves alcohol, you get to chat about a range of subjects, and there's always a chance you can win something. As well as the winning prize, there's often a consolation prize for the lowest scoring team. We didn't get either. We actually came in the most irritating position, second to last. In our defence, we were only a team of two, while all of the other teams had four to six people in them. Debs was (and still is) an amazing girl. She was gorgeous, chatty, funny, and enjoyed laughing at my jokes. It was also refreshing to be on a date with someone who was genuinely interested in the things I did. When I started talking about tai chi or Neil Young, her eyes didn't glaze over. We also discovered that we had both been at Glastonbury the same year, so we ended up chatting quite a lot about our respective experiences. I thought I was being clever by doubling up on her alcohol to try and get her more drunk. I found out later on that she was doing exactly the same thing to me, so we were both drinking doubles and triples, not realising quite why we were both getting so sozzled. At the time, Debs was working for a service design company called Plan and was involved in some fascinating projects around drones and car-sharing companies. We also chatted at length about some of her prior design projects. She had once designed a needle-free injector which I thought was incredibly creative. I was over the moon when she agreed to go on a second date with me. Obviously, I wanted to see her again, but was also chuffed that I'd succeeded in leaving a good impression. For our second date, we went to a comedy night in Angel, followed by a boozy knees-up in a cocktail bar. The rest as they say, is history.

The first meal I ever cooked for Debs was something of a disaster. She was on a very strict diet at the time. I offered to make her a Bolognese, but as she wasn't eating sugar, processed sauces or cheese, I was somewhat stumped. At least she wasn't a vegetarian; in my opinion, that's a big missed steak! My culinary skills were still pretty basic, so rather than attempt to make a suitably diet- friendly sauce, I simply elected not to do one. I also forgot to add onions, which was a bit of an error. In my defence, I was inviting Debs over to my house-share for the first time and thus was more preoccupied with tidying up and making sure the house looked vaguely presentable. Sharing a house with five other people meant that it was usually a bit of a tip, especially the kitchen area. The cobwebs that had formed on the extractor hood were such an engrained part of the kitchen that we had named the spiders that resided there. After two hours of dusting, scrubbing, and bleaching, I had run out of time to dash to the shops. Instead, I made a meal out of some fridge basics, so I think the only vegetables I added were some chopped-up carrots and diced cucumber. The hot cucumber was something that to this day she still hasn't quite gotten over. Personally, I don't see any issue with having warm cucumber, I think it's quite a nice accompaniment. People seem perfectly happy to have courgette in a bolognese which, let's be honest, is 95% the same thing. I'm convinced that one day it will be an 'in vogue food trend'. Thinking back, the meal looked pretty terrible – a plate of minced beef with some odd-looking carrots and cucumber perched on top. Bless her, she took it pretty well and managed to digest most of it.

Debs owned her own flat in-between Acton and Shepherd's Bush in West London. It was originally built to be a 'live-work' flat, with the upstairs originally designed to be an office space for people to work from home. Just after it was built, the 2007/2008 financial crash occurred, and the company struggled to sell all the units within the block after self-employment took a bit of a nosedive. Debs bought it during that period when prices were tumbling and made a nice little profit on it in the end. That's the funny thing about house cycles. You need to have a bit of luck on your side when so many factors are outside of your control. For years I put all my energies into investing in a pension and paying off my student loan, when I could have been saving for a deposit. My mindset has always been to do one thing at a time, and besides, I'd heard so many stories where people had lost huge amounts of money. Ben, for instance, had owned a flat with two of his mates, which had turned into a financial sink hole back in Brighton. I think there were some kind of drainage issues and a dispute with the neighbours over a boundary. He owned it for about ten years and actually ended up losing money on it. I remember being advised when I was at university that mortgages were a waste of money and that renting gave you much more freedom. It's funny how opinions can change so radically, depending on time and geography. If I knew then what I know now, I would have spent all my student loan on saving for a deposit and worked throughout my BA. But then again, that's all with the benefit of hindsight.

Debs' flat was in a block called Issigonis House. It was named after Alec Issigonis, a famous car designer whose most famous work was the ground-breaking development of the Mini. The flats were actually built on the site of the old Morris Minor factory. A few years later, we ended up calling our cat Ziggy as a combination of Issy and David Bowie's Ziggy Stardust alter ego. The block itself was quite nice. It had spacious wide balconies and stylish wood panelling decorating the external walls of the apartments. Some of the communal areas, however, looked a little neglected and could have had a little bit more money invested in them. The walls of the lifts, for instance, would literally wobble when you leant on them. They were silver and bendy like a 1960s Dr Who set. It seemed like the lifts would break every single week, and you would have to carry shopping up eight flights of stairs. Every year, the housing association would blame the residents for bringing up Christmas trees in the lifts. Apparently, it was the pine needles getting caught in the door mechanism that caused so many breakdowns. Any lift that can be defeated by a few measly pine needles really isn't up to the job. The biggest issue with the block was the lack of security. There was only one outer door, so it was pretty easy for people to be followed in. And the letterboxes were right at the main entrance and were easily accessible to passers-by. So, people could literally put their hands in and retrieve letters from outside the building. Debs had had her identity stolen this way, though luckily, she managed to intercept it in time by notifying her bank. The housing association did eventually end up changing the design of the letterboxes to make this more difficult for would-be thieves. Below the flats sat a small branch of Tesco. It was useful if you wanted a quick top-up shop, but it never had everything you needed. The name 'Tesco Extra' always confused me. It was that rare definition of extra that meant considerably less.

In contrast to the communal areas, the flat itself was gorgeous. Debs had designed and decorated it with a great deal of taste and precision. It was a two-bed flat, but it felt much larger due to the double height ceiling over the kitchen/living area. The upstairs section had been converted into a large bedroom with an adjoining en-suite. She was the last person in the block to be given permission for a second bathroom. There were limitations on the drainage system, so after Debs had her work completed, the council said no to anyone else doing anything similar. The bedroom had these impressive bifold doors which gave the flat a lovely open plan feel. One of her prize possessions was this hi-tech mirror that de-steamed itself and was also connected via Bluetooth with inbuilt speakers, so that you could play music through it. This was cutting edge in 2015. In reality, it was rarely used to play music through, but to this day I still find the de-steaming function awesome. Every home should have one. The flat also had a small balcony which overlooked a communal courtyard. My first impression on walking in there was that it looked like a show home. Everything seemed so perfect. You couldn't really have a bigger contrast with Mandrake Road where I was staying. It just felt 'so adult'.

Starting a new relationship is a really exciting time. I remember first meeting Debs' parents, Rob and Jen, when I was invited to a birthday dinner at a restaurant in Barnes, called 'The Depot'. They couldn't have been more welcoming and convivial if they tried. A week or so later, I was invited round their house for Friday night dinner. It was interesting seeing the enactment of Jewish traditions, as opposed to reading about them in some dusty old book at school, which up until that point was the limit of my rudimentary awareness. Thankfully, it all went well, and our first home-cooked dinner didn't become my last supper.

I recall there being a fair bit of debate in my house about taking Debs to see Slater acting in a play; it was a performance of *Salome* and involved a particular scene with a severed head. Tom was very concerned that it might be a bit too 'gory' for her. I'm not sure where he got that impression from, but it was nice of him to care. Debs' best friend, Rachel, really wasn't sure about me the first time we met. She referred to me as some type of 'dribbling fool'. I don't remember much of this, but I think we had been to two separate birthdays over the course of a day. One was for Debs, and the other was for

Rachel's then boyfriend. I had probably drunk far too much, all in the name of Dutch courage. (I was, after all, meeting a lot of new people.) Apparently, I was slurring my words and dribbling quite a lot. Great first impression!

In March 2016, Debs and I went on our first proper holiday abroad, when we decided to visit Lisbon to celebrate my birthday. Lisbon is a really interesting place, being one of the oldest cities in the world, and second oldest European capital after Athens. It pre-dates other capital cities like London and Rome by centuries. It also has the world's oldest continuously operating bookshop – The Bertrand Chiado, which has been open since 1732. The city is also famous for its relatively expansive tram network, which winds its way through the steep, narrow streets. There was one particular street where the trams passed within about five feet of people's front doors. Whilst we were walking down this particular street, we had to put our backs to the wall whilst the tram passed us by – we almost felt like breathing in. On my birthday itself, we went to this local family-run restaurant that we had been recommended. As well as cooking all the food, the family also provided the entertainment which was fado – basically, the Portuguese equivalent of flamenco music. Debs also arranged for them to bake me a cake, which I was presented with after dinner. It was colossal. I think she had assumed that they might bake a small cake with maybe two or three slices. This was enough to feed the whole restaurant, which in fact we did, offering it around to all the other diners. They had piped my name onto it in elaborate swirls of butter cream – that really was the icing on the cake. It was a great atmosphere, almost a pub lock-in, but instead it was a restaurant lock-in with live music and endless quantities of sugary sponge.

The most memorable thing that happened during that holiday was in fact something that didn't happen. For my birthday present, Debs had paid for us to go and watch one of Lisbon's main football teams, Benfica, play FC Porto. I had looked the game up a few weeks in advance and booked the tickets myself. We turned up at the stadium nice and early. It was a good hour by train to the edge of the city, so we (or rather, Debs) had planned everything to perfection. I even had a Benfica scarf. We got off at the right station, but it all felt strangely quiet – no revellers, no lads drinking beer, just a few middle-aged people carrying around shopping bags. We shrugged it off and walked to the stadium, where we assumed everyone was already congregating. Upon arrival, it was bizarrely empty. You could literally see the tumbleweed blowing through the parking lot. We walked round to where the main gates were located, and again it was completely devoid of people. We were both a bit confused. I double-checked the match on my phone; maybe I had got the time slightly wrong? Instead, I had forgotten to check if the game was home or away. The match was actually being played in Porto, over 200 miles away! It would take us at least two hours to get there, by which time we would have missed the majority of the match. I stood there with my Benfica scarf, feeling like a right plum. Debs summed it up perfectly when she turned to me and half jokingly said, 'I have never in all my life known such stupidity.'

2016 was the year of major celebrity deaths. After we got back from holiday I found out that Prince had died. I wasn't a major fan at the time, but I was still gutted, as he had been on my list of acts I wanted to see. In fact, my work colleague, Fiona, had offered me a ticket to go and watch one of his club gigs in Camden just a few weeks earlier. That was one of those instances where, looking back, you wished you'd taken the opportunity. I was still in shock from David Bowie passing away back in January. Again, he was someone that I never got the chance to witness live. Both Prince and Bowie seemed in such good health. Bowie in particular had started a bit of a creative rebirth with his last two albums, and looked incredible for his age. But it wasn't just these two. During the first four months of 2016 George Martin, Paul Daniels, Terry Wogan, Glenn Fry, Alan Rickman, and Ronnie Corbett all passed away. The year continued in much the same vein, with Muhammad Ali, Gene Wilder, George Michael, Leonard Cohen, Leon Russell, and Carrie Fisher, all kicking the bucket by the time December rolled round. There were plenty more as well – in excess of one hundred major celebrities. It almost became a running joke at work with people taking bets on who would be next.

Things had been going swimmingly over the last nine months, so in May 2016, I moved into Debs' flat. I was slightly apprehensive; after all, it's quite a big step. What if we ended up arguing all the time? What if we drove each other mad with our habits? When you don't see each other all the time, you're almost always at your best, or trying to be. But when you're living together, that isn't the case. It wasn't long before I was resisting the urge to pick my toenails whilst sitting on the sofa in my dressing gown. There needs to be a bit of give and take so that you can both feel relaxed in your environment. We are pretty similar in many ways, but we approach things very differently. For instance, we're both pretty organised, but it comes out in completely opposing ways. When we go on holiday, for example, Debs likes to pack everything a day or two before, which makes perfect sense. I struggle with this, because in the morning I always wonder if I really did pack everything, and end up taking it all out again. I prefer packing literally half an hour before we leave, so I can be sure that I haven't forgotten anything. I know that this drives Debs mad, but I can't help it. It's just the way my mind works. I was also a bit worried about her getting annoyed with all my clutter. There was a small guest room downstairs that she had very graciously let me use to store all my music bits. She also reluctantly let me keep my work desk that she absolutely detested. To be fair, it was falling to bits, but I had a strange attachment to it. When you are renting for long periods of time, I think you compensate for the lack of security by clinging onto the things you own. I gave away much of my furniture to my old housemates but was determined to keep hold of this desk. Debs' face was priceless when her dad came over and had a look at it.

'That's a lovely little desk,' he exclaimed.

'I think so, too,' I said, giving Debs a cheeky nod.

There wasn't enough space in the upstairs wardrobes, so my clothes were mostly stored downstairs as well. Her tranquil guest room was no more.

It was a lovely flat to live in, and a refreshing change having some sweeping views over the rooftops of London. From her balcony, you could just make out the London Eye glimmering in the distance. The area was another of those places that estate agents would describe as 'up and coming', which is code for 'It's not the nicest area, but if posh people keep buying here, eventually we'll price all the poor people out and it will be artisan cafés all the way.' The flat was located just outside the madness of Shepherd's Bush, so there were some pleasant places only a few minutes' away. Askew Road had a nice selection of shops, and there was a green space called Ravenscourt Park where I would sometimes go jogging. It was also pretty central and only a ten-minute drive (or an hour's walk) from Barnes, where Debbie's parents lived. I quite liked having Westfield shopping centre nearby. It was just next door to the tube station, so it was easy to pop into on my way home. It was also something of an oasis from the noise and chaos of Shepherd's Bush itself.

Shortly after I moved in with Debs, I got my first proper smartphone. I was a few blissful years behind the curve, but

Debs insisted I get one so I could join in with group messaging and WhatsApp. I guess that's the thing with technology, once you've committed, it's almost impossible to go back without feeling like you're missing out on things. To be fair, it was probably time I joined the twenty-first century, and the freedom to do things 'on the move' was a revelation. Being able to check emails on the way to work, or book a taxi through Uber, suddenly gave you a freedom that just wasn't there a few years before. As with all tech, there are positives and negatives. It's how you use it that defines to what degree your experience is either of those things. I try and ration my use as best I can. I still make a point of occasionally leaving the house without my phone, for instance. I still buy newspapers on weekdays, so my news isn't filtered through any particular platform. Without going back to the Brexit arguments, just reading news from one source that uses algorithms (i.e. Facebook) is dangerous. It gives the reader the impression that the point of view they are receiving (whether liberal, conservative, or whatever) is genuine news. The connection between social media and alarmist views has been magnified by 4G and wireless technology, with a twin sense of connectivity and anonymity that makes people feel powerful. But then again, you can also share funny cat videos, so yeah, positives and negatives.

Living in a genuinely nice environment made all the difference when it came to inviting friends over and having dinner parties. PD (pre-Debs) dinner parties could only realistically be a barbecue in the back yard or some pizza before heading out to the pub. Now I had access to real kitchen utensils – things like whisks and egg poachers (not that I very often used them, but still, it was nice to know they were there). Debs had a 'come dine with me' thing going on with her friends, where as couples we would take it in turns to cook a three-course meal for each other. These were usually themed around flavours/ingredients or more obscure things like colours and decades. Sometimes this would involve playlists or a certain style of dress. I did an 80s dinner party, for instance, with a prawn cocktail starter, *coq au vin*, and the *piéce de resistance* – a tower of Ferrero Rocher. (There was a series of 80s adverts where Ferrero Rocher was marketed as this luxury item that would be passed around at balls and cocktail parties. It would always be presented piled up on a giant pyramid, which people would respectfully take from the top.) It was quite a lot of effort to construct this golden chocolate monument. I journeyed to Hobbycraft and bought a Styrofoam pyramid, into which I then strategically positioned cocktail sticks. This gave the illusion that the chocolates were delicately balancing on top of each other, rather than being physically attached. The playlists would get more and more challenging at these dinners. An 80s playlist is pretty easy, but by the time we got to a nut-themed dinner, it became much trickier. I managed it, though, and succeeded in impressing the crowd by coming up with three hours' worth of nut-based songs. My nut-themed playlist included the following:

- *Everyone Loves A Nut* – Johnny Cash
- *Tarzan's Nuts* – Madness
- *Peanuts* – The Police
- *Coconut* – Harry Nilsson
- *Plum Nuts* – Etta James
- *Chestnuts Roasting On An Open Fire* – The Overtones
- *If This Ain't Love Then I Must Be Going Nuts* – Libby Floyd
- *In A Nutshell* – John O Atkinson
- *I'm A Nut* – Big Malo

The new commute was a bit of a pain. It was no more to endure than what most Londoners go through, but I had been spoilt by my relatively pain-free 16-minute commute on the northern line. When I lived in Tooting, it was possible to be at work within 42 minutes of waking up; I timed it once. 16 minutes to get ready, 2 minutes to make my lunch, a 5-minute walk to the tube, 16 minutes on the tube, and a 3-minute walk at the other end. I now had to get used to an hour's commute each way; it was surprisingly long, considering that we were now living on the fringes of zone 2. We were surrounded by various tube lines and stations, the district and central lines and the Overground, but they were all about a 15-20 minute walk in opposing directions. This meant getting a bus along the notorious Uxbridge Road. It was notorious for a number of reasons. The traffic could be terrible, and sometimes it was quicker to walk. Some of the people who lived along this route were crazy. There were two old guys who would drive along the road in motorized wheelchairs that were lavishly decorated with various flags and stuffed toys. They were true British eccentrics, weaving in and out of traffic and sometimes holding the buses up, much to everyone's annoyance. I read an article about them once, that they were listed in the top 10 local celebrities in and around Shey Boo. (Shey Boo is the French-sounding nickname for Shepherd's Bush, in a tongue-in-cheek attempt at glamorising the area.) The people along Uxbridge Road always seemed to be in a permanent state of loud aggression. There was always drama on those Uxbridge Road buses, particularly when people were packed in there like sardines. I recall one occasion when I made the fatal mistake of getting on a bus during a match day. The local ground was Loftus Road, the home of Queen's Park Rangers, and with all the riot police and horses keeping order, you could easily get held up in the choking traffic. This particular incident happened on a Saturday afternoon. It was boiling hot and we were sitting in this stationary log-jam when people started getting irate. The driver refused to let any passengers off as we were not yet at a bus stop. People kept arguing the point but he was intransigent. One passenger then pressed the emergency release button and a few people clambered out. This angered the driver, who straight away closed it again. So then, of course, somebody pressed the emergency button again. After a couple of goes at this, one over-zealous gentlemen stood in the middle of the doors and physically held them open, as if he were some muscle-bound 80s action star saving the day. People clambered around the sides like desperate fish escaping from a net. The driver was shouting and swearing, when another guy approached him, asked him to stand down, and claimed he was an off-duty policeman. I'm sure he probably was, but Arnold Schwarzenegger didn't seem to believe him. Then it got really heated – literally and metaphorically. There was a tussle which then turned into a full-blown fight when other people started getting involved. As you can imagine, being on a confined bus alongside pensioners and children, there was a lot of confusion with everyone shouting and a few people crying. Most people just didn't know what to do. It took a while for the situation to calm down, and eventually the doors were opened and people just got off. Incidents like that happened all the time, though that was at the more extreme end of the spectrum. Shepherd's Bush just seemed to attract a lot of loud angry people.

Later on in 2016, Debs and I briefly attempted to set up our own business. We came up with this idea of a grown-up version of the kids' game 'pass the parcel' which we named Puzzle the Parcel. The idea was that it was a social game that could be played at Christmas and other celebratory occasions, as an alternative to things like crackers. We made some prototypes and tested them with a group of friends and with my parents at Christmas that year. It seemed to go down really well, so we attempted to make a few and see if we could sell them to local shops. We also created a website, designed a logo, and got some supplies shipped in. The problem was that it was incredibly labour-intensive and also very fiddly, taking over an hour to assemble a single unit. Starting a business that involves a great deal of wrapping, when it's something I'm not very good at, was a bit of a stumbling block. I genuinely believe that it was a solid idea, and if we were a bit more risk-averse (i.e. willing to borrow large sums of money to get it produced elsewhere) we could have made a success out of it. However, with both of us having full-time jobs and looking to save money, it was a gamble we weren't prepared to take. It was probably a good thing that we didn't end up running a business together. I imagine we would have killed each other before long. In some respects, we are quite similar personalities. We're both quite determined and like to proof the doubters wrong. When I started writing this book, for instance, most people doubted I would ever finish it, and certainly didn't think I'd have the discipline to write 100,000 words (which this book is far in excess of). Debs is much the same; if someone tells her she can't do something, that seems to motivate her further. However, in other ways, particularly when it comes to planning and organisation, we're like chalk and cheese. Probably not a good basis for working as well as living together.

In August, me, Debs, Josh, and Emma went to the Wilderness festival in Oxfordshire. It was by far the most middle-class festival I had frequented. There were hot showers! They were still inside Portakabins, but running hot water after the trials of Reading and Bestival was a lathery luxury. There were various culinary feasts that professional chefs would cook up in these huge marquees, although the cost was a bit prohibitive for us. Even so, we never felt like we were missing out, as the general food stalls were also of suitably high quality. There was wild boar and venison, avocado and sourdough, and all manner of intercontinental delicacies. A first for me was seeing olive stands peppered all over a festival campsite. I think it was in the crowd for Robert Plant that I saw Mark Carney – the former Governor of the Bank of England. That was an accurate indication of the type of festival this was. The overall experience was as important and arguably more important than the music, so there were various extra-curricular activities like foraging, rabbit-skinning, archery, and trekking. There were hot tubs all alongside the main lake, which looked very inviting. We didn't actually try them out, though Emma went back a couple of years later to finally get her hot tub experience. We did go wild swimming, though – even in the height of summer, it was bloody freezing. Music-wise, it was an interesting line up. The two headliners, Robert Plant and The Flaming Lips, were great. I also enjoyed the Crystal Fighters and bizarrely thought that Charlotte Church was pretty entertaining. The highlight of the weekend was the annual cricket match that took place on the Sunday. This had a real eccentric English village feel to it, where two teams would compete to the sounds of a 'mock upper-class twit commentator' who was a hilarious hybrid of Jacob Rees-Mogg and Alan Partridge. People were encouraged to streak across the pitch, so there were quite bizarre scenes of people trying to outdo each other with their naked pitch invasions. Some people would dance, some would do gymnastics, and others would just run on with various items like bubble guns and vegetables. They would all get marked on scores out of ten. It was fantastic entertainment to get inebriated to.

August became a bit of a celebrity-spotting month for us. A week after spotting Mark Carney, I saw Wayne Rooney and we came incredibly close to playing football with him. I'll explain... 2016 was our year of weddings. I think me and Debs went to six or seven that year; we even had to turn down a couple. By the time you factor in engagement parties and stag and hen dos, it's a big time and financial commitment.

This wedding was for Debs' cousin Tanya, who was marrying her partner Steve – a big Man United fan. Tanya worked for Soho House so was able to have the wedding at Soho Farmhouse – a sprawling members' club in the Oxfordshire countryside (coincidentally just round the corner from where we had been a week earlier at Wilderness). It was one of those luxury retreat-type places that had everything – swimming pools, spas, tennis courts, and a football pitch. When we arrived, Steve had been informed that Wayne Rooney and his wife, Coleen, were staying there over the weekend. Someone in the wedding party, knowing that Steve was a massive Man U fan, had approached the staff to ask Wayne if he wanted to have a kickaround with us on the morning of the wedding. I think the answer was a 'maybe'. On the morning of the big day, a few of us trekked up to the football field in anticipation. We were going to have a game either way. Wayne, perhaps not surprisingly, didn't show up. Apparently he had been at the bar all night and wasn't feeling his best. Debs and her sister, Lou had warned me and Roger to go easy on the groom. Within about two minutes of starting the game, Roger went in for a tackle on Steve, who fell to the ground in quite a bit of discomfort. My first thought was, *Thank God it wasn't me*, and the second was, *Is he going to make it down the aisle?* It was more serious than we initially thought. The poor guy could hardly walk. Later on, he did manage to get himself up the aisle, but he was visibly hobbling. It was too painful for him to put socks on, so during the ceremony he was barefoot inside his loose-fitting wedding shoes. During the reception, Steve showed us his ankle which had swelled up like a balloon. Roger was getting a scolding from Lou, and I was sitting there feeling a little smug that I hadn't been responsible. (Usually, when there's some kind of accident, I seem to be involved.) The following day as we were leaving, Rob decided to get a group shot of us. Suddenly we all saw Wayne and Coleen driving very slowly past in their SUV. We all turned to see them while Rob, who was completely oblivious, tried to coordinate the perfect shot.

'Come on, face the camera, look this way, stop messing around...' There is a brilliant photo of the wedding party, all suited and booted, looking in the wrong direction.

Our summer holiday that year was a trip to Croatia and Montenegro. Me and Debs had our own mini break in Dubrovnik before crossing the border and meeting up with Rob, Jen, Lou, and Roger. Dubrovnik was like something straight out of a fairy-tale – an ancient walled town where all the roof cladding was the colour of clementine. It had long since expanded beyond its sixteenth century walls, but the old town itself had remained relatively unchanged. There were no cars or big-name stores, just a maze of cobbled streets and quaint little bars and restaurants. Within this labyrinth of stone, hidden pocket gardens provided respite from the burning sun. These imposing citadel-style walls surrounded the town like giant talons keeping everyone nestled safely inside. The very foundations of the town seemed to be sprouting from the rocks that held back the Adriatic Sea. HBO famously filmed the King's landing scenes for *Game of Thrones* in Dubrovnik, due to its close resemblance to a medieval fortress. It wasn't hard to see why. You could easily envisage a royal guard emerging from behind a parapet and sending you off to the tower for some minor indiscretion. Debs and I visited this small monastery, which gave us an account of the city's history: As a republic, the city of Dubrovnik was one of the first places in the world to adopt modern laws and institutions. It had a medical service set up in 1301, and one of the world's first pharmacies opened in 1317 which is still operating today. It also had one of the world's first quarantine hospitals and abolished the slavery trade in 1432, hundreds of years before the British. Walking around, it really felt like one of those 'cradle of civilisation' type settlements. After a couple of days of eating, drinking, and general lounging, we hired a car and crossed the border into Montenegro. We journeyed down to the bay of Kotor, a vast sheltered body of water with a shoreline of nearly seventy miles. It was hemmed in by two mountain ranges, the Orjen mountains to the west and the Lovcen mountains to the east. It was a stunning drive – the road clung to the base of these peaks as it twisted and turned liked an endless strand of sautéed spaghetti. It was a challenging drive – scenic but treacherous. I've seen more straight lines from a three-year-old child playing with a crayon, it was a relief when we finally arrived.

We had rented an apartment which sat at the calm water's edge, tumbling hills enclosing us in on all sides. It was a stunning backdrop to wake up to every morning. We would go for early morning swims in the lake, and me and Roger would go for occasional runs along the winding paths. Our only major excursion was to the Njegos Mausoleum. Its claim to fame was that it was the highest mausoleum in the world, resting at an impressive 1,749 metres. It was hidden away at the top of Mount Lovcen, like some secretive Tibetan monastery. It was built in 1855 for Petar Petrovic-Njegos, one of the country's former political and spiritual leaders. To the outside world, it's a strange thing to be remembered for – having your decaying body at the world's highest altitude (excluding unfortunate mountain climbers). The views were awe-inspiring, and it really felt like the roof of the world. You looked down and saw the previously mighty Bay of Kotor resembling a mere puddle. The vast cruise ships that came in to dock looked like toy boats in a child's bath.

My other abiding memory from that holiday was our desperate attempt to have a barbecue one evening. We had bought food for all six of us, which in traditional Nathan-style meant we had enough for twelve people. A mountain of meat, a sackful of salad, and a compendium of condiments, all sat there waiting to be unleashed. Just as I was about to light the grill, the weather suddenly turned. It wasn't just raining; it was a full-on electrical storm. Me, Roger, and Rob, all took it in turns battling against the elements. The wind would change direction and we would be wheeling the barbecue back and forth – to the back garden, the front garden, the side passage – anywhere for the flames not to be extinguished. I'm embarrassed to say that men do get precious over barbecues, it's not a mere cliché. It's something about the ability to control fire that brings out the caveman in us, and we were all determined, if you pardon the pun, not to cave in. There were suggestions of 'just do it in the oven', which just wouldn't do. We persevered, and in the end, after being thoroughly drenched and weather-beaten, managed to serve up a delicious spread. It was undoubtedly the most challenging barbecue I have ever attempted.

Back in Blighty, I (partially) fulfilled one of my lifelong dreams of taking part in *The Crystal Maze*. I was obsessed with it as a kid. To me, Richard O'Brien wasn't a scary creature from *The Rocky Horror Picture Show*, but a harmonica-playing, leopard skin coat-wearing eccentric who lived inside a gigantic maze with his mother. Now, that was truly living the dream. Earlier in the year, they had announced that they were bringing back the show as a live immersion experience. Around this time, immersive experiences became huge money-spinners. Things like escape rooms and Secret Cinema became hugely successful, and interactive game shows were part of this trend. They filmed the pilot for a new series there on the following day after we took part. The set then moved to larger premises, where it became the permanent base for a full TV series. It was great to watch the first televised episode, seeing people attempt the very same games we ourselves had bumbled around a few weeks earlier. Though for the record, Debs and I did notice that they simplified some of the games for the celebrity pilot. So, when we said that the games were harder in real life, they genuinely were! I managed to recruit a team of eight of us – alongside myself and Debs, it was Josh, Emma, Slater, Lorraine, Christian, and Hannah. My original thought was that we would do some proper military-style training to prepare as there was a basic assault course in our local park, but of course that never happened. Instead, in typical fashion, we hosted a Crystal Maze-themed dinner party. Each course was themed around a different zone from the programme – Aztec, Medieval, Industrial, and Futuristic. Our menu consisted of the following:

Industrial Entrée: A selection of crudités with 'industrial secret' cement dip (all the vegetables were spray-painted silver)

Aztec Starter: Tribal Mexican Bean Chilli in Taco Shells with sacrificial sour cream dip, finished off with a sandy surprise (breadcrumbs designed to look like sand)

Medieval Main: A monstrously medieval banquet of bacon-wrapped chicken thighs, gammon joint, potatoes, and boiled vegetables

Futuristic Finale: Shiny space age caramel layer cake, served with a selection of thoroughly futuristic toppings

Hats off to Debs – it was an amazing spread she prepared. After dinner, we polished up our skills by playing a long-forgotten Crystal Maze board game. I had to go all the way to Penge to get the pre-owned game from a slightly bemused family, where it was rescued from attic storage-purgatory. So, in the end, our intense training consisted of getting drunk and playing a kids' board game. Still, a bit of preparation is better than no preparation.

On the day itself, we only just got to the venue in time. Christian took it very seriously, turning up in his gym shorts. I had a Crystal Maze T-shirt, which my workmates had bought me for my birthday that year. It read 'I'd leave you locked in' underneath a picture of one of the crystals. Fate has a funny sense of humour. I was the team captain, with Debs acting as vice-captain. We'd worked out a very rough strategy of who was going to take on which types of games – physical, skill, mental, and mystery. Feraz had warned us a week earlier to avoid the medieval mystery, which we did – before it transpired that it was actually the medieval mental game that was almost impossible to solve. That became a bone of contention when I next saw him. Rather embarrassingly, I was the only one who got locked in, though I still maintain to this day that it was unjust. Still, I did win a crystal in the other game that I played. I think to have got locked in and not won any crystals would have been too humiliating to bear. Most of us retrieved one crystal – only Christian managed to complete both of his games successfully. Clearly, the wearing of the sports shorts had paid off.

The challenges that were the most fiendishly difficult were the ones where you didn't know what precisely needed doing. It's one thing to be speedy or good at maths, but quite another to think outside the box under pressure. One particular game I remember involved Slater holding a gigantic screwdriver. We assumed that one used this comically oversized prop to get all the screws out, so we were all impatiently shouting at him to get a move on. He was getting all flustered, shouting back at us, 'They're not coming out! They're not coming out!' It turned out that all you had to do was get the screws facing in the right direction. Easy when you know how. In the end, we got seven or eight crystals, which we were told was 'very average'. All in all, it was great fun, but like all these things, it would have been great to have had another go.

Another new scene that was sprouting up all over London was the 'kidult' scene – basically a concept where adults could engage in pre-pubescent activities to quench their thirst for childhood nostalgia. One of the first instigators of this was the Cereal Killer Cafe on Brick Lane, a place where grown-ups could eat bowls of sentimentally sugary breakfast cereal all day long. I popped in once on my way to Rough Trade, but couldn't bring myself to actually partake. This was rapidly followed by adult ball pits, board game cafés, UV ping-pong bars, and more wizard-themed cocktail places than you could waggle a wand at. I personally thought the crazy golf courses that various bars squeezed into their upstairs loft spaces were the most creative and enjoyable. The Victoria Tavern in Islington had a fiendishly challenging golf course that was in no way below par (ahem). Many of these places went bust in 2020, when the thought of paying £12 for a bowl of cereal or £20 for 20 minutes in a ball pit, was the last thing on people's minds.

On 31st March, 2017, my nephew, Jacob Adam Bryant was born. My brother was so relieved that he had narrowly missed April Fool's Day. Me, Debs, and my parents went round to see him a week or so later. I had held babies before, but this felt very different. Debs had the same experience with her niece, Lilah, I think. That family bond made it feel like a much more precious and personal experience. I wouldn't say that I was surprised by how good a father my brother has become (I knew he would be), but rather it's a change of behaviour that you never really expect to see. To me, he will always be my younger brother, whom I used to have pillow fights with and run around the Dane John Gardens shooting water pistols.

Jacob is adorable, and to my mind he now looks just like Matt did in those early photos from Ramsgate.

Three months after Jacob was born, Debs and I went to one of Hyde Park's annual summertime music festivals. The headline act was Phil Collins. As a general rule, I don't listen to music ironically. I would never put on an album by say, Abba or Chicago, and actively enjoy it. You can call me a Scrooge, but that cruise ship commercial frivolity has never been to my taste. The TV equivalent to me would be watching something like *Neighbours From Hell* – it can be good fun but it's not exactly inspiring. However, music-wise I do make an exception for certain 1980s hair metal and synth pop acts. Duran Duran, for instance, can be cheesy as hell, but have made some great albums, particularly after their commercial heyday. (1997's *Medazzleland* is extraordinary.) Phil Collins is another one of those who, underneath all the cheesy hits, has real talent. He came on stage to the most un-rock and roll entrance I've ever seen. He hobbled on with a walking stick and was helped over to a chair at the centre of the stage. His son, who was only sixteen at the time, was on drums and gave an incredible performance. He did the famous drum fill for *In The Air Tonight*. We also saw Mike & The Mechanics (another Genesis link), as well as Blondie and KC & The Sunshine Band. My only regret was missing Chaz & Dave on one of the other stages (one of them passed away a year later), as we didn't want to lose our prime viewing spot.

By now, I had met quite a few famous people through UAL. Earlier in the year, I had got Stik involved in one of my international speed networking events. Stik was a famous street artist, arguably the second most famous street artist at the time in Britain (after Banksy). His trademark was the painting of stick-figure people on various buildings across

London, but predominantly in Shoreditch and Hackney. Usually, these works had a political or environmental message, and would frequently fetch six-figure sums at auction houses across the capital. When he first started, he was living on the streets, so his story was one of real inspiration and an indomitable belief in the work he was creating. I met him at a talk he was giving, and managed to persuade him to come to LCC and be part of my event. That was a real coup for the college. The only negative was that he did slightly overshadow the rest of the guests at my event (none of whom were what you might call big names), so the queue for Stik was almost out the door whilst the others sat twiddling their thumbs.

I managed to overshadow that in October 2017, by somehow getting Ronnie Wood from The Rolling Stones to come and teach a painting class on one of our other sites. I came across his agent by accident, whilst being involved in another project, and just casually asked if he might be interested in being a guest for a painting class. I didn't think anything of it at the time; it was one of my many quixotic endeavours over the years. I was always approaching various people at the college who would usually turn you down with the exigencies of their busy lives taking precedence. But if you don't ask you don't get. Much to my surprise, his agent got back to me and said not only would he like to attend but he would like to lead the session, if possible. It just so happened he was going to be in central London on that day anyway. The only stipulations were that it needed to be a small group of no more than twelve, and that I and the students weren't allowed to hassle him for autographs or photos. That was all fine by me. He arrived at Chelsea College ahead of schedule, so I was able to have a bit of a chat with him. He was such a nice chap, and I managed to really impress him with my Stones' knowledge.

'What's your favourite Rolling Stones song then?' he cheekily asked whilst we were setting up the room. 'I bet it's not one of mine.'

When I answered that I was a big fan of *Black Limousine* (a Ron Wood co-write), he seemed genuinely touched. The class went really well. Truth be told, he's not the world's greatest painter, but that didn't really matter. The lucky twelve students who I enlisted really seemed to get a kick out of it. Afterwards, he gave me a copy of his new book and invited me down to his book signing later that evening, where I was able to get an autograph and some photos. All in a day's work.

Dray got married in August that year. When he told me that he had proposed, the first thing I said was, 'Not another wedding.' It probably wasn't the response he was looking for, but I just kind of blurted it out. We had been to so many over the last year or so, I had genuinely lost count. We even had two weddings either side of our holiday to Portugal, which involved going straight from one of the venues to the airport. This meant that we both had to take our wedding outfits as part of our precious luggage allowance. Dray's stag was held in Liverpool, and was a well-planned weekend of laddish activities. I tried zorbing for the first (and so far only) time. Basically, zorbing is where you are strapped into a giant inflatable ball, with your legs still free to run. It's exhausting work and incredibly hot and sweaty. We attempted a game of football whilst all dressed up as ridiculous multi-coloured balls. The hardest thing was judging distances; if you got to within one metre of each other, you would collide and go flying. The other thing I remember doing was foot golf, basically kicking a large ball across a giant golf course. I actually ended up winning a trophy for that. The wedding itself took place in a venue just outside of Guilford. It was a glorious summer's day that had that perfect wedding ambience. There was a 'pimp your prosecco' station, where you were able to add various assorted berries and straws to glam up your drink. Debs thought that was a brilliant addition, and I remember her mentally noting it down. The wedding bells were already starting to sound.

CHAPTER 13

The Palmer and his Green

HAZELWOOD LANE

On 14th June, 2017, a huge fire broke out in a council-owned block of flats in North Kensington – this was Grenfell Tower, the deadliest structural fire in Britain for nearly thirty years, with over seventy deaths. Many things were shocking about this tragedy, including the fact that this was an entirely preventable accident caused by penny-pinching and a lax attitude to health and safety when it came to some of the poorest members of our society. Grenfell Tower was just a stone's throw away from some of the richest real estate in the world – the sprawling mansions of Notting Hill, Holland Park, and Chelsea. It occurred at 1am, so most Londoners only heard the grim news the following day. That next morning when I walked across our walkway, I could see the block which had turned the colour of charcoal, still smouldering away. I hadn't properly noticed it before, but now that it was burning, it stuck out like a sore thumb on the grey London skyline. You would get the faintest whiff of smoke being carried on the breeze. The Grenfell tragedy in many ways acted as a metaphor for Tory austerity at the time. It also brought into sharp focus the inequality that existed within London. We were just in the process of trying to sell Deb's flat, which was causing her particular stress and anxiety at the time. Without wanting to sound callous, the view of the blackened shell of Grenfell was another thing that was making the experience an even bigger ordeal.

I had been considering buying my own place for a while, but only now was it starting to become feasible. My original plan to buy a flat back in Brighton had gone out the window once I had met Debs, and we agreed that we were going to buy somewhere together. We came up with some rough ideas of what it was we wanted – basically a larger family home that (ideally) we would never need to move from again. I imagine it's the same for everyone when they buy a place. The need to compromise on certain elements really makes it a challenge, especially in a crazy market like London. Top of my list was a garden. The only thing I really missed living in Debs' flat was a bit of outdoor space. She missed having a garden, too; both of us had grown up with them, so that was a no-brainer really. Space was the key thing. Somewhere that (if and when we had a family) we could grow into. Location was a bit of a secondary factor. Of course, in an ideal world, you would have both things. If I could choose to live anywhere in London, it would probably be around Angel/Highgate, but it would have been way beyond our budget for the type of place we wanted. We sat down with a map of London and looked at various areas. Central London (zones 1 & 2) was out, due to the cost. South London was ruled out because of the lack of tube lines and my personal hatred of Waterloo (the UK's busiest station). West London didn't make the cut due to the Heathrow flight path, and East London we rejected because we didn't really know anyone who lived out east. By the process of elimination, we were left with leafy North London.

We had looked at a few places during the initial stages of our search, like Streatham and Pinner, but the first place we properly considered was High Barnet. High Barnet sits at the very top of the Northern line – an old 12th century town that London had swallowed up back in the 1930s. Two of Debs' friends had recently bought there and they loved it. It had a traditional bustling high street and a beautiful art deco cinema that we have visited many times since. It also had very good transport links, with both a tube and national rail station. I can't remember how many houses we visited, maybe twelve or so. None of them quite hit the mark. They say that you know it's the right place when you instantly fall in love with somewhere, and that wasn't happening. Every house seemed to have some kind of fault, bad design, or geographic issue, that we couldn't overlook. One of the irritating things that had never occurred to me prior to house hunting, was when people did unfathomable things to increase their property's value that you would then want to remove. You would be expecting a discount to compensate for having to rip out whatever bad design they'd put in, whilst they would be expecting the opposite. One house, for instance, had a downstairs shower taking up room in a utility space. The estate agent would be selling it as a plus. 'Isn't it great to have two showers in a house?' And you would be thinking, *Maybe if you wanted to clean your dog downstairs; otherwise, it's a total waste of space.*

The worst ones were the really bad loft conversations. These were done so the owner could claim they had an extra bedroom, but when you could barely stand up in them, they were pointless and it would cost another £40,000 just to rectify. We were shown around another house by this overly enthusiastic woman who kept calling everything 'perfection'. It was far from it. She was showing us round this adequate but dated kitchen, saying, 'Every single tile is perfection.' Looking back, it was quite an interesting experience, but at the time we were wondering if we were ever going to find anywhere. We did put in offers on two separate houses in Barnet, but we were outbid on both. One was a real doer-upper which, in retrospect, I'm glad we didn't get. I think Debs and I would have killed each other if we had to sit through over a year of building works to renovate an entire house. The other was a lovely little place just round the corner from the cinema, but again fate intervened, and we were outbid.

The next area we looked at was Bounds Green. We came across it purely by accident, having decided to stop off for lunch somewhere on one of our many journeys back from High Barnet. For a while, we fell in love with this quaint little street called Myddleton Road. It was a bustling market street with mostly independent shops – bars, restaurants, and bakeries, dotted amongst antique shops and family-run businesses. I think there was some kind of community fair taking place the first time we visited. Bounds Green had the advantage of being in zone 3, thus cutting down the commuting time as well as the cost. We viewed seven or eight houses in the area, none of which were quite right for our Shangri La. One house that we saw on Russell Road had this gigantic garden, which I'd never seen the like of anywhere else in London. About 20 years earlier, British Rail wanted to sell off some of its disused railway sidings to the street that backed onto them. Only two or three of the houses agreed to buy the land, and this was one of them. The garden had this huge 'L shape' where it swerved behind the gardens of the five or six adjoining properties. It was actually too big; the upkeep would have been a full-time job in itself. You had the space to have a proper game of five-a-side football. If you Google image the area, you can very clearly see it standing out from the rest of the dwellings in the street. Garden aside, the house wasn't great. It had been done up in a really tacky and gaudy way which was to neither of our tastes, far too ostentatious for the likes of us. My most vivid memory is that it had an indoor swing suspended from the ceiling by these metal beams, so it was perching in the middle of the living room, like some humdrum performance art installation. I think it was supposed to be some kind of meditation swing. This experience was a very good lesson in not rushing into making a life-changing decision, as we slowly came to realise Bounds Green wasn't quite as pleasant as we had initially thought. When we first visited the area, it was on a bright and hot summer's day with barely a cloud in the sky. This (no pun intended) probably clouded our judgement a little. Apart from the pre-mentioned market street, nowhere else was really walkable. The area was hemmed in by the North Circular on two sides, so it felt a bit constrained. Parking was difficult, and there wasn't really a nice park or a decent supermarket nearby. I know this all sounds a bit nit-picky, but when it comes to making the biggest financial commitment of your life, I think one needs to be.

It was serendipity that we went to scout out Palmer's Green. Debs had expanded our search to look at other nearby places, and two houses popped up a couple of miles away. One of these was on Devonshire Road (an old period house which needed quite a lot of updating), and the other was on Hazelwood Lane. The strange thing about the house we eventually bought was that it didn't look anywhere near as nice in the photos, compared to real life. We had viewed quite a lot of properties by this point, and it was always the other way round. We were now used to the disappointment of clever angles and camera positioning concealing a variety of sins. When we arrived for our viewing, we couldn't believe it. The photos gave very little indication of how well laid out and spacious the place was. The owners had clearly thought they would save money by just taking the pictures themselves, which was a big error on their part. (I wouldn't say that we dismissed it from the photos, but we weren't overly excited about viewing it.) It had been on the market for a few months and had one price reduction, so potentially that photo *faux pas* may have been a factor in us eventually purchasing it. We both loved it straight away. It seemed to tick every box, and was just quirky enough for it to be interesting. It was also of a large enough size that it could be future-proofed for when we had kids. The garden was also a nice but practical size for two people who weren't very green-fingered. We initially were stunned by this huge fifty-foot-long grape vine, which wrapped itself around the garden like the flowery equivalent of a green tentacled octopus. We viewed it in late August, so there was an abundance of fruit on the vine. I think I had this strange Mediterranean fantasy where I would reach out of the kitchen window in the mornings and retrieve grapes for my breakfast. (I've only done this once, and it took a lot of stretching.) I had been carrying around this little notebook for the last twelve weeks, jotting down all the houses we viewed, and scoring them on various criteria. Once we left, we went for a deliberation drink and started scoring Hazelwood against all the others. It easily came out on top. We were off to North Africa in a couple of days' time, so we thought that would give us a bit of breathing space to think through whether or not to put an offer in.

On 1st September, we flew off on holiday to Morocco. With buying a house at the forefront of our minds, we had endeavoured to only have one relatively cheap vacation that year. One of Debs' friends had recommended this hotel on the outskirts of Marrakech, which was all-inclusive. The hotel itself was pretty plush, with a couple of swimming pools and decent accommodation. The food, however, left a lot to be desired. Debs, in fact, got food poisoning a couple of days in, which we suspected was from the trays of meat in the canteen. When these were almost empty, they would just pile more meat on top (rather than empty and clean each time), which I guess was all to do with time-saving. There is definitely a time and a place for all-inclusive resorts. If you're feeling lazy and just want to lounge around a pool most of the time, they're great. If you have a baby or young child and want it to be as easy as possible, bring it on. If, however, you want a more cultural holiday, then you're not mixing with the right people. We overheard one rather loud Scouse lady talking bluntly to the Reception staff, saying, 'I don't like Morocco. I'm just gonna stay in the hotel the whole time.' It was the kind of scene that made you feel a little ashamed to be British.

We made sure to do some excursions and a couple of shopping trips to the souks. In terms of modern development, Marrakech was amazingly unspoilt. We went to visit this small photography museum that was built around a central square open to the elements, similar to a traditional riad. There was a little rooftop café at the top, with these lovely views all over the city. It was so low-lying that you could see for miles in every direction, with all these pastel cream, yellow, and pink rooftops foregrounding the Atlas mountains glistening away in the distance. By now we had started collecting tiles from all the various countries that we had visited together. We came up with the idea after Lisbon- the spiritual home of ceramic tiles. We just thought that they were something different (and a bit less tacky) than fridge magnets. Plus, it was a fun challenge to try and locate them in shops, as often they would be of varying sizes or backed onto materials like cork. Our plan was to collect enough from various places to be able to tile a downstairs toilet. (Something we managed to do a couple of years later.) Trying to explain that we were looking for a specific type of ceramic tile in Marrakech proved to be quite a challenge. I don't think we actually got a tile whilst we were there. I suspect I ordered it online after I got home. Apart from Debs having two days of food poisoning, Marrakech was a nice break. It was whilst reclining on the sun loungers that we decided to put an offer in on Hazelwood Lane. Initially, we put in an offer way under the asking price, which got us nowhere. After a bit of back and forth, we eventually agreed on a price, and with pina coladas in hand, we were all set to go. Now it was just a case of Debs selling her flat.

I had no experience of how to sell a property. All the email correspondence going back and forth between the solicitors was just so complex that I kept losing track of it all. I was drowning in legal jargon, amortization this and encumbrance that; it was as if a thespian had swallowed a thesaurus and was regurgitating alphabet spaghetti in front of me. An email which would take me an hour to carefully construct, Debs could ping across in five painless minutes.

Originally, we used the online estate agent *Purple Bricks*. I thought that this was the future of estate agents – an online service that basically cut out the middle man and saved everyone money. We just couldn't seem to get any viewings through them, though; I think in the end we only got one person. Maybe it was something to do with the human connection; perhaps people were worried about the potential for things to go wrong and not having a dedicated agent to turn to. Maybe it still is the future, we just weren't there yet in 2017. Whatever the reason, we soon gave up on them and went for a traditional estate agents. They were called *Northfields* and based ten minutes away from the flat, down Askew Road. Debs' flat was stunning, on at a reasonable price, and had some nice features (like the double height ceiling), but we weren't getting the offers. The main reason was the financial climate attributed to the Brexit vote a few months earlier. For the first time in years, prices had started to stagnate in London. On top of that, there was the blackened shell of Grenfell Tower. But, perhaps most irritatingly, a building site had sprung up next door. They were building another block of flats adjacent to Issigonis House which was going to limit the views from the balcony somewhat. Like a giant mushroom in the middle of a perfectly manicured lawn, it was too irksome to ignore. The building plans were reasonably sympathetic to the neighbouring buildings, but when you're visiting a property, a noisy dusty building site next door doesn't give the best impression. We tried to encourage the viewings to take place on a Sunday when we knew the pneumatic drills wouldn't be going off.

We went back to visit Palmer's Green on 27th September. Our initial impressions were that it had a nice village-y feel, with a good selection of shops. Debs was very excited about a Waitrose which was on the high street, though this closed down about a month before we moved in. Oh well, we couldn't complain, we had three other equally distinguished supermarkets less than a ten-minute walk away. On our second visit, we explored the local park and had lunch at a new restaurant called Kiva which had just opened up at the end of our road. We also went back to view the property again. Having now had an offer accepted, we wanted to have a more detailed look at the house. It's very easy to be wowed by a first impression, so we double-checked a few things and asked about legal processes like building regulations. There were a few cracks that we hadn't noticed first time round, but generally the house was in a very good condition. Whilst Debs was talking to the estate agent, I had a bit of a snoop round to check for damp, which I knew was an easy thing for sellers to try and conceal. I later rang my mum up and told her that we had had an offer accepted on a house in Palmer's Green.

'It isn't Hazelwood Lane, is it? Right by the school?' That really confused me. How could she possibly know? It turned out that one of her childhood friends, Christine, lived at no. 73, literally a one-minute walk down the street. My Mum hadn't been to visit her in years, but she still remembered where it was. I actually went round to visit her house when I was about ten years old and do vaguely recall walking past

Hazelwood Junior School. It's a small world. The funny thing was, having lived most of her life there, she was now thinking of selling. Within ten months of us moving in, she had sold her house and moved up to Yorkshire. I like to think we weren't the reason for her sudden departure.

Buying a house is such a convoluted process; everything about it just seems so antiquated. A building survey makes complete sense in itself. You want an expert to write you a report detailing potential issues and defects. What you don't want is a list of everything that could possibly go wrong, to make you feel like a quivering wreck. Every point that was raised suggested that 'a pertinent buyer' would do this and do that, but we couldn't. There was no way that the current owners would let us go in and check the state of the roof, for instance. There were about fifteen references to Japanese knotweed and risks of flooding that were impossible to take seriously, and anything that would be genuinely useful to know about, they couldn't confirm one way or the other. For instance, the report stated that our bathroom ceiling 'may' contain asbestos. Great, that's no use to anyone. I realise that the people carrying out building surveys are just covering their backs, but essentially you are paying them to be vague when it matters and overly cautious when it doesn't. Still, I guess they did asbestos they could.

The people we were buying off were a nightmare. I know it's a cliché to say that buying a property is stressful, but in our case it was just unnecessarily stressful. There was nothing difficult or unusual about our situation, the people we were buying off were just incapable of communicating. It didn't help that they couldn't really speak English- only their daughter spoke it fluently. Their solicitor, who wasn't even a residential solicitor (his area of expertise was commercial purchases) also didn't speak any English and had no detailed understanding of the process. Things were getting lost in translation winding everyone up. For instance, their solicitor told them not to communicate with us directly. They took that to mean not to communicate with us at all. Debs went round there on her own and asked a couple of very basic questions and they put their hand in her face and just said 'talk to our solicitor'. I think she was just asking if they had gas safety certificates. A quick yes/no would have saved everyone a lot of time. We asked the same question on a legal survey of outstanding questions a few weeks later. Word for word this is how he responded;

"I have never been asked that before. That question is not in the spirit of the survey." It's frustrating because if another party refuse to communicate with you, there isn't really very much you can do except hang on in there.

Palmer's Green is nicknamed 'Palmer's Greek' due to the high Greek/Cypriot population. It also has quite a sizeable Turkish population, which is quite strange when you think about it. Centuries of fighting and disputes over territory, yet the Greeks and Turks ended up living in close proximity in a small area of North London. There are differing accounts as to where the name Palmer's Green originated from. In the Middle Ages, a 'Palmer' was another name for a Christian pilgrim. A hundred years ago, this would have been the last village before various pilgrims would reach the outskirts of London, so a high number of them would congregate in the local tavern, which was subsequently called 'The Pilgrim's Rest'. (It is now known as 'The Fox' pub) They would then embark upon the last stage of their journey into the big smoke. There are also local records that show a family of landowners called the 'Palmers' living in the village in 1608, so another theory is that the area is named after them. By 1800, the village had 54 dwellings, and even though the railway arrived in 1871, it was another thirty years before the area started to fully develop. Hazelwood

Lane was the first large-scale street to be built in the area, with our cluster of houses being built in 1906. Because I'm a bit of a 'pointless history' geek, I did a bit of research on when the various properties were built. From looking at Ordnance Survey maps of the time, I know that there were no settlements to the east until you get to the villages around Waltham Forest. Due to our cluster being built from west to east, there is a high chance that in 1906 our house was very briefly the most north-eastern house within present day Enfield (for a few days, anyway). Palmer's Green was then swallowed up by London's urban sprawl sometime in the 1930s.

After we moved in, I found quite a rare book on the history of the area, which made fascinating reading. I've always been interested in how urban areas change and develop over time. There are evocative black and white photos of our road as little more than a dirt track with a few isolated cottages, surrounded by open fields. I learnt some interesting titbits. For instance, there is a part of Hazelwood Lane where the style of houses drastically changes without being on a road junction (the usual boundary where architecture might change). This was due to a bomb being dropped during the Second World War and the extensive re-building needed afterwards. There also used to be a cinema on Green Lanes (the local high street) that was once known as 'London's most magnificent Picture House'.

The area isn't particularly famous for anything, though a few people of note have connections here. The poet Stevie Smith lived most of her life in Palmer's Green, and Joe Strummer (from the Clash) lived in a flat just behind our road. There is a small theatre called the 'Intimate Theatre' that is currently involved in a dispute with the local council over its ongoing viability. A huge number of actors have performed there over the years, though perhaps most famously it was the venue for David Bowie's first known paid performances – as a mime artist. It was also the setting for the world's first ever live TV transmission of a full theatre performance, in 1946. There weren't many current local celebrities that we knew of, though the actress Lindsey Coulson (who played Carol Jackson in *EastEnders*) we believe lived next door to our house until 2016. The only real celebrity (and I use the term loosely) I was aware of, was the guitarist Graham Hine, who was in the band Brett Marvin & The Thunderbolts. They had a no.2 UK hit in 1972 with *Seaside Shuffle*. I've seen him a few times since we moved in. I originally thought it was Brett Marvin himself who lived here, and although he did play locally, he wasn't actually a resident.

We had finally found a buyer for Debs' flat and were going out of our way to be accommodating for him, but not getting the same courtesy from our sellers. There were a few tears and sleepless nights for a while, particularly as we were trying to exchange and complete at the same time so that we weren't homeless in-between. Of course, every decision – or in our case, inaction – from our sellers had a knock-on effect. We had been told that we weren't in a chain, and then three weeks before completion, their solicitor contacted us and said they were trying to buy a flat for their daughter. They had the nerve to ask us to release the money to them in advance, but there was no way we were agreeing to that. We hadn't signed anything, for all we knew they could have disappeared into the sunset like John Wayne with his loot, leaving us without a legal leg to stand on. This skulduggery put the whole purchase in doubt and made for a nervous couple of weeks. Debs wrote them a very firm email saying that we were going ahead with the selling of the flat on our agreed date, with or without them. I can't remember how they responded, but we had zero trust in them by this point. We just decided to go ahead and, if necessary, put everything in storage and camp at Debs' parents for a while.

The oven was another unnecessary drama. They had obdurately refused to remove some items from the house that we had asked for, whilst other things were removed that shouldn't have been. Ovens are a little bit of a grey area, but as it was all plugged into the gas mains, it really should have stayed. It's the mean-spirited equivalent of unscrewing light bulbs. What was really irritating is that they didn't actually need it, but they were selling it to someone else. It was a very average second-hand oven so they couldn't have got more than £100 for it and we really should have been given first refusal. We would have bought it just to save ourselves the hassle of getting a temporary oven before re-doing the kitchen. There was a tick box on one of the documents that said 'I agree to leave the house in a clean and tidy condition' which they had ticked 'no' to. This gives you some indication of their mindset at the time. Even Marin, the estate agent who was dealing with our purchase was starting to tear his hair out. He was a genuinely nice guy, but we could tell he was starting to get flustered by the whole situation. I tried to break the tension one day when we were sitting in the shop. I noticed some loose-leaf tea sitting in the drinks station and asked if that was what he drank.

'Yes,' he said, 'nothing but the finest.'

'I knew you'd drink proper tea,' I responded.

He cocked his eyebrow slightly.

'Proper tea, property,' I said, trying to re-emphasise the brilliance of my pun. I got that classic weary-sounding laugh which suggested now wasn't the best time for jokes.

We had been recommended a removals company that as well as physically removing everything between locations, would also do a packing service. They sounded great but because our sellers still weren't communicating with us, we couldn't be certain of a date. The risk of losing money on a non-refundable deposit was too great, so we ended up getting this bunch of cowboys in at the last minute. In fairness, the actual packing they did was fine. There were a few personal things that we did ourselves; I wouldn't let them touch my records for instance. They came in and did the vast majority of the wrapping, boxing and stacking a couple of days before the move date. It was when they came back en masse that their ineptitude became more obvious. It was pure Laurel & Hardy. We had repeatedly told them that there were double height ceilings, so they needed to bring a ladder in order to reach some pictures. They brought said ladder, but then one of the removals men just assumed it was ours, for some reason. Unbeknown to us, early on in the job, they had wrapped it in industrial quantities of bubble wrap and placed it at the back of their lorry. They had then piled up about forty boxes of our belongings in front of it before they realised. They actually spent ten minutes looking for the ladder after I reminded them they needed it. The guy who packed it barely spoke any English, so it took ages to get to the bottom of what had happened. Rather than remove all the tightly-packed boxes, they resorted to balancing on the table with a mop, trying to get Debs' pictures off the wall, and catching them as they fell.

We arrived at the house about an hour before the removal men. We picked up the keys en route, but had no idea what to expect. Even our estate agent wasn't sure, as he hadn't heard from them in days apparently. I guess it was some small comfort to know that it wasn't just us that they weren't communicating with. He told us to brace ourselves in case the place was a complete tip. We put the keys in the door for the first time and prayed that they had actually moved out. I had visions of them sitting in the living room, saying they had changed their minds and to talk to their hands. Much to our surprise, not only had they gone, but the house was immaculate. They had got a professional cleaner in and left all the documents that we had asked for in a nice, neat pile. That bloody gas safety certificate that had caused us so much anxiety was just sitting there along with everything else we'd 'unreasonably' asked for. It was such a relief. The removals men turned up after a slight detour to pick up our spare bed from Barnes. We noticed how comical their packing had been; 'this way up' signs had been completely ignored, and the writing of contents was barely legible. One of the men had spelt kitchen as 'Kitch Them', which was hilarious. Much to our surprise, though, nothing had been broken during transit. Despite the fact that we were now living in a Greek neighbourhood, smashed crockery wasn't something we were quite ready for.

It was a strange feeling once everyone had departed. We were sitting in this new 'old house' with boxes piled up all around us. It's funny how one adapts to one's surroundings. I never remember the flat feeling cramped, but now everything was sitting here in stacks of boxes, we were both thinking, *How on earth did we fit everything in?*

I felt incredulous. It just didn't seem real that we now owned a proper sprawling house. It took a while getting used to being in different parts of it when you couldn't hear each other. In the flat, you could shout down to each other from anywhere, but now you couldn't do that as easily. During those first few days, there were a lot of 'Did you hear me/ where are you?' type conversations. Due to our courteous sellers we didn't have an oven, so our first meal was an Indian takeaway amongst all these towering boxes. It really felt like the start of a brand-new adventure. It was best not to worry about the mortgage mountain that now towered over us. Debs had been through that transition years ago with her flat, but to me it felt rather daunting. I imagine most people probably go through similar feelings. The thing to bear in mind was that it was a long-term commitment, and that inflation would slowly begin to reduce it. In thirty years' time it hopefully wouldn't seem like the crazy amount that it did in 2017. Rather than the sword of Damocles, it was an investment in our future. There is, of course, another way of looking at it: if you die in debt, you make a profit on life.

Our direct neighbours were total opposites. At no.78 was a lovely retired artist called Stephanie. Well, at least I thought that was her name. She had written her name and number on a piece of paper for us just after we moved in. Debs was convinced that she had written it as 'stafnie', or pronounced staff-a-knee. I couldn't get used to calling her that, so I always felt a bit guilty when I accidentally called her Stephanie. I got used to it after a few months, but by then we discovered that we were mistaken and her name was Stephanie all along. Name aside, she was the perfect neighbour. She was about eighty years old, but was a very lithe and determined lady. She was rather deaf, which in many ways was great for us, she never once complained about the noise if we had parties or stayed up late playing music. I would see her over the fence when she was outside in the garden and shout out to her, 'Hi Stephanie' (or stafnie), to which she would crane her neck up and look into the sky. I'd be waving my arms around like an over-enthusiastic aircraft marshal on a runway before she'd eventually see me. 'I'm awfully sorry, Chris, but I don't have my hearing aid in.' There was a lot of one-sided conversations for a while. We have been round her house on a few occasions. She always makes us tea and cake, and proudly shows us her art – usually painted pebbles or miniature beach scenes. She's a character straight out of Roald Dahl or Enid Blyton's Famous Five stories.

Liz, our other neighbour at 74 is, well, I'm not really sure what she is. We have never seen eye to eye on a number of things, despite our best efforts to be neighbourly. This book isn't really an appropriate place to list our grievances, but let's just say that tea and cake are never on the menu over there. One neighbour aside, we were really enjoying our new life in Palmer's Green. For a while it felt like being on a permanent holiday. We had moved in on 15th December, 2017, so I guess the fact that we were now both off work for Christmas, meant it didn't quite feel real yet. When our friends came over for the first time, people would say things like 'this is a proper grown-up house'. I remember Bjorn's reaction the first time he came over.

'You don't actually own all this, do you?' he asked upon entering our hallway.

I would crank the grown up-ness up a further notch on Christmas Day.

CHAPTER 14

Marriage & Mortar

Bernard Shaw described marriage as 'an alliance entered into by a man who can't sleep with the window closed and a woman who can't sleep with the window open'. I personally can sleep with the window closed but I do take his point. I proposed to Debs on 25th December. 2017. I don't think it was that much of a surprise. After all, she had given me her great-grandmother's engagement ring a few months earlier. I gave Debs her actual Christmas present, an engraved wooden wine crate, before saying that I had a small extra gift for her. This was the engagement ring which I had got resized and polished, all wrapped up in a box to look like a traditional Christmas present. I think she knew something was up, as this was at 9am on Christmas morning and I was dressed – in fact, I was wearing a shirt. She'd known me long enough to know that I would usually take advantage of any excuse not to get dressed in the mornings. Obviously, she said 'yes', and the rest was, as we say, history.

We started planning the wedding straight after New Year. At the same time, we were getting our kitchen and upstairs bathroom refitted which, looking back in retrospect, was quite a lot to organise within the space of nine months. Debs had her heart set on, if not a summer wedding, then at least a 'nice weather wedding', meaning mid- September at the latest. Planning a wedding is a lot of fun; you're basically organising a huge party. If you keep an open mind, there's a lot of creativity and personality that you can bring to it, though of course money is the thing that stops you having exactly what you want. As soon as anything has a wedding prefix at the front, the cost automatically triples. The first order of business was to find a venue and set a date. We knew we wanted it to be outside of London. The problem with having a wedding in London was that we had a large amount of our guests currently residing there. People would inevitably leave early to catch the last tube home, and so it wouldn't necessarily have that 'big adventure feel'. We wanted everyone to come away for the weekend and treat it a bit like a mini-break. We also knew that it couldn't be too far from the capital to make it impractical for people to travel to. We were especially thinking about Debs' grandparents, who were in their nineties. We had moseyed around a venue in Cornwall the year before, but rejected it for that very reason. Debs had family friends who lived in and around St Ives, a really beautiful part of the world. Being something of a hub for artists, it had quite a few connections to UAL. Perhaps most famously the sculptor Barbara Hepworth, who lived most of her life there, and whose house and gardens are now a permanent gallery. One of her works decorates the UAL building on Oxford Street. One stop along from St Ives is Carbis Bay. Debs and I stayed there on one of our visits, and went to see this elegant hotel that sat upon the beach. We weren't properly considering it at the time, but asked the staff nonetheless. They did hire out the hotel for weddings and we would have had access to our own private part of the beach. As beautiful as it would have been (especially in the height of summer), it would have been far too difficult to reach for a lot of people.

With Cornwall out of the picture, we looked at areas that were no more than a 2/2.5-hour drive from London, and came up with the idea of the Cotswolds. Again, this was somewhere that we had visited together. I've spoken to various people who have ended up traipsing round endless potential venues, so we made sure that we did plenty of assiduous online research first. And it paid off. As it turned out, the second place we visited became our wedding venue. The first place we viewed was ruled out almost straight away. It was in a picturesque little village called Boughton-on-the-Water, but was just too poky, without the 'wow factor' we were looking for. The second venue, Ellenborough Park, bowled us over straight away. So often wedding venues are corporate hotels or converted barns and outhouses, but this place was unique, with an incredibly rich history. The oldest parts of the building dated back to 1487, with an array of dukes, barons, and kings having stayed there over the next 500 years. It was once owned by Edward Law, who was the Governor of India in the 1880s. It had sweeping views overlooking Cheltenham Racecourse to the south, and of Cleeve Hill, the highest point in the Cotswolds, to the north. I think we both made our minds up there and then. Within a couple of weeks, we had booked a date. It wasn't our first choice – we were hoping for September 8th but got the following weekend, September 15th. Debs was anxious about the weather, though of course, predicting September weather in the UK is nigh on impossible. In the weeks leading up to the big day, she was constantly checking the weather forecast. It was something of a family trait. Her mum and sister would equally check all the various weather apps and then just go with whichever forecast they liked best! I could never understand that. There's no such thing as bad weather, just inappropriate clothing. As it turned out, our wedding day had much better weather than the preceding week when the heavens opened upon the fields of Gloucestershire. It was a blessing in disguise that we didn't get our preferred date in the end.

We had been to enough weddings over the last eighteen months to know what did and didn't work. We had secretly been scoring them and picking out all the various little bits that we thought worked really well. There was the pre-mentioned 'pimp your prosecco' station at Dray and Jodie's wedding, which we both thought was a nice addition. We also liked the weddings where the speeches were done in-between courses, rather than in one long go. That way, the guests weren't starving by the time the food arrived. We tried to do things a little differently where we could. Rather than having a guest book to sign, for instance, we got some laser-cut Jenga pieces, which we asked people to write on instead. We also didn't do a traditional wedding cake. I always felt that people were often a little reluctant to eat them, especially if they were already drinking or it was lavishly decorated. They looked more like forbidden fruit to me. Plus, if you had already eaten dessert, there was the danger of it being an excessive sugar overload. I had seen too many expensive half-eaten cakes at weddings. Instead, we thought we would do cupcakes. They were less messy, a bit more creative, and could be done in a variety of flavours. They were also considerably cheaper. We went to a tasting run by a local baker who made cupcakes for the Cheltenham race days. It was good fun coming up with unusual flavour cupcakes. Our weirdest flavour was 'bacon and pecan'. We also had raspberry and red wine, as well as more traditional chocolate and lemon flavours. We did have a top tier that we cut on the day but didn't end up eating until a year later, on our paper wedding anniversary.

Coming up with wedding entertainment is tricky. You need to try and avoid the feeling of enforced fun, but at the same time there are certain elements that people expect. We booked a swing and jive band that we liked the look of, called Goosebumps. We didn't know when we booked them that they were coincidentally from Canterbury. In fact, my mum had worked with one of the band members, though he was in the expanded six-piece line-up. I was tasked with booking some kind of outdoor entertainment. Originally, I had wanted fireworks, but they are notoriously expensive. I did some calculations and figured that we could probably stretch to a three-minute display. The more I looked at options, the more I thought that maybe it wasn't the best idea if we couldn't afford to do it properly. A poor firework display is often a sorry state of affairs. It also would be an easy thing for people to miss if they were dancing or in the toilet, etc. Instead, I booked a fire performer who would do four fifteen-minute slots over the course of the evening. That was a much better option; it was a more social experience and more impressive in terms of the visual impact. Our big surprise was a cabaret outfit called 'The Singing Waiters'. Neither Debs or I had ever seen this at a wedding before. They would mingle in with the actual waiters and then all of a sudden burst into song after some kind of comedy incident. In our case, they deliberately fell over with a tray of cutlery. We kept this a secret from everyone, which was surprisingly tricky to do. Debs' parents, in particular, were keen to know every detail of the day. It was also written on various spreadsheets as 'mystery guests', which kept the best man and ushers guessing for much of the day. I believe there were rumours going round that the Chuckle Brothers would be attending.

Choosing the guests for our wedding was a much tougher challenge than I thought it would be. Our basic rule (with one or two exceptions) was that both of us had to know the people attending. Our venue had space for one hundred guests, which on paper sounds like a large amount. When you break it down, however, it becomes apparent that you only make a conscious choice in regard to a very small number. One hundred guests is forty-eight people on each side, if you split it equally (which we didn't). Within that, there are fifteen or so people that you have to invite, i.e. close friends and family. Then there are the various partners, some of whom you may not necessarily be that close to. On top of that there are children, who of course count as fully-fledged guests. I think I only had ten or so spaces that were open to some kind of decision-making. Quite early on, we decided that we would only be inviting family babies. Thankfully, I didn't have that many babies on my side, but quite a few of Debs' friends did. This led to a few slightly awkward dinner table conversations. You would say things like, 'We're only inviting immediate family babies' and someone would respond, 'Oh, surely you don't mean me, though.' I appreciate how difficult it is to arrange childcare, etc., but as soon as you invite one, you end up having to invite them all. And we really didn't want a quarter of our guests to be crying babies. We gave a free pass to Mark, as he was missing the meal and only attending in the evening. In terms of my guests, almost everyone that I would have wanted to be there, turned up. The only person that I would have liked to attend but didn't was Ben, who was sadly quite ill at the time. Only one of my mates was banned, and that was Feraz. The first time that Debs had met him he had gotten rather inebriated and taken half his clothes off round her flat. Safe to say, he was not in Debs' good books, so he didn't make the cut.

Whilst we were in the midst of wedding organisation, our builder, Mariuz, started the work on the house. Mariuz was from Poland, but had been working in the UK as a freelance builder for a number of years. He just went by reputation and had done a number of building projects for Debs' family. He was great for two main reasons. Firstly, he was something of a perfectionist, who would happily discuss every little detail with you. You would come home from work and find all these little notes on the wall about the exact positionings of sockets and tiles. He would happily spend twenty minutes with you discussing the intricacies of standard bathroom sinks. Secondly, he was 'cash in hand', so not only was he undercutting other builders anyway (he sent most of the money he earned back to his family in Poland), but we also saved money on VAT. He was also a really jolly guy who worked hard and took pride in what he was doing. There were occasions when he would be labouring at ours on weekends, or working until 9pm. He really did put our beer-bellied British builders to shame.

We were having a whole new kitchen fitted, which meant everything apart from the windows and doors was being replaced. The old kitchen was fine as far as I was concerned. It was dated, done up in an early 80s mock-Mediterranean style, and wasn't what either of us wanted, but I could have lived with it for a while. The bathroom, on the other hand, did need urgent attention. I had hired in as asbestos company to remove the old Artex ceiling within a couple of weeks of moving in. The original bathroom had this flimsy shower fitting overhanging the bath, which really needed to be jettisoned. I couldn't contain my excitement about having a walk-in shower again. Debs had very cleverly designed the new bathroom to maximise on the space available. We were just able to have a bath and free-standing shower unit in there, but it was pretty tight. We had to replace the door with a bifold, so that we had additional space that wouldn't be blocked by the opening and closing of a door. There were also clever aesthetic things that Debs came up with, like the sink being floating to give the illusion of more space underneath. It's great having a designer for a wife!

It was fascinating watching Mariuz incrementally doing up the bathroom. Watching him lay all the plumbing was like watching some giant mechanical jigsaw take shape. I'm not very practical, so really envy people who are able to operate in that way. We had thought long and hard about how we would shower during the works, our ingenious idea being a big bucket and a shower hose connected via the kitchen sink. In the end, I think it was only one day that we couldn't use it. The kitchen was more of a hassle. We had moved everything we could into the living room – the fridge, toaster, kettle, and microwave – but eating and cleaning up without an oven or sink isn't straightforward. There is only so much Blitz spirit one can take before one longs for a noise-free and dust-free environment.

Around this time, I had acquired a personal trainer and started going to the gym. I was probably a bit too slim at this point, and Debs had wanted me to bulk up a bit for the wedding. I'm quite lucky in that I've never had to watch what I eat or think about my weight really; I just seem to absorb most things. (Only if I have a truly awful diet, do I accidentally put on weight.) Anyway, Debs wanted me to have a few muscles, and I was happy to give it a go. I think the spark that set me off was losing an arm wrestle to Rob, Debs' dad. I always thought I was pretty good at arm wrestling, but losing to a seventy-year-old (now) grandfather was a bit of a dent to my pride. Rob was pretty active and looked after himself, but even so, I now had a physical as well as an aesthetic goal. I had never properly used gym equipment before, so it was quite an exciting challenge. I gave up tai chi in order to properly put the effort in. At the same time, I was beginning to feel that I'd reached a bit of a dead end with it, and was thinking of trying something different anyway. I do think it's important that you enjoy what you do. Merely carrying on with things for the sake of it is an easy way to get stuck in a rut. So, having packed up tai chi, I signed up to the local Palmer's Green gym. My personal trainer was also called Chris and had been a professional boxer before becoming a trainer. He knew his stuff and was aware that the six or so months I had in which to bulk up was a tight time-frame. I would be doing the full works – personal training and at least three solo gym sessions a week, along with a strict protein-heavy diet. Gyms are strange environments. I had always been put off by the macho posing that goes on there, but this one, to its credit, wasn't like that. Yes, there were people who took it all far too seriously and lived just to show their body off to other people, but there were equally plenty of people there just to improve their cardio or lose weight. It took me a couple of sessions before I was comfortable using all the various equipment. Predominantly, I was using bench presses, pec decks, lat pulldowns, and ab machines, alongside lifting various types of weights.

My diet for a few months was basically meat (usually Heck sausages) and vegetables, alongside protein-enriched bread, eggs, whey powder and milk, with the occasional protein bar if I needed a snack. Anything else like cereal I made sure was fortified with protein, though as I quickly came to learn, anything with less than 8% was ultimately pointless. Debs and I had the same app to track what we were both eating. It actually became quite addictive scanning barcodes in shops to get the breakdown of what the food contained. It felt like being back at school, re-learning about all the different food groups and continually being surprised. I was shocked to discover, for instance, the high protein content of vegetables like spinach and asparagus. Ultimately, the training and the diet did make a noticeable difference. My arms gained a lot more muscle and I was just starting to form a six-pack by the time I stopped. It was probably about one-third of the way there, so I was more like Tupac (the American rapper). I'm sure Debs appreciated it. I quite enjoyed it, but it was a lot of work and a lot of money for very little reward. It's also a bit of a losing battle. If you want it to be permanent, you need to keep it up indefinitely. I just thought there were much more interesting things to spend my time on, I like the way I am, and ultimately life's just too short to be that vain.

By May, we were starting to see light at the end of the tunnel in terms of the wedding preparations all coming together. We had taken various trips up to Cheltenham and decided on our wedding breakfast menu. I was really excited about our pesto bread; it was some of the most mouth-wateringly delicious bread I'd ever tasted. I was so enamoured by it that I included it in my wedding speech, when I talked about putting it into white bird cages (which you sometimes see as decorative ornaments on wedding tables). I referred to it as 'bread in captivity'. Food-wise, the only thing I think we were slightly lacking in was a cheeseboard. The venue wouldn't allow us to bring our own and wanted to charge us £7 a head for theirs. As much as I would have loved a cheese board, £700 was taking the proverbial cheese biscuit.

Debs had organised all the flower arrangements and I had booked the wedding photographer. I was slightly nervous about screwing that up, as the guy I had found had only done a handful of weddings before; he was more of an experimental documentary-style photographer. I wondered whether that meant that he would be hiding in the bushy undergrowth trying to be elusive. I had visions of guests complaining about some uninvited dodgy character hiding in the shrubbery. As it turned out, he was great. He did a few of the traditional staged shots, but also a handful of interesting arty ones. There were a couple of gothic-style shots that he did of Debs under the shadow of darkness, which I thought looked great.

I had my official stag do in June, about three months before my wedding day. The reason it was so early was because Josh, the best man, thought he'd found the perfect activity. It was an 80s adult weekend in Butlins. During the summer months, they catered to kids and families, but outside of this they put on these special themed weekends. I think the weekend we went was the last one before the summer holidays kicked in. It had barely changed since my first visit in the 1990's, appearing to be cryogenically frozen in it's own naffness. We had people like Jason Donovan, Toyah Wilcox, and one of my childhood heroes, Pat Sharpe. Unfortunately, we missed all but the last two minutes of Pat Sharpe, as we were watching a rather sinister Freddie Mercury tribute act. They literally closed the curtain on us as we charged to the front of the stage with Slater shouting 'Pat! Come back!' over and over again. The best act I thought was 'Bad Manners', a ska band who rose to fame in the early eighties with their huge frontman – Buster Bloodvessel. You could see the floorboards physically shaking when he was stomping around stage, though in actual fact, he had slimmed down considerably. At his peak, when he opened a hotel in Margate called 'Fatty Towers', he was thirty-one stone. Though, to be honest, he wouldn't have looked that out of place amongst the general Butlins' clientele – there were a lot of very overweight people that weekend. On day two, all the lads dressed up in Mario costumes and we went to do real-life Mario Kart on the go-karting track. As the stag, I was dressed up as Princess Peach, along with one Mario, one toad, and one Waluigi. Unfortunately, everyone else didn't really liaise, so we had a whole troupe of Luigis. We went down a storm on the go-kart track, though, with a number of visitors filming us and asking for photos.

I had an 'unofficial second stag do' nearer to the wedding, on the same weekend that Debs had her hen down in Brighton. The main reason was due to a number of people not being able to make the original date. This was more of a casual night out affair in London, with Debs' dad tagging along for a few bars at the start of the night. Somehow, I ended up with a Dyson hoover by the end of the night. I ended up trading it with a random stranger for a bag of minstrels on my way home – classic late-night bartering.

In June and July of 2018 something extraordinary happened. The England football team put in a genuinely solid performance and made it all the way to the semi-finals of the World Cup. This was our best international football performance in over fifty years. We actually got further than the footballing giants of Brazil, Germany, Argentina, and Spain, who had all been constant thorns in our side when I was growing up. Best of all, this was no fluke; we actually deserved it, and our semi-final placing was a pretty fair reflection of how well we played. We even won a penalty shoot-out! I remember how distraught I had been when Gareth Southgate missed a penalty in 1996 crashing us out of the Euros, and now here he was, leading out a new crop of players. I think asking for England to win the World Cup the same year that I was getting married was probably too much for the gods to oblige. Still, for the first time in my lifetime, England's exit from a major tournament didn't leave me feeling deflated. I actually felt positive about the team's chances going forward.

A week before our wedding, we picked the grapes from our vine for the first time. Debs' mum accompanied her to the dress shop, whilst Rob and I spent a couple of hours picking our crop. I had worked hard that first year, learning the art of cultivating a vine. My previous experience of nurturing floral wildlife was rudimentary to say the least. None of my prior plants ever seemed to proudly burst into existence. Instead they ended up chugging into life like a creaking Southern Railways train complete with clogged toilet. I did use to enjoy giving my yucca's amusing names though, things like *Spruce Willis*, *Grant the Plant* or *Robert Plant* (from Led Zeppelin). I was determined that our grape vine would be different. Caring for it and maintaining was more work than one might imagine. It involves cutting the growth back, pruning and treating it, and encouraging the cordons (primary branches) to grow in certain directions, using wire. I had to deal with issues like grape shanking (when fruit within a bunch shrivels up), noble rot (where the grapes receive too much moisture), and various diseases like eriophyes which attack the leaves. As long as you identified these issues early on, you could stop them from spreading and infecting more of the crop. I even had to find a way to scare the ravenous wood pigeons off, my solution being a dangling Alanis Morrisette CD as a scary shiny object. As a general rule, I would tend to the vine at least once a week over the hottest months, and thoroughly cut it back every fortnight. That summer was gorgeous, with record-breaking temperatures that made it the hottest summer of my lifetime. If you took the average daily temperature and length of the heatwave into consideration, it was the hottest season since 1976. I knew by June that this would give us a bumper crop, so I made sure to maximise the number of grapes we could cultivate. Sadly, due to the dates of our wedding and honeymoon, we weren't able to take it to the local co-operative to be turned into wine. Instead, Rob and I made up some batches of jam, chutney, and grape juice. If the zombie apocalypse ever comes, we would be self-sufficient in grape-based produce for a good few weeks. We did manage to pick ten kilos the following year for Châteauneuf Du Bryant, and finally received our wine back in the autumn of 2020. They say Jesus could turn water into wine, but seeing our humble grapes transformed into this sparkling rosé was almost as impressive. It did feel like some divine miracle when we finally got to sample the alcoholic fruits of our labour.

It felt like moving house again on the day that we drove down to Cheltenham for the wedding festivities. We had so many boxes precariously piled up in the back of the car. There were table decorations, board games, signage, wedding favours, presents, vases, candles, all the suits, and of course the star of the show, Debs' wedding dress. We got there at around 11am on the Friday for the rehearsal. It felt very 'matter of fact', working out all the standing positions and timings for the bridesmaids. We had chosen the music for Debs to come down the aisle to – John Williams' score for *Jurassic Park*. I had always loved that piece of music and was slightly surprised that Debs agreed to it, but I guess if you take away the context of snapping velociraptors on the rampage, it's quite a romantic score. Like everything else, it was punctiliously planned so that Debs would come in during the crescendo. That evening, we had a slap-up meal with the wedding party, followed by a few rounds of drinks. My room was at the very top of the building's main tower. Rather than the damsel being locked away at the top of the tallest tower, it was me in a Quasimodo-type scenario. My room did rather resemble a bomb site the following morning. One of Debs' childhood friends, Dom, had bought along his dog called Marmite. (Great name for a dog!) We had spent much of that evening entertaining the guests with him, so I awoke to a banging headache, with chocolate Celebrations' wrappers covering the bed, and a bath coated in Labrador hairs.

I think one of the most difficult things about your own wedding is trying to find the time to speak to everyone. Having a Friday night dinner meant that we spent some quality time with the wedding party, but in terms of everyone else, it was probably no more than five minutes max. That morning, myself and the ushers were engaged in a lot of pacing around with spreadsheets. I was trying to brief them on what needed to be done, which was chiefly logistical things (like making sure the flowers got moved from the ceremony to the reception), but we would be constantly interrupted by people. I had factored in forty-five minutes to play a game of croquet on the lawn, but we didn't have the time for such frivolity in the end. I went in to check the table layout for the reception, and Rob was debating with the catering staff about the various permutations.

'It's all under control,' I said, pulling out reams of crumpled papers from my suit pocket. 'I've got fifteen spreadsheets here, nothing has been overlooked.'

The ceremony itself went without a hitch. Well, apart from when we actually got 'hitched'. There were a couple of noisy babies, but that was to be expected. We said our vows, which we had re-written slightly, with references to 'gin' and 'tea' – our two favourite drinks. Linked to the vows were our wedding favours, which were our own invention, gin-infused with Earl Grey tea leaves. G & Tea – get it?

Debs looked incredible in her long, flowing white dress. In the months leading up to the big day, she had been obsessed with this terribly tacky TV show called, *Say Yes to the Dress*. The premise of the show was basically women searching for their perfect wedding dress, and whether they said yes to the selected garment was the nail-biting conclusion to the show. Scintillating stuff. Anyway, after months of being subjected to this, I had a reasonable idea of what Debs would be wearing. I just didn't think she would look quite so stunning. I was pretty nervous during the ceremony, but I don't think I stumbled over any of the lines. We had rehearsed this routine of leaving the ceremony, hiding round the corner, and then coming back in via the fire exit, so people would be waiting in a suitably neat line outside. It felt a bit odd that one of the first things we were doing as a married couple was crouching behind a wall so that people couldn't see us. It was described by some as our magical disappearing act. After the 'serious stuff', I became much more relaxed and really began to enjoy the day. Being the centre of attention for a whole day is an odd sensation. It's a bit like being a kid again and having a birthday party where it seems like the whole world revolves around you. Though in all honesty, Debs was the one getting 90% of the attention.

Everyone was brilliant on that day. Josh went beyond and above his role, calming me down before the ceremony and helping out with the group shots later on. I remember giving him the rings and thinking ten years ago I would have been genuinely worried about him losing them. Slater was acting as the MC (master of ceremony) and gave it his all. I had briefed him on what needed doing, but again, he went above and beyond. He was on fine raconteur form, striding that tricky chasm of being informative and entertaining in equal measure. A couple of guests later asked me, 'Where did you hire him from?'

For some of the group shots, we used a drone. This was the first time in my life that I had properly seen a drone in action. In 2018, they were still something of a novelty, so there were a lot of ooohs and aaahs from the guests. Spike, one of Debs' friends, was an explorer and he used it to map out terrain when he was leading exhibitions, so the fact that he was able to bring it along was a great little bonus.

After all the photos, we sat down for the wedding breakfast. We had made the decision to theme the wedding tables around various games. We thought that they were quite an informal fun thing for guests to bond over. So, for instance, we had a table called 'The Catchphrasers' that had a *Catchphrase* game on the table, and 'The Articulates' with Articulate, and so on.

I thought it was amusing to name one of the lads' tables as 'The Wallies'; for their game they had *Where's Wally*?

There were lots of charming little touches during the meal. For instance, we had a couple of Jewish traditions, like drinking wine from a cup. Though we actually substituted the wine for grape juice from our own garden; somehow, that felt more appropriate. Debs and I were both quite excited to see what reaction the singing waiters would get. We spent much of the meal trying to deduce which of the waiters were real and which ones were the imposters. Rachel later confided in us that she was a bit suspicious of one of the waiting staff, as she had far too much make-up on. I would never have noticed something like that. When one of the waiters did their 'slapstick falling over routine' right in front of our table, the whole room went deathly silent. A couple of guys spun round to help, with Rachel turning to her partner and saying, 'Steve! Help him, help him.' They had thought that there had been a nasty accident and maybe he'd been impaled on a fork. When he got up and shouted out 'Surprise!' the whole room seemed to breathe a collective sigh of relief. They performed four or five karaoke songs, which took a while to get going. I think people were genuinely stunned for the first couple of numbers, but soon enough, everyone was on their feet dancing.

The first dance went by in a flash. We had been taking dancing lessons over the last few weeks, so we were reasonably confident. Our first song was Van Morrison's *Moondance*, which was a nice mid-tempo jazzy number that was fun rather than soppy. Looking back at the video, I can spot all the faults, but I don't think anyone else would have noticed. Part of the difficulty was that I was concentrating so hard on not stepping on Debs' dress, whilst still moving and keeping in time to the music. We had actually simplified the dance by taking out a couple of spins and some of the trickier steps, knowing that a dress would make it that much harder. For our first anniversary,

Debs bought me a framed picture of the lyrics, which we hung on our living room wall.

Once the first dance was over, I could finally start drinking. All I'd had up until that point was one glass of bubbles. After that, the evening seemed to fly by so quickly. I had designed the playlist, which I was determined wouldn't be the usual wedding fair. Most wedding playlists are terrible, so I tried hard to get that balance of fun but not too cheesy. To that end, there was no Abba or Bee Gees. I even said to Debs that we should have one novelty dance number, but not two. It was either the Macarena or The Village People; we went for the Village People. We had a section of Jewish music at the beginning to get the party started. We hadn't really planned it, but being hoisted up on chairs and carried over the audience was an interesting experience. You really had to hold on for dear life. There's some brilliant footage of us being vigorously shaken around by over-inebriated guests. There was also a section later on that I modelled on the predictable club playlists of our youth – the *Baywatch* soundtrack followed by Bryan Adam's *Summer of 69* and Bon Jovi's *Livin' On A Prayer*. There was a lot of pirouetting and crazy moves, particularly during my and Suri's impromptu dance-off.

What I found extraordinary about the day was how smoothly everything seemed to go. Nothing was forgotten, and everything turned up and appeared to be a success. The street food van we hired went down a storm, and the fire performer was rip-roaringly entertaining. The croquet didn't get used quite as much as we thought, but I do recall one funny moment where Spike was trying to explain the rules and get a game going, whilst Jacob (my nephew) was running around and pulling all the hoops out of the ground. Remarkably, there was no drama – usually when you put fifty to one hundred drunk people in a room together, you expect some kind of fireworks, but as far as I was aware that didn't happen. A couple of people overindulged and were throwing up, and there was a small bug going round, but that was about it. I think everyone had a great time. It really was a magical day.

The following morning, a few of us went on a cobweb-blowing walk up Cleeve Hill, followed by lunch at a local pub we had booked. I'm really glad that we spent three days in Cheltenham, as it meant the whole thing didn't sail by in a flash. The Sunday was a bit of a calm after a (very nice) storm moment. It felt very weird to be referring to Debs as my wife, and it took many months until I became comfortable with it. I'm not sure why; maybe it's because, as a term, I hardly ever hear it said. Most people in London just say partner. I would usually just go for partner as well, as 'wife' has too many old-fashioned connotations. It also took me a while to get used to us now sharing a surname: a few of Debs' letters would get opened in error when my eyes would glaze over her forename. Still, it felt great to be married after months of talking about it. Later, when we were packing everything up, we discovered that our rear tyre had developed a puncture. Luckily, we had a spare, but that did mean driving down the motorway whilst not exceeding fifty miles an hour on our journey back to Hazelsticks. We were hoping that a burst tyre wasn't some kind of metaphor for our newly sanctioned marriage.

The next day, we were jetting off on honeymoon. We had decided to go on a three-week road trip along the West Coast of America. We didn't want a honeymoon where we just lounged around and did nothing. I like lounging as much as the next person, but three weeks is a decent enough chunk of time to allow you to see a bit of the world at the same time. I planned a route that took us from San Diego (close to the Mexican border) to Los Angeles, through Nevada to Las Vegas, then up to Santa Barbara, Monterey, Big Sur, Yosemite

National Park, and finally San Francisco. The initial flight out was fine, but when we arrived in LAX for our connecting flight, I started feeling a bit unwell. We were literally just boarding our second flight when I ran off to the toilet to be sick. Debs waited by the departure gate, worrying about whether or not we would be allowed to board, whilst I was trying to be as quick as I could. After about five minutes, when I couldn't regurgitate any more, I sprinted back and we just made it. Although that flight was only an hour or so, it was a real endurance test for my gurgling stomach. Before we had even disembarked, I was throwing up again in the aeroplane toilet. I think I had caught gastroenteritis at the wedding. Debs' mum and niece were ill during the big day, and I think they may have unknowingly passed it onto me. Luckily, it was relatively brief, in that I only felt unwell for two or three days.

When we arrived at our hotel, we were obviously jet-lagged and, additionally, had been put into the wrong room, which was rather damp and situated next to the bin store. This was at 2.00 in the morning, so all I wanted to do was go to sleep. Debs wasn't very happy with the situation, but as I was feeling like death warmed-up, I didn't care. All in all, not the best start to our honeymoon. First thing in the morning, Debs went off to reception and got our room changed. It was twenty times nicer, with a panorama overlooking Mission Bay. Unfortunately, I spent much of that first day wrapped up in jumpers and trousers in 30-degree heat on the sun lounger. I don't think we ate a proper meal for the first couple of days, but by day three I was feeling a bit better.

We both loved San Diego; it had a really nice laid-back vibe. I have never been to Australia, but San Diego is what I imagine it to be like – huge stretches of sand and surfers, alongside stalls selling everything from fish tacos to flip flops. I lost count of the number of stickers I saw that said 'Life's a beach. Except in San Diego where the beach is life'. Ironically, we didn't spend much time on the beach, as I wasn't feeling well enough to sunbathe or swim in the sea. We visited the old part of the town, known simply as 'the old town', which was the first Spanish settlement on the West Coast of America. Essentially, this was the birthplace of California, with its oldest buildings (though not very old by English standards) dating back to the 1860s. We also went to Sea World, which was walkable from our hotel. We had hired a car for the trip, but had decided not to book it until we left San Diego, so it was walking or public transport all the way. America isn't really designed for walking anywhere. When I asked at the hotel reception for directions, I got some confused looks. We wanted to take a leisurely stroll there across the bay, which was just over an hour's walk, but they were adamant we should take a taxi. Apart from a five-minute stretch along a busy road, it was a nice scenic walk. Sea World was a strange juxtaposition of a traditional theme park and an animal conservation centre. Debs loved the dolphins, and the killer whales were really majestic creatures. By now they had phased out the 'theatrical killer whale shows' and replaced them with a more educational show, which was a lot kinder on the animals. It was a similar moral dilemma to visiting a zoo; animals shouldn't really be in captivity, but at least your money goes into raising awareness and conservation efforts.

After San Diego, we picked up our car and headed out on the highway. I was the first to drive, but having never driven on the other side of the road before, or indeed a car of that size, it was pretty daunting emerging onto an eight-lane highway for the first time. After a couple of hours, both of us got used to it, and it became second nature. It's a cliché, but the car infrastructure in America is something else. Absolutely everything is designed for them. We rarely came across a narrow road or a restaurant without adequate parking. No wonder Americans are car obsessed; it was just so easy. Here's an interesting bit of trivia whilst I'm on the subject of road trips. There is only one country in the world where you can travel along route 66 and go from east coast to west coast (or vice versa). Any ideas where it might be? The answer is not the U.S.A. The famous route 66 starts in Chicago, near the Great Lakes, and as such is nowhere near the East Coast of America. The answer, believe it or not, is England. The A66 goes coast-to-coast from Middlesbrough in the east to Workington in the west – the only road with 66 in the title that goes coast-to-coast anywhere in the world. Maybe for one of our big wedding anniversaries, I'll suggest that we re-enact our honeymoon with a thoroughly British road trip of Little Chefs and roadside Premier Inns.

When we got to LA, we checked in at the Hollywood Hotel, which wasn't as glamorous as it sounds. It was fine, but I chose it mainly for its proximity to the subway. For Debs' birthday, we went to watch *The Sound of Music* at the Hollywood Bowel. I had never actually seen it before, but then, not being a fan of musicals, that was hardly surprising.*

The pre-show entertainment was bizarre. I was aware that America didn't do things by halves, but this was something else; it was over an hour of people coming up on stage dressed in poorly constructed costumes from the film, in some kind of fashion parade. The audience would then cheer and whoop their approval, with very little in the way of subtlety or criticality. The one that still sticks out in my mind was this fourteen-year-old boy dressed as a female deer, complete with antlers and a

* (I just can't take musicals seriously. *Les Miserables* with Russell Crowe, for instance, is a well produced piece of cinema. Great cinematography, beautiful costumes, and first class acting, but to my mind it's all spoilt when they start bursting out in song. Like someone breaking the fourth wall, it just feels jarring being taken out of the narrative. Remove the musical element, and I think you'd have a solid film. Musicals that are actually about music seem to make more sense to me. Just my personal opinion.)

bra. (I believe it's a reference to the song *Do-Re-Mi*). The rest of our time in LA we spent doing traditional tourist things, like cycling along Venice Beach, and doing movie tours up in the Hollywood Hills. I don't think we spotted anyone famous, though we saw a bit of curtain-twitching and a gardener who was a dead ringer for Bruce Willis.

After LA, we left California, driving eastwards towards Nevada through the Mojave Desert. The landscape is like the surface of another planet—a khaki tinged terrain of boulders, burroweed and foreboding emptiness with sections of road that seem to go in a straight line forever. When the landscape is flat, it can really distort your perspective, especially when you would see a small town shimmering on the horizon. You'd think to yourself that you would be there in a jiffy, and twenty minutes later it would still be mocking you in the distance. There isn't really anywhere in Europe where you can see fifty miles stretching out in front of you in quite the same way. It was also interesting how your perception of speed would change; you would suddenly look down and see that you were doing 100 miles an hour, but without any landmarks it felt like half that speed. We made a couple of small detours en route, one of them being Bottletree Ranch. I'd seen the owner of the ranch on a Channel 4 documentary once – a real eccentric old cowboy with a beard down to his knees, a shotgun at his side, and a mangy dog following him around. He owned the world's largest glass bottle collection, having spent his life recycling them and picking them up off the highway. He'd then turned them into this huge art installation in the middle of the desert. Everywhere you looked, the punishing rays of the sun were reflecting off these sculptures of glass, projecting ultraviolet light in infinite patterns. Most of the bottles had been turned into these towering pylon-like structures, whilst others were decorated with wind chimes and moveable parts. When the wind blew, you would get this eerie whistling sound effect permeating through thousands of shards of glassware. Debs wasn't that enamoured with the whole ensemble, but I thought it was great. Sadly, the owner, Elmer, died in 2019, but I did read that someone else has now taken it over.

Of all the places we visited on our honeymoon, Las Vegas was the destination we both enjoyed the most. It was like a giant adult version of Disneyland. Walking down the strip was totally crackers, you were never quite sure of what was around the corner. We made a point of checking out all the different hotels to see what the various USPs were. The Flamingo had actual flamingos elegantly striding around the grounds; The Mirage had a volcano that erupted every thirty minutes; and The Venetian had canals and gondolas flowing through the middle of it. It was pretty surreal taking a ride on a gondola, with the gondolier singing Italian to us, whilst we drifted through this American shopping centre. The Luxor was another place we visited – a famous Egyptian-themed resort which was just a couple of hotels along from us. (I say a couple; the hotels are so large they can take up entire blocks. This, alongside the pavements which rarely go in a straight line and often divert you into the casinos, meant it was still a good fifteen-minute walk away.) The most amazing thing about The Luxor was the beam of light which protruded from the top of the pyramid high into the night sky. It's the strongest beam of light in the world, visible over 250 miles away. It's so powerful that it's used as a navigation aid by pilots at cruising altitude (as in, steer left before The Luxor sky beam).

Our hotel 'New York New York' had a roller-coaster running through it that would rattle past our window every fifteen minutes or so. Debs made a point of asking every hotel we stayed at for an upgrade. I think I asked once, but generally found it to be a bit embarrassing. When Debs asked for an upgrade at 'New York, New York', the lady behind the counter lent over and very softly said, 'Well, you have got a jacuzzi in your room, madam.' Apart from the penthouses, there wasn't really anywhere else we could upgrade to. It felt like we were living some strange fantasy dream in New York New York. I was sitting in a jacuzzi with a beer in hand, watching a roller-coaster fly past the window. The whole place was fantastic fun to visit, but as a living, breathing city, it felt weirdly lopsided, with its core designed around hedonism and recklessness. It was like a meal consisting of *amuse-bouches, entremets,* and desserts, but no main course to speak of. In terms of gambling, we didn't do very much at all, though of course we lost the small amount that we did spend. We didn't really have time to sit down and play blackjack all day; there was just so much to engage with. We went to see a Prince tribute show and took a ride out to visit the Hoover Dam. We also made a point of driving out of Nevada into Arizona, just so we could say we had visited another state.

As we were making our way up the West Coast, the weather began to turn. We found out that a few days after we left Las Vegas, it had experienced flash flooding. Debs checked her weather apps and we made the decision to abandon the Pacific Highway and head inland instead. We ended up staying on this cattle ranch for a couple of days before heading up to Yosemite. It was a shame as we missed out on some of the most beautiful parts of the trip, but the ranch was a lovely pit stop. When we checked in, we did the usual routine of mentioning that it was our honeymoon and asking for an upgrade, which we got. When we then went for dinner that evening, we saw that our table had been decorated with rose petals, which I couldn't take any credit for. The waiter then greeted us with a 'Happy Anniversary', which we felt a bit silly correcting. Then, of course, all the other waiting staff keep saying 'Happy Anniversary' to us, which we just smiled and nodded along to. The funny thing was there was a couple directly opposite us who we overhead were actually having an anniversary dinner.

'How come they get special treatment?' they muttered.

Maybe we were given their table in error, or maybe it was a genuine mistake on the receptionist's part. Either way, as it was our honeymoon, we thought it was okay to feel a bit special.

Yosemite was the only part of the trip where I screwed up the accommodation somewhat. I had made the fatal error of looking at a map, seeing this big expanse of green that I assumed was Yosemite National Park, and picking accommodation that was as central as possible. What I failed to take into account was that there were more than ten interconnected forests within the region: to the south was Sierra National Forest, and to the north, Stanislaus National Forest. The log cabin I had booked was actually in North Stanislaus Forest, although I didn't realise it at the time. It seems obvious, but it's worth remembering that America is very big- you can go spectacularly wrong if you start estimating distances. I think Debs had her suspicions as we drove in and didn't see a soul. I think in our 'campsite', only one of the other cabins had anyone boarding there. We went on a three-hour hike and didn't see a single person. In fact, whilst it was definitely the wilderness, it wasn't as spectacular as we had thought; we didn't see any rivers or mountains or anything, really. It was deathly quiet. We were looking around and thinking, 'I'm not sure what all the fuss is about.' There was no signal, so we were navigating the old-fashioned way off a paper map. When we got back, we double-checked and worked out that Yosemite Valley (the famous part) was actually a 2.5-hour drive away. Our location was more like Nosemite than Yosemite. We made the best of a bad situation and lit a rickety old barbecue using some supplies that we had bought earlier. Only then did it occur to us that we were deep in bear country and pretty much out there all on our lonesome.

We had this flimsy old chalet and I was grilling steaks on the barbecue, with this delicious smell wafting out into the forest. There was a nervous half hour where I was cooking our dinner and Debs was standing in the doorway with a torch, on bear watch. If Yogi Bear would have turned up, I suspect we would still be cowering in there now, surviving on a diet of termites and rainwater.

Having deduced that we weren't actually in Yosemite, our schedule only afforded us a day trip to go and visit what we had actually come to see. It was a five-hour round trip, and to make up for my foolish forest folly, I was driving in both directions. It became obvious as the scenery got more and more spectacular and a few other cars joined us on the road, that Stanislaus didn't hold a candle to Yosemite. We were surrounded by these granite mountains that were densely forested with pines, and from them came a multitude of streams and waterfalls flowing down the sides of the valley. We did a couple of short walks around the basin to see a few of the more famous sites. There had been a big drought that year, and as it was the tail end of summer, the water levels were shockingly low. Even Yosemite Falls had been reduced to a trickle. It is the second highest waterfall in North America, and within the fifteen or so tallest in the world. I couldn't resist clambering up the boulders within the dried-up rock bed towards the waterfall. The boulders were the size of houses, so it took a good ten minutes to climb up to the waterfall itself. Up close, I could see that it certainly wasn't a trickle; more a cascade, really. Still, I was able to put my hands underneath it and completely drench myself. It really hurt. Though, with the water dropping a distance of 2,400 feet, what was I expecting? Still, another thing to tick off my bucket list – standing underneath one of the tallest waterfalls in the world.

San Francisco was one of those places like New York that is just engrained in everyone's psyche. We found it to be rather disappointing, though. Perhaps our expectations were too high, or perhaps we had just been spoilt by the delights of LA and Vegas. For whatever reason, I just didn't like it that much. It had a massive homeless problem, the likes of which I had never seen anywhere else. We visited during the Silicon Valley tech boom, so investment and people were pouring in from all over the country. This meant that land values were skyrocketing and forcing ordinary people out. I guess the combination of escalating rents and charitable enterprises being priced out, were contributing factors to a growing homeless problem. Most cities in America could simply expand, but San Francisco was hemmed in by the sea and the protected natural areas around it. I remember we took a bus ride and came to these crossroads where there were gangs of homeless people on all four corners. On more than one occasion, people would be sprawled out on the sidewalk, and you would literally have to step over them. It was strange to have such inequality co-existing in such a relatively small area. The other thing that I found irritating were the hills. They looked impressive and gave it a unique vibe, but it made walking anywhere really difficult. I think what I disliked most about the place was that it just didn't have its own sense of character; it seemed like it was trying to be all things to all men. Parts of it were like New York, parts of it had this European ambience, and parts had this grandiose regency-type feel. Everything was physically, culturally, and architecturally hemmed in all together. It kind of had everything and nothing, all at the same time. It was by the sea, but it wasn't renowned for beaches. It had green spaces, but didn't have a real park. It was very odd.

The scenery around the city, though, was beautiful. We borrowed some bikes and cycled over the Golden Gate Bridge to get some impressive views over the bay. It was Fleet Week (an annual military parade that takes place around San

Francisco), so we got to watch a flotilla of ships sail underneath the bridge and into the harbour. On one of our last days there, we visited this forested area just beyond the bay called Muir Wood. This is one of the few areas in California where the giant redwood trees grow. Apparently, it's the moisture from the fog of the San Francisco Bay area that allows these massive trees to thrive. At over three hundred metres, they are the tallest trees in the world, as well as being some of the oldest. Just walking around these towering giants was quite humbling. They gave off this almost magical vibe that is difficult to put into words. It really felt like we were in an enchanted forest from some children's author's imagination. You could envisage pixies and talking animals scurrying around amongst the bracken.

One of the highlights of our honeymoon was visiting Alcatraz. It was strange seeing it just casually sitting there in the middle of the bay – so close to land, but at the same time virtually escape-proof. We sailed across and then spent a couple of hours wandering round and taking part in an audio tour. One of Debs' friends, whom we visited whilst over there, described it as the one of the best audio tours they had ever done. It was really interesting. You got to see all the original cells and the pipes that two of the escapees climbed down when they successfully broke out. The only thing that spoilt the trip somewhat were the biblical-like infestations of flies. These were cormorant flies which covered every surface of the island like a swarm of rampaging locusts. As we disembarked the ferry, we were all given these cardboard fans to swat away the invading irritants. After only half an hour, my arms were physically aching from all that incessant swatting. That upper arm workout was probably the most exercise I did all honeymoon. The day that we visited Alcatraz was unusual in two respects. For one thing, a contingent of the US Air Force, known as the Blue Angels, were performing an air show.

Whilst on the Rock, we witnessed the planes swooping down and doing manoeuvres over our heads. It was a bit like the US version of the Red Arrows. Also on that day, one of the retired prison guards had come in to give a talk and do a book signing. He had worked at the prison in the late 1930s, at the same time that Al Capone and Machine Gun Kelly were inmates. This was what most people seemed to ask him about. I just stood there and listened to him for a while. I remember what he said about Al Capone, that he was 'very quiet and very well behaved'. The razzmatazz of Alcatraz.

It's hard to sum up our honeymoon. We managed to cram quite a lot into those three weeks. I loved every minute of it, and after the craziness of all the wedding preparations, it was great to spend some quality time relaxing together. It did feel like the time flew by, but that always seems to be the case when you're abroad, out of work mode, and ambling around without a care in the world. It was now back to earth with a bump...

CHAPTER 15

Achtung Baby

I had always wanted kids. I think instinctively most people do. I guess it's kind of a way of ensuring your legacy – passing on your genes so a bit of you continues to live on long after you've died. A macabre thought, I know, but it's human instinct to try and stick around as long as possible. Debs and I had talked vaguely about having children, but wanted to get married first. Now we were free to properly start planning things, although as everyone knows, getting pregnant isn't an exact science. In the meantime, we did the next best thing and bought a kitten.

Coming back to the daily grind of work after a month-long fairytale existence was bound to be a bit depressing, so we thought that getting a furry feline companion would be a good remedy for that. It had been almost twenty years since my parents' dog had died, but I still missed having a pet around. I know that Debs wanted to have a cat in her old flat, but having one that can't go outdoors has always felt a bit cruel to me. Even with the breeds that like staying indoors, it always seemed a bit sad. Now that we had done most of the major works to the house, we felt it was the right time to get a pet. We got Ziggy from Wood Green Animals Charity in mid-October 2018, when she was just over two months old. We visited her when she was being housed, alongside her three brothers. They were a lot more boisterous, although after a bit of coaxing, Ziggy came out and let us play with her. We preferred to have a female cat, mainly because they were less likely to wander off, and tended to have a smaller territory than males. Although our back gardens were reasonably cat friendly, it was only six or so yards along where we were intersected by a side road. Our friends had one of their male cats killed in a road accident, so we were more reluctant to have a male. We decided pretty much straight away that we would house Ziggy. After bringing her home, it took her about twenty minutes or so until she came out of her cat basket and started exploring. She was tiny then, she could literally sit in the palm of your hand. They say that the best thing to do with a new kitten is to introduce them to one room at a time, but even on day one she was desperate to go out and explore the rest of the house. Taking her into the garden the first few times was hilarious. We borrowed a cat lead off one of our friends, and so for a week there was a daily routine of taking the cat for an evening walk. Everyone had told me that cats were resolute creatures and that even as kittens they were outdoor survivors. She was about as resolute as an empty crisp packet in the wind. She was so scared she was literally trembling, and would jump every time a leaf fluttered by. We had made a decision never to allow her in our bedroom, mainly for hygiene reasons, but also because we both have mild allergies. (It's not actually the cat hair that causes allergies, but rather the cat saliva. This can actually be remedied by feeding them a high protein diet.) We realised after a couple of days that rather than sleeping in her lovingly prepared bed, Ziggy was in fact sleeping on the bare floorboards outside our bedroom door. She clearly wanted to be as close to us as possible, so we moved her basket upstairs, and that became her favourite spot pre-Amber.

Unwrapping all our wedding gifts was great fun; it felt like Christmas had come early that year. Our house was now starting to look like a proper family home, with swanky new lamps and sparkly kitchen accessories. One of our gifts was an Alexa voice assistant, which I was a bit dubious about. It didn't appear to do anything actually useful. Sure, it looks space-age and it's fun, but other than reminders and switching between radio stations, there isn't really much else it does. I was always baffled when people would come over and get excited about it. I'm sure Debs considers me to be a bit of a technophobe, but I don't think I am. I'm just not a fan of technology that exists for the sake of it, especially when I can see that the limitations will be ironed out in a few years' time. It will be interesting to see how voice assistants develop. When they can eventually boil a kettle or tell you where you've left your phone, I might be a bit more excited. The sheer number of times that I've seen upgrades make old models redundant so quickly, is incredible. I remember in 2002 people saying it was ridiculous that I didn't have a mini disc player, so I bought one only to be told that I now needed an MP3 player. After getting that, people said that was antiquated and that I now needed an iPod. It's a perpetuating cycle that never ends. The paradox, of course, is that as newer technology evolves, what it replaces becomes increasingly harder to use. That's the reason I still have a DVD player and listen to CD's/records. I am pretty much in 100% control of what I consume, unlike say streaming from Spotify, where not only can I not listen to unauthorised releases (bootlegs etc.), but the company can take music on and off as and when they please. This actually happens with surprising regularity. Many years ago, I gave up trying to keep up with the Jones's and now just use what I think is the easiest. I actually still use an MP3 player, as it's much more convenient than using a phone to play music. There are so many advantages that I don't understand why more people don't use them. It doesn't drain the battery like an iPhone does, and will last about eight times as long without needing a charge. It's much lighter, and therefore portable, is totally free if you own the physical media, and also it doesn't matter in quite the same way if you damage/drop it, etc. Maybe there's some kind of fear around street credibility. Luckily for me, that's not something I have to worry about.

My first Halloween in Palmer's Green was a real baptism of fire. The wisdom of decorating the front of one's house in spooky spiders and creepy cobwebs, when you are situated a mere stone's throw from a primary school, is something I really should have considered. In the old flat and previous addresses, I may have got three or four trick-or-treaters over the course of an evening, but that was usually about it. I wasn't totally naive- I knew lots of young families lived nearby and envisaged maybe getting twenty or so visits from mini werewolf's and darling little Dracula's. Debs had left me some packets of sweets and given me explicit instructions not to use the jar of leftover wedding treats that were residing in our kitchen cupboard. (The last temptation of Chris). She was going out for the evening to visit her friend Sarah, whilst I stayed at home to protect the kitten. Ziggy had just about conquered her fears over falling leaves, but was in no way ready for the terrifying sounds of sugar crazed children repeatedly ringing the doorbell. Soon enough, the little monsters began to arrive and I proceeded to hand out packets of refreshers and chocolate treats. At the start I was getting up to answer the door every ten minutes or so. Then it was every five minutes, then two minutes, and soon enough it was a constant stream of visitors. After half an hour there was a literal queue of kids snaking down the street. It felt like I needed some kind of ticket allocation system as I tried to ration the remaining confectionery as best I could. When I had run out I couldn't bring myself to tell them that there wasn't anything left. This little toddler looked up at me with her empty orange bucket and puppy dog eyes. *Please Sir, Can I have some more?* she seemed to be saying. How could I resist? I went back into the kitchen and picked up the forbidden jar. *Halloween is saved!* I felt like saying as I carried the sacred jar over the front porch. The feeding frenzy resumed as our wedding sweets got handed over to the ravenous masses. Still they kept on coming, like a trail of blood thirsty zombies with no end in sight. With the wedding sweets nearly depleted I waited for the smallest of gaps and firmly closed the door. I could still hear the approaching kids from outside. As I wandered into the front room to take down some of the window decorations I had to duck, as suddenly another group of children reared into view, walked into our driveway, and approached the door. I then spent the next couple of hours hauled up in the kitchen with the trembling cat. When I was standing in the doorway, like Willy Wonka handing out golden tickets, the doorbell wasn't going off that incessantly. Now it was constantly ringing as parents and children assumed, because of the lavish decorations, that I was still running a chocolate factory. Hundreds of children must have rung our doorbell that evening. Ziggy was having a nervous breakdown and I was feeling pretty guilty that I was now enticing children in with no prospect of recompense. Debs was not very happy with me when she returned later that evening. I think I had managed to salvage a small handful of marriage sweets, but it was a pretty forlorn sight. I ordered some more the following day but I had learnt my lesson. Enticing children to knock on your door for sweets isn't a sensible strategy when you happen to live opposite a primary school.

Our cat was now growing up to be a very effective hunter. There had been quite a few ‘animal incidents’ over the last couple of years, with all manner of critters having found their way through our cat-flap – mice, frogs, birds. The worst one (so far) was the great mouse incident of 2019. It was scurrying around whilst Ziggy stalked it on one side of the kitchen, and I was crouched down on the other side with a box to apprehend it. I caught it and chucked it out, but whilst washing my hands, I heard a noise and turned around to witness her bringing it back in again! Trying to catch it for a second time proved a lot harder. I watched it run into a corner but then it just seemed to just disappear. It appeared to have pulled off an incredible vanishing trick. A couple of days later, I found out where it had gone. It had run inside the back of our subwoofer, which it had turned into its nest. It had been stealing all of Ziggy’s dry food and squirrelling it away inside the speaker. I came home one day and saw the cat looking forlornly at her bowl, wondering where all her food had gone. I picked up the subwoofer and it seemed to rattle. So, I tipped it upside down and a waterfall of pet food tumbled out all over the floor. The stupid cat had allowed this mouse to mock her by stealing all her food. I still hadn’t caught the bloody thing; despite my vigorous shaking, it must have been clinging on for dear life inside that speaker. I went through a long battle of wits with that bloody mouse. I christened him Elvis because of his healthy appetite. It was even more appropriate in the end when he got caught in a trap. I remember thinking that my only real experience of catching mice was what I’d learnt off Tom and Jerry, and Tom very rarely got his hands on the little blighter. When the kitchen started to smell, we figured out that it must now be living behind the fridge. The smell of mouse urine is really pungent. It was actually putting us off our dinner, smelling as it did like an overflowing men’s urinal on a Saturday night. I pulled the fridge out to investigate, and sure enough there was a carpet of mouse droppings. Even after cleaning it with bleach, it still stank, so I concluded that it had moved house again and was now living inside the fridge. I unscrewed the back, and sure enough, in amongst all the circuit boards and electrics, there were yet more mouse droppings. It's not easy cleaning inside the back of a fridge, around all the various wires and so forth. I would wait until Debs had gone to bed before getting on my hands and knees at midnight and scrubbing the inside with industrial quantities of cleaning products. I was incredibly careful, but the next day when I pulled it out to investigate, I yanked the entire wire out of the back. The fuse tripped and the power went off in whole house. Great! If it was the plug end, I could have re-wired it, but as it was the end that went into the fridge itself, there was no way I could fix it. We had to shift everything across the road to our friend Rachel's fridge and freezer, and then call an electrician. He managed to fix it for the princely sum of £60. That bloody mouse had caused us so much hassle, and I still hadn't caught it! A couple of days later, I finally got the bugger in a trap that was supposed to be humane but looked like a miniaturised torture contraption. The mouse was half in and half out of it, so when I put him outside in our back alley, he scurried off before I could properly release him. I was then chasing this rodent down the alley with a trap hanging off his back end, whilst Ziggy was hopping around getting very excited. After a short game of chase, I managed to catch up with Elvis and properly release him, firmly and irrevocably concluding mouse-gate.

Early in 2019, I started regularly going to a climbing centre in Finsbury Park, known as The Castle. I had been mentioning to Debs for a while that I wanted to start climbing as a sport. For Christmas, she bought me a series of lessons for a qualified climbing course. Walking into the climbing centre for the first time, I felt like a kid in a sweet shop; I just wanted to try everything. It was almost a literal as well as metaphorical feeling. The climbing walls reminded me of Liquorice Allsorts, with their various colour and shape combinations. It was as if a giant Bertie Bassett had stormed in, gone mad, and thrown his confectionery all over the walls. Like sugar-crazed ants, humans were now climbing all over them in order to get their fix. The Castle is one of the biggest climbing centres in the country, housed inside a former water pumping station which looked more like a medieval castle, hence the name. The turrets were a perfect space to house these vast climbing walls. As well as top rope climbing (the traditional method of climbing where the rope is already attached to the wall), there was also bouldering, traversing, auto belaying, and lead climbing areas, as well as an outdoor climbing space. As soon as I finished my course, I met up with a bunch of regular climbers, and once we had all bought our own equipment, we started attending every week.

The adrenaline rush that one gets from scrambling up slabs of stone is hard to describe, particularly when you really push yourself to complete a particularly challenging section of wall. I always thought I was good at climbing until I started using walls that were nothing but crevices and crimps (basically fingertip grips). Some sections we would spend weeks studying until we were able to complete them. The most difficult thing to learn is conquering your fear, particularly when it comes to falling. Deliberately flinging yourself off the top of a forty-foot wall so someone else can practise taking your weight, is counter-intuitive. By October of that year I had started lead climbing, where you attach the rope as you climb. In order to do this, you need a great deal of slack from the person holding the rope, so you can fall much further distances – sometimes as much as four or five metres. That was very nerve-racking the first few times; it's a bit like that free-fall sensation you get when you start descending from the top of a roller-coaster.

I have a tight knit group of climbers and, despite us not knowing each other all that long, we trust each other 100%. It's strange in that we wouldn't trust our closest friends in quite the same way. I remember when Rhys and I were practising a tricky technique and I was talking a bit about this book.

'You know, if I die, I want you to feel guilty,' I jokingly said.

'Sure,' he replied. 'And if your novel ends up being posthumous, I'll probably lose my credit.'

I recall one occasion when we heard shouting and the muffled sounds of crying as we were walking between walls. We ran over to see what all the commotion was about. Fearing the worst, we went over to where a small crowd had formed. People were staring up at two climbers at the top of one of the overhang sections. One of them had just proposed to his girlfriend, pulling the ring out whilst all strapped into his harness. She was crying tears of joy, but because she had let go in all of the excitement, she was now swinging back and forth unable to reach him. Every time she grabbed back onto the wall, she started crying again and slipped back off. I assumed that her drying her eyes with her bare hands meant that she had no grip. It was pretty funny watching two people that were so overcome with emotion just dangling there, unable to do very much. Two lovers separated by a carabineer and chalk dust – it was post-modern Shakespeare.

In early June of that year, we went on a week-long holiday to Cyprus. It was on the day we left that we got the amazingly exciting news that Debs was pregnant. It wasn't a great surprise to Debs' family that we were trying, so when we posted a photo on Facebook of her holding a bottle of Carlsberg, her Auntie Diana assumed that we hadn't yet been successful. It was actually a bit of a red herring, as Debs was drinking non-alcoholic beer. But it goes to show how people can keep tabs on anything through social media. There was a restaurant called the Tsiakkas Tavern that we kept going back to due to its mouth-wateringly authentic tzatziki. It was far superior to any tzatziki I've ever had at Greek restaurants in the UK – much thicker and creamier. Dipping sauces aside, the other thing the restaurant had in its favour was its sweeping views out across the ocean. As we sat at that bar looking out across the bay, I remember thinking that this felt like the end of a chapter in our lives. The last few oblique rays of sunshine were setting over the sea. That sinking sunlight was our spontaneous life of freedom being submerged by new responsibilities. It was a beautiful and poetic visual metaphor for our future.

We used Debs' pregnancy to our advantage on a horrendous boat trip that we embarked on. Knowing that I'm not the best traveller when it comes to boats, we booked a trip on a vessel that we thought would be reasonably stable (i.e. a large one) and which we believed would spend most of its voyage hugging the coastline. We even checked the weather in advance, so that we would be sailing on a day that wasn't too windy. The boat itself was lovely, with sun loungers, live music, and a buffet that would come out once we docked in a sheltered bay before the return trip. As soon as the boat got out into open water, it began rocking from side to side, and I turned my usual colour of pesto green. It wasn't just me, either. It was particularly choppy out to sea, and I noticed a few passengers who were feeling uncomfortable. Even Debs said that the journey left her feeling a bit ropey. I don't think anyone was as bad as me, though. I was clinging onto the railing at the back of the boat, trying to focus on the coastline. When we finally pulled in to Coral Bay, it was such a relief. I told Debs that there was no way that I could cope with the journey back and was literally considering 'jumping ship' to the beach, which was only a couple of hundred metres' swim. In the end, we asked the crew if we could use one of the emergency lifeboats to take us to shore, using Debs' pregnancy as an excuse, and saying it was her that didn't feel well. Before I get chastised for taking advantage of my pregnant wife, Debs actually came up with this plan. They kept offering us food before they took us, but Debs, who actually quite fancied some, refused so that we could keep up the pretence of her feeling unwell. I declined because I wouldn't be able to stomach it in the event of them not taking us to shore.

'I couldn't possibly eat in front of my wife if she can't have any,' I kept saying.

'That's so chivalrous of you,' was the response from the crew. Oh, the guilt.

There were a few concerns with us having to clamber over some rocks, but we took the risk and got the lifeboat out there. It was the right decision. We got an hour-and-a-half sunbathing on the beach instead of an hour on a swaying boat, followed by a sardine-packed bus journey back. The pregnancy card proved to be a great card to play.

During those first three months or so, Debs was pretty ill. She was feeling continually nauseous around food, so her diet (and by extension, my dinner diet) was predominantly kids' beige food – waffles, fish fingers, and such like. It was the only type of food that she seemed able to stomach. She was never physically sick, but certain foods that I would cook, especially meat, would turn her stomach. The biggest issue was the fatigue. I think for about four months, Debs went to bed earlier than me, usually around 9pm. Though, once she got into her second trimester, that eased off a bit. One of the most difficult periods was July, when we went to France for her friends' wedding, followed by a mini break in Bordeaux. Her friends had officially got married in the UK but had hired out part of this French chateau for a big party. Within a day of arriving, they had announced that they were pregnant, so without wanting to steal their thunder we thought it best to announce it also. With Debs' lack of drinking and early nights, it was going to be pretty obvious anyway. There was a deep irony about being in Bordeaux, the world-famous centre for wine, and neither of us drinking. I've never been a particular fan of wine anyway, so I was electing to drink beer most of the time. The only time I think I had a glass of wine was when I got a complimentary glass whilst visiting the Bordeaux wine museum. Luckily for Debs, they also had grape juice on tap.

I have been to relatively few funerals in my life. My grandad's (on my mum's side), I recall fairly well. They played Louis Armstrong's *What A Wonderful World* at the conclusion of the ceremony, which I found really touching. It has to be one of the most beautiful songs ever written. I would quite like for that to be played at my own funeral one day. That was also the only time that I had ever carried a coffin – something my mum asked me to do, alongside Matt and my uncles. 2019 was a first, in that I attended two funerals. Debs and I had been to a high number of weddings in the previous couple of years, and I remember Jen and Rob saying that at their age it was now funerals that they regularly attended. I wondered if this was now the start of that process. The first of these was a service for a girl I knew from Brighton. It was especially sad as she suffered from depression and had ended up taking her own life. She was only a couple of years older than me, and I'd been fairly close friends with her for a few years when I lived in Brighton, but we had lost touch after I moved away. She had a real sense of humour, and in that spirit the wake took place in a gentlemen's club – a place where all kinds of less than salubrious activities took place.

The second funeral was for Debs' grandad, Cyril. This was the first Jewish funeral that I attended. It wasn't totally unexpected, he was 98 and had been ill for a few weeks beforehand. We had gone to visit him about a week earlier, and he was very frail then. I was surprised that he held on for as long as he did. I didn't know him that well, but he was a lovely man who was always very kind and generous to the people around him. He had led an amazing life, being stationed all over the world as a soldier in the Second World War, in places like Ghana and Italy. I just wish that I could have known him for longer. The strange thing about that funeral was everyone coming up to us and congratulating us on being pregnant. It's a really odd sensation people congratulating you and saying how happy they are for you under such sad circumstances. Birth and death co-existing in the same space is such a strange juxtaposition.

By now we had started thinking about names for our daughter. It wasn't as easy as I thought it would be. Choosing names for a boy is much easier. For one thing, there are plenty of boys' names that will never go out of fashion – like James, Andrew, David, and dare I say it, Chris. Another issue is the expectation that girls' names should sound pretty. We tried to avoid fads – names that were popular but would very quickly link the child to a particular time. For instance, there were loads of girls called Kylie born in the late 1980s after Kylie Minogue, and a large number of Britneys in the early 2000s after Britney Spears. In 2018 and 2019, Olivia was really on trend due to the actress Olivia Coleman winning every acting award going. I knew of three babies called Olivia, two through work and one through Debs' friends. There were names that I liked and Debs didn't, and vice versa, often because of past acquaintances that you associated the name with. You also needed to avoid awkward or embarrassing initials. One of the contenders, once we had narrowed our name choices down to fifteen or so, was Roxanne. Without a second middle name, their initials would have been RnB. (I don't think Roxanne was ever an entirely serious choice; I found it impossible to disassociate from the Police song of the same name.)

One October evening, we sat down and did the William Burroughs' method of writing potential forenames and middle names on bits of paper, jumbling them up and then pulling them randomly out of a hat to see what did and didn't work. We both really liked the name Melody but didn't want it shortened to Mel, so tried to have it as a possible middle name. Even then, it didn't seem to work in conjunction with a first name that we could both agree upon. By the end of the year, we had narrowed the names down to our two favourites, Skyla and Amber. Amber, if you're reading this, you were very nearly a Skyla. To celebrate, we went on a 'babymoon' – supposedly a relaxed getaway for expectant mothers towards the end of their pregnancy. We had a 'Babymoon in Buckingham', which sounds like the title of a terrible Emilia Clarke rom-com.

In October, I received a letter from the police saying that I had been caught on camera speeding. That was exactly what I wanted, a fine, and half a day off work to go and attend a speed awareness course. There are very few times in your adult life when you feel like you are on the 'naughty step', but this was one of those. On the day of the course, I put the postcode into my sat-nav and drove to the venue, expecting it to be in some grotty office block or on some backwater industrial estate somewhere. I approached this magnificent Edwardian hotel just outside of London, and thought that this couldn't possibly be the right place. It had a 400-metre driveway, elaborate fountains, and rows of Bentleys all parked up. I was half expecting a harpist to rear into view as I walked up the marble steps and through the main entrance.

I must have read the letter wrong, I kept thinking to myself. Three penalty points here I come. Lo and behold, I wasn't about to gate-crash Katy Price's wedding. The course was actually being delivered in this grand five-star spa hotel. I was surprised by how much I enjoyed the day; it wasn't as condescending as I feared it might be. I re-learned some interesting facts around stopping distances and road signage, and the facilitators – two ex-policemen – were hilarious. It was like four hours of non-stop cabaret with the occasional serious bit thrown in. At the end, one of the guys said he would happily have paid £90 to voluntarily do the course. One of the policemen retorted, 'Just don't tell your friends to speed just so they can come on the course. People have done that before.'

We finished half an hour early, so just sat around drinking tea and eating biscuits. Apparently, they'd stopped people from leaving early a couple of years back, after one of the delegates was caught on camera speeding again before the course had officially finished! When I got back home, I think Debs felt that I'd enjoyed it a bit too much.

'It was supposed to be a punishment; you weren't on a jolly!'

Although the course was good fun, I still maintain it was a very over-the-top response to driving at 34mph in a 30 zone on deserted streets in the early hours. It was funny, because around that time everyone was talking about how driverless cars were going to change the world. There would be no accidents, no need for tricky parking manoeuvres, and definitely no-one being caught speeding. Up until that point, I had only seen one driverless car. It was a few months earlier when I took some of our BA Sound Arts students to the University of Greenwich to take part in a sound design project. The brief was to investigate what sounds could be added to electric vehicles to make them safer, in order for people to hear them more easily. We took turns to drive around with a massive speaker on the roof, playing around with all different types of sounds like animal noises and various bell and alarm-type music. It was whilst we were there that I saw testing being done on a driverless car. At the time, the roads around the Royal Greenwich Observatory and University were the only public roads in the country where driverless cars were allowed to be tested. I think I spent more time watching the driverless cars whiz around than with my students. It was fascinating to watch. It felt like magic – the modern-day equivalent of seeing fire for the first time, or watching television in the 1940s. *One day*, I thought, *people are going to look back and laugh that human beings were once trusted to drive themselves around at seventy miles an hour*.

On Thursday, 12th December, I sat down to watch the 2019 election, which was billed as being the most important election of our lifetime. It had basically been fought as a one-issue, (i.e. Brexit) election. Debs had her Christmas party that evening, so I sat down with a bottle of whisky and a selection box, knowing that it was going to be a long night. It had become something of a tradition for me to stay up until the early hours, and take the following day off work. I wasn't feeling particularly hopeful. I'd had a creeping sense of dread in the days leading up to it. The best I was realistically hoping for was a hung parliament, but lo and behold, millions of people voted against their own interests to give the UK the largest Tory majority since the days of Thatcher. For those of you that have never stayed up to watch an election or have erased them from your minds, in the early 2010s they were all essentially the same. They followed the same basic pattern and were rather like the stages of grief. The 2019 election was as depressingly familiar as ever, and went something like:

9pm – False Hope: You have a couple of post-work drinks and you're convinced it will go your way. Surely it will, people aren't stupid, are they? People are not going to shoot themselves in the foot. This is happening. Come on!

10pm – Exit Poll: What? That can't be right, surely. Polls are always getting this sort of thing wrong. You can never trust polls.

10.10pm – Early Evening Comedy: This is where a Lib Dem MP is so insistent the polls are wrong that he promises to eat an item of clothing live on air if they're proved true. That's something to look forward to, you think...

10.15pm – CGI Nausea: Jeremy Vine shows off his new hi-tech graphics, which consist of vomiting-inducing primary colours. It's like a cross between Super Mario Brothers, Playdays, and the world's most boring acid trip.

11pm: False Hope – part 2: The first constituencies announce their results and they're quite positive. Jump for joy! The polls were wrong! It's coming home!

Midnight – The Nigel Farage show: Nigel Farage resigns and then reverses his decision. Why is he on TV, anyway? He isn't even running. What a berk!

1am – Despair: Results start coming in thick and fast, and it's starting to look like the exit polls were right after all. The baddies are going to win again, and there's nothing you can do about it (at this point the whisky drinking really starts to intensify).

2am – Brief Respite: An MP loses his constituency to a man dressed as a rubber hippo. However, this stops being amusing as soon as the hippo says something controversial about immigrants.

5am – The Result: The results are pretty similar to what the exit poll predicted. You have lost seven hours of your life that you can never get back. The whole thing has been a complete failure, and the future is now in the toilet.

During Christmas of that year, Debs was heavily pregnant. It really is incredible what women have to go through in order to give birth. If men had to go through the same thing, then the human race would have died out centuries ago. It's not just physically giving birth, it's everything that goes with it – the sheer organisation involved with dieting, the pills, the stretching, the alcohol and caffeine abstinence, the sleeping positions, the medical check-ups, the liaising with doctors and hospitals, and all the while juggling work and home life. It's exhausting just thinking about it. Something seems to click in women's heads during pregnancy, when all of a sudden they become this multi-limbed, plate-spinning, octopus-type creature, capable of doing everything all at once. I can't even talk and make breakfast at the same time without pouring boiling water all over my cereal and bran flakes into the teapot. The only time I'd be good at spinning plates would be in a Greek restaurant. We'd started doing ante-natal courses a few weeks earlier, but I didn't feel in any way prepared. I knew about all the serious stuff, but I hadn't really given any thought to how much my life was going to change. I guess the first seeds of that change were that Christmas, when for once we weren't zipping all over the country seeing friends and family. We made one trip down to Emsworth for Christmas itself, but apart from that, everyone came to us.

Ushering in 2020 was an odd feeling. Whenever a new year rolled round, it would always take me a few weeks to get used to it. It wasn't uncommon for me to be writing the previous year in email correspondence up until February/March time. 2020 was one of those dates that always felt like the future. Films that were set in some kind of dystopian world, like *Blade Runner*, were always based around 2020. Being a nice, even number, it was always chosen as the date for various statistics involved with population growth and environmental crises. I remember vividly a lesson in GCSE Geography when we were told that the Maldives were likely to be underwater by then. It was a date that was far enough away to be detached from immediate reality, but close enough to be scary. In the end, it turned out to be something else entirely. Having said that, there's no doubt in my mind that the climate has started to shift over my lifetime. UK winters have become considerably milder over the last thirty years. I always remember thick blankets of snow in December and January when I was growing up. We would frequently go sledging as kids, and the occasional snow days (when schools would have to close) weren't exactly a rare occurrence. The soft muffling sound of virgin snow crunching underfoot as you leave the house for the first time in the morning, is one of those childhood sensations that always takes me back. All I can say is, the future is not what it used to be.

One of the (many) issues with having a pregnant wife is the guilt you feel about doing fun things on your own. When I got offered a ticket to go and watch Tottenham play Middlesbrough in the FA Cup fourth round, in their brand, spanking new stadium, I couldn't turn it down. I had been a Spurs fan for years but had never had the chance to go to a game before. The new stadium opened in April the previous year; in fact, you could see the towering cranes from Hazelwood Lane for many months after we first moved in. When we bought the house, I remember thinking it was a nice little bonus that White Hart Lane was only a couple of miles away. (Although it certainly wasn't on our shared essential criteria list). The game was actually played on 14/01/20, which was the date when Debs' pregnancy officially became full term. I had visions of Debs going into labour whilst I was stuck in a crowd of 60,000 inebriated football fans. Thankfully, that didn't happen, though I had one eye glued to my phone just in case. The stadium was incredible – a gleaming football Colosseum, which seemed to stretch up into the heavens. The match itself was a mixed bag; we won 2-1, but it was a flat overall performance. I went with Rob, Rachel, and her new boyfriend Lawrence, who had managed to secure us seats in the front section. We walked into this shiny new stadium and all gazed up at the towering terraces and the giant Spurs emblem – a golden cockerel – which sat proudly overlooking the ground. Rachel (who had never been to a professional football match before) stared up and exclaimed, 'Why is there a giant chicken on top of a basketball?' She was given the thousand-yard stare and told to never utter those words again.

It's funny how much planning goes into having a baby and yet ultimately you have no control over anything that unfolds. We had done absolutely everything – ante-natal classes, reading baby books, breathing exercises, watching DVDs, hypnobirthing sessions with Debs' auntie (who used to be a midwife), and a whole plethora of other things in preparation for the big day. After New Year's Eve, the nursery was ready, the bags were packed, and we just sat there twiddling our thumbs for a few weeks. Every time one of the couples from NCT went into hospital, we sat there waiting for the inevitable updates, praying that no-one stole our carefully thought-through name. That would have been a real 'amber alert'. The whole process was a bit like waiting for a volcano to erupt – you knew it was coming, the vibrations could be felt, and you knew that a baptism of fire awaited you. You just didn't know precisely when it was going to explode.

In reality, we had a bit of clarity, being reasonably confident that Debs was going into hospital to be induced on 29th January. Earlier scans had suggested that Amber was going to be a large baby, so in terms of safety, we were advised to go in before her due date. We got up early that morning, had a large breakfast, and made our way to Barnet Hospital. We assumed it would just take two or three days, with the plan being

I would spend the evenings at home until Debs went into active labour.

Initially, it felt like a bit of a holiday for the first three days. The bright lights, intense heat, sky blue curtains, and food being delivered to your bed, all reminded me of sunning myself in an all-inclusive resort on some tropical island somewhere. Debs, however, who was sleeping there at nights, didn't quite have the Cliff Richard summer holiday vibe. She was obviously having quite intrusive induction procedures carried out. It probably felt more like a torturous prison to her.

'Well, I'm glad you feel like you're on holiday,' she said, when I told her my thoughts after a surprisingly tasty apple crumble was delivered to her bed.

The process itself was very frustrating; nothing seemed to be working. Everyone else in our ward was being wheeled out to have their babies, whilst we spent days patiently waiting for Debs' contractions to develop. I would have liked Amber to have been born over the weekend to maximise my paternity leave, but by Sunday, 2nd February, there was still no sign. When we weren't cooped up in the ward, our time there basically consisted of lots of slow meandering along corridors, trying to bring on labour. 'Bored in the ward' I began referring to our time as. We passed the time by playing cards, watching shows on the iPad, and eavesdropping on the other patients. The midwives were a mixed bunch, who ranged all the way from fantastically warm-hearted and knowledgeable, right down to the scarily incompetent. There was one slightly older midwife who I nicknamed 'Nurse Ratchet' due to her slightly oppressive and dehumanising demeanour.Our fifth day in hospital had been our favourite birth date. 02/02/2020 is a rare example of a palindrome date, where it reads the same forwards as backwards. Now that we had missed that momentous date, we were pretty fed up. The holiday vibe had given way to prison chic, with me now staying nights as well.

I, too, was condemned to wander the Dettol-infused corridors of Barnet Hospital for all eternity.

Debs' parents had bought me in a camping mat on one of their visits, which made my sleeping arrangements that little bit more bearable. I can safely say that sleeping on the floor of a maternity ward, with continuous noise, searing temperatures, and occasionally clumsy staff stepping over you, isn't conducive to a good night's rest.

Having had no previous experience of maternity wards, I had no idea what to expect in terms of the facilities or level of care. One thing I was surprised about was the lack of provision for the fathers-to-be. Obviously, I was there to support Debs, and my comfort was of little consequence. Even so, I found it odd that I wasn't allowed tea or coffee from the drinks station, or to be able to use the showers. There was one occasion, after we had moved wards, when I actually asked one of the midwives where the nearest shower was. She stared at me and suspiciously asked who it was for. Whilst concealing the towel and washbag behind my back, I lied and said it was for my wife. As bad luck would have it, when I came back to the ward in a change of clothes and wet hair, the very same midwife was Debs' assigned carer for the day. Ouch!

'Feeling a bit fresher, are we?' I could almost hear her muttering to herself. If looks could kill, I would have been in the next bay along, also in need of medical treatment.

I have read so many stories about the NHS being underfunded and how certain parts of it are at breaking point. Until you see it with your own eyes, you don't really appreciate what an amazing job these people do under the most trying of circumstances. Although I jest about it, the majority of the midwives were brilliant, but you could see the frustration behind their eyes. I have been saying for years that we in the UK should be paying considerably more tax. The tax rate for a middle-earning UK worker in 2020 was 28%. Denmark,

Spain, France, and Belgium set their rates at 38, 40, 48, and 49% respectively. When you compare the difference in our healthcare, transport, and school systems, the difference is stark. The stumbling block, I guess, is that no normal person likes paying more tax. Perhaps somewhere in the depths of the Momentum movement, there's someone who feels a tiny frisson of joy when they see big deductions on their payslip. But the rest of us? We all know that death and taxes are the only certainties in life, and we approach them with equal trepidation. It's no wonder, therefore, that politicians spend most of their time promising they won't tax us any more. If they do dare propose tax rises, then it's always someone else – billionaires, corporations, offshore property buyers. The problem is that there is a limited number of bad guys out there, and those that exist are pretty skilled at dodging the taxman. Our public services will soon require much bigger sums of money just to keep functioning. We really should become a higher tax economy, in much the same way as most of Europe, and the Scandinavian countries in particular. With an ageing population, I don't see what exists as a viable alternative. After all, who would begrudge extra NHS funding for fathers-to-be to have access to cups of tea and hot showers.

I don't know how Debs coped for so long, being tied to the same bed day after day. I started going off the rails pretty quickly. I now understood why confinement makes people go crazy. I got excited when I saw a bottle stuck in a vending machine on one of my late-night walks! Five days became six, and Debs still hadn't gone into active labour. Most people take an average of 1.5-2 days, so we were somewhat outside the norms of a standard induction process. I was joking with the midwives about when we could claim our frequent flyer points. We eventually decided to opt for a caesarean delivery. There wasn't much more that Debs could try, and she was feeling physically and emotionally drained from the whole ordeal. We kept getting bumped off the list, as we fell between the cracks of what was an emergency caesarean and what was an elective (planned) operation. Finally, at midday on 4th February, we both got into our scrubs and made our way into the operating theatre. It wasn't what either of us had envisaged, but we were relieved that we were approaching some kind of resolution.

We had done a little bit of reading into what having a caesarean entails, but we were pretty sketchy on the details. One doesn't usually see the inside of an operating theatre. Usually the patient goes in alone and is unconscious, so us both being in there, fully aware, with twelve or so people prodding Debs, was a strange experience. We played some hypno-birthing meditations that Diana had prepared for us, and before we knew it, we were hearing soft muffled cries. We were both stunned when Amber came out after only ten or so minutes. It took another forty minutes to sew Debs back together again, but with a new baby in your arms, all that time flew by. Amber Leah Nathan Bryant was born at 12.55 on 04/02/20, weighing a perfectly healthy seven pounds and fourteen ounces. All the doctors, dietitians, and specialists, who insisted that she was too large, were all proved conclusively wrong. We had potentially spent a whole needless week in hospital because of this, but in that moment, we didn't care one jot.

Seeing your baby for the first time is an indescribable experience. Words like magical or life-affirming really don't do it justice; we were both blubbering wrecks when we saw her lifted out. Months of preparation, pain, and effort, all melted away in an instant. I felt every emotion under the sun – pride, fear, love, apprehension, joy, all bundled together. I confess that I had a quick look over the screen at Debs' stomach. It didn't look as graphic as I thought it might, just an awful lot of blood and a couple of organs on show. Nothing as bad as what you would see in a SAW film (and I've seen six of those!) The earliest photo I have of Amber is when she was less than a minute old, being weighed and checked out by the midwife. After the operation, I asked Debs what it felt like to be fully awake for intrusive abdominal surgery. Her best description of it was that it felt like someone was doing the washing-up inside her stomach.

After Debs and the baby had been cleaned up, we were whisked off to the recovery room, where we were due to rest for an hour or so. Within about five minutes, one of the midwives came in and told us we already had visitors. That was somewhat confusing. We hadn't told anyone when the procedure was booked for. Debs' parents had tried to call us, put two and two together when we didn't answer the phone, and driven up to the hospital on the off-chance that we were now a family of three. Rob was heading off to Geneva that evening, and didn't want to miss seeing his granddaughter. As luck would have it, the midwives let them in, and he got to see Amber for fifteen minutes before he jetted off for a few days. My parents came up the following day, and later that evening we were discharged. We could have stayed another night, but after eight days of being cooped up like chickens in a hen house, we had had enough. Lots of parents say that they can't believe that hospitals simply let you leave with something so tiny and helpless. I can empathise; it really does feel like you should have to sign on a dotted line, like for a parcel or something. Stepping out of those hospital doors into the cool night air was how a convict must feel after a short stay in prison. Suddenly the world is at your feet, and you don't quite know what to do with your new-found freedom.

Obviously, the 4th February, 2020, will always be synonymous with the birth of our beautiful baby daughter. The only other newsworthy event that day was the UK's first ever long-distance autonomous car journey, where a vehicle travelled 230 miles from Bedfordshire to Sunderland entirely on its own. Unbeknown to us, there was also a mysterious illness silently spreading around the globe. Amber had been born into a brave new world.

CHAPTER 16

Amber

There is nothing particularly noteworthy about Chase Side. It's your typical north London high street that winds its way through Southgate with traffic fumes and irate drivers aplenty. The shops are the usual mixture of coffee bars, fast food restaurants, betting shops, and the occasional independent retailer. I had never paid it particular attention before, but as this was the route I drove on our first journey from hospital with our baby daughter, I was scanning the environment, trying desperately to remain on high alert. I was exhausted, sleep-deprived, and on a constant look out for potholes. Debs was incredibly sore from her operation the day before, so I was trying to make the car journey as smooth as possible for her. The tiniest bump would cause her to wince, so I was going as slow as I possibly could. I think our average speed on that journey was a snail-like 15 mph. There was also the fact that we had a precious little package blissfully reclining in the back. I wasn't in the best condition to drive either. I was in that fuzzy, hazy state, over-thinking things and allowing strange thoughts to enter into my head. As I stopped at a pedestrian crossing on Chase Side and waited for the colour to change, I began to worry that we had named our daughter after a traffic light signal.

We finally got home at about 8pm that evening. As we pulled into our drive, unloaded the car, and put the key in the door, I felt a real sense of relief that we were finally home after our prolonged NHS incarceration. Once we had put Amber to sleep in her cot and had some food that wasn't irradiated hospital mush, we both had the same feeling: now what do we do? The answer was very little, at least initially. Jen had cooked stackloads of easy meals for us, which were piled into our freezer like we were hunkering down for a Canadian winter. That stash of food became a godsend over the next few weeks, as strange global forces started to impact on us.

In truth, becoming parents for the first time isn't that terrifying. We both said during that first week that it wasn't as tough as most people make it out to be. I would describe it as more of a lifestyle adjustment. It's hard work certainly, but you adapt, and after a while you settle into a routine that becomes normalised. I remember when I was at school doing my A-Levels, thinking that working a full-time job for eight hours a day seemed horrifying (school days usually ended around 3.30pm). Now I barely give it a moment's thought. It's the fear of the unknown that I think is the biggest hurdle. Having to cook for myself every day was a big deal when I was eighteen, but once you've incinerated a few chickens and boiled vegetables to within an inch of their lives, you learn from your mistakes and move on to worrying about things like whether wearing a long trench coat is as cool as you think it is. Once we had gotten over our fear of Amber suffocating in the middle of the night, and dealt with a few challenging nappies, we were all tickety-boo. We made sensible adjustments during those first few weeks, like keeping our routines flexible and not over-committing to social engagements with friends and family, but that was about it. In fact, for the first couple of weeks, Debs and I were both sleeping longer than we had in a good long while. We were regularly getting 7/8 hours sleep; it was just interrupted, elongated sleep.

The simple truth is that every baby is different. There are, in essence, no rules. Advice for new parents is a mixture of old wives' tales, subjective experience, scientific trends, and plain old rubbish, all wrapped up as wisdom, knowledge, and fact. I suspect that nearly all parents (and we are no exception) just make it up as they go along. Initially, we were both concerned about the ideal temperature in the various rooms in our house. All the advice seemed to be that the optimum temperature for a newborn baby is between sixteen and twenty Celsius, but when we double-checked with an ear thermometer, she was far too cold. Against all the advice, she seemed to be much happier in a 20-22 range. This was the first of many bits of advice that we ignored. Bringing up a baby is doing what humans have been doing for millennia – evolving and adapting to new circumstances. In many ways we are just like the inhabitants of the city of Ephesus, mentioned both here and in the prologue, just so I can unsubtly bring this book full circle.

Having complete and total responsibility for a life is a hard thing to grasp at first. All the work that one puts in is rewarding, but there's just so much of it, stretching out in front of you like the Serengeti. You've already baked the baby. Now begins the slow eighteen-year process of getting the recipe bang on. Add a generous amount of hard graft, a pinch of monotony, a dash of thanklessness, and sprinkle with a light dusting of hair-shredding insanity. Mix and repeat.

One of our pet names for Amber was 'milk face'. This was fairly self-explanatory really; she would manage to drench herself in milk whilst feeding, and then sit there looking rather tipsy afterwards. It was very cute to watch, though to me 'Milk Face' sounded like a name for the world's lamest superhero. The one X-Man who got dealt the short straw; the one that no-one could take seriously. In the blue corner, we have Wolverine, 18 pounds of muscle and claws as sharp as razors, whilst in the red corner we have Milk Face, with an ability to projectile vomit milk, and grin like a lunatic.

Watching Amber grow and develop as time went by was a continual joy. Once the days turned into weeks and then months, the changes started becoming more pronounced. Here are a few of those milestones I noted during that time:

24th February: First self-addressed letter (doctor's surgery)

25th February: Officially surpassed her birth weight

6th March: First conscious grip

9th March: First prescription

14th March: Received first library card

20th March: Amber's first deliberate smile (my birthday present)

28th March: Amber's first time sleeping through the night (7 hours+)

1st April: First injections

15th April: First time she rolled over from her front

12th May: First time consciously sucking her thumb

19th May: First time grabbing her feet

29th May: Receiving first passport

9th June: Taking the bottle for the first time

19th June: Sitting in a high chair for the first time

26th June: First time sleeping in a cot

12th July: First time eating solid food (a banana)

22nd July: Rolled over from her back for the first time

4th August: First visible tooth

7th August: Amber's first holiday/trip outside London

14th August: First time in a swing

31st August: First time sitting up unaided

15th September: First time left with a babysitter

16th September: First visit to the beach/ seaside

15th December: First time clapping

I suspect that discovering the joys of white noise is both a blessing and a curse to all new parents. The womb is a pretty noisy place to be, and as such, getting used to silence takes some doing. White noise essentially mimics some of the sound ambience of the womb, acting as a kind of audio comfort blanket. I never realised that there were so many different types. We went through three different apps, with maybe two hundred different variations. Some sounds worked more effectively than others, so there was a lot of trial and error. Not only did we need to find something that Amber could sleep to, but it had to be something that didn't drive us both mad whilst we were still sharing a room. The noise of a hairdryer is quite a common one for new parents to try, although with Amber it was never as effective as the actual hairdryer. In the end, we settled on 'airplane cabin', which by and large seemed to do the trick. Other options available included air conditioner, vacuum cleaner, and ocean waves modes. There was also the more 'out there' types of white noise, like rustling bamboo, typewriter, marshland frogs, diesel car idling, seagulls at the beech – even spaceship hum. I'm not sure how the app designers determined what spaceship hum sounded like. Basically, if it was monotonous and one frequency, it was a white noise option.

I've rewritten parts of this chapter so many times, the main reason being that a baby is a moving target. Nothing remains the same for very long. Amber was a great sleeper until she wasn't. She fed easily until she stopped feeding easily. She never cried and then she wouldn't stop crying. Of course, when you move along to a new stage, you forget the previous one. The vast majority of nights, for instance, I slept really well, but of course you're not supposed to divulge that as a new parent. Also, those nights tend not to stick in the brain. Initially, I wrote three whole pages on my issues with sleeping, which probably only lasted a couple of weeks but felt like forever at the time. Sleep is like money – you only think about it when you have too little. Then you think about it all the time, and the less you have the more you think about it. It becomes the prism through which you see the world, and nothing can exist except in relation to it. Debs had it a hundred times tougher than me. My temporary daytime lethargy was in no way equal to the conveyor belt of feeding duties that Debs was doing on a nightly basis. And then of course, once Amber had settled, Debs developed insomnia which lasted for weeks. She really was a superstar through all of this, taking motherhood and all its various challenges in her stride.

My birthday that year was a bit of a non-event. I think it was the first time in twenty years that I didn't spend it in either a restaurant or a pub. With Amber and the (spoiler alert for the next chapter) deteriorating situation in the outside world, there wasn't a huge amount that could be planned. I badly cooked us some steaks, had one beer, and then it was up the wooden hills to Bedfordshire at 8pm for Amber's night routine. It was a far cry from the hedonistic birthday nights out of years past. Not that I particularly cared. Growing older, and hopefully wiser, is just a part of life's rich tapestry. Losing my hair is a bit of a pain, but that aside, getting older is quite exciting. I can't wait to take my daughter to Legoland or teach her the rules to Settlers of Catan (one of the world's greatest board games). It's when I meet up with those friends I see less frequently that the fact we're no longer irresponsible teenage/twenty-somethings any more comes as something of a shock. Our youthful boyish looks have started to fade, dissipated in a thousand nights of excess, with no Dorian Gray-style paintings in our attics to haunt us. Still, if its a choice between eternal torment and not knowing a single song in the top 40, I would assuredly pick the latter.

Until babies can sleep in their own room, you're not really living, just kind of existing really. If you managed to carve out 1.5 or 2 hours during a particularly good nap, it was a godsend, because it meant that you could plan to do things. The lists of daily tasks that Debs and I would write for ourselves when I was working at home were incredibly dull: take the bins out, hang the washing up, that sort of thing. Anything that was a bit trickier, like a spot of DIY or some sorting of clothes, would take days or even weeks to accomplish.

By May, the bedtime routine had started to get easier. Amber began sleeping through the night and not needing to be rocked quite so rigorously.* We were very lucky that she grew quite quickly into a deep sleeper, like her Daddy. Just waking up once during the night was normal for a long time. Amber's feeding also became more controlled, so rather than uncontrollably feasting like Pacman on a pellet-guzzling rampage, she became a lot calmer. We also felt more comfortable leaving her to sleep on her own, so rather than going to bed at some ungodly early hour (7-7.30 pm was

---

* *(Note to non-parents: sleeping through the night doesn't actually mean sleeping through the night. It means seven hours of straight sleep, so waking up at 3am could be considered sleeping through).*

about the average for a while), we suddenly procured our evenings back. It's hard to describe the joy after three months of hermit-like living, to suddenly have a little bit of freedom with sensible dinner times, alcohol, and *MasterChef* back on the agenda. Sweet relief!

The four-month regression stage was something of a shock. Basically, at four months babies switch from having two stages of sleep to having the four stages that adults have. The two stages that babies are born with are the deep and regenerative stage, sometimes called 'slow wave' and the dream stage otherwise known as R.E.M. or rapid eye movement (what the band of the same title is named after). That's the reason they can fall asleep so quickly when they're young – they go straight into a peaceful deep sleep. At four months, they suddenly have two additional stages of lighter sleep to contend with, and they have to learn to transition smoothly between them. With more time spent in lighter adult sleep, they are suddenly much more prone to waking up at random times. We found that all of a sudden, our bedroom wasn't dark enough, so we moved her into the nursery. We still had our evenings, but it meant I would now be sleeping in the nursery for six weeks. Debs slept better without the white noise disturbing her, so I performed my selfless fatherly duties and crammed myself into a single bed alongside Amber. In the end, her moving into the nursery wasn't quite the joyous milestone that we thought would happen a few weeks later. Instead, it was a lot of creeping around in total darkness and being uncomfortably wedged in on a kid's bed.

The early days of bathing her were interesting. The joy of bath time doesn't really begin until a baby can consciously control their limbs. Before that, they just lie there looking confused. She was calm, and appeared to like the feeling of warm water, but I wouldn't say she was having genuine fun. She looked more like a frog about to be dissected that has just regained consciousness in the middle of a science class. When she reached the three-month stage, she was able to splash around with her legs and started reaching out for the various toys. Trying to get her neck cleaned involved a lot of distraction techniques with rubber ducks.

There's nothing quite like a baby to make a couple bicker. Through biological necessity, it's an unequal relationship from the get-go, so roles and responsibilities are always fluid. Mums have responsibility for everything except when they don't, in which case dads have 49% of the responsibility, but mums always maintain that 51% as an insurance policy. Because babies are a powder keg waiting to go off, it's all too easy to blame the other person if they try something different or suggest something that turns out not to work. On one occasion, six fateful words that I uttered – 'she doesn't need a bath tonight' – indirectly caused hours of crying and heartache, and that was just me!

Amber was developing very quickly now. The dexterity she was demonstrating in her hands was becoming quite impressive. None of the other NCT babies (who were all older than her) were anywhere near that level of development. Maybe the terrible global crisis that was unfolding was having one positive impact on us, Amber was getting more mummy and daddy time than she might otherwise have got. We tried to keep life as normal as possible for her by replicating what we would have been doing in the outside world. For instance, as all the swimming pools were now closed, we ordered our own inflatable pool and set it up in the garden. All the fun of the swimming pool, just without the chlorine, rip-off parking, and additional screaming kids. It was a mission to get it suitably warmed up, though. It was impossible to attach our hose to the kitchen tap for warm water, so multiple shuttle runs carrying kettles and buckets were required. It was a bit like an extended crystal maze game, but the prize was a warm outdoor bath. I think I spent about two hours of traipsing up and down the garden with water for ten minutes of Amber splashing around. Now that's dedicated parenting!

One of the interesting things to get your head around with a new baby is trying to lose one's sense of self-consciousness. I think that naturally comes a lot easier to mothers. It's tricky, but you have to. Trying to sing *Ob-La Di, Ob-La-Da* over and over again would be impossible otherwise. There's lots of nonsensical rhymes that I imagine will be forever burned into my brain. Here's just one example that we would sing to Amber whilst giving her a leg massage:

> Wibble Wobble, Wibble wobble, jelly on a plate
> Wibble Wobble, Wibble wobble, jelly on a plate
> Let's wibble to the left and wobble to the right
> Wibble all day and wobble all night

Creeping around one's own house is another of those strange things that happens when you have a baby. It's not just the keeping quiet, it's modifying where and how you carry out your behaviour. There's the obvious things like taking phone calls in other rooms, but it's the amalgamation of all the little things that's interesting. I realised it had now become instinctive during one of Amber's kitchen naps, when I opened the fridge to retrieve a peach melba yoghurt. It was a set of four, the kind where you have to snap an individual yoghurt off. I took all four yoghurts into the downstairs toilet just so I could snap one off before returning the remaining three. There was also the realisation that my 'baby talk' was becoming so ingrained that I was now accidentally using it in adult situations. One night for instance, when Debs had finished eating a lovingly prepared king prawn stew, I turned to her and said 'Good girl'. It sounded beyond patronising; the kind of thing Mickey Rooney might have said in some shockingly chauvinistic Hollywood picture. I can safely say that the king prawns weren't the only thing that were stewing that evening.

By now I was starting to understand all the nuances to the different types of crying. Debs had become an expert at this. I was a mere novice, but I could pick out some of them. It's true that when you don't have that bond, a baby crying is the most irritating sound in the world. To the untrained ear, they all basically sound the same. Case in point: when sitting on an aeroplane for hours on end, you don't think to yourself, *That's a 'lavish attention on me' cry.* You think to yourself, *Jesus, how much longer can this possibly go on for?* It's grating and irritating, like nails down a chalk board or Katie Hopkins trying to write a balanced argument. When you have unrequited love, that crying morphs into a strange form of language. In the absence of speech, it's how babies communicate. Just to name a few: there's the attention cry, the uncomfortable cry, the feed me cry, the tired cry, the overtired cry, even the why am I crying cry.

Amber receiving her first passport should have been a joyous occasion. Instead, it was somewhat marred when we unwrapped it and saw that it was blue. We had applied for her passport before the deadline when the government switched them from the EU burgundy colour that Debs and I had both grown up with. Unfortunately, it got held up by the Covid-19 crisis and was among the first of the new passports to be issued without the EU insignia. It shouldn't have bothered me as much as it did, but the blue seemed to symbolise racism, intolerance, and a shrinking of freedoms. It was a visible symbol that, unlike us, Amber wouldn't be gifted the automatic privilege of living and working anywhere in Europe. I guess there was a time, many decades ago, when it didn't infer those things, and soon enough it would again come to be seen as standard.

It's fascinating watching babies learn about the world around them. Everything is brand new and gets taken at face value. Even without the ability to speak, babies are hilarious. Blow a raspberry and Amber would recoil in shock, wipe her face with a muslin and she would get more excited than a dog loose in a butcher's shop. Then there was the ever-versatile peekaboo game, which would provide hours of baby friendly entertainment. We started playing her different types of music as she began to react more to sounds. I played her the exact record that I remember my parents playing for me when I was around five years old – a collection of children's novelty songs called 'All Aboard'. It had numbers by people like Bernard Cribbins, Benny Hill, and Charlie Drake. *Nellie The Elephant* by Mandy Miller appeared to be her favourite. Amazingly, thirty years after all that incessant spinning, it still played perfectly.

Rocking a baby to sleep is one of the most infuriating things anyone can do. I'm sure other parents can attest to how complex and soul-destroying this can be. It requires patience, strength, agility, and stamina – the key attributes to all martial arts, now that I think about it. The stress is hard to describe if you haven't had to do this whilst sleep-deprived in the middle of the night. Thankfully, this became a relatively rare occurrence once Amber was a little older, but even so, it stays with you like a war wound. Rocking Amber to sleep would take about twenty minutes. I'll rephrase that: if done correctly, it would take about twenty minutes. Those vexing minutes can easily feel like an hour when you can't see a clock. Frequently, it was longer, and if you failed to get her to sleep you had to start again. It wouldn't be an extra few minutes, either; she would be wide awake and you would need to start from scratch with the full process. You're in the pitch black for the whole time. Not the usual night darkness, but total darkness with the blackout blinds and curtains. The kind of darkness that would make Batman shudder. You can't see the baby, so you can't tell if they have their eyes closed or for how long they've drifted off. You need to rely on instinct and pick up on non-visual cues, like how floppy their arms are. You can't check your phone, as any light source risks waking them up, so you stand there gently rocking, trying to count in your head. Counting to 1200 in the pitch black is one of the least stimulating things anyone can do. You can't scratch, sneeze, yawn, or cough, which becomes a real mental battle. You also start to ache if you get the positioning slightly wrong. A small weight imbalance and you can end up with a dead arm. I would start off rocking vigorously, whilst gently bouncing and ssshhing her to the count of three. Once she had stopped crying and/or wriggling, I would slowly stop the ssshhing and begin to reduce the bouncing. This would take about ten or so minutes. Then, with much gentler swaying, I would creep towards the cot as slowly and stealthily as I could. I would then reduce the rocking, and just stand with her in my arms for a few more minutes. The next stage was lowering her down, whilst adjusting my hand that was supporting her head, so I didn't get it trapped underneath her. If I managed to do all that, the nail-biting conclusion would be exiting the room without making a sound. Usually, I would crouch on the floor for a couple of minutes, barely daring to breathe, before I made a bolt for the door. I reckon I only succeeded in getting her to sleep first time in maybe, 40% of my attempts. You would feel absolutely crushed if you had done all of that, only for her to wake up crying at the very end. Or, as happened to me on one maddening occasion, someone deciding to ring my phone at the crucial juncture. The best parallel I can think of for this whole procedure is someone trying to defuse a bomb; one false move and it's game over. A baby going off isn't quite a life or death situation, but it certainly feels like it if you've been waiting 45 minutes to go to the toilet. Oh, the ineffable mystery of baby's sleeping patterns.

We couldn't wait to start Amber on proper food. Everything to do with a baby is all about routine, so you long for new things to help break up the monotony a bit. Starting a baby on solid food is one of the big ones. Debs was so excited to start cooking her meals and experimenting with different texture and flavour combinations. The very first thing she ate was some chopped-up banana, though in reality, 50% went on the floor, 45% got grounded into a sloppy pulp down her clothes, and maybe 5% got ingested. Banana drama indeed. Her first proper meal was sweet potato with Greek yoghurt and avocado. This was all part of baby-led weaning, the idea being that you place food for babies in front of them and allow them to help themselves. It was real food from the get-go for Amber – no mush, no baby foods, no force-feeding, none of that 'here comes the aeroplane nonsense', and none of those unnecessarily cute pots that decorate supermarket shelves. I can't take any credit for this; it was all Debs' doing. She had done a large amount of reading on the benefits of baby-led weaning, which I casually skim read after her. It actually makes perfect sense. Unless they're ill, babies don't need to be force-fed. When babies can pick up food, explore textures, and decide what they prefer, a lot of the stress is taken out of the feeding process. They're also less likely to become fussy eaters, as they associate mealtimes with fun and exploring, not having a plastic spoon rammed down their throat. They also learn about portion control, and because they decide how much they eat, they're likely to have a better metabolism when they grow up. I suspect that a lot of the ideas around specific baby foods and purées are tied in with the advertising and marketing industries. It's probably the same guy who convinced millions of people to pay £2 for a bottle of the same stuff that comes out of your tap for free. She learned how to use a spoon incredibly quickly. As long as the food was sloppy enough to stick, like a bolognese or Weetabix, she was pretty proficient at spoon-feeding herself. She was even able to use both hands by six months of age. Amber-dexterous, I used to call it.

It's amazing how quickly one gets used to nappies. Mother Nature is very clever. At the start, they are not a big ordeal. You are somehow lulled into a false sense of serenity with the early milk-based ones, which we in the NCT man cave (not my term) used to say reminded us of slightly burnt Horlicks. It's a hell of a shock a few months later when they start moving on to solid food. Out of nowhere, you are suddenly faced with something so toxic it makes the previous ones seem like a visit to the Selfridges' perfume counter.

We didn't witness the first time that Amber properly rolled over (from her back onto her front). It was in the early hours of the morning. Debs just glanced at the monitor and noticed that Amber was now on her front, looking a bit confused. She must have pulled herself around using the bars on the cot as leverage. We thought that was now it, she would be rolling here, there, and everywhere. But she didn't. Smugly satisfied that she could now roll, she didn't want us to bear witness to it. We also missed the second time that she rolled over nearly two weeks later; this time it was during the day, when we were having lunch with Matt and Katy in the garden. Finally, a further three weeks later, it was third time lucky and we got to see her rolling in front of our eyes.

We had a mini celebration for Amber's six-month birthday in August. It felt like we had now reached a major milestone. The hardest of the hard work was now hopefully behind us. We had a slice of carrot cake and blew out the best match to a half candle I could find. A few days later, we were off on a mini break to Cambridgeshire – the first time Amber had left the confines of the M25. We really needed some time away just to recharge our batteries after the craziest six months of our lives. We stayed in this lodge on a working farm just outside of Chippenham. We had our own private hot tub on the outdoor terrace, which provided welcome moments of opulence in-between all the Amber-related duties. They, of course, never stop, even on holiday. In your own house, it's just an accepted part of life, but elsewhere, all the baby paraphernalia – the food, beakers, washing, nappies, and toys – stick out like a Dick Van Dyke cockney accent. Trying to clean with a baby around is like raking up leaves during a hurricane, so you just relax around the chaos. Sipping on champagne and savouring strawberries, whilst sinking into the sauna, felt heavenly during her naps. This was now our new normal, and in spite of the brevity, the baby, and the budget-busting board, we did come away relaxed and refreshed. Six months down, 210 to go.

CHAPTER 17

The Year the Earth Stood Still

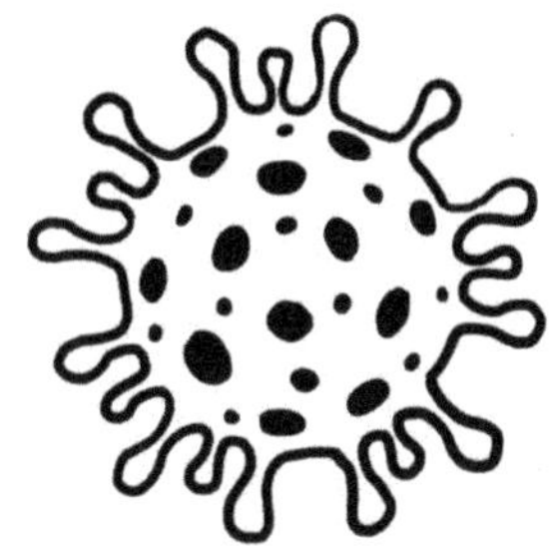

When I first started writing this book, I never imagined that I'd end on a chapter with such a doom-laden title as 'The Year the Earth Stood Still'. And yet, that is essentially what happened to the world in 2020. It was like God had pressed a gigantic pause button on his heavenly remote control. Slowly but surely, everything ground to a halt in the biggest global event since the Second World War. Just as I was about to finish this book, the Covid-19 crisis reared its ugly head, and caused me to re-assess a lot of things that I had written. Suddenly Brexit didn't seem that big a deal and the frivolous tone of some of the earlier chapters no longer felt appropriate. Hindsight, of course, is a wonderful thing. I did a small amount of rewriting, but ultimately decided to leave most of what I had written unaltered. That was then, and this is now.

The term 'crisis' derives from the Greek word 'krisis', meaning decision or judgement. A crisis can conclude well or badly, but the point is that its outcome is fundamentally uncertain. To experience a crisis is to inhabit a world that is temporarily up for grabs. One where the normal rules no longer apply and there is no certainty about how we will emerge at the other end. Living through a crisis that will be forever defined in history, is fascinating. Much like the 2001 attacks, this felt momentous, a game-changer that would be discussed at dinner parties for years to come – the first truly global pandemic in over a hundred years.

The first I heard about the crisis was early in January, when reports began coming out of the Chinese city of Wuhan about a mysterious illness that was causing severe cases of pneumonia. These cases were all traced back to a seafood wholesale market, where scientists deduced that a virus which had originated in bats had jumped into the human population. Like most people in the UK, I barely gave it a moment's thought. Without wanting to sound callous, it just sounded like another strange illness that would burn itself out in a land far, far away. There had been so many diseases over the last twenty years that hadn't amounted to anything like the scale that the doom-mongers and survival nutters were always suggesting. There was the SARS outbreak in 2003, followed by Ebola in 2014, and MERS in 2015-18, none of which were major stories in Europe. The only thing I remember about SARS is that some of the bands I followed at the time shortened a few tours. The sad truth is that if it didn't impact on America or Europe, it wasn't considered big news. Initially, Covid-19 was the latest in a long line of infections that a few people might mutter under their breath as being a serious threat to society. However, if they continued to talk about it, you would assume they were some kind of Bear Grylls wannabe with four hundred cans of chickpeas in their larder and a makeshift bunker in their garden. Of all the conversational taboos that exist in British culture, pessimistic pandemic views were almost on a plateau with earnings and political persuasions before the crisis. I think prior to 2020, I'd heard more people claim that Paul McCartney reached his full creative potential in Wings than talk about their worries around infectious illnesses. Debs and I obviously had other reasons to be distracted at the time; we had just experienced our own mini-lockdown in hospital, and were now getting used to life with a squealing baby.

By early February, the city of Wuhan had been put under strict quarantine, but cases had already spread to Thailand, the Philippines, the United States, and Italy. By February 9th, the death toll from Covid-19 in China alone exceeded the number of people killed worldwide by SARS. The major turning point I recall was when cases in Europe started to sky rocket in March, particularly in Italy, where the exponential growth rate was terrifying. A couple of weeks later, all sixty million people in the country went into lockdown. Suddenly it became the number one workplace topic of conversation. At the college, we had a high number of international students from every corner of the globe flying back and forth during the Easter break, so we had started making serious disaster response plans about what to do in the event of an outbreak at LCC. What I really objected to at the time was the undercurrent of racism that seemed to infect every news story, with terms like 'foreign virus' or 'Chinese flu'. These kinds of terms tend to stick in the head and do more harm than good. One of the reasons the 1918 flu came to be known as the 'Spanish' flu was because Spain was neutral in the war and didn't censor its press. The US, Britain, and France – all of which had the flu before Spain – kept it out of the newspapers at first to avoid damaging morale. Spain took the brunt of the blame and anger through heated geopolitics rather than rational argument. It was equally unwise to blame China in 2020. Although the virus originated from a Wuhan food market, there were many countries in the world where equally dubious, and far worse food safety practices were observed. With 1.5 billion people (19% of the world population), the chances of a new virus coming from China were one-in-five, purely in statistical terms alone. Globalisation and the interconnected world that we live in are the reason that the virus spread so swiftly and effectively. Cheap air travel and global tourism didn't originate in China. Ultimately, the source of the outbreak didn't matter. As Sting famously sang, 'We share the same biology, regardless of ideology.'

The Chinese students at work were having a particularly torrid time, being stigmatised by their peers. Wearing face masks around the college meant they really stood out. In many Asian cultures, the wearing of face masks is a common occurrence; it's as conventional as the wearing of hats in the UK. (It's not just avoiding pollution and illness, but also the idea of Qi and breathing techniques, as well as fears around skin bleaching. Whereas people in the West tend to want to tan to appear darker, people in the East will often avoid sun exposure to appear lighter.) Many of the Chinese students were worried about the UK and EU students not taking the outbreak seriously, and didn't understand why they weren't wearing masks, so there was a sense of double standards. They felt they were taking the appropriate steps to protect themselves and others, whilst at the same time, taking the brunt of others' vitriol.

The gauntlet of opinions ran the whole spectrum of responses from 'do nothing' to 'follow Italy's example as soon as possible'. Many people couldn't quite comprehend what was happening; maybe at some subconscious level people thought that this kind of thing could never happen in the UK. It was as likely as us winning the Eurovision song contest. The problem that every country had to contend with was that there was no proven effective response. This was a brand-new virus, related to other Coronavirus illnesses like the common cold and SARS, but unique in terms of its spread, incubation, and infection rate. In about 20% of cases, there were no symptoms whatsoever, so people could spread it to others without even realising it. Other people could suffer severe symptoms, and for an unlucky few, death by asphyxiation – a horribly painful and protracted way to go. Then there was the long-term damage that it could potentially cause to the heart, lungs, kidneys, and even blood vessels, of the people who recovered. About three months down the line, this started to become more obvious, with people recovering and then relapsing. Later on came the worry that Covid-19 might have permanent health impacts that would only come to light months or even years later.

It took a while for the severity of the virus spread to fully sink in. Through normal behaviour, the average person infected 2.5 others within five days. Within a further twenty-five days, those people would go on to infect another 400. The exponential growth was such that, if left unchecked, 80% of the country could become infected, equating to 7.4 million hospitalisations and nearly half a million deaths within the course of a few short months. This would have been on top of all the other deaths from ongoing ailments, not to mention cancelled operations and postponed treatments. Simply put, there weren't enough hospitals, doctors, beds, or equipment, for even a fraction of that amount. The figure for the number of UK-wide hospital beds was something in the region of 170,000, and this was already at full capacity in 2020. Even if the beds were all miraculously emptied, tens of thousands of people would die through lack of respirators and other equipment. What was available wouldn't cover even 5% of the hospitalisations that would be needed. This was a pandemic on a truly unprecedented scale, and every country faced similar challenges. Once that sank in, public opinion and behaviour slowly started to change. Everyone was frantically scrambling to get a vaccine developed as soon as possible, but that wouldn't be available for at least a year. The only interim solution was the concept of social distancing. This became the buzzword of 2020. The idea was that people would need to be physically separated from each other as much as possible to flatten the peak of infection and leave the NHS more able to cope with a smaller, but still substantial, number of cases. Boris Johnson, the clown prince, was suddenly thrown into the role of national spokesman for the country's biggest crisis in living memory. It was painful to watch him address the nation, woefully out of his depth, with his floppy fringe unable to hide the fear behind his eyes. This was a man so spineless he'd make a jellyfish look upstanding, and yet here he was attempting to reassure everyone that the situation was under control. The bluff and bluster he'd used to con millions of people into thinking Brexit was a great idea, was of no use now. It's hard to make people laugh when you're telling them that tens of thousands of people are going to die, the country is going into lockdown, millions of people are about to lose their jobs, and that the freedoms of a liberal democracy are being withdrawn. It was totally the right thing to do (the alternative was too horrible to contemplate), but there was a real sense of dramatic irony that the walking embodiment of a public school-educated classical philologist was now overseeing a real-life Greek tragedy.

Everything we took for granted about our way of life slowly started to grind to a halt. The modern world is so interconnected that if you remove one piece, everything else sways like a Jenga tower in a storm. First, it was the cancellation of big films. The first major one I recall being the latest James Bond film, which was postponed for an unspecified time. This was then followed by anything which had obviously large gatherings – i.e. various sporting events and concert tours. The English Premier League being suspended was a real wake-up call for millions of football-loving souls up and down the country. This was the first time since the Second World War that a campaign had not been completed. Glastonbury, Eurovision, and the suspension of the filming of various soap operas soon followed. Employers were advised to let their staff work from home wherever possible; my last date in the office being the 16th March. I had already felt like I'd had so much disruption. I hadn't worked a full week in the three months' prior, due to a combination of Christmas, an office move, hospital visits, paternity leave, staff strikes, student strikes, and even a bomb scare which caused the whole college to be evacuated. Coronavirus was the giant cherry on top of an already collapsing cake. Between early December 2019 and June 2020, I didn't manage one full week of work. Initially, the whole university being sent home was one massive shock which took a few days to process. Because of the new social distancing restrictions, everything would have to be done remotely, including teaching. This meant shifting our entire course portfolio onto a digital online learning model. We had a three-week window over Easter before teaching was due to recommence, essentially doing five years' worth of work within fifteen days. We had no idea what the future held, but at least for now our jobs were secure.

Me, Debs, and Amber, went into social isolation on the day I started working from home. Essentially, this meant no contact with anyone else for at least twelve weeks. This was what the government was advising; it was the socially responsible thing to do, and of course we had a baby who hadn't had any of her injections yet. The long-term effects of the virus were still unknown, so we wanted to take every possible precaution. The advice was to stay at least two metres away from anyone else by avoiding crowded places like restaurants, bars, and shops. Slowly but surely, these all started to close, as the restrictions got tighter and tighter. When pubs – the historical cornerstone of British social life – were forced to shut, it felt like the very fabric of society was collapsing in on itself. Schools started to cease teaching, out of a fear of children transmitting the virus to others, whilst big name stores, gyms, and even some public parks started shutting up shop whilst public transport was pared back significantly. The government then followed the example of our European neighbours and banned all mass gatherings, which would be enforced by the police. These were extraordinarily draconian measures, but as the number of confirmed cases and deaths continued their upward trajectory, people's mindsets started to shift. You would be surprised by the sheer number of things that could be considered mass gatherings. Weddings, choirs, evening classes, concerts, markets, nursery care, and even picnics in the park, were now all off the agenda. In an address to the nation, we were told that apart from key workers, the only reason to leave the house was to get essential supplies of food and medicine. You were also allowed to go out once a day for exercise, and that was pretty much it for outdoor pursuits.

Everything felt unbelievable and overwhelming but paradoxically familiar, as if we'd walked into an old recurring dream. In a way, we had. We'd seen it before on TV and in Blockbusters. We knew roughly what it would be like, and somehow that made the encounter not less strange but more so. The 2011 film *Contagion* was so close to the bone that it was morbidly fascinating. I watched it a few weeks after lockdown commenced, and everything in it, from the origin of the virus to the discussion of the R number (the rate at which the virus reproduced), was spot on. Parts of it were indistinguishable from a factual documentary on the crisis.

This was life imitating art in the most macabre way possible. Life as we knew it was over for now; the blurry outline of something new was emerging before our disbelieving eyes. Barely a fortnight ago, all we had to do was wash our hands. Now the whole country was in a medically-induced coma, almost all usual life suspended to save the patient.

In many ways, we were very lucky. We were lucky in that I could work remotely, and Debs was still on maternity leave. Unlike large numbers of the population, we wouldn't be taking an additional hit to our wages. We were lucky that we had Amber to keep us busy, and of course we were fortunate to have a nice house and a garden, thus reducing the symptoms of cabin fever somewhat. I felt sorry for friends and colleagues who were cooped up in tiny flats across the capital, with no work to keep them from going stir crazy. Usually people with babies and young children look on in envy at those who are young, free, and single, but in a nationwide lockdown, I was grateful for the distraction. Everyone had some kind of major disruption story. The fickle finger of fate had cursed those who were in the process of buying houses or planning weddings. Debs' cousin, Alice, called us up when the wedding venue she had booked for her special day went into administration. Fortunately for them, they had a further fourteen months or so to make alternative arrangements. Some people just ploughed on anyway and said their nuptials in front of virtual guests. Rather than a shotgun wedding, people were having lockdown weddings. Someone else I knew had booked a trip of a lifetime holiday, costing many tens of thousands of pounds, and only discovered that her partner hadn't paid for any travel insurance once the Covid-19 crisis was underway. I think the divorce proceedings were started not long after.

During the start of the crisis, my mum was travelling around Holland on an art gallery tour with her friend, completely oblivious. It just so happened that the Netherlands was one of the last countries in Europe to start shutting down, and without access to a smartphone or a TV, neither of them could comprehend the severity of the situation. My mum's friend Bernie, Matt, and I, all rang her up, trying to encourage them both to come home as various countries started shutting their borders. They thought I was exaggerating. Although most of the galleries they had gone to see were shut, the coffee bars and shops of Amsterdam were still packed to the rafters. In fairness, the whole situation sounded fanciful. Every day brought new developments that a couple of weeks earlier would have seemed implausible. In the UK, we were all refreshing the news, not out of a sense of civic duty but because everything was coming in so thick and fast. Imagine telling someone a month earlier that: schools would be closed, public gatherings cancelled, and hundreds of millions of people around the world would be out of work. In certain places, landlords would not be collecting rent, or banks collecting mortgage payments, and that the homeless would be allowed to stay in hotels free of charge. Large swathes of the world would be collaborating, with various degrees of coercion and nudging, on a shared project of keeping at least two metres between each other wherever possible. Would you have believed what you were hearing? On one of the occasions when I rang my mum up to give her an update, she asked if I was drunk. Eventually, and perhaps not co-incidentally, at the end of the holiday the truth dawned on them as I was scanning the depleted Eurostar timetables. I called them up to give them the skeleton schedule of what was still running. They arrived back at St Pancras the following day to a very different London than the one they'd left behind.

I never thought in my lifetime that obtaining food would be so challenging. One of the more unpleasant side-effects of the Covid-19 crisis was the 'every man for himself' mentality that some people contracted when it came to acquiring food.

During those first couple of weeks, as things got progressively more serious, people started panic buying and raiding the supermarket shelves for non-perishable goods. For a while there was a nationwide shortage of toilet roll, as people piled their trolleys high with all the soft fluffy sheets they could get their hands on. Pasta, tinned goods, and eggs also vanished, as people started hoarding these things in massive numbers. After the first couple of days, I stopped going to the bigger supermarkets; it was like the wild west in North London. The queues snaked round the entire store, with people arguing and vociferously refusing to believe that the self-service queues could possibly have over a hundred people in them. Others still crammed in, as tightly packed as possible, because no matter how desperate things got, the unique British anxiety that someone would misinterpret a small gap in the queue as being the start of a new one was always omnipresent. Morrisons resembled a Mexican stand-off, with everyone eyeing each other suspiciously, permanently on edge about being in such close contact in these everlasting lines. Meanwhile, the carrier bags that blew across the entrance way resembled branded twenty-first century tumbleweed. The empty shelves that had been decimated earlier in the day only added to the sense of panic that was etched on everyone's faces. I saw people physically racing elderly customers to those last few precious tins of chopped tomatoes. Other people were strolling around like John Wayne, with their tins of tuna, trying to rise above all the kerfuffle. The irony, of course, was there wasn't a genuine shortage of food. It was the inevitable consequence of the UK's 'just in time supply chains'. In order to save money on storage, staffing. and transportation. the food industry operated a policy of just stocking enough produce to meet the standard needs of the population. They had been caught with their guard down. as people raced to the shops like it was 9.30pm on Christmas Eve, having realised they didn't have a turkey to go with their delicious stuffing and cranberry sauce. It was a vicious cycle, where panic buying caused more panic buying, as people thought everything would eventually run out.

I ended up going to the smaller shops – the convenience stores and health food specialists, where you could still obtain most things. Debs and I refused to panic buy. It was selfish, unnecessary, and ultimately self-defeating. There were people with genuine dietary needs who needed things like gluten-free pasta or, in our case, long life almond milk (Debs was going on a dairy detox, because we suspected Amber might have a mild lactose allergy). Besides, rather than seeing the supermarket shelves as half empty, you could look upon them as being half full. Plus, I imagine the mentality of someone who hoards excessive amounts of food isn't one of calm and rational thought. If you were genuinely worried about supply shortages, no amount of chickpeas or quilted Andrex was ever going to soothe that nagging fear at the back of your mind. Incidentally, I could never understand why toilet roll was the first thing people seemed to reach for when it came to hoarding. There were so many alternatives – kitchen roll, the *Daily Mail*, Piers Morgan's endless memoirs. (Verbal diarrhoea helping to clear up the real thing.) The one thing that made me really angry was people stripping the shelves of supermarkets and pharmacies of paracetamol. The vast majority would clearly be sitting in the back of bathroom cabinets until their expiry date kicked in, in a few years' time. You really did start to worry for the elderly and those in genuine need. In the end, supermarkets began getting a grip on the situation, limiting the number of products people could buy, and operating limits on the number of customers in store at any one time.

The flip-side to all this selfish behaviour were the outbreaks of altruism which restored one's faith in humanity. Neighbours posted various offers of help through each other's letterboxes, and people swapped food items when things were running low. We gave some of our excess eggs to Stephanie, our next-door neighbour, who in turn baked us some Passover biscuits. Debs swapped items in the park with her friend Alliea which, before the crisis, would have looked suspiciously like a drug deal. Staying six feet apart, Alliea threw Debs a package containing pasta, whilst Debs left her some home-made banana muffins. Drop completed, they then went on their merry way. This resurgence in community spirit was a happy side-effect of the crisis. Now that people couldn't physically see each other, they started making more of an effort to stay in touch. The online traffic on platforms like Skype, Zoom, Teams, and Google Hangouts, went through the roof. We did virtual dinners, virtual murder mysteries, and virtual pub quizzes with our friends. As part of one of our early lockdown quizzes, I did a memory round where I paraded twenty or so items across the camera in homage to the *Generation Game* conveyor belt challenge.

One evening it was decided that there would be a nationwide applause for all the NHS and healthcare workers who were battling to stay on top of the crisis. Being on the front-line of a pandemic, exposed to infection, and having to decide who lived and who died, was not a role that anyone would relish. At 8pm one evening, millions of people showed their gratitude by opening their front doors or standing on their balconies, and clapped, cheered, and banged saucepans. It was quite a bittersweet moment to step outside on Hazelwood Lane and see people disengaged from each other but engaged in celebration. We were together but apart. Later on, this became a bit of a weekly ritual.

The Covid-19 crisis was relentless; there was nothing it didn't impact on. The BBC news morphed from being about a variety of news stories to a Covid-19 awareness-raising channel. They would now start bulletins by saying, 'Here are the latest Coranavirus headlines.' There was no end to the statistics, death rates, symptom trackers, and home testing/vaccine updates from around the world. The first time I saw TV presenters sitting six feet apart on the sofa, it looked weird, but as the weeks and months rolled on, it became normalised. You got used to seeing pictures of airports looking like parking lots, and central London resembling a ghost town. Because you weren't supposed to physically go elsewhere, the news became your gateway to the outside world.

Humour always helps in a crisis. I very nearly titled this chapter 'The year the bin went out more than us.' When Rachel and Lawrence came over to ours for a chat one day, I got the tape measure out and marked six feet on the floor, where we could maintain our social distancing but still have a good chinwag. As they remarked at the time, it felt like an episode of *Black Mirror*. There was also the time when I came back home and said I had a case of corona, before pulling out a small case of corona beers. I deliberately got that brand just so I could make that exquisitely-timed joke. There were all manner of weird and wonderful regulations that were introduced all over the world. In Mauritius, for instance, people were given allocated shopping days according to their surname. April Fool's Day was essentially abandoned that year; what was happening in real life was strange enough. Everyone was on edge, so an ill-judged prank could severely backfire. On the other hand, a harmless little joke would just fly under the radar. If someone had posted a story about, say, KFC deciding to use ostrich as the meat in their nuggets, people would have just shrugged their shoulders and gone straight back to refreshing the news about Covid-19. When the truth is stranger than fiction, it's hard to push buttons.

By the start of April, a quarter of the world's population – nearly two billion people – were under lockdown. India's decision to enforce strict curfew measures on its vast population meant that one-in-four people were now living under tough restrictions on movement and social contact. Although these felt like unique and strange times, London wasn't a stranger to virus outbreaks. It has a deep buried history of plague laws, wardens wandering the streets, crosses on doors, and houses all shuttered and bolted. When parts of central London were being excavated for Crossrail, the constructors unearthed huge plague pits buried beneath Liverpool Street. The crisis of 2020 wasn't some unlucky one-off event; pandemics are something that we have dealt with for millennia. Knowing that this was in an inescapable fact of life provided a few small crumbs of comfort. Perhaps the old adage that the only things certain in life are death and taxes should be amended to include occasional pandemics.

Going out for walks was challenging with Amber in tow. Whether it was a pram or a sling, you were very conscious how less nimble you were, particularly on narrow pavements and pinch points like the entrances to parks. Trying to stay two metres apart from anyone else was fine in theory, but in reality, if it was mid-afternoon on a gorgeous sunny day, everyone else would have the same idea. The basic problem was that some people took it less seriously than others, or even worse, simply didn't care enough. Even with a baby, nine times out of ten it would be us who had to cross the road to avoid people or swerve into side streets to let people pass. It reminded me of one of those mobile games where coloured bricks fly towards you and you have to sidestep to avoid them. We were constantly on alert, so it was less a pleasant meandering stroll and more a game of high-stakes chicken.

On one of our lunchtime walks, we witnessed the police patrolling Broomfield Park, checking that people weren't flouting the rules. If what people were doing didn't count as exercise, then it was a big slap on the wrists. It was astonishing how many people were obliviously sunbathing or having picnics. Some people had cottoned onto these patrols and would have a back-up exercise regime just in case the boys in blue turned up unexpectedly. We saw people like this sunbathing or chatting who would then jump to attention when the police drove up. A bat and ball would mysteriously appear, or they were suddenly in full 'Rocky mode' doing press ups and planks. It was oddly embarrassing to watch. Seeing fully grown adults doing something so transparent and juvenile – rather like when young kids cover their eyes and think that you can't see them – was just bizarre. There was also a sense of injustice that most people were trying so hard to follow the rules so that we could get back to some sense of normality as soon as possible, whilst a small minority were breaching them for their own selfish reasons. The reality is that for any self-isolation or quarantine to work, people need to be compliant. This depends on a level of emotional intelligence that seemed to be somewhat lacking at times in North London. The resilience of those who refuse to change their behaviour after, say, a terror attack – the people who go out, anyway – was of absolutely no use in this situation. The virus didn't care about individuals' bravery, politics, or views on globalisation. It didn't care if you trusted the government or hated Brexit, whether you were a catastrophist or a conspiracy theorist, all it cared about was surviving by infecting as many people as possible.

Another thing the virus was good at was magnifying the behaviour of already stupid people to embarrassingly blatant proportions. I don't need to go into the details of what a complete ignoramus Donald Trump was at the time. Well, maybe I will go into a few details. Blaming the World Health Organisation for the pandemic in America and withdrawing funding, was a low blow – the equivalent of a boxer repeatedly punching a hapless victim in the groin and then blaming the gloves. Then, of course, there was the brutal irony of Mexico banning Americans from crossing the border. This, at a time when Trump had initiated a hateful campaign to kick undocumented Mexicans out of the country and build, in his words, 'a big beautiful wall'. It must have been a big dent to his pride when the tables turned and suddenly it was the Mexicans who were scared of millions of uninsured Americans heading south. He didn't even seem to understand what Covid-19 was, calling it a genius for dodging antibiotics. Whilst antibiotic resistant bacteria is a cause for concern, this had absolutely nothing to do with the Coronavirus, which you may have gathered from its name, is a virus, not a bacteria. There were literally millions of young children who understood this better than the President. Quite how people managed to keep a straight face at his 'press conferences' was always beyond me. I kept on expecting a Ceausescu moment, where people could no longer keep up the pretence. To this day, I still can't comprehend the thought process behind those people who voted him in. Was it a practical joke that went too far? The last 'press conference' of his I watched was two hours of non-sequiturs, half-finished sentences, unanswered questions, and ill-informed waffle. He ended it by suggesting we should all drink bleach to cure the virus. Imagine watching all that and thinking, *I'm glad he's in charge*. You might as well shave a chimpanzee, stick him in a tanning booth, and graft a dead squirrel to his head; you would get about the same amount of sense. Actually, I stand corrected. A chimpanzee wouldn't be dumb enough to drink bleach.

The importance of routine in all our lives is seriously undervalued. When the days blend into one another and there's very little difference between a weekday and the weekend, things can start to feel claustrophobic very quickly. Time seems to become thick and amorphous, like walking through treacle in slow motion. Rather like being on an aeroplane, the secret is to plan your time and break it into manageable chunks, so that it feels like you've achieved something. Even if it was only a spot of cleaning or some baking, that mild fulfilment really helped alleviate that sense of confinement that was in danger of making us all go a bit loopy. When we weren't working or looking after Amber, we would indulge in a bit of 'me time'. Debs would do her painting by numbers and home workouts with the exercise guru of the year, Joe Wicks. I would do a spot of gardening, writing, and in one of my more bored moments, the growing of a lockdown beard.

It's interesting how quickly the way we were living our lives became normalised. We hadn't stepped into the doorway of a single shop for weeks; everything we needed was being delivered. The sight of opening the front door to see a delivery man in a mask, standing eight feet back, was alarming at first, but over time it became as accepted as the colour of the sky. Storing parcels in our hallway for 72 hours required a filing system, so you knew exactly in what order to open things to avoid potential transmission. We were literally trying to avoid it like the plague.

I would only walk down Palmer's Green high street in the evening when the street was as empty as a Donald Trump fan club meeting. 90% of the shops were indefinitely closed, either with their shutters up or encased in protective layers of MDF, with hastily printed signs saying that they hoped to be back in business soon. Some of the stores that were still open had garish paint markings on the floor, telling you where to stand if you were queuing to get into a particular shop. Barclays had stuck these branded circular discs on the pavement outside, which again separated people when queuing to get into the bank. It rather looked like the pavement had caught a case of the measles – perhaps appropriately, this virus-based infographic was helping to stop the spread of the real thing. (These things became much more commonplace later on.) It was quite sad seeing our little high street reduced to a food and medicine distribution shuttle run. My evening exercise was usually a two-mile circular walk, which took me down the high street, along Alderman's Hill, up to Southgate Green, and then back home via the suburban streets around Fox Lane. I barely ever saw anyone; even at 8pm on a Saturday night, I could probably count on one hand the number of people that were out and about. I was so acclimatised to the situation that seeing people was actually exciting. I mentally noted every person I saw on those walks. Two people chatting outside a fish and chip shop was now the pinnacle of human activity. I was actually missing those minor anti-social incidents that stick in the brain – a group of raucous teenagers messing around outside McDonalds, a couple of alcoholics drinking Strongbow on a bench, or a spot of minor road rage. I guess the teenagers were now getting takeaway McDonald's, the alcoholics were drinking Strongbow in their living rooms, and road rage was now confined to the virtual world of PlayStation 3.

It was astonishing how far the virus spread in such a short period of time. Only three weeks on from India's lockdown, and now half the world's population (over four billion) were under containment to try and slow the pandemic. Everyone knew that the numbers of people infected were much larger than what were being reported. Because the NHS was only counting people that were tested in hospitals, the number of people who had the illness and the number of people who sadly died would never truly be known. We were 99% confident that Jen had contracted it from her friend who was a confirmed case. Because she isolated at home and didn't go into hospital, she wasn't officially counted as a case. Equally, I knew of two cases at LCC (whilst I was still going into work) that were not reported. In all likelihood, there were far more but my understanding was that UAL wanted it kept quiet, at least until the term ended. It was later estimated that during the peak as many as 100,000 people in the UK were contracting the virus daily. I didn't know anyone within my social circle who wasn't affected in some way. I was chatting to Ritchie, who was now working as a landscape gardener back in Jersey. Being a small island, I assumed they might have escaped the wrath of Covid-19. As it turned out, they had quite a high number of cases- even an isolated piece of land adrift in the English Channel wasn't safe.

By the end of April, there were no major countries that didn't have an outbreak. There were only eleven tiny island nations that remained Coranavirus-free. It was probably no co-incidence that ten of these were the ten least visited places on earth – the majority being inaccessible and self-sufficient slithers of land in the Pacific Ocean. Most people had never heard of them; again, probably the reason they remained virus-free. They were Kiribati, Lesotho, the Marshall Islands, Micronesia, Nauru, Palau, Samoa, the Solomon islands, Tonga, Tuvalu, and Vanuatu.

It wasn't all doom and gloom. There were positives from the whole saga. The environment, for one, was flourishing, with wildlife starting to encroach on the fringes of human environments. There were reports from all over the world of wildlife which hadn't been seen for decades. In Venice, for instance, dolphins were seen swimming through the deserted canals of the city. In Harold Hill in East London, deer had found their way onto the deserted streets and were making themselves at home in people's front gardens. Markedly less exciting, but I for one noticed much larger populations of butterflies in our garden that spring. A few months later, one of my work colleagues, Gifty, was amongst the first people to set foot back in the university post-lockdown. The powers-that-be had decided to allow staff one day where they could briefly pop back in to retrieve any belongings that had been left during the mad rush to leave. I had an online meeting with her later the same day, where she described the scene to me. Upon entering the building with the estates team, they discovered that a family of foxes, a scurry of squirrels, and a flock of pigeons, had all moved into the vacant premises. Dens, nests, and bird poo, were rampant amongst the college corridors. The building was just one of many across London that had started to resemble a nature reserve.

There was also a dramatic fall in nitrogen dioxide levels in cities all over the world, as industry and transport were temporarily mothballed. In London, levels fell by about 60%, meaning that emissions were at their lowest since the 1950s. The air in Palmer's Green became cleaner and fresher, with the distant roar of the North Circular reduced to a slow trickle of background noise. Electricity consumption also fell. It was estimated that global electricity demand was down by more than 20% throughout 2020, the biggest drop since the Great Depression of the 1930s. It was as if Mother Nature was enjoying a well-deserved breather.

One early evening, I heard a wren chirping loudly in the matted ivy that clung to the trees along Alderman's Hill. What was unusual, I realised, was that I could actually hear its birdsong clearly. Normally, it would be muffled by the incessant rumble of traffic, which had all but been extinguished. I thought to myself that this shouldn't seem unusual. It's funny how things appear impossible until they actually happen. When they do, you begin to start questioning a lot of things. Before Covid-19, we accepted the dominance of traffic noise as an inevitable consequence of city life. Now that we had sampled an alternative urban ambience, would people be happy to go back to the way it once was? Sadly, the answer was yes, but for a short while anything seemed possible.

Another positive was the strange sense of liberation in the suspension of more or less everything. Any fashions, hobbies, or sets of priorities that one might have had and considered dull or cumbersome before March 2020, you were no longer beholden to. When else in life can one go for months on end without setting an alarm clock or worrying about the clothes you wear. People who always complained about a lack of 'me time' suddenly had it in spades. If you let it consume you, the novelty would quickly wear off, but if you embraced it, there was paradoxically a real sense of freedom in being locked inside.

The UK government started to get a grip on the situation with the building of specialist field hospitals to start taking in excess patients. The first of these to open was the NHS Nightingale, which utilised the space inside London's Excel Centre, comprising of 100 acres and space for up to 4000 beds. Spike, one of Debs' friends and our wedding videographer, bravely volunteered to work as a clinical support worker there. By the time he finished his training, the number of serious cases had begun to go into decline, so he was never actually needed during that first wave. He did, however, take part in a trial for one of the new experimental Covid drugs and helped assist the patients during the later second wave. As well as hospitals, various drive-through Covid testing facilities started popping up all over the place. Twickenham rugby stadium was one such place that was converted for this purpose.

The 21st April that year was another date for the history books. This was the first day in nearly 75 years (since 1946) when there were no cruise ships or ocean liners carrying passengers at sea anywhere in the world. There had been a huge scramble to bring cruise ship passengers home amid the pandemic – many of whom had spent weeks being refused entry at various countries, for fear of carrying the virus. After this date, a small number of vessels were quarantined, with their crew sheltering in various harbours and ports across the globe. But when on 21st April the *Costa Deliziosa* docked at the Italian port of Genoa, the seas were emptied of all their cruise ships and their 26 million annual passengers.

May and June were long hard slogs. Everyone was understandably anxious to get some clarity on when things might start returning to normal. It was clear that the number of cases and deaths were flatlining, so the policy of social distancing did seem to be working. The term 'exit strategy' was being bandied around households up and down the country. As we kept being reminded on the Government's daily briefings, there were no good options or easy answers. If everyone simply went back to their previous behaviour, the virus would start re-infecting people again, there would be a second wave, and we would be back in lockdown faster than Boris Johnson could say Châteauneuf-du-Pape. What was needed was a gradual, staged response, based on scientific evidence and a bit of creative thinking. Human trials had recently started on a possible vaccine that was being developed at Oxford University, so everyone was waiting with bated breath.

It seemed as though we were all now existing inside an Edward Hopper painting. For the uninitiated, Edward Hopper was an American 1920s painter who depicted the isolation of modern living. A man bereft in his apartment, lonely shop workers, and people sitting far apart in a diner, were all famous motifs he used throughout his career. Whilst F. Scott Fitzgerald was writing about the party people of the jazz age, Hopper painted people who looked like they'd never been to a party in their lives. Towering urban buildings where everyone lived in self-contained apartments were brand new back then, so the fabric of modern cities changed almost overnight into a machine that churned out solitude. A hundred years on, and history seemed to be repeating itself. You could see the soaring skyscrapers of Canary Wharf and the City from Broomfield Park, built for thousands of workers but you knew were now virtually deserted. There's something slightly unnerving about giant monuments that don't fulfil their function. Like Chernobyl or a wild west ghost town, if urban environments don't have people to occupy them, they become extraordinarily creepy very quickly.

It was fascinating watching the advertising industry desperately trying in vain to adjust to this new reality. Friedrich Nietzsche once said that we need to affirm life rather than deny it. To deny life is to pretend that it isn't what it is. To affirm life is to look at everything, no matter how uncomfortable or frightened it makes us, and say, 'That is life.' Historically, advertising had always denied real life, with its perfectly skinned, continually smiling, carefree models, always slim and healthy in spite of the artery-clogging fried food they were consuming in front of the viewer. Then, all of a sudden, they began to start reflecting reality – admittedly in small doses, but it was incredibly jarring. The number of advertisements that pre-Covid would depict people having fun in large social gatherings was huge. Now, that escapism was superseded by reality. People were no longer going to parks to share a KFC bargain bucket, but were getting it delivered to their homes. Supermarkets would advertise their brands with shoppers wearing masks. Advertising was no longer selling you a dream life, but reflecting back to you some semblance of reality. Personally, I was waiting for Canon to start using the slogan 'Look photogenic during the pandemic'.

One of the big moral conundrums involved in a nationwide lockdown was determining when it was okay to bend or even break the rules. Sometimes the positives of seeing someone would outweigh the risks. Debs' cousin, Tanya, came over to deliver us some baby bits and bobs for Amber. These were a mixture of clothes, toys, and a seated baby bath that her daughter, Tallulah, had grown out of. To have bought all that stuff brand new would have cost us hundreds of pounds, not been environmentally friendly (certainly in terms of plastic), and wasn't really feasible for a courier to deliver. We were very sensible, and took suitable precautions like unlocking the garden gate so Tanya could get into our garden via the back alleyway, and trying to remain at least six feet apart. It's a strange feeling trying to socially distance whilst being hospitable. Body language that infers you would rather someone wasn't near you isn't conducive to a relaxed catch-up with friends or family. Debs made Tanya a coffee in a cardboard cup, which was then strategically placed at a midway point on our garden table. She could only see Amber (whom she had never met before) from a distance, and of course wasn't allowed to come inside, so even an emergency toilet trip was out of the question. This might seem like overkill, but her partner, Steve, who worked for the *Guardian* newspaper, was still going into his office. (One of the very few people outside of NHS workers that we knew of.) This was exactly the kind of scenario that allowed the virus to silently spread, but by taking the proper precautions we knew we were safe, even if we were technically breaking the law.

One of the first things that tentatively started re-opening were tips and recycling centres. Incidences of fly tipping had increased dramatically since the lockdown came into effect. It was an obvious consequence, really. If you had a large amount of materials to discard, what could you, as an unscrupulous person, do if nationwide every tip was closed? The government came to the conclusion that it was a relatively safe thing to re-open. After all, people don't go to the dump to hang about and socialise. Most people unload their car as quickly as they can and then skedaddle off to somewhere that doesn't smell like a two-week-old nappy bin on a hot summer's day.

By now, the financial costs of the pandemic were mind-boggling. The government was effectively now paying the wages of nearly a quarter of the UK workforce. 6.3 million people (23%) had applied for the UK's job retention scheme, where the government would pay 80% of workers' wages, up to £2500 a month. That was on top of the additional 1.8 million new Universal Credit claims. Economic production had ground to a halt, as even those that could still work weren't being as productive or efficient as they would in normal circumstances. Many other countries had similar schemes, which did make you wonder how on earth we were going to pay all this money back. After all, this was global borrowing on a stratospheric scale. The world was bracing itself for the biggest economic crisis in living memory.

Although I was reasonably content working from home, I was missing my colleagues. Virtual meetings simply weren't a good enough substitute for the real thing. I was perhaps fortunate in that I had less meetings than many others, but even, so fatigue was starting to creep in. Zoom had rapidly attained the status of a verb, and the phrase that described its pernicious effect was not far behind. 'Zoom fatigue' was our innate response to staring at a grid of faces for hours on end. When we all meet in person, human beings will subconsciously process body language, tone of voice, facial expressions, and various other non-verbal cues. On screen, we expend much more energy trying (often in vain) to pick up on these cues. In an office, a couple of seconds of silence may go unnoticed, but in the virtual world it can make you feel on edge. Did I say something wrong? Why have they steered the conversation away? Was that joke I just made slightly inappropriate? You begin to long for genuine face-to-face interaction.

Covid-19 should have been an apolitical event. You may have noticed that there was barely a whiff of politics so far in this chapter, mainly because I never thought that the blame game was particularly helpful. Also, though mistakes were made, I thought that the government did a reasonable job at handling the crisis. I didn't think at the start that another party would have handled it much better. Hindsight, of course, is a wonderful thing; to have the gift of hindsight is to play God. By and large, I was vaguely happy with the course the government was charting, and then all of a sudden something peculiar started happening. The government deliberately started giving vague, contradictory, and in some cases dangerous advice. Political game-playing had now entered the arena.

Everyone was on the same page for the first three months. Until a vaccine or effective treatment was readily available, the best course of action to reduce fatalities and stop the spread of the virus was for numbers to be driven as low as possible through social distancing. An app was being developed, whereby people could report their symptoms and those that they had been in contact with. This became known as test, track and trace. Once the cases were in the low hundreds and deaths in single figures, the virus would be brought under control. This was the approach that countries like Germany and South Korea were taking. It made perfect sense and would save many thousands of lives. It was a long hard slog, but it was simple and effective. That was where we all thought we were going. Then one night, Boris Johnson came on TV to address the nation, and told the country that restrictions were being gradually eased. He then proceeded to give one of the most shambolic speeches I have ever witnessed. I didn't understand the new rules. I watched the speech, followed up on the BBC news, and even read the whole sixty-page legislation document that went through parliament (even with a newborn, I had plenty of time to kill), and I still didn't understand it. No-one I knew could figure it out either, it became a running joke for the next couple of days. I could safely say that 99.9% of the country couldn't grasp the new rules. People no longer needed to 'stay at home', but to 'stay alert'. People should go to work if they could, but not use public transport, unless of course they couldn't. People could leave the house for unlimited amounts of exercise in some parts of the country, but not all of it. One member of one household could see one member of another household, but only in a public place. Nannies and nurseries could look after multiple children, but grandparents weren't allowed to look after their own grandchild. Oh, and of all the things people were crying out for, it was decided that golf courses should re-open. It was bizarre, made no sense, and confused everybody. Be alert at work! Catch the virus as a sustainable rate! If you go to Cumbria, you will be killed! Strange times indeed.

In a time of crisis, people want the honest complex facts, coupled with very simple instructions on what to do about them. Instead, the government oversimplified the facts and complicated the advice. It's a bit like a teacher not completing the whole syllabus, and in the week before the exam spending every lesson insisting on going over revision techniques and exam etiquette. I knew instantly that as result of these bizarre rules, infections would stop falling within two to three weeks. A larger-scale return to work without the ability to test, trace, and isolate, risked creating super-spreader events. It took me a couple of days to get my head around what was happening. What were the government playing at?

The Tories had decided to give up on the science and instead focus its collective energies on political survival. It seemed their ultimate goal was to retain power rather than save lives. They had very shrewdly calculated the maximum number of deaths they could get away with causing by relaxing restrictions earlier than was wise. Their goal was to appease their voter base by getting the economy moving again. By making their advice ambiguous, they could pass the blame onto individual behaviour. They were forcing people back into work with a 'Don't say we didn't warn you' type message. The emphasis had shifted from national collective endeavour to individual fault. The Tories were trying to push responsibility for whether we lived or died from themselves onto everyone else, but without giving the public the tools or the information to make the right decisions – all of the responsibility but none of the power. They had failed to reach a sufficient level of testing, failed to launch the test and trace app, and were starting to fall out of favour with the general public. At this point, we were in the unenviable position of having the third highest number of cases in the world. With their backs to the walls, their last card to play was in appeasing their traditionally wealthy voters. They themselves wouldn't be entering the fray. It was, of course, the blue-collar workers who were going back to work first – the construction workers, security guards, and factory operatives, all of whom were guinea pigs using a transport system that was plainly unsafe at this point. Workplaces could enforce social distancing with relative ease. A bit of money and creative thinking were all that was required. People's journeys into their workplace were more problematic. You could have all the protection and safeguards in the world, but if you were packed into a rush-hour train, you were plainly exposed to risk. Those that had the luxury of working from home or could drive to work, were shielded. This was class division cruelly exposed by government policy. The working poor didn't matter; businesses could always get more workers, and funerals were far cheaper than medical care. I imagine that others like me felt immense amounts of guilt, pressure, relief, and luck. You were sitting at home nice and cosy whilst all the while the Tories were acting like First World War generals sending the infantry over the top to do their dirty work. If the guilt ever got too much for them, they could always go and play a round of golf in their recently re-opened private members' clubs. Such disdain for one's fellow man was despicable. That, in a nutshell, is why I despise the Tories and will never vote Conservative.

This was the point when we stopped religiously following the government's advice. It was safer not to. No-one was going to tell me that I could catch a packed tube train but not see people that I trusted. I also stopped watching the daily briefings, because I could no longer handle the government twisting and manipulating the facts. The positive spin they were putting on the data felt like a sick joke. Did you know that in early 2020 you had a 30% chance of dying if you ended up in a British hospital with Covid-19? That's roughly the same overall mortality rate as Ebola in West Africa in 2014. Safe to say, that was never mentioned during these briefings. On the first day that some of the restrictions were eased, the news showed people crowding onto buses at Finsbury Park. There appeared to be the same amount of jostling and grappling as there is during a Premier League corner kick. *Not the best start*, I thought, *to a new normal of social distancing*. We elected to do what we thought was best for our health and sanity. We began to see Rob and Jen again, and Debs started going out for walks with her NCT friends.

When garden centres started re-opening, news broadcasters were delighted that they had a new story to run. There hadn't so much been slow news days over the last few weeks, but rather groundhog news days. I literally watched forty minutes of prime-time news, where a reporter and a manager trudged the length and breadth of a garden centre, explaining all the new safeguards. They talked about car parking, the trolley system, and even how the height of certain plants could obscure people's vision and make distancing more dangerous. They talked about why certain areas were sealed off, sanitation, and how hand-washing stations were strategically deployed at various points. There was even a whole section devoted to how people should wait patiently at the checkouts, which really tapped into the classic British queue mentality. It was a bit like those old Pathe features, where an incredibly posh gentleman would explain how to use an escalator or what a microwave did. I thought that if I were inclined to record this and show it to people in twenty years' time, they would never believe that this was real. Without the proper context, it would come across as very strange. There were plenty more 'clutching at news' news stories – the non-appearance of the Glastonbury Festival, for instance. I watched Michael Eavis sitting in a field, talking about it not happening that year. Something not happening is the opposite of news, I remember thinking to myself.

There was now a steady trickle of things starting to re-open. It was inevitable; at some point, people had to come out of hiding. I thought it was far too soon, but at least it was being done tentatively. We were still playing cat and mouse with the virus, and to be clear, we were the mice. Everything had to be reconfigured to meet social distancing requirements. There were either limits on the number of people allowed in certain spaces, or floor markings and separate areas so people could avoid coming into contact with each other. Schools were very controversial. Some decided to re-open as soon as the government allowed it, but many didn't. At the start, it was just Reception, Year 1, and Year 6. I had no idea how teachers were going to prevent five and six-year-olds from running around and playing with each other. You would see pictures of children in these chalk circles, where it looked more like a military discipline camp than a school playground. There was so much misinformation and speculation around the role that children played in potentially spreading the virus. Some parents were relieved that some schools were starting to open, whilst others were horrified by the prospect. The truth was that no-one knew for sure how dangerous it potentially was. It was such an odd feeling having this huge question mark dangling over every facet of one's life. The fact that there wasn't one person on the entire planet who conclusively understood this virus just didn't compute with people. I think we as a species are fascinated by the unknown, the escapism of unsolved murders, the existence of aliens, and so forth. However, when major unknowns impact on our way of life, we crave instant answers. I'm sure that they will come in due course, but at the time, the decision around schools was one giant roll of the dice. In many ways, those few weeks before the summer holidays kicked in were a dry run for the opening of schools proper in September.

In mid-June the government finally brought in quarantine rules for travellers to and from the UK. Amid the global pandemic, arrivals at UK airports were 99% down compared to the previous year. Arrivals by boat and via the Channel Tunnel were down 97 and 98% respectively. However, the feeling was that as restrictions were gradually eased both at home and abroad, those numbers would begin to increase. As domestic cases of Covid-19 were now broadly static, imported cases would begin to make up a larger number of the percentage total. A fourteen-day quarantine period was introduced for 'risky countries', where passengers would need to tell the authorities where they would be staying upon arrival, with fines imposed on people if they were found to be disregarding the rules. There were predictable howls of outrage from the travel industry, but I thought it was necessary. You didn't want to encourage holidaymakers and non-essential travel during these uncertain times. The rules were softened over time for certain countries, but when outbreaks resurfaced, as they later did in Spain and France, the quarantine periods were reimposed. Going anywhere abroad was now something of a calculated risk. Instead of sun, sea, and sand, it was stress, sanitiser, and steriliser. I couldn't understand why anyone was bothering. I personally couldn't handle the illogicality. If I couldn't have friends over for dinner, why was it okay for me to be on a packed flight with two hundred strangers? I knew that expecting consistency from a government led by Boris Johnson – a man who isn't even consistent about how many children he has fathered – was a fool's errand, but weren't we supposed to be suppressing the virus, not giving it lifts around the continent in planes? Debs and I had already resigned ourselves to a staycation that year.

The football season had finally resumed, albeit behind closed doors. I sat down to watch Bournemouth V Crystal Palace – the first time in thirty-two years that a top flight match had been shown on terrestrial TV. It wasn't the most exciting game, a fairly straightforward 2-0 victory for Crystal Palace, but the morbid curiosity of seeing a game in this strange new world made it must-watch TV. It was an eerie spectacle with everything being so cautious – no ball boys, no celebrations, no handshakes, and a socially distanced subs bench. The biggest difference, of course, was that there were no crowds. Football without fans is rather like fish without chips, or Laurel without Hardy; it just didn't make sense. Apart from the coaching staff, security, and TV broadcasters, the stadiums during this end of season run were all pretty much deserted. The strangest sensation was hearing the artificial crowd noise that was overlaid so there wasn't total silence during the games. It was so grating. Like an own-brand box of cornflakes, it just screamed its own inauthenticity. It's a pretty complex business making believable crowd noise that doesn't distract from the on-the-pitch antics. Some added nuance would have made all the difference so that the groans at a half-fluffed chance sounded moderately miffed rather than stolen from a livid crowd during a missed Southgate penalty.

Some sense of normality was now starting to re-emerge through the hazy fog of lockdown. Non-essential shops were allowed to re-open as long as they could demonstrate that they were 'Covid secure'. From the 4th July (the so-called British Independence Day), a number of restaurants, pubs, and galleries – armed with masks, hand sanitizers, and floor markings – began welcoming back customers. The streets were starting to fill up again, but if there's one thing guaranteed to make you more uneasy than a deserted high street in a pandemic, it was one which appeared relatively normal only at first glance. Upon closer inspection, everything was just slightly off; a kind of 'village of the damned' vibe where, behind the nervous smiles (if shoppers weren't wearing masks), you could sense the bubbling tension.

On the positive front, the first proven treatment – Dexamethasone – which was shown to cut deaths by around 30%, was now being used up and down the country. There was also the encouraging news that New Zealand had become the first major country to entirely eradicate the virus. All the restrictions had been lifted, and they were now returning to a normal way of life. This only lasted for about three months before a couple of small clusters emerged, but it did at least suggest that Covid-19 wasn't entirely insurmountable.

Elsewhere, the global picture was mixed. The epicentre of the pandemic had now moved to Latin America. Now that Europe had managed to get something of a grip on the situation, global attention was focusing on poorer developing countries who were even less well equipped than we were. Brazil's numbers of infections and deaths were going through the roof, so much so that the government started removing data from its official website. This was a calculated political move from its right-wing leader. The United States was still the worst affected individual country with approximately 70,000 official cases being declared daily. By comparison, the UK's 600 cases a day seemed like small fry. Even with a population five times the size, their epidemic was about twenty times worse than ours (with numbers still rising).

Later that month Debs and I braved going to a pub beer garden for the first time in months. We went to one of our favourite local taverns, The Cherry Tree on Southgate Green. We chose it because, although we weren't yet comfortable enough to go inside a pub, it had an expansive beer garden at the front so was the perfect place for a trial run in these strange times. We knew that the tables were far enough apart and that there was ample space for Amber and her pushchair. Months earlier, I had envisaged a victorious post-pandemic pub pint, but it was none of those things. It wasn't really a full pub experience, and I didn't actually have a pint – rather a mixed berry gin and tonic. It may have been post-lockdown but the pandemic itself was still ongoing. The beer garden was run with military discipline. You now needed to book to go into almost all pubs, so that they had your details on file. We hadn't actually made a reservation, but as there were a couple of free tables, that wasn't an issue. I had to give the barman my contact details before they would even take our order. The idea being that if the pub were to have a confirmed case of Covid within the next few days, everyone who visited would be contacted and told to isolate. Essentially, private businesses were now required to do the work of healthcare professionals if they wanted to remain open. They explained the rules to me, how it was one-in-one-out to the building itself, and how everything was now table service. There was no going up to the bar and being allowed to peruse what was on tap. When they brought the drinks over, the waiter wasn't even allowed to place the glasses on the table; you had to physically take them from the tray and place them down. It was a peculiar experience: on one hand, perfectly pleasant, but on the other, it was strangely functional. There was now a set way of doing things and that was that; it felt a little bit like being back at school. You even had to double-check with the staff if you wanted to go to the toilet. That, dear reader, is the story of Amber's first visit to a pub.

On one gloriously sunny day whilst out for a stroll, I popped into a local newsagents to retrieve a parcel for Debs. Whilst I was waiting patiently in the queue, the phone rang. One of the ladies behind the counter picked it up, then seemed to freeze and shouted, 'Enfield!' The three staff in the shop all started panicking and running around. *Who was it?* I wondered. Was Harry Enfield on his way down to sign for a package which they were then going to pass off as an autograph and sell to the highest bidder? It turned out Enfield was the marginally less exciting Enfield Council, who were sweeping up and down the high street checking that staff and customers were wearing their masks. *But this is London in 2020*, I thought, *not Chicago during prohibition.* How have we got to the stage of such fear and panic that shop workers are practically throwing themselves under their counters in terror? I would always wear a mask in shops. I thought it was a sensible and reassuring thing to do, and it was hardly a major hassle wearing one for a couple of minutes. If I thought that balancing a strawberry blancmange on top of my head would make a difference and help us get back to normality quicker, I would gladly have rolled up my sleeves and whipped one up in our kitchen to use as fashionably fruity headgear. But I knew that not everyone felt that way. Plenty of people don't like strawberry blancmange, and equally, plenty of people don't like wearing masks. It's one thing to advise and encourage, but quite another to make compulsory. It's always better to educate and inform than to try and enforce something that's totally unenforceable. Keeping apart as much as possible was the only proven way to reduce the transmission of Covid.

This whole fuss around masks seemed to muddy the waters and lulled people into a false sense of security. Put it this way, being alone on a bus with no-one else bar the driver without a face covering, though technically illegal, was far safer than being in a busy shop with everyone wearing masks. I was watching all these shop workers frantically running round, thinking that common sense had gone out the window. I thought about how damaging this kind of thing was for human relations, particularly impressionable young children. Fear kills everything, and it kills nothing more quickly than reason and humanity. Yes, we were living through dark times, but the worst thing you could do was let the fear consume you.

You were aware that you were now acclimatised to the whole situation when crowded scenes of people would make you shudder. Whether it was some re-run of a travel programme, or a past performance of a gig or a football match that you were watching, there were always the same thoughts circling at the back of your mind. You would be thinking, *Wow, that's so many people in a confined space*, or *I can't believe that was normal a few months ago*. While compiling the photos for this book, I got slightly nostalgic for feeling safe in large crowds – particularly the photo of me amongst 100,000 revellers at Glastonbury.

August and September brought yet more developments in the ever-evolving world of Covid. Finally, we had a test that could confirm within two hours whether or not a person had the illness. The previous tests had taken an average of 24 hours, but could often take up to 72 to come back from the lab. This was a game-changer that meant cases could be identified and acted upon far quicker. There was also a sense that the much-touted phrase 'the new normal' was starting to apply to things that had previously been thought of as impossible whilst the virus was still circulating. The BBC

Proms went ahead at the Royal Albert Hall with a physically-distanced orchestra and no live audience. It worked fine without spectators, though of course the ambience was very different. The strangest thing, with me not being particularly knowledgeable about classical music, was not knowing when a piece of music was supposed to end. Usually, the gentle murmurings of light audience applause were the indication as to whether it was a tacet or the conclusion to a piece. Who knew that silence could be so distracting?

We had one proper holiday in 2020 – a jaunt down to Watergate Bay in Cornwall. Going on holiday during a pandemic is a very strange sensation. I initially thought it was a bad omen that our lodgings – the Watergate Bay Hotel – were named after an infamous political scandal. If it all went Pete Tong, I wondered if we would end up referring to our trip as Watergate-gate. I didn't want to be a hypocrite. The thought of going somewhere to relax and unwind during a time of crisis felt a bit selfish, but at the same time we were helping the UK tourist industry which was being battered from all sides. If anything, our indecision was just mirroring all the confusion that was sweeping through the country. A few days before we left, the government introduced a new law whereby people weren't allowed to meet up publicly or privately in groups any larger than six. There were exceptions for schools, workplaces, and a few other specialist areas, but generally speaking you now couldn't meet up with more than five others for any social or leisure reasons. Cases of the virus were stubbornly creeping up, so something needed to be done to prevent the situation from spiralling out of control again. Like so many things during that year, it was a good idea that was badly executed. For one thing, there was no consideration given to the size of a family. A couple who had four children, for instance, weren't legally allowed to meet with anyone else, if they were all together. Another issue was that babies and toddlers counted as fully-fledged adults, so during our Cornish getaway, Amber and Lilah were counted in the same way that we all were. This meant we were a group of eight, which caused us a bit of a logistical headache during mealtimes. Sometimes we had to sit on separate tables, sometimes we would be looking for adjoining tables to give the illusion of group distancing, and other times we could be together if the children were sleeping. It was farcical really. That aside, being in Cornwall was rather like being in a state of dreamlike detachment, at least temporarily. The hotel was fantastic, the scenery stunning, and the company exquisite. Seeing Amber splashing around in a proper swimming pool and playing on a sandy beach for the first time, were joyous sights to witness. We were wallowing in the last vestiges of summer just before the autumnal air blew in to bring us all back to reality.

At long last, we were starting to make plans to go back to work. Lockdown hadn't so much redrawn the workplace for millions of people, rather it had chewed it up like a broken printer. Before Covid-19, I thought remote working sounded blissful, and in small doses it was. By now, I was longing for chats in the staff kitchen and to be amongst the whirr of photocopiers and the incessant typing of colleagues. Initially, the plan was that I would go back for two days a week, and in an exciting development, I would be getting my own office. The start of the new academic year had been delayed until 20th October (a month later than usual) to allow us, as an institution, more time to adapt to this changing world. Blended learning was now the term being bandied up and down universities across the country, whereby students would do a mixture of online and campus-based learning. We had redrawn our course portfolio so that only 33% of our students would be on campus at any one time. Two days a week, each student could be physically present on site, which meant our building only needed to deal with 1800, rather than potentially 5500 students at a time. I wouldn't even be scratching the surface if I were to tell you the innumerable issues this was throwing up. Every student was still paying their full tuition fees – a hefty investment – and being strictly limited to two days on campus, with all the restrictions on libraries, support, studios, and technical spaces that this entailed. Online provision could fill the void for some, but for others... let's just say that value for money took something of a pounding.

I was literally a few short days from returning to work when all of a sudden, our plans were thrown into yet more turmoil. Cases had started to rise again, and it appeared that the much talked about second wave of infections was now coming to fruition. A second national lockdown was now being seriously discussed, and after weeks of kicking the can down the road, this finally swung into action on 4th November. It was described by many shops, who relied on this period of festive trading, as *The Nightmare Before Christmas*. Lockdown 2.0, as it became known, was the sequel that no one wanted, but at least this time we had more of an idea of what to expect. It was a mutual decision that I now wouldn't be returning to work for the foreseeable future, certainly not until the tail end of 2021. The health of me and my family had to come first. A limited number of staff were now working on site, but only these deemed to be absolutely essential. A skeleton crew for a, if not quite sinking, then certainly stationary ship. This truly was the year the earth stood still.

There will be a vaccine or an effective treatment very soon, I have no doubt. I can't think of any non-neurological diseases that don't have one or the other. With so many potential drugs being tested across the world and hundreds of millions being spent, the chances are close to 100% that one or more will hit the jackpot. With all that global collective brainpower and the pillars that support capitalism coming under threat, it's inevitable. Also worth bearing in mind is that it's not necessary for a vaccine to be 100% effective. The seasonal flu vaccine, I'm told, is somewhere within the region of 50-60% effective, and that works fine. The more pressing issue, I suspect, will be logistical. How do you handle distribution, convince populations it's safe, and make it affordable across the globe? There's still a long way to go in this crisis, with plenty more bumps in the road ahead. It woes me slightly to end this book on something of a cliff-hanger, but publishing deadlines await. Things may appear bleak at the moment, but it takes darkness to see the stars. By the time you're reading this, this will hopefully all be ancient history.

I was seeing my office for the first time in months. It was being beamed into my kitchen on a live feed from a college iPad. It reminded me of those documentaries where people go suited and booted into nuclear exclusion zones to film things that wouldn't be safe for others to witness in person. Rather than the Geiger counters and spent fuel rods of Chernobyl, I was viewing the lever arch files and photocopy toner of the LCC academic support office. A colleague from our estates team was over-enthusiastically waving the iPad around the room as if he were trying to swat a fly. I had asked him if he could locate some files for me, so he was opening various cupboards and shuffling through my bulging collection of ring binders. It was slightly surreal watching him enter my deserted office, and then talking him through how to gain access to everything. The code to the office hadn't changed, and the door swung open in the same creaky fashion it always had. The PCs and Macs stood there, a thin layer of dust residing upon them. Everything else was as it was – the coat stand, the bookshelf, the coffee mug stains, all present and correct. It was frozen in time, as if the last eight months were nothing but a dream. As Shakespeare once remarked, 'a dream itself is but a shadow'. That shadow of darkness seemed to lift as he opened the window blinds and the light flooded back in. He peered into my mug and showed me the only obvious sign of the passing of time. In my haste to leave I had neglected to cleanse my cup, which was now sprouting a swampy forest of basil green growth. I had cultivated penicillin for a new era. It was then I had another of those strange moments. *Perhaps,* I thought, *the answer to Coronavirus had always been here. The cure for Covid-19 had been residing in my cup all this time...*

Au Revoir

And so we have reached the end of our journey. This book took me nearly two and a half years to complete. It's incredible to think how much my life has changed just over that time, as I now sit here with Amber resting serenely in my lap. She is blissfully unaware that Daddy has completed his first novel and is sitting all smug, waiting for the publishing cheques that will never arrive. In a way, it was almost inevitable. The first chapter was about me being born, and the (nearly) last about the birth of my daughter. Things have come full circle, if you will. It's been quite a therapeutic process jotting down all my thoughts and memories over the last thirty-or-so years. You recall something that triggers another memory that you hadn't thought about for twenty years. It's like having the contents of your head emptied and scattered across the kitchen floor whilst you're scrambling around trying to piece it all together. There was a point one evening, when Debs had gone to bed, where my thoughts were literally spread across the floor. I laid these large sheets of paper out and attempted to work out month by month what I did in any given year. It was colour-coded with flowcharts and links to other events. It was a colossal amount of stuff – much of it non-interesting, but still colossal. Wading through it all and trying to pick out stuff that you think others might find engrossing, was incredibly challenging. To my mind, writing an interesting book is a bit like taking a decent photo – you just need to focus on what you think is important. Editing this book was also an arduous process; there were so many stories that couldn't find a home in any of these chapters. If I've missed something out or not mentioned you by name, please be assured it's nothing personal. The dynamics involved in writing a coherent narrative inevitably results in things falling by the wayside. (I even considered editing out this section on editing.) This book really is the tip of the iceberg, with my first draft being considerably longer than the edition that you now hold in your hands. I could easily have written 300,000 words and split it across two volumes, but I didn't think it would have been as interesting as this condensed single edition. Besides, I wanted to keep some things back so that there were plenty more stories left to tell. Maybe I'll end up writing another book in thirty-six years time. Watch this space...

Chris Bryant

CPSIA information can be obtained
at www.ICGtesting.com
Printed in the USA
BVHW090431250521
608002BV00012B/2255

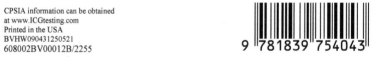